The Praeger Handbook of Education and Psychology

Volume 3

Edited by JOE L. KINCHELOE AND
RAYMOND A. HORN Jr.

Shirley R. Steinberg, *Associate Editor*

 PRAEGER

Westport, Connecticut
London

433233

MAR 2 6 2008

Library of Congress Cataloging-in-Publication Data

The Praeger handbook of education and psychology / edited by Joe L. Kincheloe and
Raymond A. Horn Jr.
    v.   cm.
   Includes bibliographical references and index.
   ISBN 0–313–33122–7 (set : alk. paper)—ISBN 0–313–33123–5 (vol 1 : alk. paper)—
   ISBN 0–313–33124–3 (vol 2 : alk. paper)—ISBN 0–313–34056–0 (vol 3 : alk. paper)—
   ISBN 0–313–34057–9 (vol 4 : alk. paper)   1. Educational psychology—Handbooks, manuals, etc.
   I. Kincheloe, Joe L.   II. Horn, R. A. (Raymond A.)
  LB1051.P635   2007
  371.4–dc22   2006031061

British Library Cataloguing in Publication Data is available.

Library of Congress Catalog Card Number: 2006031061
ISBN: 0–313–33122–7 (set)
        0–313–33123–5 (vol. 1)
        0–313–33124–3 (vol. 2)
        0–313–34056–0 (vol. 3)
        0–313–34057–9 (vol. 4)

First published in 2007

Praeger Publishers, 88 Post Road West, Westport, CT 06881
An imprint of Greenwood Publishing Group, Inc.
www.praeger.com

Printed in the United States of America

The paper used in this book complies with the
Permanent Paper Standard issued by the National
Information Standards Organization (Z39.48–1984).

10 9 8 7 6 5 4 3 2 1

Contents

VOLUME 2

PART III   ISSUES IN EDUCATION AND PSYCHOLOGY

Constructivism

Creativity

Criticality

Culture/Cultural Studies

Developmentalism

Educational Purpose

VOLUME 3

Enactivism

Knowledge Work

Learning

Memory

Mind

Psychoanalysis

Race, Class, and Gender

VOLUME 4

Situated Cognition

Teaching

CHAPTER 56

Complexity Science, Ecology, and Enactivism

BRENT DAVIS AND DENNIS SUMARA

COMPLEXITY SCIENCE: THE STUDY OF *EMERGENT* AND *STRUCTURE DETERMINED* SYSTEMS

Complexity science is a nascent field of study that defines itself more in terms of *what it investigates* than *how it investigates*. It focuses on the question of how relatively simple components in a system can come together into more sophisticated, more capable unities—and how, in turn, those grander unities affect the actions and characters of their components. One intertwined set of examples includes cells that cohere into organs that cohere into bodies that cohere into social groupings that cohere into societies.

Complexity science first arose in the confluence of very diverse fields, many of which had begun to appear in the physical sciences in the mid–twentieth century, including cybernetics, systems theory, artificial intelligence, and nonlinear dynamics. More recently, complexity theories have come to be taken up and developed in the social sciences in many and various ways, ranging from the highly technical, philosophical, narrative, and more recently the applied. In fact, interest in what are now described as complex phenomena pre-date the emergence of complexity science by more than a century. Complex sensibilities were well represented in Charles Darwin's studies of the intertwined evolutions of species, in Frederich Engel's discussions of social collectives, and in Jane Jacobs' characterization of living (and dying) cities. Many dozens of examples could be cited, in both the physical and the social sciences.

There are some important qualities that are common to all complex forms. Most important, complex phenomena are *emergent*: they self-organize. Coherent collective behaviors and characters emerge in the activities and interactivities of individual agents. Such self-organized forms can spontaneously arise and evolve without leaders, goals, or plans. This quality of transcendent collectivity—of being "more than the some of the parts"—is useful for drawing a further distinction between analytic science and complexity science. Complexity science does more than argue for a new category of phenomena; it asserts that reductionist analytic methods are not sufficient to understand such phenomena. Complexity scientists (or complexivists) contend that unpredictable behaviors and new laws arise as more complex systems emerge, and those systems must thus be studied at the levels of their emergence. They cannot be understood in terms of lower-level activities.

Complex phenomena are also *structure determined*; they are able to adapt themselves to maintain their coherence in the face of changing circumstances. Phrased differently, they embody their histories. That means that, unlike mechanical systems, complex systems can be highly unpredictable. They are thus better described in terms of Darwinian evolution than Newtonian mechanics. The property of structure determinism helps to explain why classical experimental methods, encumbered by the criterion of replicability, are not particularly useful to study complexity. For reasons that might never be apparent, similar complex systems can respond very differently to identical circumstances. In fact, the *same* system can respond differently to virtually identical conditions—since the system, not the conditions, determines the response.

COMPLEXITY SCIENCE AND SOCIAL SCIENCES RESEARCH

Within the arts, humanities and social sciences, complexivist sensibilities have begun to show up in an array of new subdisciplines whose titles transgress traditional disciplinary boundaries, including, for instance, social cybernetics, ecopsychology, neurophenomenology, and biological psychiatry. These titles are explicit in their acknowledgment of the biological roots of personal knowing, the cultural nature of collective knowledge, and the more-than-human contexts of human activity.

The notions of emergence and structure determinism mark important breaks of complexity science sensibilities from the assumptions and emphases that oriented much of the work in social sciences in general, and psychology in particular, through the twentieth century. For example, the notion of emergence might be interpreted as a problematization (if not an outright rejection) of the tendency to think of the individual as the proper site of learning and cognition. For the complexivist, all complex phenomena are learners. Cells, bodily organs, social groupings, societies, species—among other nested, co-implicated forms—are all cognitive agents. They obey similar adaptive dynamics, albeit at very different time scales; they all exist far from equilibrium; and they all arise from and have the potential to contribute to the emergence to other orders of complexity.

These realizations have prompted descriptions that often violate a rule of psychological research—namely, the avoidance of anthropomorphic expressions (see, e.g., *The Publication Manual of the American Psychological Association*, 2001). Individual human qualities and intentions are not to be applied or ascribed to nonhuman, subhuman, or superhuman events. Despite this interdiction, complexivists contend that it might be quite appropriate to describe complex adaptive systems, such as classrooms and societies, in terms of moods, personalities, beliefs, and so on.

In a further break from psychology, and specifically behaviorist psychology, the notion of structure determinism represents a challenge to the thoroughly critiqued, but still pervasive assumption that experience *causes* learning. For the complexivist, learning is not a change in behavior due to experience; it is a change in structure that contributes to the ongoing coherence of the learner. Learning depends on experience, but it is determined by the learner's structure, not by the experience.

The notion of *structure* is critical here. Invoking the biological definition, structure is understood as a system's ever-evolving form. The brain's structure, for example, is more than just the biological organization that was present at birth, simply because the brain is constantly changing. Each event of learning entails a physical transformation whereby subsequent events of learning are met by a different brain. The word *structure*, then, refers to the physically embodied, biological–experiential history of a system.

Through most of its brief history, complexity science has been focused on efforts to better understand the emergent and self-determining character of structures, understood in the sense described in the preceding paragraph. The principal strategies in such study have been close observations of actual complex systems and computer modeling. For the most part, this work has been descriptive in nature, through which researchers have attempted to identify features and conditions that are common to complex systems. More recently, there has been an increased emphasis among complexivists on the deliberate creation and nurturing of complex systems. This shift has been a significant one for domains like psychology and education, where the concern is not just with understanding complex behavior, but with affecting it. To this end, several key conditions that are necessary for self-organization and ongoing adaptation have been identified. For example, for complexity to arise, systems must have considerable redundancy among agents (to enable interactivity), some level of diversity (to enable novel responses), a means by which agents can affect one another, and a distributed, decentralized control structure. We return to a discussion of some of these pragmatic considerations of complexity science research after we introduce two closely related discourse fields, ecology and enactivism.

ECOLOGY: THE STUDY OF RELATIONSHIPS

Complexity science has helped to legitimate a topic that had almost become taboo in Western academia: transcendence. The ideas that higher-order unities can emerge spontaneously and that they obey their own rules simply do not fit with the mindset of analytic science, oriented as it is by quests for basic parts and universal laws.

However, despite its contribution to discussions of interconnectivity and transcendence, complexity science has retained some of the attitude of analytic science around matters of how arguments are presented, what constitutes evidence, and so on. This is not to say that complexity scientists are unaware of their participations in cultural and natural forms. Quite the contrary, such issues are prominent (see, e.g., Varela et al., 1991). Nevertheless, the moves to collect humans, hearts, social collectives, anthills, and the biosphere (among other forms) into the same category and to redescribe them in terms of systems rather than machines reveal that, conceptually, complexity science has maintained aspects of the detached modern scientific attitude in which questions of meaning and morals are left un- or underaddressed.

In many ways, this continued evasion is odd. Complexity asserts that our knowledge systems are rooted in our physical forms—and that those forms, in turn, are engaged in ongoing cyclings of matter with all other living forms. Oriented by this realization, through studies of complexity, science has mounted a case against itself. Accumulated evidence points to the possibility that many current personal, cultural, and planetary distresses can be traced to scientifically enabled human activities. It does not seem unreasonable to suggest that something other than an—or, at least, in addition to—explanation-seeking, possibility-oriented scientific attitude is required for an effective response. Knowledge is useful here, but one might argue that a certain wisdom is needed.

In particular, an ecological philosophy or ecosophy (from the Greek *sophia*, "wisdom") may be needed. This is the sort of thinking that underpins deep ecology, a movement that encourages a shift in how we experience the more-than-human world. Departing from most environmentalist discourses, which continue to frame humanity's relationship to the more-than-human in terms of management and overseeing, deep ecology begins with the assertion that life in all forms is inherently valuable. In other words, within deep ecology, the role of humanity is not understood in terms of stewardship, but of mindfulness and ethical action. A tenet of deep ecology is that humanity has the "right" to draw on planetary resources only to satisfy vital needs—which is a much more radical stance than the one taken within more popular sustainability discourses. For many deep ecologists, there is also an explicit political agenda that includes calls to reduce human populations, to rethink the Western corporate obsessions for endless economic growth, to move toward smaller-scale modes of production, and to embrace more local governance structures. A major recommendation in the deep ecological agenda is bioregionalism, a movement toward region-appropriate lifestyles and production activities.

Attentiveness to situation is a prominent theme in ecological discourses. Ecopsychology, for example, is oriented by the assertion that widespread feelings of personal isolation and collective dysfunction are mainly rooted in people's separations from the natural world, as opposed to separations from other humans or imagined selves, as posited within much of contemporary psychological research. The main therapeutic tool of ecopsychologists is reconnection to nature. Another emergent discourse is ecofeminism, in which it is argued that prevailing worldviews are not just *anthropocentric* (human-dominant) but *androcentric* (male-dominant). Proponents note close correspondences between the beliefs and structures that contribute to the oppression of women and those that contribute to the oppression of nature. In effect, ecofeminists, along with deep ecologists, argue that anti-oppression discourses and movements should include the category of nature along with race, class, gender, and sexuality.

The issue of how humans discriminate themselves from other living forms is common across many branches of Western thought. For example, across ancient mystical and religious systems, the human tends to be distinguished from the nonhuman by virtue of a soul. In Enlightenment-era rationalist and empiricist discourses, the means of differentiation is the faculty of reason, which is often assumed (inappropriately) to be a strictly human competency. Across such twentieth-century discourses as structuralism and poststructuralism, humans are set apart by language and other capacities for symbolically mediated interaction. For complexivists, the human brain is frequently cited as the most sophisticated structure that is known, and human consciousness and social systems are often described as the highest known forms of organization.

Across most ecological movements, this apparent need to discriminate between the human and the not-human is interrupted. This point is true of deep ecology, ecopsychology, and ecofeminism. And it is particularly true of those ecological discourses that are clustered under the umbrella term of ecospirituality, some of which have pressed toward modes of description and engagement that are highly reminiscent of ancient mystical traditions and that represent a dramatic break from the sensibilities that frame most research in psychology.

Ecospiritual movements have found a perhaps surprising ally in recent neurological research. There is mounting evidence that humans are physiologically predisposed to mystical and spiritual experiences—that is, to such feelings or sensations as timelessness, boundlessness, transcendence, and oneness that have been commonly associated with spiritual events (Newberg et al., 2001). Until quite recently, the psychological explanation for mystical and religious experience was that the experience was in some sort of pathological state such as a neurosis, a psychosis, or another problem with brain function. (In fact, the American Psychiatric Association listed "strong religious belief" as a mental disorder until 1994.) The associated assumption, that the mystic or religious zealot is prone to losing touch with reality, has proven problematic on several levels. Psychology has been unable to prove the assumption that spiritual experience is the product of delusional minds. On the contrary, it appears that those who experience genuine mystical states or who live devoted religious lives tend to have much higher levels of psychological health than the general population. There is further evidence that mystical experiences are quite unlike psychotic states. The latter tend toward confused and even terrifying hallucinations; the former tend to be described with such terms as serenity, wholeness, and love (Newberg et al., 2001).

Such events, in fact, may not be all that unusual. Virtually everyone can recall an experience of being lost in a book, immersed in an activity, or caught up in a crowd. Such experiences can also be induced and enhanced through repetitive, rhythmic activity—which should perhaps not be surprising. The explicit purpose of most rituals is to "lift" participants from their respective isolations into something greater than themselves. As it turns out, there is a neurological basis for these sorts of responses. Such activities affect parts of the brain that are associated with reason and the imagined boundaries of the self. To oversimplify, when the dichotomizing tendencies of logic and self-identification are relaxed, the sensations associated with mystical experience emerge.

It is one thing to say that something of this sort can happen, and quite another to address the questions of why it happens at all and why it is so common. Why might humans be physiologically predisposed to feelings of transcendence? Among the many answers that are possible to these questions, one response has a particular intuitive appeal: It happens because there *are* transcendent unities, of which we are always and already part. In being aware of their selves and of nature, humans are one of the means by which nature is conscious of itself. Human thoughts are not about the cosmos, they are parts of the cosmos—and so the universe changes when something as seemingly small and insignificant as a thought changes. These convictions are at the core of emergent ecospiritual movements. The defining feature of ecospirituality is an attitude of respect and entanglement with all living forms. This sort of attitude is represented in almost every ancient spiritual tradition, theistic and nontheistic alike.

The word *spiritual* has been redefined somewhat within ecospiritual movements. Classically, in modern and Western settings, spiritual is used in contradistinction to the physical and is associated with disembodiment, ideality, and denial of the worldly. This sense of spirituality also tends to be framed in contrast to a scientific attitude in which spirituality is thought to be about unquestioned faith, whereas science is seen to be concerned with unquestionable evidence. This cluster of distinctions is usually erased in ecospiritual discourses, which are structured around the recollection that matters of the spirit are, literally, matters of breathing. Derived from the Latin *spiritus*, "breath," the spiritual is about constant physical connection to and material exchange with an animate world. (The word *psyche*, the root of psychology, has a similar origin—from the Greek *psukhe*, "breath.")

Once again, this attitude seems to be as much about a recovery of an ancient understanding as it is about the emergence of a new one. Historians, anthropologists, and cultural commentators have reported on many indications of deep ecological sensibilities across cultures and societies. Unfortunately, when these sorts of beliefs were interpreted by Europeans to reach indigenous cultures— both evangelical Christian missionaries and rational-empiricist researchers—references to spirits and souls could only be heard in terms of ignorance and mystical delusion. However, such a belief is very much in keeping with emergent ecological understanding. It is about lateral or outward relationships as opposed to forward or upward grasping.

The underlying attitude is one of *participation*, a word used by anthropologists to describe the animistic aspects of indigenous people's and oral cultures' worldviews. The term has been picked up in the current phrase, "participatory epistemology"—which is used to refer to any theory that asserts that all aspects of the world, animate and inanimate, participate with humanity in the ongoing project of knowledge production. The whole is understood to unfold from and to be enfolded in the part(icipant). In a word, within participatory epistemologies, the central issue is meaning.

ENACTIVISM: AN ECO-COMPLEXIVIST DISCOURSE

Enactivism (Varela et al., 1991) begins with a redefinition of *cognition*, in terms similar to the scientific definition of complexity. Cognition is understood as ongoing processes of adaptive activity. As with complex systems, the cognizing agent can be seen as an autonomous form or as an agent that is behaviorally coupled to other agents and, hence, part of a grander form. An implication is that cognition is not seen to occur strictly inside an agent. Cognition, rather, is used to refer to all active processes—internal and external to the cognizing agent—that are part of its ongoing adaptive actions. The processes of cognition are the processes of life.

As with all complexity and ecological discourses, enactivism rejects the assumption of a core, essential, inner self. Instead, personal identity is seen to arise in the complex mix of biological predisposition, physical affect, social circumstance, and cultural context as the agent copes with the contingencies of existence. The term *enactivism* is intended to highlight the notion that identities and knowledge are not ideal forms, but enactments—that is, embodied in the nested interactivities of dynamic forms. Life and learning are thus understood in terms of explorations of ever-evolving landscapes of possibility and of selecting (not necessarily consciously) actions that are adequate to situations.

A further aspect of enactivism, and one that is particularly relevant in discussions of human cognition, is the notion of languaging. Understood in complexity terms, language is an emergent phenomenon that exceeds the agents who language. It arises in the interactions of agents and, in turn, conditions the interactions of agents. The gerund *languaging* (versus the noun *language*) is used to point to the open-endedness of language. Like knowing–knowledge, doing–action, and being–existence, languaging–language is in no way a finished form. It is constantly arising and adapting.

A key aspect of languaging is recursivity. Humans have the capacity to language about language—an endlessly elaborative process that seems to be vital to knowledge production and to the emergence of consciousness (see Donald, 2001). Our abilities to self-reference—that is, to cleave our individual selves from one another and from our contexts—is clearly amplified by, if not rooted in, our language. In this regard, enactivism has much in common with twentieth-century poststructuralist and many postmodern discourses. The main differences have to do with attitudes toward scientific inquiry and persistent reminders that we are biological beings whose habits of interpretation, while enabled by sophisticated languaging capacities, are conditioned by the way humanity evolved in and is coupled to a physical world. Even humanity's most abstract conceptual achievements are understood to be tethered to the ground of biologically conditioned experience.

COMPLEXITY, ECOLOGY, ENACTIVISM, AND THE PRAGMATICS OF TRANSFORMATION

Through most of the twentieth century, it was not uncommon to encounter descriptions of psychology as the "science of education." With the pervasive assumption that psychology was the only domain devoted to the study of learning, most major faculties, colleges, and schools of education in North America came to be organized around departments of educational psychology.

Such organizational structures continue to be common, even though a host of other fields and discourses have entered the discussion on the nature of learning and learners. Indeed, whereas psychology once dominated, among educationists it now plays a minor role.

At present, the influence of psychology on discussions of learning and teaching is perhaps most prominently represented in Piagetian-based theories of child development and children's construction of understanding. These constructivist theories are typically considered alongside social constructionist and critical theories, and they are commonly critiqued for their failure to attend to the social and cultural character of knowledge and identity.

Complexity science offers another frame for considering the complementarities and incongruities of these sorts of theories. It offers that constructivism, constructionism, and critical theories—among a host of others currently represented—might be distinguished as each being concerned with a particular body. Constructivism is focused on the individual, biological body.

Social constructionisms are concerned with epistemic bodies—that is, bodies of knowledge, social corpi, and so on. Critical theories deal in the main with the body politic. These bodies are nested, and each is dynamic and adaptive. Regardless of which one is brought into focus, similar sorts of recursive, self-maintaining processes seem to be at work. Understood in such terms, individual knowing, collective knowledge, and cultural identity are three nested, intertwining, self-similar aspects of one ever-evolving whole.

However, following a core complexivist principle, these phenomena cannot be reduced to or collapsed into one another. At each level of organization, different possibilities arise and different rules emerge. Complexivists thus avoid debates around matters of the relative worth of different discourses on learning. Instead they are more oriented by the question, On which levels (or in which domains) is a particular theory an explanation? Constructivism, for instance, does not work as an explanation on the level of cultural evolution. Similarly, critical theory and cultural studies tend to offer little to help make sense of an individual's construal of a particular concept.

This nested interpretation of cognition can be extended in both the micro and macro directions. On the subhuman level, for instance, recent complexity-oriented medical research has underscored that the body's organs are relatively autonomous and cognitive unities. The immune system, for example, is not a cause–effect mechanism, but a self-transforming agent that learns, forgets, hypothesizes, errs, recovers, recognizes, and rejects in a complex dance with other bodily subagents. The brain, similarly, is not a static form, but a vibrantly changing system that follows a nested organization: Neurons are clustered into minicolumns, minicolumns into macrocolumns, macrocolumns into cortical areas, cortical areas into hemispheres—and, at every level, agents interact with and affect other agents.

On the supra-cultural level, to understand humanity as a species, one must attend to the web of relationships in the global ecosystem. Metaphorically, humanity might be understood as one among many organs in the body of the biosphere, engaged with other organ-species in the emergence of collective possibility. Invested in every human—woven through our biological beings—is a trace of our species' history and its implicatedness in the planet.

Returning to the level of the individual, then, one's cognition is not just the product of her or his experiences. It is also a reflection of the emergence of the species. To ignore or to downplay the biological, in the complex-ecological view, is to seriously restrict any discussion of what learning is and how it might happen. This is not to say that the biological must be given priority, merely that humans are both biological and cultural beings. Each of us is, all at once, a collective of agents, a coherent unity, and a part of other emergent unities. It is for this reason that complexity science is a useful discourse for those interested in matters of knowledge, learning, and teaching. Complexity science straddles the classical institutional break of the sciences and the humanities. As such, those psychologists and educators who have embraced complexity have found it necessary to assume an inter- or transdisciplinary attitude (hence the spate of "new" areas of study, such as neuropsychology, ecopsychology, and cultural psychology).

Educationally, complexity science has also prompted attentions to levels of structural unity that lie *between* the individual and society, not just beyond them. For instance, a common, everyday conversation turns out to be a complex event. Although participants in a conversation are rarely aware of it, slowed video recordings of their interactions reveal a complex choreography of action. Speech patterns are precisely synchronized with subtle body movements that are acutely sensitive to events in the surroundings. The choreography is so tight that a conversation can properly be described as a coupling of individuals' attentional systems.

The same sort of *structural coupling*—that is, of intimate entangling of one's attentions and activities with another's—is observed in parents' actions as they assist in their children's learning of language and various fine motor skills. Exquisite choreographies of activity emerge as a parent offers subtle cues or assistance, maintaining a delicate balance between too much and too little help. What is surprising, as highlighted in follow-up interviews with parents, is that this extraordinary process of coupling one's actions to another's can occur without conscious knowledge. When asked about prompts given and assistance offered, most parents are unable to provide rationales for their actions. In fact, parents are often at a greater loss when asked to explain how and when they learned to teach in this complex, participatory manner—an observation that has prompted the suggestion that humans are *natural* teachers. We are biologically, not just culturally, predisposed to engage with others in ways that can properly be called teaching.

Joint attention—that is, the interlocking of two or more consciousnesses—is the foundation of all deliberate efforts to teach. As Donald (2001) points out, "human cultures are powerful pedagogues because their members regulate one another's attention, through a maze of cultural conventions." However, it is one thing to note that humans have these capacities to engage, and quite another to assert some sort of utility for the rigidly organized and prescriptive context of the modern classroom. How might the teacher go about structurally coupling with 30 (or 300!) students at the same time around an issue that may not be a particularly engaging topic of conversation?

On the first part of this question, it turns out that we are always already structurally coupled to one another. Harris (1998) makes this point in a review and reinterpretation of a substantial psychological literature around the emergence of individual identity. To perhaps overtruncate her argument, the evidence seems to suggest that the major influences in the emergence of identity are genetics and one's peer group. Compared to the influences of friends and age-mates, parents and early family life play a minor role. Harris reasons that this difference in influence arises in the fact that the child's main task is not to become a successful adult, but to be a successful child—to fit in, to be part of the group, to not stand out. In other words, the child (and, for that matter, the adult) is oriented toward structurally coupling with others. This phenomenon is perhaps better examined on the group level, as a tendency toward social self-organization.

The classroom teacher can thus count on this tendency to be already in place. Eavesdropping on almost any lunchtime school staffroom conversation will confirm this point. Teachers commonly refer to classrooms of learners as coherent unities—that have intentions, habits, and other personality traits. The difficulty, however, is that such collectivity rarely emerges around engagements with a subject matter, but around the common and continuous project of fitting in. The question thus remains, How might a teacher concerned with a prescribed curriculum topic invoke the capacities and tendencies of learners to come together into grander cognitive unities? This is a question that is only starting to be answered. One strategy that seems to hold some promise has been to structure classroom activities in ways that ensure the presence of the conditions that are necessary for complex emergence—a matter that we develop elsewhere (Davis et al., 2000).

One of these conditions merits special mention here: *decentralized control*. In complexity terms, learning is an emergent event. That is, learning can only be defined in the process of engagement. In classroom terms, the understandings and interpretations that are generated cannot be completely prestated but must be allowed to unfold. Control of outcomes, that is, must be decentralized. They must to some extent emerge and be sustained through shared projects, not through prescribed learning objectives, linear lesson plans, or rigid management strategies. Complexity cannot be scripted.

Applied to schooling, the condition of decentralized control should be interpreted neither as a condemnation of the teacher-centered classroom nor as an endorsement of the student-centered classroom. Rather, it represents a critique of an assumption that is common to both those structures—namely, that the site of learning is the individual. As complexity science asserts, the capacity to learn is a defining quality of all complex unities. One must thus be clear on the nature of the complex unities that are desired in the classroom. Such unities are concerned with the generation of knowledge and the development understanding—meaning that the focus should not be on teachers or learners, but on collective possibilities for interpretation.

Unfortunately, a vocabulary to frame complexivist teaching has yet to emerge. At the moment, it is much easier to talk about what such teaching is *not* rather than what it is or might be. For example, it is not prescriptive, detached, or predictable. It cannot expect the same results with different groups. It cannot assume that complex possibilities will in fact emerge. Furthermore, this manner of teaching is not a matter of orchestrating; once again, complex emergence cannot be managed into existence. However, complexivist teaching might be described as a sort of *improvising*, in the jazz music sense of engaging attentively and responsively with others in a collective project. Another term that might be used to describe teaching is *occasioning*. In its original sense, *occasioning* referred to the way that surprising possibilities can arise when things are allowed to fall together. The word is useful for foregrounding the participatory and emergent natures of learning engagements as it points to both the deliberate and the accidental qualities of teaching.

The role of the student is also reconceived by complexivists. Departing from popular discourses, complexity science does not use notions of margins, fringes, and peripheries to describe complex systems. In fact, such constructs make little sense when systems are understood as nested within systems. This alternative geometry prompts the suggestion that students are not neophytes, initiates, or novices that are to be incorporated into an established order. Rather, like teachers, they are participants—and, in fact, play profound roles in shaping the forms that are popularly seen to shape them.

Ecological discourses have a similar disdain for notions of marginalization. They also share with complexity a conviction that all forms and events are intimately intertwined. However, for ecologists, this conviction has prompted more of a concern for ethical know-how than practical know-how. Ethical action is understood here as contextually appropriate behavior that may or may not be—and usually is not—consciously mediated (Varela, 1999).

The suggestion that ethics may not be consciously mediated was actually first developed within twentieth-century structuralist and poststructuralist discourses. Ethics have been argued to be matters of collective accord, of tacit social contract. Ethical codes, that is, are seen by some critical and cultural theorists as largely arbitrary sets of rules deployed to maintain existing social orders. However, despite the departure from the commonsense conviction that ethics are ideal and universal, these interpretations maintain one usually unquestioned delimitation—namely, that ethics tend to be understood in terms of interactions of humans with other humans.

Ecological discourses ask us to consider questions of ethics within the more-than-human world, rather than limiting discussions to the space of human concern. This sort of shift is timely, given such developments as the now-apparent role of human activity in ecosystems, the prospect of pulling biological evolution into the space of the conscious and the volitional through genetic engineering, and the emergence of technologies that amplify our potential impact on the planet. These concerns are added to those already foregrounded within critical discourses, including, for instance, the decline of cultural diversity, ever-widening gaps between have and have-not nations, and persistent social inequities rooted in perceived differences among races, classes, and other means of distinguishing one human from another.

Varela (1999) explains that ethical action arises in a deep appreciation of the virtuality of one's own identity—knowledge that one's self is a fluid, always-emergent, biological–cultural form. Knowing, doing, and being are inseparable. One might thus embody a conception of the self as pregiven and eternal and, hence, not implicated in the events of the physical realm. Or one might embody a conception of self as situated and emergent and, hence, complicit with events in the physical realm. Ethical action flows out of this latter sort of enactment. Ethical know-how is neither instinctive nor based on principles that are woven into the fabric of the universe. Rather, it is a mode of ongoing coping, a responsiveness to what is appropriate here and now.

As for what this ethical action might mean for living, generally, and teaching, specifically, many ecological discourses advocate an attitude of mindful participation (Varela et al., 1991) in the unfolding of personal and collective identities, culture, intercultural space, and the biosphere. In some important ways, the notion of mindful participation harkens back to the mystical traditions that prompted teaching to be described in the terms *educing* and *educating*—literally, of drawing out. A teaching that is informed by ecological sensibilities might be understood in similar terms, although selves would be understood as emergent possibilities rather than pregiven but unactualized potentials.

As might be expected, a consistent and broadly accepted vocabulary has not yet emerged for this sort of ecological–ethical attitude toward teaching. Some terms have been suggested that are resonant with the principles of ethical know-how: *tact*, *caring*, and *pedagogical thoughtfulness*. Significantly, these notions often point more to attitudes of teachers than to the pragmatics of teaching. To that end, one that is particularly useful for describing the teacher's activity in the classroom is *conversing*. The word is derived from the Latin *convertio*, "living together," and thus resonates with the notion of *oikos*, "household," that is echoed in the contemporary prefix, *eco-*. A conversation is an emergent form, one whose outcome is never prespecified and one that is sensitive to contingencies.

Recent neurophysiological research supports the use of the term *conversing* to describe teaching. When engaged in conversations, our working memories are vastly larger than they are on our own. We are able to recall more detail, to juggle more issues, to represent more complex ideas, and to maintain better focus than when alone (Donald, 2001). Part of the reason is that conversations involve interlocking consciousnesses—a quality of interpersonal engagement that is all but ignored in the traditional, radically individuated classroom.

Extending this notion of interlocking subjectivities, ecologists might seek to elaborate the complexivist suggestion that the classroom should be recast as a collective unity. However, a problem with this suggestion is that it says very little about the role of the teacher beyond responsibilities for ensuring that the conditions necessary for complex emergence are in place. In ecological terms, the role of the teacher in the classroom collective might be understood in more explicit terms as analogous to the role of consciousness in an individual.

To elaborate, despite popular assumption, our consciousnesses do not direct our thoughts and actions. In fact, for the most part, consciousness operates more as commentator than orchestrator (Donald, 2001). However, consciousness does play an important role in orienting attentions— that is, through differential attention, in selecting among the options for action and interpretation that are available to the conscious agent. Succinctly, consciousness does not direct, but it does orient. Such is the role of the teacher in the complexity-eco-minded classroom: attending to and selecting from among those possibilities that present themselves to her or his awareness. In this sense, teaching is about *minding*—being mindful in, being conscious of, being the consciousness of—the collective.

TERMS FOR READERS

Complexity (science)—the study of adaptive, self-organizing systems—or, more colloquially, the study of living systems—or, more educationally, the study of learning systems.

Ecology—derived from the Greek *oikos*, "household," ecology is the study of relationships. It is often distinguished from *environmentalism*, a term seen to imply a separation between agent and setting. Ecology assumes no such separation and understands agents to be aspects of their contexts.

Emergence—a process by which autonomous agents self-organize into a grander system that is itself a complex agent. Emergence is a bottom-up phenomenon through which transcendent unities arise without the aid of instructions or leaders.

Enactivism—a perspective on cognition that asserts (a) the possibilities for new perception are conditioned by the actions that are enabled by established perceptions, and (b) an agent's cognitive structures (which might be thought of as the "space of the possible" for the agent, as conditioned by its biological–experiential history) emerge from repetitions and patterns in the agent's engagements with its world. The term *enactivism* is intended to foreground the central assertion that identities and knowledge are not preexistent, but enacted.

Structural Coupling—(also referred to as coevolution, cospecification, mutual specification, consensual coordination of action) the comingling of complex agents' ongoing histories; the intimate entangling of one's emergent activity with another's. (See *structure*.)

Structure—the embodied (and constantly unfolding) history of a complex agent. The structures of living systems are understood to be influenced by both biology and experience—with experience playing more significant roles in more complex systems.

Structure Determinism—used to refer to the manner in which *complex agents* respond when perturbed. The manner of response is determined by the agent's *structure*, not by the perturbation. That is, a complex agent's response is dependent on, but not determined by, environmental influences. The same can be said of the components that comprise a complex unity. The properties of those components depend on the system in which they are located—in contrast to the components of a noncomplex system, in which the parts do not change depending on whether they are part of that system.

REFERENCES

American Psychological Association. (2001). *Publication Manual of the American Psychological Association* (5th ed.). Washington, DC: American Psychological Association.

Davis, B., Sumara, D., and Luce-Kapler, R. (2000). *Engaging Minds: Learning and Teaching in a Complex World*. Mahwah, NJ: Lawrence Erlbaum.

Donald, M. (2001). *A Mind So Rare: The Evolution of Human Consciousness*. New York: W. W. Norton.

Harris, J. R. (1998). *The Nurture Assumption: Why Children Turn Out the Way They Do*. New York: The Free Press.

Newberg, A., D'Aquili, E., and Rause, V. (2001). *Why God Won't Go Away: Brain Science and the Biology of Belief*. New York: Ballantine.

Varela, F. (1999). *Ethical Know-How: Action, Wisdom, and Cognition*. Stanford, CA: Stanford University Press.

Varela, F., Thompson, E., and Rosch, E. (1991). *The Embodied Mind: Cognitive Science and Human Experience*. Cambridge, MA: The MIT Press.

CHAPTER 57

Providing a Warrant for Constructivist Practice: The Contribution of Francisco Varela

JEANETTE BOPRY

This chapter will trace the chronology of the development of Varela's enactive framework beginning with his collaboration on autopoiesis theory with his mentor Humberto Maturana, the development of autonomous systems theory as a category within which to place autopoiesis as a special case, and finally enaction as a framework within which these theories work as a matter of course. I will explain important terms: autopoiesis, organization, organizational closure, structure, structural determination, structural coupling, and effective action. Finally, I will discuss the implications of the framework for theorists and practitioners concerned with teaching, learning, and cognition. Special attention will be paid to the following: the concept of information, the rejection of the representational hypothesis and the metaphor of transmission, and the related rejection of prescription.

Francisco Varela (1943–2001) considered himself both a scientist and an epistemologist. He is credited with being able to move easily between hard science and philosophy (both Western and Eastern). He was instrumental, for example, in organizing a series of semiannual meetings between cognitive scientists and the Dalai Lama. His epistemological position is the result of his reflection on the scientific work in which he engaged both with his mentor Humberto Maturana and in his own right. He is credited with both the development of autonomous systems theory and with the development of the enactive framework. The enactive framework is important because it provides an alternative to representational realism. The framework can be used to provide a warrant for constructivist practice and to ensure that such practice is epistemologically consistent. Enaction is not simply a reaction to the representational one, but the result of attempts to understand the results of scientific work that calls the representational framework into question. Enaction is of primary interest in this chapter, but it cannot be dealt with effectively without reference to autonomous systems theory or to his collaboration with Humberto Maturana on autopoiesis theory, which provides the basic concepts and terminology for the enactive framework.

AUTOPOIESIS THEORY AND AUTONOMOUS SYSTEMS THEORY

Varela became known initially for his collaboration with Humberto Maturana on autopoiesis theory. According to autopoiesis theory all living systems are self-producing: All of the component parts and processes that comprise the living system are manufactured within the boundaries of the system itself. The cell is the prototypical example of autopoiesis as its organization is characterized by *closed* or circular processes of production. The concept of *organizational closure* was powerful enough to begin to influence practitioners in fields other than biology. Unfortunately because the form of closure Maturana and Varela described was autopoietic, it was this form of closure that people tried to import into other fields, so one that would read of communication producing communication, laws producing laws, etc. [This is an improper translation because people are important mediators in both instances: people produce communication, people produce laws.] Instead of choosing the common term *autonomy*, Maturana and Varela had coined the term *autopoiesis* specifically to distinguish living from nonliving systems. Such importations at best muddied the intended distinction; at worst they caused nonliving systems (e.g., social systems) to be treated as if they were living systems, something Maturana and Varela coined the term *autopoiesis* in order to avoid. The application of the organismic metaphor to social systems can result in people being considered mere component parts of larger living entities, the survival of which takes precedence over the survival of the people (now relegated to the status of interchangeable parts) that comprise it. This misuse of autopoiesis theory led Varela to develop the autonomous systems theory, which makes it possible to deal with the concept of organizational closure without limiting it to processes of production. Organizational closure is the criterion characteristic of all autonomous systems; autopoiesis is a special case of autonomy. Autonomous systems theory and autopoiesis theory share concepts and terminology that are relevant to the enactive framework. These require some explanation as their meanings are not intuitive. In particular, the terms *organization* and *structure*, which in everyday English are often used interchangeably, have specific and distinct meanings.

BASIC CONCEPTS UNDERLYING THE ENACTIVE FRAMEWORK

Organization and Structure

Organization is the set of relationships that must be present for something to exist as a member of any given class or category of entity. Take for example a geometric figure, the square. The organization of a square is a closed figure on a single plane composed of four equal sides connected at right angles. This definition includes both the properties of the components of the square (four equal sides) and the relationships inhering between them (closed, on a single plane, connected by right angles). The organization of the square is instantiated in all actual examples of that class of systems. All figures that have this organization will be recognized as squares.

Any actual example of an organization is a structure. Our square may be made of pencil lines, built of wood, built of plastic, etc. I can replace all the wood parts of my square with plastic parts and still have a square. If, however, I change the angle at which the sides of the figure connect, I have changed the organization of the figure and it is no longer a square. Organization and structure, therefore, are complementary concepts. Organization requires a physical structure, and any structure is an instance of some organization. Organization is the source of the identity of a system.

Organizational Closure—Autonomous Systems

Systems are divided into two major categories: closed or self-referred (autonomous), and open or other-referred (allonomous). An autonomous system is any system exhibiting a circular or closed organization. This type of organization allows no inputs or outputs. An allonomous system exhibits linear or open organization and allows inputs to and outputs from the system.

For example, the heart is an organ that is organized to process blood, the input–output process is essential to its organization.

In order to determine if a system is autonomous we must be able to observe its component parts. Organizational closure requires a system made up of a network of components that interact so that they

1. recursively recreate the interactions that brought them about in the first place, and
2. establish themselves as a unity by creating a boundary and using it as a means of separation from the background.

Autonomous systems come in a variety of forms, only a small number of these are autopoietic. The nervous system is an example of an organizationally closed system that is not a living system (it is a component of a living system). The organizational closure (circularity) of the nervous system takes the form "neuronal activity leads only to more neuronal activity." The nervous system cannot be considered autopoietic because it does not produce the components that comprise it. Social systems can be interpreted as organizationally closed systems of coordinated behaviors that are reproduced over time by their members. Language is also considered an autonomous system because it can only be described in language. In "Autonomy and Autopoiesis," Varela (1981) gives other examples of autonomous systems, including descriptions of events, rearrangements of elements, and computations of all kinds. Any autonomous system will tend to interact with the environment in such a manner as to preserve its identity.

A most important distinction between allonomous and autonomous systems is that informational interactions are essentially different in the two types of systems. A primary metaphor for allonomous systems is the *computer gestalt*: input, process, output. We interact with allonomous systems through instructions. Meaning is seen as contained in the correspondence between the representation and what it represents rather than in the system. A cognitive system belonging to the allonomous systems category (e.g., a computer) brings only syntactic (structural, grammatical) processing to this interaction. In the case of autonomous systems, meaning is provided by the cognitive system itself as determined by its own structural properties—through interpretation not through input. So, the cognitive system operates semantically, with meaning. In this regard information is what Varela has referred to as *in-formation*. In place of the computer gestalt, the primary metaphor for autonomous systems is the conversation.

The computer gestalt is the primary metaphor of cognitivism and information-processing theories. It is important to keep in mind that when this metaphor is applied to cognitive systems they are being treated as allonomous systems. In autopoiesis theory, all living systems are cognitive systems (cognition is the operation of living systems), but not all cognitive systems are living systems. So, to treat a living cognitive system as allonomous is to treat it as a nonliving entity, what Heinz von Foerster refers to as a *trivial machine*. While this type of interaction is possible, it demonstrates a basic disregard, even lack of respect, for the identity of the system.

Structural Determination

A system's organization cannot change without a change to its identity. If a living system stops producing its own components it dies. But systems undergo change all the time and the distinction between organization and structure becomes critical. Structure determines the range of interactions a system may have with its environment and any changes a system can undergo. Change in a system may be triggered by the environment, but it is not caused by the environment. Changes in the structure of a unity can come from two possible sources: its *internal dynamics* and *continuous interactions* with an environment. Both types of interaction are determined by the properties of its structure; a system can only engage in the kinds of interactions its structure makes possible. If this seems counterintuitive, consider that structural determination is very much a part of our commonsense understanding of everyday experience. When I press the accelerator in my car and nothing happens, I do not blame my foot, I understand the problem to be related to the structure of the car. The concept of structural determination provides a biological foundation for the notion that we construct reality, construct our own perceptions, and construct what we call knowledge.

For cognitive systems the combination of *organizational closure* plus *structural determination* has important implications. Organizational closure makes it impossible for information to be transmitted through, or picked up from, the environment. Structural determination makes information possible. Information is a construction, an interpretation made by a cognitive system, one that has been triggered by an interaction with the environment or some other cognitive system. This is apparent in our recognition that animals perceive the world very differently than we do and that this is related to differences in perceptual makeup. Dogs, bats, and birds all have their own ways of seeing the world. Yet, we do not say that they see the world incorrectly, just that they see the world differently. Cognitive systems do not create their perceptions out of whole cloth. The environment constrains the range of perceptions that a member of any given species may have.

Perceptions are the result of the interaction of a cognitive system with an environment. The environment perturbs the nervous system (triggers a response) but does not provide the response (determine the reaction). The cognitive system responds, not to the environment but to the deformation the environment has triggered in the system itself. In other words, my description of a sunset is not a description of an external phenomenon as much as it is a description of my own visual field. That you and I have similar responses to the same sunset is a testament to similarities in our physical and cultural makeup: We describe the deformation to our cognitive systems triggered by the sunset in much the same way. But, given organizational closure and structural determination, how is it that we are able to talk about the sunset at all? The answer to that question lies in *structural coupling*.

Structural Coupling

When a system interacts with the environment it undergoes structural change, and so does the environment. Just as is the case with the system, any change in the environment is dependent upon its structural properties. When a unity is in continuous interaction with an environment, so that there is a mutual triggering of structural change over time that is stable in nature, the unity and the environment are said to be structurally coupled. This process is more commonly referred to as adaptation. The process is recursive in that the changes in A triggered by B will trigger changes in B that will trigger changes in A, etc. Two unities may also become structurally coupled. When this happens they act as environment for each other. If two unities remain structurally coupled over time their ontogenies (life histories) intertwine. Cells that are structurally coupled may form metacellular entities; organisms that are structurally coupled may form social groupings. There is no plan, no design, being followed that determines the results of structural coupling. This is a historical process, a process of drift. As long as the structural changes mutually selected in each other result in the conservation of the organization of the unities, the unities will carry on in co-ontogenic drift.

Social Phenomena

When two autopoietic entities are structurally coupled in such a way that their life histories intertwine, a new phenomenal domain arises: a social domain. This form of structural coupling

Figure 57.1
Levels of Experience

Reflective
Description
Observation
Unreflective
Thrownness

is close to universal, but takes different forms in different species. What is common to all social phenomena is that they become the medium in which the autopoiesis of participating organisms occurs. All social phenomena require the coordination of behavior, which is provided through the mechanism of structural coupling. All behavioral patterns that are learned and that are stable through generations are cultural behaviors.

Language.   Communication is a form of coordinated behavior. Communicative behavior that is learned, as opposed to instinctive, is linguistic. Many animal species generate linguistic domains (use signs). In their coordination of linguistic behaviors, human beings generate language (recognize that they use signs and communicate about the signs themselves). Language is the glue that holds *human* social interaction together. Its development signals the emergence of a phenomenal domain that is unique to humans and which coevolves with language: the observer.

The Observer.   The term *observer* as used by Varela approximates Heidegger's term *Dasein*. The observer is the human "way of being in the world." The observer is able to observe and communicate about its own linguistic states. It is within the domains of language and the observer rather than in the cognitive domain of the nervous system that representations come into play; they are a construction that facilitates communication between observers. Language is the glue that holds human social interaction together.

Social interaction depends upon structural coupling. Structural coupling makes it possible for the living system to enter a social domain, and eventually to develop the domains of the observer and language that make the consensual specification of a reality possible. The notion of structural coupling replaces the notion of the transmission of information. This is important in understanding experience.

Levels of Experience

The emergence of new phenomenal domains suggest different levels of experience (Figure 57.1). These levels of experience are each organizationally closed domains that do not intersect, so that what happens in one domain is unknown to the others except through structural coupling. So, while we can observe ourselves or others engaged in some common unreflective activity, the observation is an interpretation of that activity and is not isomorphic to it. We can describe our observations in language, but again this description is not an exact representation of the observation but an interpretation of it. Through structural coupling these domains perturb each other and interpret the ways the other perturbs them. Higher levels of experience depend upon, but do not intersect with, lower levels. The level of observation depends upon unreflective activity, but within it such activity acts as a perturbation or a trigger for interpretation. Descriptions are attempts to put observations into language, and again they are not equivalent to the observation. It is fundamental to the enactive position that everything that is said is said by someone. Actor cannot be divorced from action, observer from observation, describer from description.

ENACTION

Rejecting the Representational Hypothesis

The enactive framework has not come about as the result of philosophical musing alone. Maturana and Varela engaged in scientific work in neurophysiology and, more recently, for Varela at least, immunology. The enactive framework came about in part as a necessary component of understanding the results of their own research; dealing with the shortcomings cognitive scientists have just begun to acknowledge with cognitivism. The need for a new framework as an alternative to representational realism became apparent to Maturana in the 1960s when his work on color vision led him to realize that activity in the retina could be more easily correlated with the experience of the perceiver than with the physical stimuli present in the environment. If the representational hypothesis were correct then the color of an object, say an orange, should appear differently under fluorescent (blue) light than it does in the sunlight (full spectrum). However, our experience of the color orange is the same in both environments. In order to account for the problem posed by color vision Maturana came to the conclusion that perception cannot be considered as the grasping of an external reality, but rather as the specification of one. The representational hypothesis works only if there is a pre-given world to represent; if perception specifies the world, the representational hypothesis must be rejected. When Varela joined Maturana both recognized how their work posed a direct challenge to the representational hypothesis, but it was left to Varela to formally codify an alternative. The enactive framework is the result.

Cognitive science developed within the representational realist framework has a number of acknowledged drawbacks. Serial processing is one of these; another is the notion of memory as an entity stored in specific locations in the brain. These are important problems, but Varela points to the inability of cognitive science in a representational framework to account for a large percentage of cognition, what we refer to as *common sense*.

The Enactive Framework

If we do not interact with the world through representation, what mechanism do we use? The main thrust of the enactive framework is that the primary way we interact with the world is through action. As I move about I interact with the world: I *bump* into things. In bumping into things my perceptual systems become deformed. I interpret this deformation and project it back onto the *outside* as environment.

This position has currency in recent developments in artificial intelligence. The roving robots sent to Mars to collect samples and the small autonomous vacuum sweeping system currently being marketed in the United States are examples. The enactive position is nonfoundational: it does not assume a preexisting world (realist position) or a preexisting mind (idealist position).

Constructing a Reality

The nervous system is a closed system of neuronal activity (neuronal activity leads only to more neuronal activity). It cannot be instructed by the environment: information cannot be input to or output from it. The living system structurally coupled to a nervous system does not pick up information from the environment; instead, it interprets its interactions with the environment. These interpretations may be triggered by the environment, but they are determined by the structure of the living system. In this way, I may say that what I see is not the world outside, but my own visual field. Thus, the nervous system is incapable of making a distinction between perception and hallucination. While one might think that the closure of the nervous system means that the specification of a reality is an individualistic and solipsistic matter; in fact, this cannot be the case. It is, ironically, the very fact that the operation of the nervous system is solipsistic that makes this impossible. Since an individual alone cannot make this distinction, a social consensus is required. The determination of a reality, then, depends upon social interaction, an understanding that what is perceived by oneself is also perceived by others. We share a reality because we have cospecified it through the coordination of our actions with the actions of others. This can lead to the specification of many different realities because it is an activity that can be engaged by a small group as easily as a large group. So one may speak of *multi-verses* in place of a *uni-verse*.

By focusing on interaction rather than representation, Varela has avoided the mind–body, physical–mental dualism. Existence and interpretation are the same thing. Those things that we label information, knowledge, and semantic content are constructions, structurally determined products of structural coupling. They have no independent existence. So, we may say that reality is both socially determined and dependent upon the interpretation of individuals. It is the creation of the process of inquiry rather than discovered through inquiry.

Effective action

Effective action is simply successful ways of being-in-the-world. More precisely, it is the history of structural coupling that brings forth a world in such a manner as permits the continued integrity of the systems involved. Effective action is metaphorically a conversation; maintaining the continued integrity of the system requires keeping that conversation going. Survival is proof of effective action. Within this framework, information, knowledge, and semantic content are all constructions of the cognitive system and products of structural coupling. They are effective to the extent that they permit the continued integrity of the system. What we call knowledge is effective action within a given domain. What is called *content* in the representational framework becomes part of the environment through which we must wend our way.

Communication

Seen from a representational perspective, communication is deterministic. The responsibility for understanding lies with the sender. The process is easy if the sender is competent at transmitting semantic content. Within the enactive framework, on the other hand, communication requires effort and patience. It is a reciprocal process of interpretation and reflexive understanding. I must interpret what my partner is saying, I must interpret my partner's understanding of what I am saying, and I must interpret my partner's understanding of my understanding of what he is saying, etc. The process is like the experience of looking in a three-way mirror, where the images go on into infinity. The involved parties will assume they share an understanding until such time as their *conversation* breaks down, then, and only then, they will engage in a problem-solving process to get the conversation back on track if they consider the effort worthwhile. Communication within this framework requires mutual respect—it is impossible unless both parties are willing to make a space for the other in their lives.

GENERAL IMPLICATIONS

Abandon the Transmission Model with Its Container Metaphor

The most obvious implication is that we must abandon the transmission model of communication. This is troublesome because the English language conspires against us. We talk of sending information, or putting information into messages that can be sent. We put knowledge into books and other vehicles of conveyance. Meaning is referred to as contained in words or sentences. We admonish our students not to read too much into test items, etc.

One of the implications of the transmission model is that the sender is responsible for the understanding of the receiver. If he crafts his message correctly it will not be misunderstood. If we extend this to instruction we can see how it is that teachers are considered to be responsible for learning in their students. If instruction is the transmission of knowledge (and/or information) then the teacher (as sender) is the responsible party. This is something that has not escaped the notice of students who often describe *learning* as something that someone does to them rather than as something for which they are responsible.

An implication of the container metaphor is that information and knowledge can be contained in words, books, tools, and other devices. Within the enactive framework knowledge is effective action within a domain. It cannot be contained. It is better to think of such material as indices of the intelligent activity of their creators. Anything that might be considered input, like presentational material, has only the potential to function as a perturbation, a trigger for neuronal activity, that results in a change of state determined by the structure of any individual that interacts with such material.

The transmission model can function only in a representational environment, where the world outside is pre-given, where information and even knowledge are pre-given. In an environment where interaction brings forth both the knower and the world to be known, we cannot speak of transmission, we must speak of structural coupling, of bringing forth through interaction.

Information Is a Construction

Many constructivists, generally those who refer to themselves as moderate constructivists, consider knowledge a construction, while considering information an entity with independent existence. To take the position that knowledge (or meaning) is constructed from information that is picked up or transferred from the environment is to consider the cognitive system simultaneously allonomous and autonomous. From an enactive standpoint, this is illogical. Information is what Varela has referred to as *in-formation*: an interpretation, a construction. Information cannot be picked up from the environment; rather it emerges as regularities within our cognitive activity. We interpret these regularities as facts.

Intelligence Is an Ability to Join or Create Shared Worlds of Meaning

Within the representational framework intelligence is equated with problem solving. Within the enactive framework, intelligence is measured by the ability to join and the ability to create shared worlds of understanding. Sharing in this context does not denote isomorphic or identical understanding; rather it means that a conversation can be conducted on a given topic without breakdown. As we carry on the conversation we may *assume* we have the same understanding and we may *behave* as if there is one. The longer we can carry on this conversation, the greater our confidence may become in this isomorphism. Such interaction allows us to coordinate behavior with others. We generally become aware that understanding is not isomorphic only when the conversation breaks down. To stand Bateson's definition of distinction on its head, a successful conversation is one in which the differences make no difference.

Becoming a member of any preexisting community and taking on the values and commitments of its members is the prototypical example of joining a shared world of understanding. Examples include our family, local community, schools, professions, etc. Creating new worlds of understanding may seem more remote, the activity of scientists, explorers, artists, and even politicians who push the frontiers of knowledge. I suggest, however, that this activity is not really so remote. It seems to be a natural part of the adolescent journey into adulthood. Hip-hop culture seems a good example of this form of creation. Each generation of American youth seems to have generated some new understanding that has had an impact on the culture at large.

PEDAGOGICAL IMPLICATIONS

The enactive framework, dealing as it does explicitly with issues of cognition, has implications for educators, in terms of both how we understand learners and learning and how we approach the process of design for learning.

Implications of Organizational Closure and Structural Determination

Learning is very much under the control of, and the responsibility of, the learner. The educator orients or points learners in desired directions. The symbol systems we use (e.g., language) are not conveyers of meaning; they are orienting devices. They effectively constrain, but do not determine, the possible interpretations that can be made by another of a given situation. In pedagogical interaction attention needs to be placed on learner understandings. Educators may also ask learners to reflect upon their own learning, to experience it as a learner-owned construction.

Implications of Structural Coupling

The foundation of the relationship between educators and learners is structural coupling. The excellent educator is one who is well adapted to his or her charges, and the students, in turn, are well adapted to their educator. The most obvious implication is that learners need to be provided opportunities for structural coupling that are consistent with learning goals. The converse is also true: the environment must scaffold the teacher's understanding of the learner's experience. As a history of structural coupling involves not just changes in the living system, but in the environment as well, learners should be provided an environment rich enough to afford reorganization by the learner (learners as designers) in pursuit of his or her learning goals.

Implications Effective Action

In addition to pointing learners in particular directions, educators also act as mediators between learners and the worlds of meaning to which they have oriented their charges. Worlds of meaning are metaphorically conversations among the members that comprise these worlds. Educators scaffold the ability of learners to enter into conversation with members of these worlds, to engage in effective action within the domains these worlds encompass. This suggests that learners have access to various communities of practice and other ongoing worlds of shared understanding. It is important to remember that the classroom is an environment in which learners can create their own shared worlds of understanding and their own communities of practice. While this activity is already present in the classroom, the educator may wish to make it visible so that learners may experience it reflexively. Contributing to the development of this shared world once it is visible requires that the environment be rich enough to afford problem setting as well as problem solving.

DESIGN IMPLICATIONS

Problems with Prescription

When I prescribe I create a number of problems from the enactive perspective. First of all, we know that instruction (transmission of information or knowledge) is not possible. So, prescription is a matter of so constraining the possibilities available to learners that their responses will fall into a narrow and predictable range. We effectively eliminate the possibility for a diverse range of responses, and for unusual or creative responses. Furthermore, when I expect students to limit what they learn to what I already know (or is provided as part of my design), I am treating them as an extension of my own cognition. This is an essentially oppressive activity. For learners, following another's prescription puts that person at the center of their cognitive activity, they follow that person's trajectory, not their own. You allow yourself to be used as a trivial machine. Every person needs to feel at the center of their own cognition. Finally, when I predetermine what my student may learn and further limit it to what is already known, I deny my charges the opportunity to make a valuable contribution to a community of importance to them. If I pretend that my prescriptions are the correct, or best, way of engaging a domain of knowledge I discourage learners from taking multiple perspectives on a given way of knowing. Those behaviors that we say we cherish most in learners: responsibility, creativity, and a critical stance are possible only when learners find themselves at the center of their own cognition.

Proscription as an Alternative

Proscription has a different logic than prescription. Prescription puts us in a place where what is not allowed is forbidden, proscription a place where what is not forbidden is allowed. One can argue, for example, that the viability of the U.S. constitution depends on its proscriptive logic. What is not specifically proscribed by law is permissible, and rights not specifically granted to the federal government belong to states or to individuals. In addition, the making of certain kinds of laws is expressly forbidden. If we consider what makes two cultures distinct, it is obvious that they offer their members different life experiences. We cannot know what we do not experience. We are enculturated through the proscription of certain experiences. While no culture can prescribe that all its members have a given set of experiences, cultures can establish taboos or experiences that are not allowed, or, even more effectively, cultures can simply ignore the possibility of certain experiences. Issues related to values are central to a proscriptive logic.

While design by telling people what not to do seem unpalatable, it is less constraining than prescription which tells people what to do. When I prescribe a series of steps for someone else to follow, I am proscribing an unknown set of alternatives. There is no mechanism for questioning what I have proscribed. When I set constraints by proscribing certain steps, I am providing guidance, but not determining how a goal may be reached. By naming what is proscribed, I am making the proscribed visible and open to question. What would otherwise be invisible may be critically analyzed. Proscription does not define a correct route to attainment of some goal, making the discovery of new alternatives possible, so learners in such an environment are constantly challenged to be creative.

Proscription can be seen as a humanistic alternative to prescription, because it determines what will not happen rather than what will happen, thereby allowing for diversity in practice. Proscription also seems to be a component of the process of creativity: Creative artists take account of the constraints of a given situation, often turning those constraints to their advantage. Within the enactive framework the concept of creativity is brought into the foreground: context and common sense are the essence of creative cognition. Common sense is defined as an individual's bodily and social history and this context provides the constraints imposed in a given situation. What matters is to maintain a history of effective action even while the obstacles or constraints that one encounters change.

Learners as Designers

It seems impractical to expect prescription to totally disappear. Novice members of communities of shared understanding will continue to rely upon the instructions of more expert members as part of the price of admittance to the community. There are alternatives to remedying the most onerous problems with it, however. In the example I just provided, the choice to accept a subordinate position is likely to be taken on willingly and novices may have some flexibility in the selection of experts they work with. That submission is willing does not ensure that the relationship is not oppressive. One can, however, encourage learners to create prescriptions for themselves with the understanding that such prescriptions will undergo constant revision as the learner's expertise improves.

REFERENCES

Maturana, H. R., and Varela, F. J. (1980). *Autopoiesis and Cognition*. London: D. Reidel.

Varela, F. J. (1992). Whence perceptual meaning? A cartography of current ideas. In F. J. Varela & J. Dupuy (Eds.), *Understanding Origins* (pp. 235–271). Dordrecht: Kluwer.

———. (1981). Autonomy and autopoiesis. In G. Roth & H. Schwegler (Eds.), *Self-Organizing Systems* (pp. 14–23). Frankfurt: Campus Verlag.

Varela, F. J., Thompson, E., and Rosch, E. (1991). *The Embodied Mind*. Cambridge, MA: The MIT Press.

CHAPTER 58

Action Research and Educational Psychology

DEBORAH S. BROWN

Throughout the twentieth century, educators advocated the notion of teachers conducting research on their own practice or engaging in what has become known as action research. The fact that the popularity of action research has waxed and waned over the last hundred years or so does not make it any less important In fact, the paradigm shift evidenced in the action research movement is indicative of the overall epistemological shift in the field of educational psychology often described as postmodern and constructivist in nature.

AN OVERVIEW OF THE HISTORY OF ACTION RESEARCH

Before exploring this paradigm shift in greater detail, the historical context for teachers conducting action research in the twenty-first century will be overviewed. The first mention of action research in the teacher education literature dates back to 1908, when it was advocated as a means of improving the quality of teachers and teaching. However, with the advent of group intelligence testing, calls for the experimental study of classroom problems became more commonplace; by the 1920s and 1930s university-level educators were encouraged to employ the scientific method to study classroom problems. The major alternative voice in this period was that of John Dewey, who in 1929 argued that teachers should study pedagogical problems through inquiry. Echoed in Dewey's writing was the sentiment that logically, teachers were the most appropriate persons to validate the results of scientific studies.

Despite the influence of Dewey and progressivism, it was not until the 1940s, as World War II came to a close and our nation focused once again on domestic social problems, that the popularity of action research reemerged, led by such figures as Kurt Lewin. Stephen Corey of Columbia University is credited with bringing the term into the domain of educators with his claim that action research would lead to teachers making better instructional decisions. However, by the late 1950s university educators questioned its legitimacy and action research again fell out of vogue. It was replaced by university-driven research framed by the process–product paradigm, which emphasized the quantitative study of classroom events.

In the late 1970s action research once again became popular as university researchers were criticized for turning teachers off to educational research that was rift with technical language;

furthermore, it was argued that researchers had created a disconnect with teachers because "teachers were studied down" by a research community that often appeared to teachers as elitist and too far removed from everyday practice. Hence, it became popular to argue for collaborative educational research between university researchers and teachers with teacher parity as a prime goal. A qualitative research paradigm that viewed the teacher as the focus of research, instead of classroom events, was now in favor.

Enjoying a resurgence in popularity, in the 1980s action research was promoted as a means of empowerment and professionalism for teachers; by the early 1990s, at this time Donald Schon's notion of teacher as reflective practitioner depicted teacher research as both a collegial and public examination of problems related to practice. According to this view, action research served to combine the processes of curriculum development, teaching, evaluation, research, and professional development. As such, the division between the roles of teacher and that of researcher became intricately intertwined. This reflective practitioner perspective clashed with the traditional teacher craft culture, which viewed teacher research as a threat to teacher privacy and authority and argued that the role of teacher should take priority over that of researcher.

In contrast to Schon's version of practical action research, emancipatory or critical action research was advocated during the same time frame by authors such as Stephen Kemmis. In critical action research, teacher research must be critically grounded in that it must consider the sociocultural, historical, and political contexts of schools in an effort to identify those aspects of the dominant social order that pose barriers to the work of teachers. Seen in this light, action research entailed teachers' arranging themselves into research communities, fostering both teacher autonomy and group decision making. Most recently, in this vein, action research has been proposed as a means of school renewal and change focused around on-site collaborative decisions.

PARADIGM SHIFTS AND CONCEPTUAL FRAMEWORKS

Throughout the twentieth century the field of educational psychology in general was characterized by a similar series of paradigm shifts. For most of the twentieth century the field was dominated by positivistic, experimental, and process–product studies of teaching conducted mainly by university-based researchers who saw themselves as research experts. It was not until the 1970s and 1980s that ethnographic, naturalistic, and qualitative studies of phenomena besides observable behavior were accepted into mainstream educational psychology; even then in some segments of the field these methods were presumed to be inferior to those of a quantitative nature.

The paradigm shift that began in the 1970s sprung from new research in cognitive psychology on topics such as the information processing model and situated cognition. Research on teacher cognition represented the continuation of this focus among researchers interested in studying teaching. In the 1970s and 1980s places such as the Institute for Research on Teaching at Michigan State University led the way in conducting groundbreaking studies of multiple facets of teacher cognition, including teacher decision making, teacher planning, as well as research on teachers' knowledge and beliefs. This laid the foundation for uniting the teacher-as-decision-maker focus with the teacher empowerment movement of the 1980s. The latter movement contended that in order for teachers to truly be empowered there needed to be on-site research at the local school level that occurred hand in glove with on-site decision making led largely by classroom teachers.

The 1980s also heralded the parallel popularity of multiculturalism and the notion of teacher-as-change agent; the latter view held that teachers had the responsibility to challenge the status quo and thereby work to remedy social injustice and equity issues in schools. At the same time, Lev Vygotsky's social constructivist perspective was becoming popular in educational psychology circles. Like Lewin, Vygotsky had argued that psychological and educational phenomena should be studied as occurring within a larger historical, ever-changing, sociocultural context. This view certainly complemented both the political nature of the teacher empowerment movement as well as the emerging interdisciplinary focus of qualitative research as represented by such new fields as educational anthropology.

Another relatively new approach to educational problems—offered by Dr. Mel Levine—also represented the merging of another discipline with that of educational psychology. Levine's phenomenological approach advocated that educators develop neurodevelopmental profiles of students instead of using labels. The profiles would in essence consist of a balance sheet of individual strengths and weaknesses along with a description of the "goodness of fit" between these and the tasks a child is asked to do. Levine believed teachers are in the best position to observe, describe, and respond to differences in learning; he viewed teachers' engagement in action research as a prerequisite task to effective teaching and learning.

The merging of these paradigm shifts in educational psychology along with the rising popularity of action research has resulted in some interesting new directions in the 1980s, 1990s, and beyond. Lee Shulman and others called for practical craft knowledge (or the knowledge of teaching acquired as a result of examining one's own practice) to be considered along with traditional research on teaching as comprising the knowledge base of educational psychology. Shulman and others have argued that both teachers and university researchers have a legitimate place. The university researcher can help to fit action research findings into a larger theoretical framework whereas the classroom-teacher-as-action-researcher tests if findings from the larger research literature are effective in practice. Much of the next section will contain illustrations of this latter point.

DEFINING THE NATURE AND TYPES OF ACTION RESEARCH

It is most important to remember that action research represents a systematic tradition through which teachers are able to communicate to their colleagues insights about some aspect of the teaching–learning process. One form of action research is conceptual in nature and consists of the analysis of ideas and generation of theories; teacher essays on classroom life, on the philosophy of schooling, or on the nature of research itself may fit this category. A second form of action research is empirical in nature and focused on implementing and studying an innovation. The first step in this type of action research is that teachers identify the problem to be studied. This conceptualization stage entails delineating the specific research question(s) to be answered. Next, the teacher-researcher selects research methods to be employed in the data collection process. In the implementation phase the teacher carries out a change in their own teaching behavior and measures the results. Often teachers study changes in student achievement, attitude, and/or behavior. Finally, in the interpretation phase, teachers analyze the results of the action research; it is at this point that they judge the effectiveness of the teaching–learning process under study and determine actions to be taken as a result.

There are several different approaches to doing action research that focus on the study of an innovation. Action research may involve an individual teacher or a small collaborative group of teachers, or it may be schoolwide in nature and involve a host of school professionals. Action research exists on a continuum with regard to the extent to which its goal is to achieve equity for students, revitalize the school organization as a collective problem-solving unit, and improve collegiality among teachers and school staff members. One common element across the different types of action research is the notion of disciplined inquiry designed to answer a practical question.

In terms of action research conducted by individual teachers, several illustrations follow. For example, one teacher may be interested in documenting her students' perceptions of a cooperative learning model she is piloting. A second teacher may want to discern the effectiveness of teaching language skills by using daily reading and writing workshops instead of using a basal reader. A third teacher may investigate if the use of a brain-based teaching approach in math is comparable to a traditional teaching approach.

Teachers may also pair together or work in small groups to conduct an action research project. For example, a high school English teacher and a kindergarten teacher who pair their students in a reading and tutoring program may team together to study the results. Or a cross-disciplinary grade-level team of four may embark on a research project to document the effectiveness of student journal writing across the curriculum. In a third context, a teacher may share portions of a videotaped lesson in which he is trying out an innovative teaching method with several colleagues, asking them to record and discuss their reactions to it.

In some settings it may be more appropriate to conduct schoolwide action research. For instance, this may be done in order to assess the perceptions of administrators, counselors, teachers, and students with regard to a new middle school advisor–advisee program. Or a study may be done to determine the effectiveness of a new schoolwide discipline plan. Alternatively, an entire school district may become involved in action research, as has been the case in the Madison Metropolitan School District in Wisconsin under the leadership of Ken Zeichner; teachers in this district became involved in action research studies on topics such as race and gender equity as well as assessment.

Another type of action research involves coresearching with students. For instance, a teacher may ask his special needs students to talk and write about their perceptions of what it is like to be included in a regular education classroom. Another teacher, struggling with how to make reading more enjoyable for her students, may decide to ask her students for their solutions. In a high school concerned about the dropout rate, students may be selected to interview their classmates about both what they find interesting and what boring in school. The students tape the conversations and also participate in analyzing the data.

In addition to these different types of action research, numerous action research projects have been conducted by pre-service teachers, student teachers, as well as cooperating teachers. For instance, pre-service teachers in a social studies methods course may develop and administer surveys designed to ascertain the nature of both the social studies curriculum and social studies instruction in a local school district. Or pre-service teachers may each be asked to interview five elementary students after asking the question "What is writing?" The pre-service teachers may be encouraged to take notes as well as tape-record the interviews where possible. Transcripts of the interviews could then be produced and analyzed for reoccurring themes.

Secondary student teachers may design and administer a survey to determine their students' learning style preferences as well as to track whether certain sections of students had a majority learning style preference. A middle school student teacher may want to study how helpful concept maps are in terms of her students' comprehension of scientific concepts. An elementary student teacher may be interested in assessing the impact of sharing student portfolios in parent–teacher conferences with regard to parental understanding of student strengths and weaknesses.

Cooperating teachers may have myriad action research interests. These may include completing observational checklists designed to assess the quality of teaching and documenting how the results change over the student teaching assignment. Or, it may be that a group of cooperating teachers are interviewed to glean their perceptions about areas they believe their student teachers lack adequate preparation in; the results of such a project may be shared with university supervisors at a local college campus.

PARADIGM SHIFTS IN EDUCATIONAL RESEARCH AND ACTION RESEARCH

Even though the paradigm shift evidenced in the growing acceptance of qualitative methods by the 1980s paralleled the resurgence of action research methods, action research can be conducted by using either qualitative or quantitative methods. In fact, many authors contend that the most effective action research incorporates both qualitative and quantitative methods. When selecting a method it is critical that teachers determine why it would be of value and if it addresses their research question(s). The following section delineates the array of qualitative methods available to those who do action research.

Qualitative Action Research Methods

There are numerous qualitative methods available to the teacher-researcher. Qualitative research is much more concerned with the description of the context in which natural events take place than is quantitative research. Some qualitative methods involve observational techniques using research logs or journals to record anecdotal notes and personal recollections. Other observational techniques include observational checklists and rating scales, tape recordings, videotapes, as well as interview notes and field notes.

Nonobservational qualitative techniques include attitude scales, questionnaires, individual and focus group interviews, and demonstrations of student performance. Another nonobservational data source entails the analysis of archival data such as records of attendance, dropout rates, suspension rates, discipline referrals, grade distributions, and the number and percentage of students labeled in the various special education categories. In addition, archival data may include documents such as school board reports, curriculum guides, district and state tests, accreditation reports, or needs assessments. In terms of credibility, triangulation, or using at least three different types of data, is more credible than using only one data source from the qualitative perspective.

Quantitative Action Research Methods

Quantitative methods may include reporting quantitative data using descriptive statistics such as the mean, median, mode, range, and standard deviation. A variety of pretest/posttest comparison group designs could be used. Or teacher-researchers could use within-subject designs in which the individual student is the point for comparison such as time series design in which baseline data are collected describing the target behavior prior to the use of the intervention. Next, the teacher introduces the intervention and collects data describing the behavior of the student. The teacher then compares baseline data with data collected during the intervention phase. Repeated and frequent measures are collected in both the baseline and intervention phases. If comparisons of these data show dramatic differences, then the researcher concludes that the intervention caused the behavior differences.

Resolution of Research Paradigm Clashes

It is argued here that both qualitative and quantitative research methods may be appropriate for use in the conduct of action research. One reason for this view is that many educational researchers contend that the use of the two categories of methods described above is not a sequential process, but rather a parallel process. That is to say, techniques from both methods may be useful in answering research questions. For instance, in an action research study designed to assess the effectiveness of cooperative learning, a pretest/posttest group design may be used in which a teacher computes typical gain scores on the postassessment measure as compared to the preassessment measure after cooperative learning is used. To determine why cooperative learning was either effective or ineffective, collecting additional qualitative data may be of value, such as assessing student and teacher perceptions about cooperative learning by using attitude surveys. Observations of classroom teaching may further serve to answer action research questions. In this case, deciding on the method to use was not an either/or choice.

A second rationale for considering both methods involves the realities of the workplace in which teachers live; certainly the quantitative analysis of test scores is a way of life for most modern-day educators. However, the addition of qualitative data enables the teacher-researcher to depict the context in which the quantitative data were collected and provide a lens through which to understand the limitations of solely relying on test score data. With the current focus on test scores, it may be that both sets of data are needed to convince others of the social inequities present in schools.

Thirdly, educators in the twenty-first century will likely be involved in both conducting and sharing the results of case study action research; in compiling case research relevant to one's own students and setting, both quantitative and qualitative data may be necessary. The sharing of case research with school professionals who work in other contexts is similar to the sharing of cases among both law and medical professionals.

Some have held that a focus on research methodology often belies a more serious disagreement in terms of educational epistemology. For this reason, two markedly different perspectives on the philosophy pertaining to how an educator knows what he or she claims to know will be reviewed in the next section.

PARADIGM SHIFTS IN EDUCATIONAL EPISTEMOLOGY AND ACTION RESEARCH

The larger question remains as to how the two different educational epistemological views will be reconciled when it comes to conducting action research. Before speaking to this, the nature of the differences in these two views will be examined.

Positivism

Positivists contend that knowledge exists outside of the self and can be objectively observed and measured. In the field of educational psychology, the influence of positivism is best represented in the behavioristic paradigm that became so influential in the 1940s through the early 1970s. For the behaviorist, learning is defined solely in terms of changes in students' observable behaviors assessed by using quantitative methods. It is assumed that in studying the student, no value judgments will be made. Positivism contends that all knowledge is determined by the teacher, who defines appropriate and inappropriate behavior; controlling student behavior is seen as the central act of teaching. Behavioristic classrooms are often described as teacher-centered.

Positivism is predicated on the notion that a teacher's job is to teach finite skills that build into a competency as evidenced in the cognitive domain of Bloom's taxonomy of objectives. Positivistic teachers use authoritarian discipline methods such as assertive discipline; in this approach, teachers control student behavior by employing consequences such as positive and negative reinforcement. The teacher takes responsibility for conveying the curriculum to students; the curriculum is influenced heavily by external forces such as administrators, textbook manufacturers, and state and local requirements. Tests used to assess student progress often report success or failure in terms of percentages and based on comparisons made with other students. Conforming to instructions, rules, performance standards, and expectations is emphasized in a behavioristic classroom.

Constructivism

In contrast, constructivists believe that knowledge is subjectively determined and highly personal, arising out of experiences that are unique to the individual. In the field of educational psychology the influence of constructivism is evidenced in the humanistic, cognitive, and social constructivist paradigms. The humanistic paradigm was introduced as early as the 1960s, while cognitivism dominated in the late 1970s through early 1990s; through the 1990s and into the twenty-first century, social constructivism has superceded cognitivism in terms of influence. For a constructivist teacher, both knowledge and learning goals are constructed by the student; hence constructivism entails a student-centered approach to learning. The teacher's job is to facilitate personal learning by creating a community of learners of which each student is an important member.

Constructivism is based on the notion that students must put knowledge together based on experiences and expand that knowledge through interaction with others and personal reflection. Thus, constructivist teachers place a premium on the use of cooperative learning and teaching students metacognitive study strategies. In a constructivist classroom students are presented with relevant problematic situations in which they can experiment in a search for their own answers. A constructivist teacher is likely to have students determine their own behavioral standards by having them participate in making classroom rules and resolve discipline problems through the use of class meetings and open and reflective dialogue and problem solving. The constructivist teacher maintains his or her right to determine specific instructional goals and challenges students to set their own personal goals for learning. Assessment tools focus on individual growth as seen in portfolio assessment rather than on student placement within the class population. Self-evaluation and peer evaluation are stressed.

RESOLUTION OF EPISTEMOLOGICAL PARADIGM CLASHES

Clearly the notion of teachers doing action research on first glance smacks more of constructivism than positivism. In fact, in Great Britain the emergence of action research was viewed as an alternative paradigm to that of positivism, which was rejected at the time because it was viewed as an external means of controlling teachers. Secondly, the conceptual framework from which action research originated was constructivist in nature. Dewey envisioned the teacher as one who constructed a complex understanding of teaching and learning by engaging in teacher research instead of solely accepting what authorities tell them works. Thirdly, in action research teachers continue to learn and grow by reflecting on and self-evaluating their own practice, often with the involvement of students and colleagues as coresearchers. The action-researcher determines his or her own research questions and research design on the basis of local needs. These reoccurring themes are constructivist in nature.

Yet it would be a mistake to completely discount the influence of positivism on action research. A critical part of doing some forms of empirical action research consists of being able to narrow the parameters of the study to focus on a set of manageable questions that lend themselves to some manageable form of interpretation and assessment. And sometimes, albeit not in every case, this process entails operationalizing concepts and measures. This process does not necessarily preclude the teacher-researcher's examination of his or her own assumptions, the assumptions of other researchers, multiple frames of reference, and whose interests are served by the action research. This process of operationalization also need not preclude the collection of qualitative data, which may be useful in depicting the sociopolitical and cultural context in which the action research study is conducted.

Another possible slice of positivism that may be helpful to teacher-researchers is the use and/or modification of assessment measures adapted from so-called authorities in the field; some of the most appropriate designs in action research may have been developed in the context of the quantitative perspective. Some of these quantitative designs may produce results consistent with postmodern goals such as illuminating social justice and equity issues. Would teacher-researchers be unable to consider the results of such research valid because they were based on quantitative-data–gathering procedures? Such questions should convey the absurdity of defining action research as an exclusively constructivist process.

Certainly, pieces of the positivistic tradition have something of value to contribute to action research. Perhaps a more difficult issue to resolve is the notion advanced by some that teacher-researchers must uniformly adopt a critically grounded postmodern perspective. While it is of great value for teachers to view their own action research from multiple perspectives and continually question their own assumptions and those of others, should the goal of all action research be of a postmodern nature, designed to resist the dominant culture perspective and illuminate social justice and equity issues? Does it follow that in failing to challenge the status quo in every action research endeavor, one automatically endorses it? Perhaps a more realistic goal is that those who conduct action research consistently and thoroughly document the sociopolitical and cultural context in which the action research takes place.

Is it possible to construe action research as a socially constructed act and yet permit the major player in that act, the classroom teacher, the freedom to define its goals and design as appropriate to the local setting? If the goal of action research is to empower teachers to engage in continuous inquiry about their teaching so that they can reflect upon and improve their own work and situations, is it appropriate for those outside of schools to define action research in exclusively political terms that classroom teachers may or may not concur with? Perhaps our field would do well to minimize the role that external factors such as the standards movement, university requirements, and mandates from central office project coordinators play in the development and conceptualization of action research. It could also be argued that until larger issues are remedied, such as changing the face of the teaching force to incorporate more diversity, action research will not in and of itself be a process that can effectively address social justice and equity issues in schooling.

The study of epistemology also may shed light on how to resolve epistemological paradigm clashes. In a new model that describes the development of epistemological understanding, Kuhn, Cheney, and Weinstock (2000) contend that mature epistemological understanding is the coordination of objective and subjective ways of knowing. According to these authors, initially the objective way of knowing dominates to the exclusion of the subjective. Then, in a dramatic shift, the subjective way of knowing supercedes that of the objective, with the latter being excluded. Finally, in mature epistemological understanding, the two ways of knowing are coordinate; this entails arriving at a balance between the objective and subjective in which one does not overpower the other. It is striking as to how much this new conceptualization of intellectual development parallels the history of thought relative to action research. In the first part of the last century, educational research was framed from almost an exclusively objective view, which in turn served to frame how action research was viewed. In the last several decades of the last century, educational researchers became more accepting of the notion of subjective types of research. That being the case, as we begin the twenty-first century, many authors who write about action research now take almost an exclusively subjective view of research.

Might it be the case that as we progress through the twenty-first century, a mature conceptualization of action research will emerge with the achievement of a balance between the objective and subjective ways of knowing? Perhaps the resolution then of epistemological paradigm clashes ultimately resides in the development of mature epistemological understanding, which unfolds developmentally and over time at both the individual and collective levels. Indeed the field of educational psychology, and cognitive psychology in particular, offers us a most valuable lens through which to understand how action research may evolve and unfold during the twenty-first century.

ETHICAL ISSUES AND PROFESSIONAL RESPONSIBILITY

As action research has become more commonplace in schools, more attention has shifted in recent years to a host of ethical issues. The following section will overview ethical issues surrounding the conduct of action research, the ownership of action research data, support for teachers to engage in action research, and the potential politicizing of action research.

Ethical Issues about Action Research Process and Data

One concern often mentioned by critics of action research is the notion of teachers "doing research" on their students. Unlike large-scale studies, typically action research does not involve the random assignment of students to treatment conditions, which may disadvantage students who receive less effective treatments. It is also important to remember that in action research the performance of students is studied during their regular participation in the education process. Thus, no student is denied opportunities based on this type of research. In fact, since the treatment would likely be taking place anyway, it could be argued that it would be unethical to not evaluate its effectiveness. And once the treatment is demonstrated to be effective, it can be used with other students who did not initially receive it.

A second ethical concern pertains to issues involving confidentiality. The argument as to whether school-based data are the private domain of the educator or part of the public domain belies the discussion of this issue. Those who espouse the former view contend it is vital that data be reported only in an aggregated format and that when teachers write about their schools and students they use pseudonyms to protect their identities. Alternatively, those who see school-based data as public argue that decontextualized, impersonal, and aggregated data limit the ability to arrive at sound judgments about practice in particular contexts. Those who contend that school-based data are part of the public domain also propose some ethical safeguards including the presentation of alternative descriptions, interpretations, and explanations of events.

A third and related issue to that of confidentiality is that of ownership of the data. As stated above, some contend all school-based data belong to the public. Alternatively, others view ownership largely as a function of the level of the action research study. In individual teacher action research, it is the teacher and students who are the owners. As the research team expands—to perhaps several teachers or a team of teachers—then all of the teachers involved and their students own the data. In schoolwide action research, it can be argued that the entire school staff owns the data. With the growing popularity of action research, more and more districts have policies about the aforementioned issues.

This is also the case with regard to another central ethical concern as to how the action research data should be shared. The sharing of data on an informal basis within the school is often encouraged because an issue one teacher faces is most likely encountered by other teachers in the same school. This sharing could occur within teacher study groups as teams of teachers meet together to design, collect, analyze, and report their data or through teacher professional development activities such as in-services in which teachers report their data to either the school or perhaps before the entire district. In addition, teachers can share the results of action research in the form of scrapbooks, self-evaluative journals, lesson plans, curriculum designs or models, or through videos and exhibitions.

The sharing of action research data on a more formal basis could occur in an array of formats. Teachers may write narratives in which they report their research using a story telling format. Or, written reports may be compiled for the school district. It may be that an action research study is written up as a project or even thesis as part of a university requirement. Other written vehicles for sharing action research may be in the form of a paper presented at a professional conference or an article written for a professional journal. Middle school science teachers who participated in the Science FEAT program in Florida and Georgia, along with university collaborators, published a monograph containing action research papers. Increasingly, action research reports are available on a variety of Web sites as well.

Ethical Issues in Terms of Providing Adequate Support to Do Action Research

Toward the end of the twentieth century, it became popular to argue that action research belonged at the centerpiece of professional development activities. It would seem that in this context, school district administrators would be in the best of positions to garner the supports needed for teachers to do action research.

One of the most important supports that could be provided for teachers who wish to do action research is time. The argument for extending necessary time should be buttressed by the presupposition that teacher research cannot be easily separated from the rest of the teaching process as it serves to combine curriculum development, teaching, evaluation, research, and professional development. Time could be allocated as part of the in-service program, part of faculty or departmental meeting times, paid release time, after school meetings, or summer workshops. It is critical that a large block of time be provided in order to sufficiently study the complex process of teaching.

In addition, administrators could play a pivotal role in making resources available for teacher research by encouraging teachers to apply for mini-grants and sponsoring grant writing seminars. Administrators must also promote a climate of collegial inquiry and collaboration within a school building. Affirming the sharing of action research results and providing venues for publishing the results of action research would be two powerful ways in which to do this. A peer support structure that permits teachers the freedom to take risks in a safe climate also needs to be fostered by the school administration. In essence, the notion of teacher-as-reflective-practitioner needs to replace that of the traditional teacher craft culture; in the former the collegial and public examination of school problems is viewed as a natural and necessary part of the teaching process. In this new culture, novice teachers could be provided with mentor teachers who serve as models of reflective inquiry, both sharing the results of their own action research and helping novices to design and implement action research that addresses the novice teacher's needs. Teacher study teams could serve to match teachers with common research interests.

The Potential Politicizing of Action Research

Although administrative support for action research is imperative, some have argued recently that teachers must be aware of the possibility that local administrators may usurp teachers' places in the design and purpose of action research. For example, a central office administrator may be looking for a way to legitimize a new language arts program or a superintendent may be consumed with raising assessment scores connected to the standards movement. In such circumstances as these and because of the hierarchical political structure of schools and districts, it is likely that nonteachers in positions of power may seize the opportunity to co-opt the action research process and resulting data. Teachers, especially those who are untenured, will no doubt be at least somewhat compelled to comply with administrator wishes. Particularly in cases where administrator and teacher goals conflict, this scenario poses quite the conundrum for classroom teachers. If such issues become a systemic part of how schools and districts function, perhaps teacher unions may need to play a role in their resolution.

Another larger-scale aspect of this issue potentially may occur relative to the standards movement at both the state and national levels. If the self-interests of local administrators lead them to attempt to co-opt teacher research, certainly the self-interests of politicians could lead them to meander in the same direction. This is a particularly troublesome scenario in that in the early years of the twenty-first century, some would argue that politicians have already usurped the role of educators in making decisions of significant consequence to student learning and welfare. In addition, this is disturbing if one agrees that instead of measuring knowledge, standardized assessments connected with the standards movement measure a student's familiarity with the culture of testing as well as their familiarity with the culture of an institution still largely controlled by those from dominant cultural groups. Perhaps the postmodern perspective makes its best case around such issues as these. How these issues are resolved will, in part, depend on how larger political debates unfold.

FUTURE DIRECTIONS OF ACTION RESEARCH IN THE CONTEXT OF EDUCATIONAL PSYCHOLOGY

In the initial years of the twenty-first century, increasingly attention has shifted to the question as to how we can translate practitioner knowledge, based on teachers' action research, into professional knowledge that can be easily understood and publicly disseminated. An analogy has been drawn to the profession of medicine where physicians rely on case literature or reports from other physicians who have tried and refined new ways of treating illnesses as well as case law in which lawyers follow the interpretations of laws as they progress through the court system.

One method proposed for establishing this professional knowledge base is to have teacher-researchers generate and test both hypotheses and local theories about the ways in which daily lessons impact student learning. With the daily lesson as the unit of analysis, it is argued that examples of teaching can be stored and disseminated through the use of video technologies. Hiebert et al. (2002) have recently contended that this approach may be of help in providing concrete illustrations of practices studied in teacher research to other practitioners; in fact, this may be a useful adjunct to written descriptions of practice that are often too vague in nature for another teacher who wishes to replicate these in their own teaching. By having the daily lesson stored in this way other teachers could ponder how the results of action research could be readily connected to specific content in their own curriculum.

Another advantage of this proposal is that practices studied in action research could be continually evaluated by other teachers who would implement and test them in many different types of local contexts. With repeated observations conducted over multiple trials, knowledge is said to become more trustworthy as teachers modify practices to fit their local contexts. At the local level, professional development could be provided for teachers through participation in action research; one way this could be organized is through teachers' membership in lesson study groups. In these groups teachers design a lesson and have one member of the group implement it while the other members observe what works and does not work as a means of revising the lesson. After additional teachers in the group try out the revised lesson on their students, the lesson continues to undergo refinement. At the end of the process, documentation of the lessons could be disseminated to other professionals. This approach, in fact, represents a combination of an emphasis on repeated observations rooted in positivism and an emphasis on teacher inquiry and collaboration rooted in Dewey's work and constructivism.

In the twenty-first century the substance and organization of teacher research needs to be linked to the voluminous research base in educational psychology. Research on topics including race and gender equity, brain-based teaching, as well as social constructivist practices could provide a starting point for the substance of such teacher research. The emerging practitioner knowledge base then needs to be integrated into the extant literature, which is currently organized into several different types of knowledge: pedagogical knowledge, pedagogical content knowledge, and knowledge about students. Hiebert et al. (2002) propose that as these knowledge bases are fused according to the type of problem the knowledge is meant to address, then teacher research can play a vital role in the professional development of teachers. This should occur throughout teachers' professional life spans, beginning with pre-service teachers' observations and subsequent reflections about the practices they observe. Hopefully, this will provide the foundation for action research to become part of the routine dialogue between cooperating teachers and student teachers as they contemplate effective practice. Likewise, teacher research should also undergird the mentorship of novice as well as veteran teachers.

REFERENCES

Corey, S. (1949). Curriculum development through action research. *Educational Leadership*, 7(3), 147–153.

Dewey, J. (1933). *How We Think: A Restatement of the Relation of Reflective Thinking to Educative Process.* Chicago: Henry Regnery.

Hiebert, J., Gallimore, R., and Stigler, J. (2002, July). A knowledge base for the profession of teaching: What would one look like and how would we get one? *Educational Researcher*, 31(5), 3–15.

Kemmis, S. (1993). Action research and social movement: A challenge for policy research. *Educational Policy Archives*, 1(1). Retrieved August 15, 2006, from http://epaa.asu.edu/epaa.v1n1.html.

Kuhn, D., Cheney, R., and Weinstock, M. (2000). The development of epistemological understanding. *Cognitive Development*, 15, 309–328.

Lewin, K. (1946). Action research and minority problems. In *Resolving Social Conflicts: Selected Papers on Group Dynamics* (compiled in 1948). New York: Harper and Row.

Schon, D. A. (1987). *Educating the Reflective Practitioner.* San Francisco: Jossey Bass.

Shulman, L. (1986). Those who understand: Knowledge growth in teaching. *Educational Researcher*, 15(2), 4–14.

Zeichner, K., and Caro-Bruce, C. (1998). *Classroom Action Research: The Nature and Impact of an Action Research Professional Development Program in One Urban School District.* Final Report to the Spencer Foundation.

CHAPTER 59

Beyond the "Qualitative/Quantitative" Dichotomy: Pragmatics, Genre Studies and Other Linguistic Methodologies in Education Research

SUSAN GEROFSKY

Studies in educational psychology most often analyze complex situations in education by collecting the results of tests and questionnaires, analyzing these results statistically and drawing conclusions from statistical findings. Occasionally, educational psychologists use qualitative, ethnographic studies to obtain a "thicker" description of a situation where a complex web of relationships affects results.

In this chapter, I describe a "third way" of doing research in educational psychology, and suggest that there may well be multiple methodologies yet to be explored that will give useful and interesting results in this field.

The research methodology I describe here is based in linguistics, the philosophy of language, and an interdisciplinary formulation of genre theory. Since many of the situations studied in educational psychology involve linguistic artifacts (interview results, written output, conversations, classroom discourse, etc.), ignoring the insights available through linguistics, and particularly linguistic pragmatics, may mean that valuable opportunities for rigorous analysis and deeper understanding are often missed.

In many faculties of education in North America, graduate students are required to take two methodology courses: quantitative methods and qualitative methods. Often these are the only two research methodology courses offered, and the implied message to new researchers is that one's research techniques must fall into one or the other of these two camps.

Quantitative methods courses deal with ways of collecting data in the form of numbers or quantities, and teach students how to use statistical methods to analyze, represent, and interpret these numerical data. The rigorous methods of mathematical statistics are imported into the field of educational research, and are applied in much the same way as they are in other research fields ranging from biology and metallurgy to sociology, psychology, and other social sciences. Quantitative methods necessarily deal only in those data that can be made numerical; if it can be counted, it "counts," and if not, it doesn't. The mathematical rigor of quantitative research gives it the cachet of a "hard science" in some circles—testable, reproducible, evidence-based, reliable, rational, and, by extension, unassailable. It is available only to those who are initiated through a background education in statistics, and it favors an unemotional, detached attitude. A great deal of educational psychology research has traditionally used quantitative, statistical methods and the language of experimental science.

For some researchers, frustrations have arisen with quantitative methods in education on several accounts. For one, even those who have made a commitment to using statistical methods may often find results that they, as informed observers, find "significant" (i.e., important, telling, useful, helpful, noteworthy) but that do not achieve the rigorous status of "statistical significance." The conclusions of many statistically based papers in educational research contain results deemed "significant *to us*," and researchers' informed intuitions may well be correct in spotting important data trends, even if they are not technically "statistical trends."

Even among those who feel in tune with quantitative methods, there is a worry that a great many readers of academic journals skip over the actual data and data analysis that forms the bulk of quantitative-based papers, reading only the abstract, the introduction, and the brief concluding remarks. This may happen because of readers' time constraints, a lack of training in statistical methods, or a lack of interest in the important but "plodding" details. Many readers want to "cut to the chase," but this may mean that studies are often accepted wholesale, without rigorous examination by most readers, inadvertently promoting an *anti*-scientific attitude of mind.

Other frustrations with quantitative methods arise because of the fact that not everything important can be counted, and much of what is necessarily left out of quantitative studies forms an important part of human life and educational interaction. Stories, emotions, hunches, artistic and linguistic expressions, the "flavor" or mood of an incident, contextual and biographical features in which interactions are embedded—all these important features and more are difficult to include in statistical studies. For many education researchers, the uncountable elements may be the very essence of the educational phenomenon they want to study, yet these are disallowed by the methods of quantitative research. Besides, such features are often relegated to the status of "soft" data—subjective, nonverifiable, irreproducible, nonrational.

To address the exclusion of the noncountable from quantitative studies, education has borrowed and adopted qualitative methodologies from other social sciences and humanities over the past twenty years or so. Particularly prevalent are methods adopted from anthropology, especially ethnomethodolgy and participant-observer research. Related methods of journaling and autobiographical writing are related to literary studies as well as anthropology.

Ethnomethodology and participant-observer research developed from the methods of anthropologists who in earlier, colonial times, would aim to live with an "exotic" foreign people or tribe as a solo researcher for a matter of months or years, finding bilingual informants to help bridge gaps in culture and understanding, and gradually learning the mores, kinship patterns, power structures, and religion of the group. By being accepted into the group, and yet functioning at least partially as an outside observer at all times, the anthropologist could retain some degree of objectivity and still have "insider" insights. By taking copious field notes, accompanied by drawings, diagrams, photos, artifacts, recorded speech and stories, etc., the researcher could bring a degree of rigor and an evidence base to what was often necessarily a subjective and solitary study. Triangulation, in the form of corroborating research by others, or at least several sources of evidence to support a particular conclusion, could lend a higher degree of reliability to the study.

In recent years, anthropologists have turned much of their research focus away from the study of remote "exotic" tribes (of which there are few remaining anyway) and turned toward the subcultures and cultural phenomena of their own societies. In this way, a modern anthropologist might study women mountain climbers, skateboarding youth, or the cultural status of meat as a symbol. By "making strange" the unexamined phenomena of one's own culture, the anthropologist may act as an ethnographer, a participant-observer, in a context close to home.

In a similar way, qualitative researchers in education have begun to turn an anthropologist's eye, ear, and field notebook to the phenomena of teaching, learning, and schooling. Researchers in a qualitative study may spend long periods of time observing and participating in a classroom or other learning situation, acknowledging their own "insider/outsider" status and the fact that subjective and objective points of view are inextricably interwoven in such a study. Field notes and reports, including multiple observations, transcribed recordings, photos, artifacts, student work and so on to provide triangulation, may often run into many hundreds of pages. Biographical, contextual, and autobiographical material may take a prominent role in such studies. Autobiographies of teachers, students, and administrators have recently been given the status of the ultimate "participant-observer" report, in which the event studied and participated in is one's own life and career.

Like the quantitative reports, these papers run the risk of being little read simply because they are so long. Many time-pressed or impatient readers will jump from the abstract and introduction to the concluding pages, missing the evidence that gives validity and substance to the study. Ethnographic researchers face the problem that they are necessarily creating the theoretical framework for their study in the course of conducting the study, and because of this, it is difficult to know in advance which evidence should be given the most weight, or even whether one detail *should* be stressed at the expense of another. Worries about the role of the researcher, and the ways in which the participant-observer's very presence changes the phenomenon, are often part of the dilemma of qualitative research methods. Many qualitative researchers in education are beset by overwhelming anxieties about their own unconscious prejudices, race/class/gender identities, power relationships to those studied, and guilt related to present and historical positions of privilege. Quite a number of qualitative studies are fraught with researchers' sense of culpability in perpetuating colonializing relationships to some degree, and even with the researcher's desire to "disappear" as a presence at the research scene.

Both quantitative and qualitative methods have produced illuminating studies in education and educational psychology over many years, and both approaches have validity in different realms. Nonetheless, I want to argue that it is too simplistic to divide the world of educational research along the rather crude "quality vs. quantity" fault line. In truth, there is a *multiplicity* of research methods available in education, and it is misleading to direct new scholars to a choice of only two approaches.

My own work has used interdisciplinary research methods based on genre theory and linguistic pragmatics for research in education. I would like to present these methods as a new approach (among the many others possible) that could open up educational research to ways of thinking and analysis, and potentially enrich the scope of research in our field.

Linguistics, the study of language, has many branches that focus on the analysis of language on different levels; for example, *phonetics* studies the sounds of language, *phonemics* the distribution rules of those sounds, *syntax* studies word order and sentence composition, *semantics* looks at fields of word meanings, and so on. The branch of linguistics that I have found most useful as a methodological tool in education is *pragmatics*.

Pragmatics studies "language in use." In other words, pragmatics makes the connection between actual utterances (either spoken or written) and their lived context. This distinguishes pragmatics from many other branches of linguistics like, for example, syntax, which theorizes about the structure of idealized sentences, without regard for their speaker or audience, the context in which they might arise, or even whether or not they might actually be uttered in any particular context.

Educational studies largely deal with actual learning and teaching situations, replete with complex interactions and numerous real-life contingencies and lived contexts. While more abstract theoretical linguistic concepts may prove useful in educational studies, I think that the ideas of linguistic pragmatics are generally a closer fit to the aims of educational research.

Pragmatics provides rigorous analytical tools for the analysis of various aspects of language in context. Subcategories of pragmatics include

- addressivity
- reference
- deixis
- implicature
- relevance
- speech act theory
- presupposition
- schema theory
- metaphor
- politeness
- discourse analysis and conversational structure.

Many of these subcategories are directly related to the concerns of educational researchers studying the linguistic artifacts of teaching and learning: lectures, classroom discussions and verbal interactions, student writing, textbooks and curriculum materials, and so on. I will give a brief description of each of these subcategories; further elaboration can be found in the reference sources given at the end of this chapter. I will also describe ways that pragmatics along with genre theory can provide a dynamic methodology for educational studies, different from both "quantitative" and "qualitative" models.

The issue of *addressivity* was first raised by the Russian literary theorist and linguist M. M. Bakhtin. Addressivity interrogates the relationship between speaker (or writer) and audience, and asks how this relationship is reflected in the language of the utterance. Interestingly, the audience may be actual (as in a teacher speaking directly to a class), hypothetical (a radio announcer broadcasting to a real but unseen audience), or entirely imagined (a person writing a piece to be sealed in a time capsule). Nonetheless, utterances are always addressed *to* an audience, and the nature of that audience affects the language of the utterance.

Reference looks at the objects, persons, places, times, and so on referred to by words and phrases in an utterance. Some very interesting work has been done, for example, in looking at the referents for common pronouns like *we* and *you* in an educational context, since any particular use of *we* might include or exclude the audience, and *you* has a wide range of referents, ranging from the generic (similar to the generic use of *one* as a pronoun), to the second person singular or plural, which may include or exclude various members of the audience.

Reference goes beyond pronouns to look at the referents for nouns, verbs, time words, etc. The concepts of reference and *deixis* are closely related. Deixis, or indexicality, studies the way words "point" to things. For example, time deixis looks at verb tense, time adverbials, and other time words to establish a model of the concept of time in the utterance in relationship to a "deictic centre," the *coding time*, or time when the utterance is supposed to have taken place. Deixis can also deal with persons, places, and objects "pointed to," and even to words that point to the nature of the speaker, the audience, or the utterance itself in a self-reflexive mode (in a metapragmatic or metaconversational move).

Implicature looks at what is implied by an utterance in context, apart from the literal meaning of the words used. Since implicature takes into account social and power relationships between speaker and audience, it is a particularly useful kind of analysis in educational research. Implicature is based on the notion of cooperative principles in conversation, without which nonliteral meanings would be impossible to fathom. Philosopher of language H. P. Grice's four basic maxims of conversational cooperation establish a foundation for further studies in implicature, which include the concepts of *relevance*, conversational logic, and the "flouting of Gricean maxims" (i.e., uncooperative conversation, as in a testimony in a court of law which may be *literally* true while at the same time using conversational conventions to imply untrue extended meanings).

Speech act theory, based largely on the work of philosophers of language J. L. Austin and John Searle, looks at the kind of language used when we "do things with words," and contrasts this to the kind of language that can be assigned a "truth value" (i.e., a statement that can be labelled either true or false). Examples of speech acts involve situations where the utterance itself constitutes an action in the world—for example, "I second that motion," or "I sentence you to three years in prison." Speech acts have *force*, which Austin analyzes as *locutionary, illocutionary*, or *perlocutionary*, depending on the joint intentions of the speaker and the audience. Intentionality plays an important role in the analysis of speech acts, an idea that lends itself readily to the study of educational interactions, as the intentions of the parties involved (teachers, students, administrators, parents, legislators, etc.) and (mis)interpretations of mutual intentions often vary widely, and may be analyzed in the language produced.

Presupposition and its broader cultural analysis, *schema theory*, relate the interpretation of utterances to the audience's background knowledge, cultural predilections, foundational myths, and "commonsense" structurings of the world within a particular culture or subculture. Presupposition and schema theory relate strongly to studies of learners' construction of new knowledge, and to misinterpretations of teachers' intentions based on students' and teachers' differing presupposed schema or background knowledge. The study of presupposition is useful in dealing with cross-cultural differences of interpretation based on varying culturally established worldviews.

Metaphor, along with category theory (from anthropology), deals with the nonliteral use of language and the ways in which individuals and cultures give imagery and organization to experiences and ideas. Within a particular individual's speech, the use of metaphor, irony, and categories gives an insight into conscious and unconscious analogies in that person's understanding. Across a culture, extended metaphors influence individuals' unconscious, "commonsense" structuring of their culturally mediated world. In educational studies, metaphor is both a productive means of bringing analogies into play in introducing new concepts, and at the same time a limitation to new thought through the imposition of old categories and images.

Discourse structure and the related area of *politeness* look at discourse in terms of the social relationships involved (power relationships, kinship, social distance or intimacy, respect markers) and analyze structural features that either reinforce or disrupt these relationships. Phenomena such as turn-taking, the use of personal pronouns, active and passive voice, pauses, reasoning strategies, and face-saving strategies can be analyzed to reveal shifting relationships of power and deference in an interaction. Discourse analysis has been used in many studies of conversational interactions in education to analyze, for example, the effectiveness of group work within a community of learners or to understand power relationships in the classroom.

In addition to the analytical tools provided by linguistic pragmatics, I am particularly interested in using the broader category of *genre analysis* as part of a language-based methodology in education. Genre analysis has its origins in a number of different disciplines, including linguistic pragmatics and, equally important, film studies, literary theory, anthropology, and folklore studies.

Genre theory looks at the "types," or stereotyped forms, of discourse within a particular culture. These "types" or *genres* can be analyzed for the constellation of features that characterize them, for the relationships among utterances of the same genre, for the process of generation of new genres, the lingering effects of earlier generic utterances, the breaking of generic conventions, and the effects of generic structuring within a culture. For example, film studies may look at the evolving genre of "the horror film"; folklorists might study "hitchhiker tales" in modern urban folklore. Some of my own studies in mathematics education have looked at mathematical word problems and at first-year university calculus lectures as genres. Education establishes many spoken and written genres as varied as "the programmed reading primer," "the spelling test," "the public speaking contest," "the lab report," and "illicit notes passed in class." The nature of these genres, both linguistic and contextual, the multiple intentions involved, and the way genres structure our expectations and perceptions, offer a kind of structured study that is neither strictly quantitative (i.e., statistical) nor qualitative (i.e., narrative), but allows for both intellectual rigor and intuitive creativity in seeing connections, implications, and potential alternatives.

Peter Grundy, in his book *Doing Pragmatics* (cited in the references below), gives a partial list of investigable topics in applied pragmatics, all of which have possible applications within education research. His list includes

- conversational strategies
- studies of power, distance, and politeness
- the construction of audience by a speaker
- coauthorship of conversations by speakers
- the acquisition of pragmatics by children and by second-language learners
- intercultural pragmatics
- the relationship between context and the way talk is organized
- ethnomethodological accounts of language use
- metapragmatic and metasequential phenomena
- "folk views" of talk—investigating people's beliefs about the pragmatic uses of language
- the analysis of misunderstandings, and how people work to "repair" the situation when talk goes wrong
- the identification of genres and study of the structure of a particular genre.

I would like to add to this list one further extension of pragmatic/genre studies that has been particularly useful to me in researching types of talk and writing in education. As well as identifying and analyzing the structure of a particular educational genre, I am interested in finding analogies among different genres within a culture, whether educational or not, to find resonances and metaphorical connections across generic categories. For example, I have found structural analogies among "the initial calculus lecture," the "hard-sell sales pitch," and "infant-directed speech," a connection which implies that the audience for a calculus lecture hears and interprets the resonance of these other genres (unconsciously) embedded in the lecturer's utterance patterns. Similarly, the genre of "mathematical word problem" carries generic echoes of riddles, parables and ancient social puzzles. By looking at the contemporary genres of education "as if" they were framed within structurally related cultural forms, we may find insight into culturally bound constraints, but also openings and opportunities for reframing generic forms in education.

Opening up the field of educational psychology to a variety of relevant methodologies drawn from interdisciplinary sources (including, but not restricted to those described here) offers educational psychologists the chance to broaden the scope of the field, to consider a wider range of phenomena and to find fresh insights into complex situations.

A researcher's choice of methods in data collection and analysis necessarily narrows the available subject matter and analytical perspectives. This is not a bad thing in itself, since a particular study must be delimited in order to be manageable. However, any field of study that restricts its methods too narrowly may eventually exclude interesting, important phenomena and perspectives. Allowing new research methodologies to be developed in the field can provide an opening to allow exciting new insights and even new subjects of research to enliven and revitalize the field of educational psychology. These and other new methodologies will help educational psychology to grow in its scope and explanatory power.

FURTHER READING

Davis, S. (Ed.). (1991). *Pragmatics: A Reader*. Oxford: Oxford University Press.

Grundy, P. (2000). *Doing Pragmatics*. London: Arnold.

Levinson, S. C. (1987). *Pragmatics*. Cambridge: Cambridge University Press.

Swales, J. M. (1990). *Genre Analysis*. Cambridge: Cambridge University Press.

CHAPTER 60

Knowledge in a Reconceptualized Educational Environment

RAYMOND A. HORN JR.

In the current climate of No Child Left Behind (NCLB), public knowledge of the educational process has been limited by the sound byte simplicity of the political rhetoric concerning education. Specifically, substantial discussion about issues concerning knowledge, such as what constitutes valid knowledge and how knowledge is produced or acquired, is left to the experts and the others who the experts invite into the conversations. The result of these expert-driven discussions is the determination of educational policy about knowledge, and the subsequent mandated curriculum that is based on this sanctioned knowledge. Seldom are administrators, teachers, students, and parents brought into this formative conversation. The proposition that conversation about knowledge is best left to experts who have little contact with the schools, but are closely aligned to economic, political, and cultural special interests, has created a situation where public participation by all educational stakeholders is limited to discussions about how the teaching and assessment of externally mandated knowledge can be facilitated through the actions of administrators, teachers, students, and parents. The result of this lack of public participation in the conversation that forms epistemological policy is the tacit assumption by the public that there simply are no issues concerning knowledge that need to be discussed, except high-profile and politically charged value issues such as evolution, intelligent design, and creationism. This conversational situation facilitates public acceptance of the positivist assertion that there is empirically objective and valid knowledge that simply needs to be transmitted to or discovered by teachers and students. Another outcome is that the public is not aware of the constructivist nature of knowledge, and of the very different values and consequences that are attached to the different ways that knowledge is produced.

The lack of public conversation about knowledge is indicative of the positivist and conservative control of education. This strategy of control is significant for a number of reasons. First, this colonization of knowledge allows curriculum to be viewed only from a technical rational aspect of education that masks the politically significant values and outcomes attached to different views of curriculum. In this context, standardized curriculum, which is inherently value-laden and has significant consequences for those who must learn this curriculum, is posed as representing a consensus about which meanings and interpretations of reality are true and valid. Second, this imposed and misleading consensus about curriculum aligns with specific instruction, assessment, and class management strategies that synergetically promote one ideological, economic, political, and cultural position about the nature of education and, subsequently, society. Consequently, this promotion of one worldview facilitates the attempted domination of society by this worldview.

A reconceptualized view of education challenges this attempt to gain power through the manipulation of the educational process. The most fundamental aspect of this challenge is to engage the issues of what constitutes valid knowledge, how knowledge is produced and acquired, and the consequences of the possible answers to these issues. Reconceptualists recognize the fundamental truth that knowledge, like all aspects of education, is political. This chapter will explore how a reconceptualized view of teaching and learning would influence these issues about knowledge in the educational environment. The result of a reconceptualized view of knowledge would not be the silencing of stakeholder voices, but instead would be a rich and inclusive conversation that would further result in a view of knowledge that would promote an educational system devoted to the promotion of social justice, an ethic of caring, and participatory democracy.

WHAT CONSTITUTES VALID KNOWLEDGE?

Unlike an empirically based technical rational educational system that promotes only selected empirically generated knowledge, which supports the promotion of a conservative dominant culture, a reconceptualized view of knowledge is diverse, egalitarian, and critical in its intent. A reconceptualized perspective values all forms of knowledge. This inclusiveness is essential if the complexity of education is to be fully engaged. A reconceptual view maintains that no one form of knowledge can provide a full and accurate understanding of a natural or social phenomenon. Knowledge produced by individuals who represent different philosophies, ideologies, methodologies, and sociocultural contexts contributes to a broader and deeper understanding of a complex phenomenon.

Besides the formal knowledge empirically generated by the scientific method, knowledge that is indigenous to individuals who are not part of the culture of Western science is also valued by a reconceptualized view of education. Often, these indigenous cultures have been subjugated by positivist-oriented cultures that consequently determined the indigenous knowledge to be inferior to their formal empirical knowledge. In this case, the domination of one worldview and one knowledge production process sharply limits the potential to engage complexity.

In relation to knowledge and its representation in school curriculum, this process of domination and subjugation can be seen in current educational policy and practice. Any standards and accountability system that is driven by standardized testing and imposed on individual schools by a political body is an example of the determination by that controlling group of what constitutes correct and valid curricular knowledge. In situations like this, phenomenological complexity cannot be fully engaged because teachers and students are now restricted to specific information and inquiry processes. For instance, if there is a specific answer as to whether Woodrow Wilson was a conservative or liberal President of the United States, students' investigation into this complex historical situation will be simplistically restricted to only the information that can lead to the predetermined correct answer. Lost in this potentially rich and critical inquiry into history will be all of the information that contradicts such a simplistic answer. In this case, the potentially diverse student answers that represent a high and critical level of engagement of the historical evidence will be subjugated to the predetermined view of those in control of the curriculum.

Besides the formal knowledge presented through textbooks, video presentations, and teacher lectures, all learners bring personal knowledge to the learning situation. This personal knowledge, whether accurate or inaccurate, mediates and informs the learning process. Because of this, a reconceptualized view of education allows personal knowledge to become part of the conversation and critiquing process that occurs in a classroom that seeks authentic, relevant, and complex understandings. How students have seen and experienced life presents an opportunity for pedagogical connections to be made that enhance student learning through authentic and relevant connections between their lives and curricular knowledge. However, to be truly authentic and relevant, the students' use of their personal knowledge must have the potential to conclude in answers that may deviate from a simplistic predetermined answer.

In addition, educators have practical knowledge gained through their experience. In educational situations dominated by a technical rational perspective, this experiential knowledge is viewed as a confounding variable and subsequently displaced by scripted, teacher-proof lessons that are generalized to all schools. What is denied is the contextual uniqueness of all classrooms and schools, and what is lost is the contextually unique understanding of their own place that individual school administrators and teachers can bring to their practice. The result of this loss of experiential knowledge is the implementation of a decontextualized process of administration and teaching that is neither authentic nor relevant and that subsequently disallows any recognition or engagement of the broader and deeper complexity of the learning process and environment.

Another difference between the technical rational and reconceptualized views of valid knowledge lies in the valuation of formal and informal knowledge. As previously explained, technical rational systems value the formal knowledge derived from empirical scientific investigations. In addition, educational knowledge is restricted to the knowledge that directly applies to each traditional discipline as determined by the gatekeepers of that discipline. Of course, within each discipline there is contentious debate over what constitutes valid knowledge. Currently in science, a debate rages over the teaching of evolution, intelligent design, and creationism. The social sciences have experienced similar debates over representations of historical, economic, and political events. The resolution of these debates dictates the content of standardized curriculum and assessments, as well as the content of textbooks. However, a reconceptualized view expands the idea of knowledge to include all of the other knowledge that is part of all educational experiences. This knowledge is represented by the objects of research found in the field of cultural studies. In this field, knowledge produced by and represented in popular culture, mass media, business-promoted educational programs, and any other aspect of human activity is considered valid knowledge that must be critically engaged. As the hidden curriculum, this nonformal knowledge not only permeates all schools and pedagogical contexts, but also actively mediates and informs all teaching and learning.

So, what constitutes valid knowledge? Is it only empirically derived formal knowledge, or is indigenous, personal, and practical knowledge also valid? A reconceptualized view of learning answers this question in this way. The validity of all knowledge is situational and contextual. What this means is that whether knowledge is correct or incorrect depends on how the context in which the knowledge is situated is defined. For instance, 5 plus 5 equals 10 if the context is that of a base 10 system. However, if the contextual base is different, then 10 may not be the correct answer. Is nuclear power beneficial to humankind? This question will have different answers depending on how broad the conversation is allowed to be. As the context is broadened and the complexity of the conversation increases, the answer to the question will change. Even in seemingly irrefutable laws of physics, correct answers depend on whether the question is posed within a macro or micro context. In the end, the validity of an answer is closely aligned to the level of complexity that is allowed in the answering process.

A reconceptualized view of teaching and learning pragmatically recognizes this situational aspect of knowledge. In some situations where the context is tightly and narrowly defined, there are correct answers. However, in more loosely bound contexts that require higher-order thinking, the correctness of answers is not so easily ensured. This is so because higher-order thinking requires an expansion of the context and an embracing and welcoming of epistemological complexity that in turn problematizes simplistic solutions. In a reconceptual view, what really increases the complexity is the requirement of critical knowledge and a critical critique of knowledge. Based on the assumption that no knowledge is value-free because it always exists within a human context that brings values into the reading of the meaning of the knowledge, reconceptual education requires a continuous analysis of how all knowledge is situated in relation to a concern for social justice, caring, and democratic participation. Whether formal, indigenous, personal, or practical, all knowledge must be critically critiqued. This critical component adds another dimension to the issue of validity. Is knowledge valid if it is unjust, uncaring, or undemocratic? The answer to this question automatically requires an expansion of the boundaries in which the knowledge is situated. This expansion removes the knowledge from a contextually limited reductionist view, and repositions it within the greater complexity of human activity.

A RECONCEPTUALIZED PERSPECTIVE ON KNOWLEDGE PRODUCTION AND ACQUISITION

As discussed, empirical scientific method can provide a technical understanding of a natural phenomenon, but not provide an understanding of the social, cultural, economic, political, and historical contexts that implicitly affect its socially constructed meaning and use. Likewise in relation to social phenomena, neither quantitative, qualitative, nor any other isolated use of analysis, synthesis, or evaluation methodologies can by itself uncover the diverse contexts, origins, and patterns that contribute to the complexity of the phenomenon. Therefore, the acquisition of knowledge through a diversity of research methodologies is a necessary condition of a reconceptual view that strives to engage the full complexity of a phenomenon. In addition, in a reconceptual engagement of complexity, all of the knowledge that is produced and the processes used in knowledge production must be subjected to a rigorous critical interrogation. This interrogation is an essential activity that continues the engagement of complexity through the ongoing expansion of etymological knowledge, context, pattern detection, and other analysis, synthesis, and evaluation processes.

A fundamental reconceptualist understanding of knowledge production is that all production is a socially constructivist process. Grounded in the work of individuals such as Piaget, Vygotsky, Bruner, and Dewey, this means that individuals and individuals in interaction with their social environment actively participate in the construction of knowledge or meaning. Moving beyond the individual constructivism of Piaget to the Vygotskian understanding that knowledge is constructed within social interactions and a cultural context, a reconceptual view recognizes the role played by the individual as well as the individual's social environment in the knowledge production process. This constructivist analysis of learning is in contrast to the positivist assertion that knowledge exists outside of the learner—that the known and the knower are separate. This assertion is challenged by constructivists, who maintain that because the learner is an active participant in the learning process and the construction of knowledge, the known and the knower are inseparable.

Reconceptual education is also critically constructivist. Critical constructivism is a synthesis of critical theory and social constructivism in that the knowledge that is socially constructed must be critically interrogated in order for the individual to become aware of the consequences of the knowledge in relation to social justice, an ethic of caring, and participatory democracy. Critical constructivism requires critical thinking. However, in this case, critical thinking is not the narrowly applied use of higher-order thinking skills found in the reductionist thinking of technical rational education, but the critical interrogation of the constructed knowledge and the processes used in this construction. In the critical constructivist process, all aspects of the construction of knowledge are critically interrogated, including the individual's involvement, the aspects of the social environment involved in the construction process, the processes used in the construction, and the consequences of the constructed knowledge or meaning. When involved in critical constructivist activity, individuals utilize diverse and multiple methodologies to uncover the deep and hidden critical ramifications of the knowledge that they constructed. Among these methods is a critical reflection not only on the knowledge that was produced and the processes employed in the construction, but also on their own participation in the construction and the subsequent consequences of their actions in relation to this constructed knowledge. The critical constructivist process results in knowledge about knowledge, knowledge about self, and knowledge about one's critical interaction with others. Critical constructivists also understand that knowledge production is connected to the actions that one takes. For instance, the idea of praxis involves a sequence of action, critical reflection, and subsequent action based on this reflection. Critical constructivism adds the imperative of an awareness of how power is manifested in a situation and how power is potentially rearranged through our actions. Critical constructivists continuously reflect on how power arrangements affect a concern for social justice, an ethic of caring, and participatory democracy.

Finally, an important characteristic of reconceptualized teaching and learning is a continuous emphasis on research by all educational stakeholders. In a reconceptualized environment, teachers are researchers. They research their subject matter, their pedagogy, and their students. As researchers, they understand the necessity to effectively and situationally employ diverse research methods. As teacher researchers in a reconceptualized environment, they understand that in addition to technical effectiveness they need to employ a pedagogy that is just, caring, and democratic. Understanding the critical value of research, they promote the knowledge, skill, and opportunity for their students to become student researchers. Through research that is based on critical awareness, they and their students expand the complexity of teaching and learning. In this critical constructivist context, research takes on an emancipatory goal—the liberation of both teacher and student through greater critical understanding of the knowledge that they construct and the actions that they take.

THE POLITICS OF KNOWLEDGE

Starting from the assumption that all human activity is political, the process of knowledge production is the key to political control and the emancipation from oppression. Knowledge production in both technical rational and reconceptualized educational systems is politicized. In the former, a rigorous control over the validity of knowledge and the production process creates an opportunity to exercise societal control through the education of children. If this control is aligned with other efforts of control through economic, political, cultural, and social interests, a powerful agenda can be constructed to implement a specific view of the organization and functioning of society. Likewise, a reconceptual view of education can attempt to accomplish the same. However, the significant difference between the two lies in the role of the individual.

In technical rational perspectives, individuals are seen as resources or entities that if properly prepared will consciously or unconsciously support the agenda of the dominant group. Control of knowledge production (i.e., curriculum, instruction, and assessment) creates the potential for compliance with the canon of the dominant group. On the other hand, reconceptualized teaching and learning facilitates the development of critically aware and literate individuals who through the critical knowledge, skills, and dispositions acquired in a reconceptualized educational environment experience a greater degree of intellectual freedom from the control of special interests. In addition, this intellectual freedom creates the potential for action that can be emancipatory and critical.

The different political agendas of technical rational and reconceptualized views of education can be seen in the assimilation versus diversity issue in public education. Proponents of assimilation see the purpose of education as the construction of a homogenized society that is grounded in one perspective that aligns with their ideological position. In this case, correct or valid knowledge is that which promotes the economic, cultural, social, and political perspectives that allow a reproduction of their ideological position. Knowledge production is viewed as an activity that must be closely controlled so that only certain knowledge or representations of knowledge become the norm. The aspects of educational psychology that are identified as relevant foundations for educational theory and practice are those that will produce the desired outcome.

In contrast, proponents of diversity see the purpose of education as the construction of critically aware individuals who have the disposition and capacity to think independently and take action that is based on a concern for social justice, caring, and participatory democracy. The inherent consequence of this educational purpose is a pluralistic society that values difference and diversity, and acts to promote empowerment and emancipation from oppression. In this case, correct or valid knowledge is viewed as an ongoing construction that must be continuously scrutinized in relation to its critical consequences. Knowledge is not viewed as value-neutral but value-laden, not external to the knower but inseparable from the knower. Knowledge production is viewed as a political activity that must be constantly and critically interrogated to determine the economic, cultural, social, and political perspectives and their consequences. The aspects of educational psychology that are identified as relevant foundations for educational theory and practice are those that contribute to the construction of a just, caring, and democratic citizenry and society.

CHAPTER 61

Critical Epistemology: An Alternative Lens on Education and Intelligence

ANNE BROWNSTEIN

WHAT *IS* THE PROBLEM?

I can't do anything with these kids. They're unwilling to learn.
Why do we have to learn this?
I don't know how many are going to pass despite all the drilling they have.
Why can't we study something that matters?

While working as an assistant principal in a New York City public high school, I was at a loss for how to respond to what appeared to be the *dispossession* between teachers and students and the teaching/learning experience revealed by questions such as the above directed to me when I visited classrooms. Unfortunately, I regularly observed evidence of this dispossession in student behavior: students continuously talking off-topic or taking pictures of one another on the sly with their cell phones during instruction, wandering out of class, or slowly strolling halls with bathroom passes. Teacher behavior likewise attested to their dispossession from teaching/learning experience judging from the daily flow of calls to security to escort particularly noncompliant students to the dean's office and low teacher attendance at school. By perplexing contrast, however, during lunch periods and before and after school, what I observed was quite different: students and teachers pleasantly greeting one another, laughing, and talking together about daily events or shared interests. I couldn't make sense of it all. What was happening in the classroom to turn teachers and students into adversaries both of one another and the teaching/learning experience, and what could I do to help fix the problem? Moreover, what *was* the problem?

We educators are not alone in our profound concern about what does (or does not) go on in the schools. It should be obvious to anyone living in this country that there is a widely held perception that the United States' educational system is in crisis. One has only to turn to the media to discover that it is commonly believed both in popular and political circles that the problems facing education can be attributed to one, some, or all of the following "causes": teachers don't know what they're doing; kids don't respect their teachers; educational standards are too low; and we need to return to "the basics." While for a long time I agreed with the above assertions, I now no longer believe they are "causes" of the problem, but symptomatic of problems arising from much more complex issues of what and how we conceive of truth, knowledge, intelligence, and ultimately the purpose of education.

Fundamental to understanding the causes of the failure of our educational system is to uncover the traditional assumptions underlying the thinking of critics and even supporters of education in this country, as well as our own. This requires that we look closely at our conceptions of how the human brain works, how learning takes place, what we consider worth learning, and how we assess intelligence. In short, we must reexamine our most deeply held beliefs about the kind of human beings we are teaching our children to be and the role of schools in achieving that goal.

In pursuing the above line of inquiry we discover inevitably that so much of what we consider "true" about how the brain thinks and learns is derived from the dominant mechanistic tradition of educational psychology. This tradition, which reduces the brain to the simplistic metaphor of a computer that uploads and downloads information on command if the right sequence of buttons are pressed, has resulted in producing a vast population of teachers and students dispossessed from the teaching/learning experience by imprisoning the conception of what humanity is and the role of education in its development. If we earnestly are committed to providing all children with a meaningful, joyous, and empowering education, we need to redefine the problem by acknowledging fundamental misconceptions born of the tradition of mechanistic educational psychology that are embedded in the current dominant educational structure. Educational "failure" is not to be found in the teachers and students: It's within the dominant traditional tightly bound notions of the brain, knowledge, truth, and intelligence that have subsumed and misguided even the most well-intended educational efforts.

The study of critical epistemology has enabled me to begin to understand what I had regarded as teacher and student dispossession from the teaching/learning experience. Rather than assume that the teachers and/or students are somehow to blame, I now interpret their disengaged behavior as an act of resistance to the ultimately dehumanizing and professionally deskilling effect of a state-imposed standards-driven curriculum and assessment régime, one that demands that teachers instruct "the facts" with little or no room for creativity, and worse, with little or no opportunity to evaluate and question the value of what is taught. Although I am loath to admit it, I was formerly likely to attribute the disturbing phenomena I observed to a fundamental lack of teaching ability and/or the insurmountable and debilitating effect of socioeconomic issues of the students' backgrounds. Perhaps in some cases my analysis may have been accurate. Even so, I am convinced that the behaviors I observed can be better understood in terms of the far-reaching and powerful legacy of the effects that traditional mechanistic educational psychology have on virtually every aspect of how we "do" education, from teacher training and curriculum design to the physical appearance of classrooms, buildings, and how teacher and student behaviors are regulated. To begin to address the "problem" in education today, we must uncover the underlying ideological and epistemological paradigms inscribed in teaching and learning that have served not only to create a sense of dispossession between teachers and students and the teaching/learning experience, but also understand how these have served to reinforce dominant power structures and class/cultural inequalities in this society. For some, and most likely for those who firmly believe in the absolute merit of traditional mechanistic educational psychology and the structures it has produced, this may be a very unsettling process.

My objective in writing here is to trace the historical derivation of the dominant ideological and epistemological frameworks underlying traditional (positivistic, Western, white, male) education, and postmodern responses to these frameworks. If successful, I hope that students of traditional mechanistic educational psychology and others will gain insight into understanding why so much of what takes place in most educational settings is experienced as frustration, apathy, and despair. Moreover, I hope to respond to those critics who are only too willing, as I had been, to blame teachers and students for the failure of teachers to instruct and students to learn anything truly exhilarating or useful in school.

HOW DO WE QUESTION THE TRUTH?

So, what is *critical epistemology*? As I am using this compound term, critical epistemology is a theoretical and philosophical framework that allows us to examine not only how knowledge and truth ("the facts") are produced, but also to apprehend issues of power embedded in what is presented as "fact." Critical epistemology is a framework that allows us to consider questions such as the following: What is truth? If there are many versions of the truth, whose version do we accept, and why do we choose to accept one version over others? Can information be neutral, and if not, how can we recognize when it is not? Who "wins" or "loses" as a result of a particular version of the truth?

Some readers of the above, particularly students of traditional mechanistic educational psychology, may be scratching their heads wondering how considering such questions may be at all relevant to gaining insight into what is blighting contemporary education in the United States. Some perhaps may feel annoyed or outraged by the endeavor to question what "truth" is, particularly within a critical theoretical framework that demands that we scrutinize all knowledge within the temporal, political, cultural, gendered contexts in which it is produced and disseminated. However, if we hope to begin to address what broadly has become regarded as the "failure" of teachers to teach and students to learn in our current educational system, we must begin to examine the questions raised by a critical epistemological perspective.

To start, consider the following: Seldom are those of us who have dwelled as students or teachers for any length of time in educational settings ever asked to consider where our conceptions of knowledge or intelligence come from, nor have we been presented with opportunities to reflect on the possibility that there are oblique sociopolitical agendas embedded in the "truths" disseminated both inside and outside of the school experience. More often, as teachers we come to understand that in order to be successful in our careers we must comport ourselves as "neutral" deliverers of information and to regard our students as "receptacles" for whatever we teach. Worse, in most traditional school settings students quickly learn that passive, unquestioning behavior is much more likely to be rewarded than behavior that actively challenges the status quo. However, stepping back and peering in through the lens provided by critical epistemology, we might begin to wonder not only how the teaching/learning experience came to be this way for so many of us, but also whose agenda the pretense of a neutral and passive educational structure serves.

Essential to the critical epistemological approach is the assertion that all knowledge is *constructed*, that is, produced by human beings interacting within particular social and physical environments during specific time periods. As such, the process by which we come to understand and accept some things as "fact" and others not is by definition the product of human beings perceiving and trying to make sense of the world within the historical, political, cultural, gendered, ideological web of reality in which they live. Following this reasoning, as will be discussed later, even those phenomena that can be "proven" by "scientific method" is a reflection not only of the multiple complex contexts within which the "method" is constructed and used to establish "fact," but also a reflection of the personal web of reality in which the individual researcher is situated. Similar to the study of phenomenology (the study of phenomena as they are constructed by human consciousness), critical epistemology requires us to consider the "phenomenon" of knowledge construction and dissemination not only in terms of the larger context of the multilayered, intersecting social, political, ideological, temporal web of reality in which these phenomena take place, but also to reflect on our individual position to this complex web.

In the spirit of the above and by way of example, I will pause a moment to situate myself in relationship to the topic at hand. Raised in an intellectually and economically privileged university community, I entered the field of education as a form of social action. Jewish, female, and liberal, as a teacher I was particularly committed to providing a classroom environment for the highly diverse populations I taught and tried to engage every student's interest and imagination by experimenting with new ways to teach the proscribed curriculum. Believing that classroom tone was enhanced or inhibited by the physical arrangement of space, I was particularly interested in creating a spatially "equitable" environment. This belief was translated into a physical arrangement of seating that required students to face one another and me in a circular group so that we could all participate in egalitarian discussion. At the outset of my career, while I would have agreed with Kincheloe that every dimension and every form of educational practice are politically contested spaces, not once did I pause to examine the epistemological and ideological beliefs underlying my instruction to try to discern potential invisible forces operating in the name of democracy and justice but ultimately serving to reinforce the oppressive nature of what I taught. Therefore, like many teachers who arrange their classrooms to facilitate face-to-face discussion among students to foster egalitarian interaction, in the end I still taught the fundamentally monological state-authored curriculum that was firmly grounded in assumptions about the human brain derived from traditional mechanistic educational psychology, a curriculum that only recently I have come to recognize as representing a far-from-neutral or democratic worldview. Besides this, I attempted to present politically "neutral" instruction even though how I taught my classes was founded in my own firm belief that students needed to cultivate work-oriented skills and a culturally "sanctioned" knowledge base to participate competitively in a market economy. Had I been cognizant of it at the time, I would have realized I was promoting not only some form of neoconservative or neoliberal capitalist agenda, but also a very limited perspective of what "valuable" knowledge is. Regretfully, only now am I aware of my role in reinforcing the ideology of the dominant culture via the state-approved curriculum and my neoconservative/neoliberal capitalist orientation, both of which I presented as value-free and "true." Eager to please me and/or concerned for their grades, seldom did any students challenge the ideologies embedded in the curriculum and my instruction. I regarded the few who did as radical recalcitrants, and although I tried to persuade these students to compromise, all chose to fail my class rather than "buy into" what I was "selling." Similarly, I have seen many caring, well-intentioned teachers employ instructional strategies that were democratic in physical structure only and that were ultimately undermined by the same fundamentally unquestioned/unquestionable monological standards-driven curriculum and the teacher's veiled or unconscious ideological beliefs. I now understand that "noncompliant" students (usually nonwhite, non-Western, and poor) invariably fail under an education system that requires teachers to unquestioningly inculcate "facts" born of the ideology of the dominant class. Unequipped to have meaningful conversations with our students about the issues of power that are embedded in the curriculum and where our conceptions of knowledge and intelligence come from, we instructors would be a lot more honest if we arranged our rooms in a way that reflected the monological nature of what we taught and expected our students to accept ideologically. At least we would not confuse ourselves or delude the vast majority of our students with the notion, as Kincheloe has argued, that if the method of information delivery is democratic, then so is the epistemology and ideology underlying it.

IS SCIENCE NEUTRAL?

If we were to assign blame to a single cause of the current crisis in education, it would be the assumption that Western science—that is, the framework and methods by which we perceive and measure all phenomena—allows us to produce objective, neutral, true, and hence universal data about all there is to know in the world. In education, this assumption is embodied in particular by the tradition of mechanistic educational psychology, the consequences of which can be found not only in the narrow way we construct curriculum (i.e., the selection of "facts" and skills that are taught), but also how we determine what intelligence is (i.e., the "neutral" testing standards to assess aptitude). While I am not asserting that we should completely discard Western science (and by extension, all educational psychology) as a means of learning more about human beings and the world, it is important that we understand it as *one* approach, and one that is embedded in a complex historical, cultural, and ultimately political context.

Western science, the traditional system of knowledge production in the United States, has dominated our thinking for so long that it may be hard to see it merely as a single approach among many. Known also as positivistic epistemology, Western science was born in Europe during the Modern Period and is characterized by the significant epistemological changes that occurred during the Scientific Revolution of the sixteenth and seventeenth centuries when scientific thought (reason) was elevated to the pinnacle of how human beings can and should explore/explain all phenomena. Thanks to Descartes, who asserted that the world can be best understood by being "broken down" and applying scientific method/reason to understanding each of its constituent parts, knowledge came to be regarded as "something out there waiting to be discovered." By reducing every phenomenon to a "part" or "thing-in-itself," free of relationships to other phenomenon and devoid of any social, historical, and cultural context, modernist thinkers firmly posited that there was no relationship between the *knower* and the *known*. This view led to the conception of the world as a mechanical system divided into two realms: the internal world of sensation and an objective world composed of natural phenomena, a conception that led to a litany of other false dichotomies. Contributing to the notion that knowledge is context-free and independent of the human beings who "discover" it, Newton extended Descartes' theories by describing time and space as absolutes. Later, Bacon contributed to the reinforcement of the exalted status of scientific thought by establishing the supremacy of reason over imagination. In short, modernist thinkers deified rationality by asserting that scientific method—"rational" because of its attention to applying scientific procedures (methodology) to measure all phenomena—could produce data that was human-bias- and context-free. Following this line of thinking, modernist thinkers were firmly convinced that certainty is possible, and when enough scientific research is produced, human beings will finally have understood reality well enough to forgo further research.

Constructed and promulgated by members of the dominant Western, white, male society, modernist epistemology represents a distinctly limited and limiting perspective, one in which scientific method is used to the exclusion of all other approaches in establishing what constitutes the "truth" or "facts." This Cartesian–Newtonian–Baconian epistemology, known from the nineteenth century onwards as positivism, subsumed not only the thinking and scholarly activities of the culturally, economically, politically, militarily dominant Western nations in which it was born and cultivated, but also was disseminated and inculcated via the pedagogical practice and learning institutions of these countries and those countries/cultures conquered and colonized by them. Through this process, a single, hegemonic view of the world emerged, one in which scientifically discovered "facts" were established and affirmed of comprising a "universal, one true reality." The belief in the supremacy of "objective" science necessarily inhered the impossibility of the value or "validity" of any other culture's knowledges and knowledge-producing system. The primary objective of the education system of the dominant (and typically colonizing) culture not only was used as a means of reinforcing the dominant, Western, white, male, positivistic epistemology of a "universal one true reality," but also was used as a means of silencing and in many cases obliterating all subjugated (non-Western, nonwhite, female, indigenous) knowledges and epistemologies. Establishing "the facts" became the responsibility of scientifically trained academicians. As a result, teachers became responsible merely for delivering the "facts" and not for producing them: In turn, students became responsible for "receiving the facts" and not interpreting/questioning or otherwise making sense of them. Ultimately dispossessed of whatever other knowledges they may have had before entering the education system as well as the ability to produce knowledge through the teaching/learning experience, it seems inevitable that both teachers and students should come to feel and behave adversely to what they are expected to "do" together in the classroom.

Unfortunately, how education is traditionally conceived was not the only domain affected by Western science. Approaching human thinking as an "object" that can be dismantled and understood in terms of its component "parts," traditional mechanistic educational psychologists and cognitive scientists have endeavored to define intelligence by applying positivistic methods to the human mind, the primary objective being to "quantify" intelligence, which they narrowly defined as performing certain "thinking" tasks on demand. One devastating consequence of this approach was the utter dismissal and denigration of human emotion, physical sensation, intuition, and spontaneous improvisation, without which it is nearly impossible to imagine being able to "think" or lead a healthy, interesting, and successful life. Another terrible outcome of this positivistic approach was that it also led to the development of "objective" measurements such as the Binet–Stanford IQ test, the Standardized Achievement Test, and a variety of other assessments designed to "quantify" human learning. These tests are predicated on the assumption that if schools, teachers and students are doing their jobs, one can measure what students know on the basis of how they perform in the decontextualized setting of an examination room. On closer analysis, however, Bourdieu among others has suggested that these tests reveal more about the values and cultural assumptions of those who construct the tests and the students' familiarity with cultural norms (including the curricular "facts") of the dominant class than they do about the critical and creative qualities of how students process and apply what they know. In short, in their efforts to analyze the human mind in terms of very narrow mathematical and psychometric measurements that essentially reduce intelligence to quantifying how many "facts" one knows during a decontextualized test, traditional mechanistic educational psychologists and cognitive scientists fail to recognize, as Varela (1992) has pointed out, the value and importance of the nuances, subtleties, and ambiguities by which some of the most spontaneous creative and abstract thinking is characterized and enacted throughout lived experience. Assessed in this manner, it is no wonder that many students feel misunderstood and ultimately insulted by traditional instruction and evaluation.

The simplistic curriculum design and intelligence assessment standards provided by educational "experts"—those followers of traditional mechanistic educational psychology and cognitive science—ultimately have served to undermine education in this country. It is inevitable that teachers and students, excluded from research and knowledge-producing activities in the daily teaching/learning experience and constrained by highly limited definitions of what intelligence is, feel dispossessed from what they are expected to "do" while in the classroom. So long as teachers are regarded as unskilled taskmasters responsible for inculcating a static set of state-sanctioned scientifically produced "facts," the sheer boredom and disempowerment that accompanies this approach will continue to result in professional dissatisfaction and burnout. Likewise, so long as students are expected to be unquestioning recipients and parrots of such an education, there will continue to be "winners" (compliant students) and "losers" (noncompliant ones) in the educational process. Within the current traditional positivistic, Western, white, male framework that underlies education in this country, it is now clear to me that the primary objective of schooling is to reinforce the dominant culture/class structure while ensuring the continued subjugation of marginalized (nonpositivistic, non-Western, nonwhite, nonmale) voices that would challenge its authority. As such, much of our educational system facilitated a dominant belief in traditional mechanist educational psychology, has become a bleak, spirit-breaking institution destined to exacerbate and expand the unjust distribution of knowledge and power between the dominant and subjugated classes that comprise U.S. society. Is this really the kind of society we hope to foster through our educational system and, if so, how can a democracy survive when we educate our children this way?

ARE THERE ALTERNATIVES?

The vast majority of educators I have come to know in New York City are committed to critical pedagogy, that is, to engaging in teaching and providing learning experiences that foster social justice and equality. New York City educators are hardly alone in their commitment: Those interested in critical pedagogy everywhere understand that in order to remedy an unjust educational system there must be a significant paradigm shift in terms of the ideological orientation of schools. To create a just society, schools must welcome and cultivate the rich experiences and knowledges students bring to the learning environment. Schools must educate students to evaluate ideas critically, a process that not only requires understanding the complexity of the contexts in which knowledge is produced, but also that allows for ambiguity and the possibility of multiple interpretations of the truth. How knowledge is produced and disseminated both inside and outside of the schools must be understood in terms of its relationship to societal power structures. Moreover, individuals need to understand how to put ideas into action. The myth of teacher and curriculum ideological "neutrality" can no longer be accepted. In short, we must search far beyond traditional mechanistic educational psychology to resolve complex educational issues as it completely ignores these essential sociopolitical issues.

Under the current framework, teachers are expected to be merely neutral information deliverers. Those interested in critical pedagogy understand that no human activity is ever bias- or context-free. In fact, the concept of the ideology-free teacher can be seen as a conflation/extension of the idea that all knowledge is "neutral," a notion that derives from modernist thinkers. Ultimately, for critical pedagogues the objective of education is to teach students how to resist the harmful effects of dominant power and empower the marginalized and exploited, activities that must include everything from engaging such individuals in a rigorous pursuit of empowering education to a more equitable distribution of wealth. As challenging as this may seem, it is perhaps the only means by which one can hope to ease the failure and suffering that characterize both the teachers' and students' experiences in schools that will carry over later into society as widespread suffering of the disempowered social classes and as a potential force in undermining our democratic system of government.

The current unjust, limited, and limiting epistemology and ideology found in the U.S. educational system cannot be expected to exist forever without resistance. As Giroux and many others have asserted, human beings have agency, the ability to actively resist the oppressive forces designed to control and limit their behavior. As a result of mid–twentieth-century social and cultural movements (i.e., feminist, African, and Native American), the evident failure of education to serve large diverse populations of students, and the spread of works by critical theorists of the Frankfurt school, new perspectives have developed in resistance to the oppressive force of the "culture of positivism" on education. Often labeled as "postdiscourses" because they question the modernist, scientific, Western approach to knowledge production and distribution, two significant theoretical orientations have emerged: critical theory and complexity theory. Critical theorists are principally concerned with power and its just distribution. Complexity theorists are principally concerned with the interplay/relationship of multiple forces (i.e., gendered, social, temporal, cultural, etc.) that comprise and have an effect on all phenomena, and understand that no phenomenon can be understood in isolation or "unto itself": every phenomenon must be regarded as a part of a totality of multiple aspects/influences/forces, all of which have an effect on one another and in relationship to one another. The theoretical approaches of these two postdiscourses (which also include poststructural, postcolonial, and postformalist ones) have significant implications for education. Taken together, however, those interested in *critical complex pedagogy* understand not only the relationship between power and how knowledge is produced and distributed, but also the multilogical, human-constructed, and therefore ambiguous nature of the truth. In sum, critical complex pedagogy seriously challenges reductionistic epistemologies and the oppressive ideologies inscribed in them.

Refuting traditional mechanistic educational psychology and the supremacy of the positivistic Cartesian–Newtonian–Baconian epistemology—that is, the exclusive use of scientific and mathematical methods to measure and quantify the world and its phenomena as a means to "discovering" and "understanding it"—is fundamental to bringing about the necessary paradigm shift to address the oppressive dominant Western ideologies embedded in curriculum and instruction that have led to the above-described dispossession of teachers and students in the teaching/learning experience. Providing hope, several theorists have emerged to offer epistemological and ideological alternatives. These alternatives provide the means of transforming schools from dehumanizing and disempowering institutions to ones in which both teachers and students can reclaim and reaffirm the "validity" of the knowledges of their own sociocultural backgrounds, as well as engage in acts of producing and understanding knowledges in terms of their complexity.

Phenomenology, the study of phenomena in the world as they are constructed by our consciousness, provides a means of reuniting the "knower" to the "known" by asserting the significance of the world's phenomena as they are constructed by human consciousness. Unconcerned primarily with the nomological or factual aspects of some state of affairs, the phenomenological epistemological approach requires that we inquire about the nature of phenomenon as meaningfully *experienced*. In reestablishing that there is a relationship between human beings and the world in which we live, and focusing on lived experience as a means of discerning meaning, phenomenologists such as Van Manen (1990) ultimately attempt to understand what it means to be human. The significance of phenomenology to pedagogy is that it reintroduces the intimate relationship of human beings to other human beings, the environment, and all of world's phenomena, thereby providing a means for students and teachers to draw on their own lived experiences and to share these to create meaning via the teaching/learning experience. In short, phenomenology empowers teachers and students to become researchers of their own lived experience, a process through which they produce knowledge for themselves instead of merely delivering or receiving scientifically produced "facts" as knowledge.

By definition, phenomenology requires that we eschew the positivistic notion of the universal "certainty of knowledge." Hermeneutics, the branch of philosophy concerned with human understanding and the interpretation of texts (i.e., written, spoken, works of art, events, etc.) is particularly useful in this pursuit. For phenomenological hermeneutists, one must accept that all knowledge is interpretation. As Madison (1988) has suggested, the "truth" is a human construction, an interpretation that comes down to and is no more than saying it is generally accepted by a community of interpreters. In this framework, scientific knowledge is viewed not as a passive copying of reality but rather as a single means of constructing reality. In significant contrast to positivistic epistemology, phenomenological hermeneutists present scientific methodology as *one* way in which reality is creatively interpreted, granting no more "validity" than any other mode of interpretation or access to absolute reality and truth.

The notion of reality as a contextually dependent human construction born of interpretation and not of empirical, scientific method raises many important and potentially upsetting epistemological questions such as, How can we know anything for certain? How do we know what the truth is? Is all truth relativistic (i.e., relative to the limited nature of the mind, conditions of knowing, individuals and groups of "knowers")? Must we accept all interpretation as the truth?

Following Madison, dethroning positivistic epistemological approaches in favor of hermeneutic (interpretive) ones does not mean that we reject all standards for evaluating what is "true." In answer to these questions, phenomenological hermeneutists such as Madison assert that it is not to science but to *rhetoric* or *the theory of persuasive argumentation* that interpretation should look for its theoretical and methodological grounding. What is pedagogically significant about this epistemological approach is that it allows teachers and students to respect the epistemologies of a diversity of cultures, genders, races, and religions that comprise a typical classroom by dialogically examining and understanding the nature of "truth" in terms of multilogical (i.e., non-Western, female, etc.) perspectives. In short, phenomenological hermeneutics welcomes a broad range of knowledges and interpretative systems for understanding the world, including those that may have completely different conceptions of time, space, history, and social values.

While integrating phenomenological and hermeneutic epistemologies into pedagogical practice are essential in making the shift from the positivistic paradigm to that of complexity in education, critically complex pedagogues also understand how important it is that teachers and students understand how schools have been used as mechanisms for reproducing the ideology of dominant power structures, a process that by necessity oppresses subjugated/"indigenous" cultures and their knowledges. Moreover, critically complex pedagogy is not only concerned with these issues, but also with how education can become a transformative force in improving the human condition. Giroux's *Pedagogy and the Power of Hope* and Kincheloe and Semali's *What Is Indigenous Knowledge?* (1999) specifically address these issues, but before discussing these it is important first to define a few terms.

There is no definitive set of characteristics (essences) that characterize who is and isn't "indigenous." Contrary to essentialist assertions, there is no "natural" category of indigenous persons. It is important to understand this concept, as indigeneity manifests itself within diverse and often hybridized ranges; and there is, of course, great differences among individuals who theoretically belong to this same group. *Indigenous*, as defined by the World Council of Indigenous Peoples in Kincheloe and Semali, describes such individuals who occupied lands prior to populations who now share or claim such territories and possess distinct language and culture. By extension, *indigenous knowledge* refers to knowledges produced in a specific social context and employed by lay people in their everyday lives. In returning to the question of who "qualifies" as indigenous, it should be clear that there is a great deal of cultural/historical/racial/ethic/linguistic diversity among how indigenous peoples identify themselves or are identified by others. Suffice to say that given the above definitions, in terms of this country one can make an argument that indigenous peoples comprise the majority of those attending urban public schools.

Critical complex theorists interested in pedagogy such as Kincheloe, Semali, and Giroux address schools as institutions that oppress subjugated/indigenous cultures and knowledges through ideologies that are tacitly expressed through curriculum and instructional practices. For Kincheloe and Semali, oppressive forces that shape us have formed the identities of both the powerful and the exploited. By seeking out the ideological forces that construct student perceptions of school and the impact such perceptions have on their school experiences, they offer a means of analyzing the process by which this happens to understand why students succeed or fail in school. The authors assert the superiority of indigenous knowledges over dominant positivistic epistemological paradigm—one that asserts the "certainty of knowledge": Following complexity theory, Kincheloe and Semali demonstrate that many indigenous epistemologies are not uncomfortable with a lack of certainty about the social world and world of nature, because they have no need to solve all mysteries about the world they operate *with* and in. Indeed, indigenous knowledges as they are presented by these authors provide clear examples of the epistemology of complexity when applied to classroom teaching/learning, epistemologies that value phenomenological lived experience and hermeneutic, interpretative ways of knowing over the traditional positivistic approach. This is not to say that they suggest that schools completely dispose of scientific (positivistic) ways of knowing. By contrast, they assert that *transformative scientists* understand that any science is a social construction, produced in a particular culture and specific historical era, an understanding shared by phenomenological hermeneutists, complexity theorists, as well as other scholars and proponents of indigenous knowledges. In sum, inclusion of indigenous knowledges in education serves two essential purposes: (a) providing a means of understanding the world from a variety of different epistemological orientations and (b) promoting a more democratic ideology by reinforcing the notion that understanding the world via the knowledge systems of indigenous (subjugated) peoples have value for everyone.

Giroux's *Pedagogy and the Politics of Hope* (1997) offers a response to the reductionistic notion that schools are necessarily and hopelessly subordinate to political, economic, and social power structures by demonstrating both the oppressive and potentially emancipatory forces of the process of schooling. Giroux asserts that we all participate in ideology on conscious, subconscious, and material levels, but that we are not necessarily imprisoned in it: human beings have "agency"—the ability to resist and transform the ideologies that oppress us. To begin to address social injustices and transform society, Giroux believes that critical educators need to (a) become aware of the extent to which ideologies exert a force over our belief systems and behaviors and (b) enable students to become critically aware of these forces. Giroux (in keeping with the post-discourses of other theorists), views positivism as antithetical to developing students to participate in a critical democracy (society as a struggle for just distribution of knowledge and power) since the mode of reasoning embedded in the culture of positivism cannot reflect on meaning, value, or anything that cannot be verified in the empirical tradition. To counter this tradition, Giroux argues that teachers need to regard themselves as transformative intellectuals who help students acquire critical knowledge about basic societal structures such as the economy, the state, the workplace, and mass culture. To do this, teachers and students need to become aware that ideology operates at the level of lived experience signified in material practices produced within certain historical, existential, and class traditions. In sum, it can be said that for Giroux, to be liberated from the oppressive ideologies of society (reproduced and reinforced in schooling, institutions, mass media, and culture), students and teachers must become producers of their own knowledge, drawing on epistemologies such as phenomenology, hermeneutics, and complexity theory in their efforts to become critical not only of themselves but also of the society at large.

WHAT NEXT?

Without question, the current system of education is in crisis in this country. Conservative "solutions" to the problem, steeped as they are in the "scientific data" of traditional mechanist educational psychology, have taken the form of reactionary measures such as those embodied by the No Child Left Behind legislation. Similar to other educational efforts predicated on dominant Western, white, male, epistemology and ideology, these measures are certain to broaden even further the chasm between the dominant elite minority and vast marginalized majority that comprise this country. Rather than try to return to a mythical Golden Age of education that never existed except in our imagination, we must honestly examine the purpose of teaching and learning and our goals in educating the young. Gaining a greater understanding of the oblique agendas embedded in how we go about schooling via familiarity with the study of critical epistemology is an integral first step in this process. We must optimistically redefine what the primary objective of education should be, beginning with the question of what kind of society we hope to create. Mindful of the seriously debilitating limitations of mechanistic educational psychology that traditionally has been the basis for how we construct intelligence and knowledge, we must boldly seek alternative perspectives and approaches that attempt to understand the complexity and richness of all of human experience.

Understanding critical epistemology allows us to see that teaching and learning are *not* "neutral" activities—more than anything else, this is one area that traditional mechanistic educational psychology has overlooked. Ultimately, we must ask ourselves what kind of human being we hope to inspire and nurture through education: Are we interested in educating all of our children to become members of a critical citizenry capable of sustaining democracy, or subservient members of the labor force and consumer society? At its best, education can provide the joys of discovery, intellectual empowerment, and freedom. Above all, providing students with an educational experience that achieve these should be the starting point for all educational reforms we undertake in the future.

SUGGESTED READING

Bourdieu, P., and Passeron, J.-C. (1990). *Reproduction in Education* (2nd ed.). New York: Sage.

George, J. (1999). Indigenous knowledge as a component of the school curriculum. In L. Semali and J. Kincheloe (Eds.), *What Is Indigenous Knowledge?* (pp. 79–94). New York: Falmer Press.

Giroux, H. (1997). *Pedagogy and the Politics of Hope*. Boulder: Westview Press.

Kincheloe, J. (2004). *Critical Pedagogy Primer*. New York: Peter Lang.

Kincheloe, J. (2001). *Getting Beyond the Facts*. New York: Peter Lang.

Kincheloe, J. (1999). Trouble ahead, trouble behind: Grounding the post-formal critique of educational psychology. In S. Steinberg, J. Kincheloe, and P. Hinchey (Eds.), *The Post-formal Reader: Cognition and Education* (pp. 4–54). New York: Falmer Press.

Madison, G. B. (1988). *The Hermeneutics of Postmodernity: Figures and Themes*. Bloomington: Indiana University Press.

Semali, L., and Kincheloe, J. (Eds.). (1999). *What Is Indigenous Knowledge?* New York: Falmer Press.

Van Manen, M. (1990). *Researching Lived Experience*. Albany: SUNY Press.

Varela, F. (1992). *Ethical Know-How*. Stanford: Stanford University Press.

CHAPTER 62

Dialogism: The Diagotic Turn in the Social Sciences

ADRIANA AUBERT AND MARTA SOLER

The concept of dialogism implies a focus on dialogue and communication in the explanation of society, social relations, and personal development. Dialogism is not a new concept but recovers a tradition of looking at the social dimension of the self, from the perspective of cognition and action. In *The Pedagogy of the Heart*, for instance, Freire argues that dialogism is *inherent of human nature, and a requirement for democracy*, and in this statement he is telling us two important ideas. On the one hand, human beings are social—since the day of birth they seek for interactions—and they use dialogue to make meanings, to acquire knowledge and skills, and to perform actions. On the other hand, to live together in society on the basis of equal rights, humans need to talk to each other and come to agreements. Agreements come from dialogue, not from imposition. We can find contributions to the dialogic perspective from different disciplines and scientific traditions that try to explain human beings and society (i.e., how we are, behave, learn, interact, and understand our world and others). The social sciences, in fact, were born in the eighteenth century, when people wanted to know themselves in order to be able to govern themselves, giving way to enlightenment and what we know as Modernity. That is why some intellectuals argue that the modern current of thought had a dialogic origin that claimed people's agency, but was lost through the bureaucratization of democratic institutions. The loss of meaning in society that Weber already denounced can be overcome by recovering that dialogic origin, and this is what many contemporary social scientists, across disciplines, have done and are doing today.

Furthermore, some explain that there is a dialogic turn in the social sciences and in the society, which coincide both with the latest changes in society and the latest move in the social, cognitive, educational theory and in the way we do research in these fields. While the linguistic turn implied a move from the philosophy of conscience to the philosophy of language—that is, a shift from focusing on a subject's consciousness to focusing on the role of language to explain human action and thought—the dialogic turn implies a move toward intersubjectivity.

In the twenty-first century, our world is increasingly dialogic: interactions among different people are key for personal and collective projects and for a peaceful coexistence in a society that belongs to everybody. Recent social changes such as the technological revolution and globalization (i.e., economic, social, and cultural globalization) are expanding the feeling of risk and uncertainty in the lives of many people, while at the same time we face a broader plurality of options to choose our own lives and construct our own biographies. This new social environment provokes, on the one hand, individualization, as a person's role in society is not defined only by his or her gender, status, or cultural tradition. However, individualization does not equate to individualism or alienation, rather to a growth in communication, as people usually decide with those with whom they live, work, and have relationships.

The dialogization of our environment is provoking a dialogic turn in the social sciences and research. Flecha et al. (2003) explain this phenomenon in their analysis of contemporary sociological theory, and also argue that the dialogic turn can be seen in a wide range of disciplines: philosophy, psychology, education, sociology, linguistics, anthropology, women studies, etc. Particularly, in the field of educational psychology we find a recovering of dialogic perspectives both in developmental psychology and language acquisition, as well as new proposals of dialogic learning and action in educational practice. Researchers from different disciplines are proposing transformative solutions to social problems that are grounded in communication and mutual recognition, taking into account the dialogic potential of current society. Therefore, we can see that diverse authors have included the dialogic nature of language and human condition in their theories (Bakhtin, Mead, Vygostky), and others have also used intersubjectivity to be able to explain society, and stressed dialogue as the needed requirement for different people to live together in society (Habermas, Freire, Beck).

Furthermore, when moving to the field of education, we see that due to the mentioned social changes, learning has also changed. In the information society, learning is less related to what happens within a classroom and increasingly associated with the coordination of the diverse learning events that take place in the different spaces in which children interact with others: in the classroom, in the school, in the home, in the street. Therefore, improving learning implies taking into account all these spaces of interaction and development, achieving continuity between school and life.

The dialogic approach to learning is framed by the social interactions among people mediated through language. It assumes that there are different forms of knowledge that people bring to the learning process, recognizing their capacity to further their knowledge and achieve the knowledge and skills needed to fully participate in current society. Dialogic learning thus implies intersubjectivity: diverse people exchanging ideas, acquiring and producing knowledge, and creating new meanings that transform both the language and the content of their lives. From this dialogic perspective, the learning process is not only understood as an individual and internal process, but also inextricably linked to the multiple interactions that take place in diverse social and cultural environments. This process can be defined through seven principles—egalitarian dialogue, cultural intelligence, transformation, instrumental dimension, creation of meaning, solidarity, and equality of differences—that also lay the ground for democratic and egalitarian education, orienting school practice toward excellent outcomes for everyone, regardless of their age, culture, socioeconomic status, or previous schooling.

In fact, it is precisely because society is becoming dialogic that the concept of learning is also turning dialogic and recovering the interactionist tradition that existed previously (although not often recognized as such) within the field of educational psychology. A clear example is the work of Vygostky, Luria, and their Russian contemporaries. Their work was not broadly known within the international scientific community until some American scholars like Michael Cole, Sylvia Scribner, and Barbara Rogoff, among others, recovered them in the seventies and further developed a socio-cultural-historical approach in the analysis of different contexts. Now, this approach is still present and their focus on agents' interactions stressed. For instance, Scribner's studies on practical thought in workplace environments are today a reference in adult education theory and practice. Rogoff's studies about learning in nonschool contexts (like rural Guatemala) through guided participation sheds light today on communities as learning spaces and the relevance of family participation. Cultural psychology, as Cole argues, has a past and a present, and his own work today, from cultural-historical activity theory, proposes forms of intervention with excluded children or low achievers, based on interactivity. Another example is the work of George H. Mead on symbolic interactionism. His theory on the development of the self in society through both nonverbal and symbolic communication has been an important contribution to Habermas's theory of communicative action, and it is recovering relevance again today in social psychology, media, and linguistic studies.

The current dialogic turn of society and the need for new learning approaches is thus emphasizing a dialogic perspective in many relevant contributions to the field of educational and social psychology.

DIALOGIC TURN IN SOCIETY AND IN THE SOCIAL SCIENCES

Dialogue is increasingly permeating and influencing all social spheres today, from the world of work, to the economy, to the definition of new lifestyles. If industrial society was the framework for the development of traditional modernity—a perspective based on instrumental rationality, science, and the creation of rights and norms—the current information society offers the opportunity to live in a dialogic modernity, which includes a rationality grounded in dialogue and consensus among all subjects rather than the imposition of a few (i.e., experts or hegemonic cultures).

Dialogue in Our Lives

The old patterns and norms that used to guide our lives in the industrial society lost their legitimacy in current society. Increasingly, we need dialogue and communication to make decisions about our lives and our future. Traditional models in the context of the family, education, politics, labor, etc., are increasingly being questioned. Dialogue and communication are the elements that are being used in the orientation of our actions and our lives. For instance, while the father used to take decisions in the family, it is now becoming usual for parents and children to have to agree on issues such as what TV channel to watch, negotiating curfews, or the distribution of chores at home.

Furthermore, society is opening up to new cultural exchanges, values, and social norms. If we look at the private domain, there are many new possibilities. For instance, people can choose whether to marry in a particular traditional religious ceremony or to create a ceremony that merges rituals and meanings from two different religions. They can also decide not to have any ceremony at all, or may be to go later on to the justice of the peace and legalize their emotional bond before having a child. There are also single-parent families and families who live apart together. Authors like Ulrich Beck and Elisabeth Beck-Gernsheim or Anthony Giddens have discussed how these "new" types of relationships and families emerge, how they coexist in the same communities with "traditional" types, and how they are becoming socially accepted, notwithstanding a number of personal and social conflicts that often arise.

In the field of school education, teachers must also negotiate and reach consensus with their students about the activities and knowledge to work on. In the same way the authority shifts in the homes, when teachers try to impose their criteria using their position, they often find students who do not respect this authority and conflicts arise. Often, the solution has been the opposite pole, becoming a laissez-faire teacher focusing on "motivating" activities to engage these students. The increase of dialogue, however, does not imply watering down the curriculum, and families and students do ask for quality and even dare to challenge educators with their own knowledge.

Furthermore, people also ask for and seek out more dialogue, negotiation, and agreements with the so-called experts or professionals in diverse social contexts, such as health, politics, labor, or education. There are no experts with the whole truth, as everybody can contribute to knowledge and can contribute arguments from different experiences and resources. Some authors like Ulrich Beck have described this phenomenon of questioning the professionals—or not attributing them the whole truth—the *de-monopolization of expert knowledge*. Now, if I have a health problem, I will go to the doctor, but I also will hook on the Internet for information about this problem and the possible medical treatments that exist in the world. The same happens in education. Teachers do not have the whole truth and, moreover, information is public, free, and easy to get on the Web. Students can access it and challenge the teacher or raise questions. They can also work as a team, and reach out to more and richer information after reflecting on it. A new way of teaching is needed in which students are not recipients of knowledge but creators of knowledge through peer work and teacher guidance. This reflects the idea of dialogic inquiry in the classrooms, drawing from the work of Gordon Wells. The de-monopolization of expert knowledge demonstrates the dialogization of our lives in society.

Dialogue in the Institutions

Many institutions that were initially born to serve the citizens have become highly bureaucratized and provide little or no opportunity for people to interact. Schools are a clear example of this. However, people today are claiming their agency; they ask for open dialogue and to have their voices represented in decision-making spaces. A clear example is the World Social Forum, and the way people are getting organized through social movements worldwide to have a say in global politics to make "another world possible." Citizens also claim for more transparency in national and local politics and they go to the streets again. In the field of education, for instance, families and neighbors want to participate in deciding the school they want for their children and what sort of education must be guaranteed within it.

Education is thus moving away from unilateral actions of "experts" and increasingly becoming defined through consensus and dialogue between a whole educational community. Active participation of family members and communities in general is one of the priorities for many schools today. Many are also promoting dialogic approaches to learning in order to overcome dropout, failure, and exclusion. Along these lines, concepts like learning communities, communities of practice, or school–community partnerships are increasingly present in this field.

The more systems decide how people should live and relate to each other, without including them in the decision-making process, the more these people lose freedom and meaning in their lives. Habermas conceptualized the process of bureaucratization of systems as the *systemic colonization of lifeworld*. Habermas describes society as a dual relationship between the lifeworld and the systems, which influence each other. The *lifeworld* is the context of relationships and communication among people, such as the above-mentioned daily interactions and negotiations. The systems are the institutions and social structures, like the government, the family, or the school system. Systems emerge from the lifeworld, as people create structure and normative rules to live together. Other authors like Giddens or Freire also provide this double conceptualization of society that includes subject (or agency) and structure.

Social movements (agency) are recovering the communicative grammar of the colonized lifeworld through increased dialogue. Political and governmental institutions must then respond to people's demands for transparency and radicalization of democracy. Elster contends that there is a revival of the idea of deliberative democracy, or what he describes as the process of "collective decision making with the participation of all who will be affected by the decision . . . by means of arguments offered *by* and *to* participants who are committed to the values of rationality and impartiality." Furthermore, current research policies are acquiring new orientations to bring research closer to the real needs of society. Ultimately, social projects and popular proposals are oriented toward including citizen's voices and extending citizen participation. These are some more examples of the dialogic turn in society.

Dialogue in Social Theory

The changes taking place in our daily lives, systems and institutions are expressions of the dialogic tendency of society. This is at the same time influencing how researchers and academics analyze society, conduct research, and how they produce theories that help to explain society and human relations. Habermas, for instance, affirms this link when he contends that the communicative perspective is not a mere theoretical or intellectual invention, but that it arises from real social phenomenon. Diverse authors have reflected on the nature of communication and dialogue in our society, as well as in our developmental processes as organisms, persons, souls, subjects, or people in the world. This look at intersubjective communication is at the basis of diverse disciplines. At the same time, authors committed to the overcoming of social inequalities analyze the strong connection between dialogic processes and social change, and write about it in order to support the transformative proposals that are emerging from social movements and agents.

Critical intellectuals who analyze the current changes in society argue that this dialogic tendency has inspired democratic revolutions throughout history. For instance, Habermas compares the dialogic spirit of information society with the bourgeois–socialist liberation movements and the American civil rights movement. Castells compares it with the revolutionary spirit of the sixties. He states that "the emphasis on interactivity, on networking, and the relentless pursuit of new technological breakthroughs . . . was clearly in discontinuity with the somewhat cautious tradition of the corporate world. The information technology revolution half-consciously diffused through the material culture of our society the libertarian spirit that flourished in the 1960s movements." In his early work (*Pedagogy of the Oppressed*), Freire discusses the existence of both dialogic and antidialogic actions in our society. Later, in the late nineties, he states that "one of the most important tasks for progressive intellectuals is to demystify postmodern discourses with respect to the inexorability of this situation [reproduction of power]." He considered postmodern discourses led to immobilization. Rather than just denouncing power structures he proposed announcing transformative actions—led by agents in dialogue—that contribute to social change. Authors like Habermas and Freire have been accused of being utopian idealists. However, they respond by reiterating that their dialogic project is not a theoretical invention but a reflection of the dialogic practices that people have already developed in their everyday lives. Although they never worked together, neither met, they coincide in their proposals of dialogic action to further democratic relations. Both propose a theory that explains how dialogic actions take place and what sorts of action promote understanding, cultural creation, and liberation, and opposing that, what actions negate the possibility for dialogue and promote distortion communication and the reproduction of power.

Moreover, this dialogic turn is shown in the fact that intellectuals are including dialogue with social actors when they conduct research and produce scientific knowledge about society. There is no methodological relevant gap between the interpretations of researchers and that of the social actors. They are not just informants, but they interpret their own realities from their own worldviews. It is in this sense that theory and scientific research are being reoriented and becoming more. As a consequence of the dialogic turn, researchers and intellectuals also see the need to work from an interdisciplinary approach, to provide answers that consider social phenomena as a whole, and to work with social agents to be able to understand reality closely and create better proposals of action.

DIALOGISM IN PSYCHOLOGY AND LANGUAGE

In the information society, learning depends more on the coordination of the interactions that take place in the different contexts in which children learn, than on what happens solely within a classroom or a formal education setting. As pointed out, there are many contributions from the field of psychology that have precisely stressed the dialogic nature of learning and the relevance of social interaction, in the process of both learning and becoming a person in society. They place intersubjectivity as a key point in their theories, although it is often expressed in different terminology. In this section, we will introduce the dialogic perspective in the socio-cultural-historical and symbolic interactionist traditions. Besides, on the other hand, the assumption of universal capacity for language is a prior requirement to understand the strength of dialogue and interaction in cognitive development.

Universal Faculty

All people are born with the faculty to learn, and develop skills and knowledge in diverse social and cultural contexts of activity. Habermas defends that people are capable of language and action. Therefore, people have the capacity to communicate, express ideas, thoughts, provide arguments, reach agreements, and coordinate actions, regardless of their social, linguistic, or cultural condition. In the dialogue, it is not so important whether we speak the same code, but the validity claims we hold and our intention to reach understanding. Drawing from speech acts theory (Austin, Searle), we contend that every time we say something we are doing something, and therefore, people's words, utterances, and communicative intentions are strongly linked to actions.

Noam Chomsky, whose work is in the field of linguistics, stands out especially for his theoretical conception of linguistic competencies. This conception, in contrast to the structuralist perspective of language, is defined as generative. It starts from the premise that all human beings are capable of generating new language (expressions, responses, etc). He departs from generative linguistics and the assumption that there is a universal grammar. According to Chomsky, all people have an innate language faculty (that he later defines as "I-language") but different productions or outputs, which will ultimately depend on their social interactions. People therefore develop different productions depending on the contexts in which they interact, that is, different language and language codes. Assuming universality and innate common grammar, we come to the conclusion that everyone possesses the capability to communicate and develop new language codes and knowledge through interactions.

Symbolic Interactionism

Meaning is not part of what we see or the emotions we feel; there is a social dimension to it. Meaning creation can be modified and changed in the interpretive process that a person develops through social interaction. George H. Mead, the main representative from symbolic interactionism (a school in social psychology that grew in Chicago), analyzes the relationship between the self and the social. He suggested that the person can only be understood as a member of a society, and his or her thoughts and soul are a result of a process of social development, mediated by language.

Each individual acquires cultural roles and patterns through interactions and is situated within a concrete sociohistorical context. Mead argues that the *self* is made up of interrelationships between *I* (reactions of the organism in response to other's actions) and *me* (the attitudes taken on by the I). The self is determined by the images others attribute to me. The self-image is then the result of a dialogue between what we are and what the people with whom we interact think about us. Therefore, the interactions that educators generate in the school environment have a great influence on the process of dismantling social biases internalized by the children, as well as on the transformational process of the excluding patterns and roles that were developed earlier in life. Social interactions have a direct influence on how children experience education and the very school.

If I am convinced that I will not do well in the exam, I will probably perform badly, but if the professor tells me so, I will probably collapse. When a teacher interacts with a child who thinks that she or he cannot learn like the rest, the child will internalize the teachers' attitude and will construct a "me" that includes low expectations about her or his own learning capacity and an image of failure. Teachers' expectations are transmitted through language, gestures, and symbols in school interactions (dialogues). They are crucial for the development of children's selves.

Interactions in Diverse Sociocultural Environments

All people have the capacity to learn and they do so in very different contexts. Drawing from this idea, Vygotsky developed the concept of practical thinking, to refer to what children learn by doing. Practical intelligence must be taken into account in order to explain learning and development both inside and outside the school settings. In fact, the concept of practical intelligence, as mentioned, was later recovered by psychologists, who questioned the reductionism of intelligence to academic intelligence, and the many skills people develop through their daily life experiences (see the work of Scribner, Gardner, Stenberg, etc.). Vygostky considers that practical intelligence and speech are complementary functions, and he also links action to communication: often we talk about our actions, and both speech and action is connected to our thought. He argues that language and action spring from the same complex psychological function. Children begin by getting a grasp of their environment—on which they will build their intellect—through language. Thus, linguistic interaction is what forms the person (although authors like Mead include nonlinguistic interactions in the same process).

Vygotsky's sociocultural theory provides a contribution to the dialogic approach to learning. He argues that all higher-order psychological mental functions are social relations that have been internalized. He proposes a double function: a first stage of learning that is interpsychological (dialogue mediated by language), and a second stage in which this is internalized and becomes an intrapsychological process. Therefore, knowledge is first created from intersubjectivity and later brought into an individual, internal plane. When children need to solve a problem (as part of a school activity) and they do not know how to do it, they often ask the teacher, and they also ask their peers. When they had to solve the problem in a group, they often generate more knowledge and go deeper in learning and understanding. Those who are educators can think of many examples from school practice in which children constantly interact among themselves to solve the task. Authors like Gordon Wells have developed this perspective in the classroom with the concept of *dialogic inquiry*. Classroom dialogues among peers and with adults are verbal reasoning that will become intrapsychological functions, that is, thought.

Vygostky saw in education a tool for transformation of his society; he believed in changing the psychological processes through the transformation of the context. He states that "learning which is oriented toward developmental levels that have been already reached is ineffective," and continues, arguing that "an essential feature of learning is that it creates the zone of proximal development; that is, learning awakens a variety of internal developmental processes that are able to operate when [the person] is interacting with people in his environment and in cooperation with his peers." Vygotksy describes the Zone of Proximal Development as the differential between the actual learning and the potential learning to be attained with the help of other people. The dialogic nature of learning is also stressed in this concept. There are educational implications: if all learners can develop their potential with the support of teachers, relatives, and peers, by transforming the context—that is, school organization, family participation, community projects and volunteering in the school, family literacy, etc.—there will be an improvement of the learning process, creating challenging and rich learning environments that overcome discontinuities between schools and communities enhance children's development. The consolidation of evidence about dialogism in the theories of human development and psychology, and the recovery of these ideas in the field of education, is promoting the dialogic turn in educational institutions we mentioned before, a perspective that counts on communities and dialogue to improve school achievement.

Language, Literacy, and Dialogicity

A key reference in the discussion of dialogism in the field of literacy theory and linguistics is Mikhail Bakhtin. The perspective of Bakhtin on dialogicity is complex, as after his most important work *Problems in the Poetry of Dostoievski*, he dedicated the rest of his life to reflect about dialogism and polyphony (multiple voices) in the reading of the novel and the literary texts. While his reflections are complex in general, Bakhtin's term of *dialogicity* derives from the simple act of dialogue, the linguistic exchange of "give–take" between two people, brought to the reading of a text. Bakhtin departs from a fundamental problem in the philosophy of language: language holds some ambiguity because people produce speech from different worldviews (language philosophers have also discussed this problem, like Wittgenstein addressing language games or Austin reflecting on the consequences of "infelicity" in speech acts). While poststructuralist authors would explain this ambiguity as the inability of words to represent precise meanings or a demonstration of the subjectivity of language, Bakhtin argues that this ambiguity demonstrates that we need to create meanings dialogically with others.

Bakhtin challenged the monologic way of interpreting text and understanding truth in the rationalist philosophy of modernity. Instead, he proposed to unite the utopian perspective of modernity with the utopian socialism and claimed for the dialogic experience of human beings making meaning with other people of text and realities. In his analyses he reflects on the dialogic nature of a novel, and on the dialogic process that lies behind any single written or spoken utterance. In one of his latest essays on speech genres he stated that "the utterance is a link in the chain of speech communication and cannot be broken off from the preceding links that determine it." According to this, any interpretation is the result of previous dialogues in which the participant has been interacting with others throughout his or her life.

Some scholars have used Bakhtin's dialogics to explain the concept of *intertextuality* (each text is the result of the interaction of many texts). This concept, however, is closer to deconstructionist perspectives than to dialogic proposals. Through deconstruction, Derrida defends the death of the author, that is, any text can be deconstructed and read differently in different contexts and by different people. Furthermore, images, actions, realities, etc. are text. Opposed to this approach, Bakhtin proposes dialogic interpretation of the novel as interactions among subjects that we internalize, rather than interactions among texts. In fact, he conceives human life as a dialogic process in which we find meaning only through our interactions with others. In general, dialogic relations are more than a mere exchange of words: they are universal phenomena present in all manifestations and discourses of human life that have meaning.

TERMS FOR READERS

Dialogic modernity—Is a current of thought that trusts in the capacity of all people to act in order to transform social reality. It is an intellectual project of radicalization of democracy by extending the egalitarian dialogue to diverse groups and people. Traditional modernity had a project of democracy but decided by a few and imposed to the rest. Hegemonic positions and the attached process of bureaucratization of democratic institutions led to a reaction against modernity: the postmodern thought. Postmodernism, however, not only countered hegemony, but also the democratic project. Dialogic modernity gives back the center to social agents by promoting egalitarian dialogue. This is today at the basis of most relevant contemporary theories in the social sciences.

Dialogic turn—A "turn" implies a shift in the way of analyzing society and social relations within the different disciplines in the social sciences. The dialogic turn therefore defines the inclusion of dialogue in these analyses. Intellectuals talk about a "linguistic turn" in philosophy that implied the inclusion of language use (pragmatics), overcoming theories focused on subject's conscience. The "dialogic turn" overcomes constructivism by focusing on subject's interactions. Furthermore, dialogue has a greater role in current society and there is a shift in how people create meaning and make decisions in many spheres of life.

Information society—Since the beginning of the seventies, there has been a technological revolution that has transformed the basis of economy and forms of production, organization of labor, cultural creation, social relations, and society in general. In the current society, the key for success is increasingly the capacity to select and process relevant information. In informational economy the raw material for productivity and growth is creation of knowledge through information processing. There was a first phase of information society in which access to information and the Net was crucial to avoid social exclusion (described as "social Darwinism"). At the beginning of the twenty-first century, the push from NGOs and excluded countries (but also from informational capitalism), leads to a move toward creating an information society for all.

Intersubjectivity—Is the interaction among subjects that are capable of language and action. In their everyday practices, people use communicative ways of reasoning (interactions) to structure their lifeworld on the basis of understanding others and agreement. They negotiate meanings with other people through these interactions. Intersubjectivity is not the addition of individual subjectivities, but a reflective process that produces new meanings. A person's thoughts and conscience come from the social interaction with other people; it is not individual. The concept of intersubjectivity stresses agency, and the power of social agents in communication to change social reality.

SUGGESTED READING

Bakhtin, M. M. (1981). *The Dialogic Imagination. Four Essays.* Austin, TX: University of Texas Press.

Flecha, R., Gomez, J., and Puigvert, L. (2003). *Contemporary Sociological Theory.* New York: Peter Lang.

Habermas, J. (1984). *The Theory of Communicative Action. Reason and the Rationalization of Society.* Boston, MA: Beacon Press.

Mead, G. H. (1962). *Mind, Self, & Society, from the Standpoint of a Social Behaviorist.* Chicago, IL: Chicago University Press.

CHAPTER 63

Experiential Learning

TARA FENWICK

Experiential learning is arguably one of the most important contemporary areas of scholarship in educational psychology. *Informal learning*, *prior learning*, and *practice-based learning* are terms used in different contexts to refer to experiential learning. The tradition of experiential learning in educational psychology has emphasized examination of actual *learning processes* going on in experience, which has influenced important changes in educational practices. The focus on *experience* has foregrounded difficulties and multiple dimensions to consider in theorizing the very nature of human experience and knowledge production that unfold in different sociopolitical contexts. Despite the debates around defining experiential learning, most would agree that experiential learning recognizes and celebrates knowledge generated outside institutions. If learning can be defined as change or transformation, in the sense of expanding human possibilities and action, experiential learning is expansion that challenges the hegemonic logic of expert knowledge. Experiential learning refuses disciplinary knowledge claims of universal validity, and resists knowledge authority based solely on scientific evidence. This is why the concept of experiential learning remains significant in educational research and practice, despite conceptual problems in the experiential learning discourse that will be discussed further on.

In the field of educational psychology, descriptions of experiential learning have tended to be inherently positive, and the experiential learning movement has successfully championed learners' personal knowledge and lived experience. Experiential activity or dialogue emphasizing participants' experience is by now common in formal education programs. Over twenty major associations internationally are devoted to experiential education. Informal (experiential) learning is increasingly the focus of analysis in workplace learning and community-based education. Since the writing of progressive educators such as John Dewey and Eduard Lindeman and throughout the twentieth century, experiential learning in practice was intended to be radical, to challenge prevailing orthodoxy that worthwhile knowledge is canonical and that legitimate education is planned and monitored by professionals.

This chapter is a modified version of an article that appeared in *Studies in the Education of Adults*, volume 35 issue 2. The permission of the editor is gratefully acknowledged.

CONCEPTUAL AND PRACTICAL PROBLEMS IN THE EXPERIENTIAL LEARNING TRADITION

As critics have contended, the educational tradition of experiential learning has developed its own unfortunate orthodoxies. These may stem at least partly from the division of body and mind in the experiential learning discourse. With the educational emphasis on learning through *reflection* on experience, the body in some respects is removed from the central process of learning, along with the body's embeddedness in its social, material, and cultural activities. Learning is thus harvested from bodies in action. Further educational procedures associated with experiential learning measure, commodify, and credential experience according to normalizing categories. The purpose of experience is often determined by its relevancy to either existing knowledge disciplines or to the workplace. Even those who challenge this colonization of experience and call for emancipation have been accused of appropriating experiential learning. That is, their critical pedagogy approaches—educating individuals' life experience through critical consciousness-raising—have been criticized as distrusting "raw" experience and treating individuals as blind dupes of their socialization. Recent analysts focus instead on how educators can position themselves within the complex webs of experiential learning, particularly when they are committed to political purposes of widening participation, equality of opportunity and freedom from exploitation.

The following section outlines four contested issues of theory and practice that have arisen around the experiential learning tradition in educational psychology: the separation of mind from body, the emphasis on reflection, managerial practices, and exclusionary aspects of experiential learning as it is treated in education. Following this section, three contemporary approaches to understanding experiential learning are presented, all based on embodied understandings of learning that view the individual as participants enmeshed in subsystems and suprasystems of biology, culture, and action. These three include a coemergent perspective offered by complexity science: a psychoanalytic perspective focusing on dynamics of desire, and a social action perspective emanating from social movement theory. Together, these contemporary, interdisciplinary orientations offer important directions toward reconceptualizing experiential learning in educational psychology.

SEPARATION OF MIND FROM BODY IN THE EXPERIENTIAL LEARNING TRADITION

Feminists have long disparaged the Cartesian separation of mind and body in a Western epistemological tradition that privileges mental detachment: the observation and calculation of the world from a disembodied, rational subject. This split is visible in experiential learning theories and programs. David Kolb popularized the assumption that experience is "concrete" and split from reflection as though doing and thinking are separate states. He depicted experiential learning as a cycle beginning with a concrete experience, followed by the individual's reflective observation, then abstract conceptualization on this experience to create learning, culminating in active experimentation to apply the learning to a new concrete experience. Since Kolb published *Experiential Learning* in 1984, 378 journal articles and 140 doctoral theses report studies that applied this model uncritically to study people's experiences. What becomes emphasized are the supposed conceptual lessons gained from experience, quickly stripped of location and embeddedness in the material and social conditions that produced the knowledge. What is excised from these lessons is the body, with its desires, messiness, actions, culture, and politics. In the movement to rationalize experiential learning, argue some, the body is not so much transcended as rendered invisible.

This split sustains other dualisms such as the binary of formal/informal learning, which some contend is problematic in the way it centres schooling and implies that nonschooled learning is less significant. The term *experiential learning* is similarly problematic, for no manner of learning can be defensibly classified as other, as *not* experiential, unless experience is confined narrowly to sensual or kinesthetic activity. Person is often split from environment in conceptualizations of learning, with context or place portrayed as an inert container in which people perform their actions. Even situated cognition, which first attempted to challenge acquisition models of institutional learning by theorizing learning as participation fully entwined in the actions, objects, and relations of a community of practice has been depoliticized in its contemporary uses. The community of practice and environment of learning are often treated as resources from which the learning subject excavates useful experiences (i.e., for organizational productivity), and "participation" as unproblematic engagement of people in activity. The primary dualisms of body and mind, and subject and object, underpinning such conceptions of learning are also at the root of rational logic. Thus experience comes to be viewed as a commodity, and people as fragmented learning minds.

EDUCATION'S EMPHASIS ON REFLECTION-ON-EXPERIENCE

A second theoretical problem arising from this body–mind dualism is the continuing emphasis on mentalist reflection in experiential learning, evident in the popularity of pedagogical approaches such as "reflective practice" and reflective dialogue as an obligatory learning activity in experiential education. In such renderings, reflection is treated as the conduit from event to knowledge, transforming "raw" experience into worthwhile learning. Critics such as Elana Michelson (1996) argue that emphasis on reflection centers learning in an individual rational knowledge-making mind. This individual mind is implied to rise above ongoing action, interactions, and sensation to fix both experience and a singular self that possess the experience.

Reflection orders, clarifies, manages and disciplines experience—which internalizes relations of ruling. Perhaps this is precisely why individuals find refuge in reflective periods, to creating meaning and pattern in chaotic fragments of experiences, through narratives, snapshots, justifications, or causal patterning. People try to manage the uncertainty and undecidability of their experiences by imposing reflective structures on them.

But basing experiential learning theory on this personal predilection of meaning making produces a somewhat myopic conception of learning. Individual mental representations of events become prominent, static, and separated from the interdependent commotion of people together in action with objects and language. Experience is cast as a fixed thing, separated from knowledge-making processes, yet reflection itself is experienced, and experience as event cannot be separated from our imaginative interpretation and reinterpretation of the event. We might ask where are we standing when we "reflect"? Experience itself is knowledge-driven and cannot be known outside socially available meanings. What is imagined to be "experience" is rooted in social discourses that influence how problems are perceived and named, which experiences become visible, how they are interpreted, and what knowledge they are considered to yield. Those interested in how language, audience, purpose, and identity make the reflective act itself a performance of remembered experience, rather than a realist representation of it. Thus the "meaning" of lived experience is undecidable, because it is constantly being produced anew.

These insights show the limitations of viewing learning as a matter of deriving prescriptions for future actions from "authentic" memories of a "concrete" experience. First, these memories depend upon those truths that can be acknowledged within particular cultural values and politics. Second, many slippages between the named and the invisible occur in meaning-making, and further disjunctions occur between the so-called learner and those other readers of experience who allot themselves the authority to do so under the title of educator. Third, concrete experiences do not exist separate from other life experiences, from identity, or from ongoing social networks of interaction.

EDUCATION'S MANAGEMENT OF EXPERIENTIAL LEARNING

A third issue that continues to trouble critics is the management of experiential learning that has arisen in education, employing disciplinary mechanisms of language, measurement, and knowledge legitimation. Many have argued critically that the Assessment of Prior Experiential Learning (APEL; also known as Prior Learning Assessment or Recognition of Prior Learning) creates a disjuncture between private experience and public discourse, which produces a fundamental paradox when the private journey of discovery and learning is brought under public scrutiny and adjudication. The assessment process compels individuals to construct a self to fit the APEL dimensions, and celebrates individualistic achievement: "learners are what they have done." People's experience becomes divided into preset categories of visible/invisible, which regulates how people see themselves and their knowledge.

Assessment processes employed in experiential learning reveal the contested terrain that is engaged when educators insert themselves, and their pedagogical categories and ideologies, into complex nets and structures of experience. Valuing experience may be a well-intentioned gesture to diminish the power of institutionalized knowledge, but ultimately renders local knowledge into institutional vocabulary. Worse, the exercise may be directed by an impulse to recognize then proceed to liberate people from illusions that their own experiences are believed to have produced. When experiential learning is judged and managed, both "experience" and human subjectivity are translated into calculable resources serving what are ultimately utilitarian notions of knowledge. This calculation of experience has become a central occupation in the workplace of the so-called knowledge economy. In the new work order, working *is* learning. Experiential learning in particular has become the new form of labor—learning new identities, knowledges, texts, and textual practices. Workers' knowledge that is rooted in the objects and activities of material labor, a history of social interactions, shifting subjectivity, spontaneous invention, and transgression is appropriated and recast in rational, stable terms.

EXCLUSIONARY ASPECTS OF EDUCATION'S APPROACH TO EXPERIENTIAL LEARNING

Ultimately the educational disembodiment of experiential learning, with its emphases on rational reflection, management, and measurement of experience, creates exclusions. People, psyches, knowledges, and cultures are excluded through normative approaches to experiential learning that determine which sorts of experiences are educative, developmental, knowledge-producing, and worth enhancing. Some have argued that in the categories typically used to study or accredit experiential learning, the strong influence of capitalist production is immediately apparent. Work experience is prominent, usually characterized as paid employment. Long-term unemployment, nonsalaried or contingent work, and low-income routinized jobs do not usually produce the rich sorts of experiential work learning that excites researchers of informal learning. Experiences depend partly on inhabited environments and bodily capacity. Those who have been socially, physically, economically, or politically excluded from particular experiences may be judged as lacking social capital, remedied through expanding their access to "rich" experiences and networks. But this approach colonizes their own knowledge, reifies the normalizing categories of the middle class, whose values control the dominant cultural meanings, and perpetuates an acquisitive conception of experience as *capital* to be obtained and parlayed into credit, income, or profit.

Excluded are realms of experiential learning that do not correspond to knowledge categories most recognized in education, such as disciplinary knowledge driving curriculum areas, technical vocational knowledge, communicative knowledge (understanding people and society), or moral-emancipatory knowledge (discerning systemic injustice, inequities, and one's implication in these). Sexuality, desire and fantasy, for example, tend to be ignored in educational discourses of experiential learning. Nonconscious and intuitive knowledge, knowledge of micro-negotiations within systems that struggles in bodies and discourses, and knowledge without voice or subject that lives in collective action also tend to be bracketed out of these discourses.

CONTEMPORARY APPROACHES TO UNDERSTANDING EXPERIENTIAL LEARNING

Given these four problems in educational theory of experiential learning of mind–body separation, emphasis on reflection, managerial disciplines, and exclusion, why not simply jettison the experiential learning discourse? The short answer is that its democratic intents are important in an institutionalized world where the cult of credentialing challenges any knowledge generated outside market usefulness. Experience focuses on the messy problems and tedious practices of everyday life which continue to run counter to the logic, language, and disciplines of science and the academy, particularly those privileging the rational and, increasingly, the linguistic and discursive. Experience exceeds language and rationality, because it emphasizes the crucial locatedness of bodies in material reality that cannot be dismissed as a solely linguistic construction, as certain forms of postmodern thought would try to do. Indeed, this signifier of *experiential* learning is useful to challenge assumptions about the nature of reality and of experience. When reexamined in terms of its textures and movements, attention to experience has the potential to unlock a liberal humanist preoccupation with individual minds, knowledge canons, and rational reflection, and shift the focus to embodied, collective knowledge emerging in moments and webs of everyday action.

The embodiment of experiential learning is an ancient concept: indigenous ways of knowing, for example, have maintained that spirit, mind, and body are not separated in experience, that learning is more focused on being than doing, and that experiential knowledge is produced within the collective, not the individual, mind. For example, a Canadian researcher named Julia Cruishank shows how the life stories and knowledge development of the Yukon First Nations people are completely entangled with the glaciers around which they live. The glaciers are not inert environment, but alive and moving, rumbling and responding to small human actions; the lines between human and nonhuman, and social history and natural history, are fluid. Writers on Africentric knowledge, so named to distinguish it from eurocentric perspectives that fragment and rationalize experience, have also shown how learning is embodied and rooted in collective historic experiences of oppression, pain, and love which are inseparable from the emotional, the spiritual, and the natural. The difference here from mentalist or reflection-dependent understandings of experiential learning is accepting the moment of experiential learning as occurring *within* action, within and among bodies. An embodied approach understands the sensual body as a site of learning itself, rather than as a raw producer of data that the mind will fashion into knowledge formations.

Embodiment however must not be mistaken for essentializing the individual physical body. The body's surfaces can be misleading; while sites for sensuality, they are neither identifiers nor boundaries separating what is inside from what is outside. The core conceptual shift of an embodied experiential learning is from a *learning subject* to the larger collective, to the systems of culture, history, social relations, and nature in which everyday bodies, subjectivities, and lives are enacted. This shift is toward what some call a "complexified" view of cognition, casting experiential learning as something that various commentators have characterized as "participative," "distributed," or "complex, organic" learning processes constituted in systems of practice. Complexity science, examining webs of action linking humans and nonhumans in complex adaptive systems, is one area of contemporary theory and research that informs an embodied view of experiential learning. A second area focuses on the dynamics of desire currently being explored in feminist and psychoanalytic learning theory. A third area studies learning as struggle evolving in the body politic, evident in social action movements.

These three perspectives are outlined in the following section. All three emphasize fluidity between actions, bodies, identities, objects, and environments. They point to complexities and contradictions in experiential learning that can be obscured through paradigms of transparent reality, individual meaning making, or domination and oppression. All three share a focus on learning as complex choreography transpiring at different nested levels of complex systems adapting to and affecting one another: bodily subsystems; the person or body biologic; collectivities of social bodies and bodies of knowledge; society or the body politic; and the planetary body. (These nested system levels are described by Brent Davis, Dennis Sumara, and Rebecca Luce-Kapler in their book *Engaging Minds: Learning and Teaching in a Complex World* [2000].)

COEMERGENCE: EXPERIENTIAL LEARNING AS COLLECTIVE PARTICIPATION IN COMPLEX SYSTEMS

Discussions of embodied learning informed by complexity science highlight the phenomenon of coemergence in complex adaptive systems. The first premise is that the systems represented by person and context are inseparable, and the second that change occurs from emerging systems affected by the intentional tinkering of one with the other. Humans are completely interconnected with the systems in which they act through a series of "structural couplings." That is, when two systems coincide, the "perturbations" of one system excites responses in the structural dynamics of the other. The resultant "coupling" creates a new transcendent unity of action and identities that could not have been achieved independently by either participant. These dynamics are described in detail by Francesco Varela, E. Thompson, and Eleanor Rosch in their book *The Embodied Mind: Cognitive Science and Experience* (1991).

A workplace project or a classroom discussion, for example, is a collective activity in which interaction both enfolds and renders visible the participants, the objects mediating their actions and dialogue, the problem space that they define together, and the emerging plan or solution they devise. As each person contributes, she changes the interactions and the emerging object of focus; other participants are changed, the relational space among them all changes, and the looping back changes the contributor's actions and subject position within the collective activity. This is "mutual specification," the fundamental dynamic of systems constantly engaging in joint action and interaction. The "environment" and the "learner" emerge together in the process of cognition, although this is a false dichotomy: *context* is not a separate background for any particular system such as an individual actor.

Most of this complex joint action leaks out of individual attempts to control behavior through critical reflection. And yet, individual reconstructions of events too often focus on the learning *figure* and ignore the complex interactions as "background." Complexity theory interrupts the natural tendency to seek clear lines between figures and grounds, and focuses on the *relationships* binding humans and nonhumans (persons, material objects, mediating tools, environments, ideas) together in multiple fluctuations in complex systems.

All complex adaptive systems in which human beings are implicated learn, whether at micro-levels such as immune systems or at macro-levels such as weather patterns, a forest or the stock market. Human beings are part of these larger systems that are continuously learning, and bear characteristics of the larger patterns, like the single fern leaf resembling the whole fern plant. But individuals also participate, contributing through multiple interactions at micro-levels. At the subsystem level, for example, the human immune system, like organs and other subhuman systems, functions as an autonomous learning system that remembers, forgets, hypothesizes, errs, recovers, and adapts. The outcome of all these dynamic interactions of a system's parts is unpredictable and inventive. The key to a healthy system—able to adapt creatively to changing conditions—is diversity among its parts, whose interactions form patterns of their own.

Learning is thus cast as continuous invention and exploration, produced through the relations among consciousness, identity, action and interaction, objects, and structural dynamics of complex systems. New possibilities for action are constantly emerging among the interactions of complex systems, and cognition occurs in the possibility for unpredictable shared action. Knowledge cannot be contained in any one element or dimension of a system, for knowledge is constantly emerging and spilling into other systems. For example, studies of safety knowledge in the workplace show that experiential learning emerges and circulates through exchanges among both human and nonhuman elements in a net of action. The foreman negotiates the language of the assessment report with the industrial inspector, the equipment embeds a history of use possibilities and constraints, deadlines and weather conditions pressure a particular job, and workers adapt a tool or safety procedure for particular problems—depending on who is watching. No actor has an essential self outside a given network: nothing is given in the order of things, but performs itself into existence.

Such studies of objects, people, and learning as coemerging systems are helping to challenge our conceptual subject–object splits, refusing the notion that learning is a product of experience, and showing ways to recognize how learning is woven into fully embodied nets of ongoing action, invention, social relations, and history in complex systems.

DESIRE: NEGOTIATING SUBSYSTEM DYNAMICS

Embodied systems of behavior and knowledge also are influenced in part by dynamics of desire, love, and hate, according to psychoanalytic theorists of learning. These analysts suggest that learning should focus less on reported meanings and motivations and more on what is occurring under the surface of daily encounters: things resisted and ignored, the nature of longings and lack, and the slippages among action, intention, perception of self, and experience. Psychoanalytic learning theory shares the position of complexity theory that experience is not contained in the body, and that the individual mind does not perceive the totality of micro-interactions in which it participates. One particular contribution of psychoanalytic learning theory is highlighting desire for and resistance to different objects, which can be argued to occur in both micro-interactions and in larger movements of coemergence. Desire may be manifested in longings to possess or be possessed by another, creating urges to act toward such longings. The complex influence of these urges on consequent actions arguably affects the directions in which systems involving humans coemerge.

For educational theorists working with these psychoanalytic concepts, desire and learning come together in daily, disturbing experiential encounters carried on at psychic levels that individuals manage to ignore using various cognitive strategies. But while these levels can't be known directly, their interactions interfere with intentions and conscious perception of direct experience. These workings constantly bother the (individual and collective) mind, producing breaches between acts and wishes. Despite varied and creative defenses against confronting these breaches, the conscious mind is forced to notice random paradoxes and contradictions of experience, and uncanny slips into sudden awareness of difficult truths about itself. These truths are what learning theorists such as Deborah Britzman call "lost subjects," those parts of self and its communities that people resist, then try to reclaim and want to explore, but are afraid to. Full knowledge of these lost and perhaps disturbing subjects jeopardizes the conscious sense of identity as self-determined, sensible, and knowledgeable. But in learning processes, individuals and groups notice the breaches between acts, dreams, and responsibility. Learning is coming to tolerate conflicting desires, while recovering the subjects that are repressed from the terror of full self-knowledge. The implicit difficulty in learning from experience—forcing people to tolerate frustration and uncertainty, to reconsider meanings of past experiences and change their relationship to their past knowledge—is the unconscious "hatred of development" it produces. But desire points not only to knowing resisted ("active ignorance" in Britzman's terms), but also to what Sylvia Gherardi describes as passionate knowing, to pleasure-seeking, to sensing lack, and pursuing objects. These dynamics influence the direction and shape of coemergent communities and action.

Experiential learning is thus posed as the opposite of acquiring transparent experience—it is entering and *working through* the profound conflicts of all the desiring events burbling within experience that comprise "difficult knowledge." This psychoanalytic perspective may ultimately imply a somewhat deterministic conception of humans helplessly controlled by simple drives or by a mysterious "unconsciousness." Nonetheless, the important effects of desire in learning are undeniable. Psychoanalytic theory offers useful analytic tools that highlight, in human participation in systems of experience, the learning dynamics of working through psychic conflicts at the fulcrum of desire.

STRUGGLE: DISEQUILIBRIUM AND CHANGE EMERGING IN COMPLEX SYSTEMS

Some proponents of critical or emancipatory pedagogy believe that experience must be educated, that individuals are overdetermined by received meanings that reproduce existing oppressions and inequalities. They argue that emphasis on experiential or informal learning depoliticizes the core purpose of education. Certainly many cultural systems, unless interrupted, continue to produce toxic or exploitive conditions that benefit a few members at the expense of many. However, the assumption that dynamics of struggle bubbling within systems are seduced into silence until released through (proper) education is self-serving and arrogant on the part of critical educators. The emancipatory position is challenged by some commentators as representing people as dupes of ideology, puppets of overdetermined social structures.

Furthermore, emancipatory learning models that depend on critical rational detachment from one's sociocultural webs of experience appear to overlook the fact that detachment is never possible even if it were desirable. Rational critique of individuals' culturally located beliefs is itself inescapably embedded in their historical nets of discourse and action.

In fact, complexity science shows that complex adaptive systems generate the seeds of their own transformation. According to complexity theory, learning is the continuous improvisation of alternate actions and responses to new possibilities and changing circumstances that emerge, undertaken by the system's parts. More sudden transformation can occur in response to a major shock to the system, throwing it into disequilibrium. A shock might originate in abrasions with external systems, or through amplification (through feedback loops) of disturbances occurring within a system. Computer-generated images of systems undergoing disequilibrium show that they exhibit a phase of swinging between extremes, before self-organizing gradually into a new pattern or identity that can continue cohabiting with and adapting to the other systems in their environments. Examples of social disequilibrium abound in social movements. The diverse patterns of growth and activity of such movements defy explanation limited to notions of educating consciousness. Multiple interactions at different systemic levels leading out from disturbance, influenced by system shocks, desire, diversity among system parts, and mediators such as Internet communication, are evident in recent movements such as transnational advocacy networks protesting multilateral-trade agreements. People are not necessarily docile dupes of capitalism. They struggle against forces that threaten their freedom.

Social action demonstrates processes of collective experiential learning that emerge through struggle. Case studies of social action refute notions of rational critical deliberation that reframes "distorted understandings" and "false ideology." Radical transformation of both social order and consciousness, as praxis or dialectic of thought and action, appears to be embedded in complex systems interacting, adapting, and influencing one another: the body politic, diverse collective bodies, and persons as body biologic. In other words, as people enact solidarity, strategizing and learning together about unjust social arrangements in a choreography of action, they recognize new problems and possibilities for action. Each action opens alternate micro-worlds, while expanding people's confidence and recognition of the group's capacity to influence other systems. This experiential learning is continually inventive, and also filled with conflict and contradiction.

Then, how is the educator implicated in these processes? Radical action emerges in social movements in ways that it cannot in schools and postsecondary institutions, themselves contested spaces of transformative and reproductive impulses, to create spaces for inventive transgressive knowledge and alternate visions for society. Some have argued that an important catalyst for radical impulse within education institutions lies in its alliance with social movements: just as institutions need the political energy and grounded struggle that social action engenders, social movements need the resources of formal education. This might be not just a plea for collaboration, but also perhaps as a complexified awareness that struggle and social change is possible when educators view themselves as diverse parts of the system, not its rescuer, and when mutual interaction and adaptation is enabled with other system parts.

These theoretical dimensions of coemergence, desire, and struggle explored through complexity science, feminist/psychoanalytic theory, and collective social action encourage a view beyond individual learning subjects separate from the objects of their environments and the objects of their thoughts, to understand knowledge as constantly enacted as they move through the world. They focus on the *relations*, not the components, of systems, for learning is produced within the evolving relationships among particularities that are dynamic and unpredictable. They help explain how part and whole cospecify one another, and how participation in any shared action contributes to the very conditions that shape these identities.

These dimensions offer a way out of the individualization and fragmentation that can lead to commodification of experiential learning in the classroom and the workplace. They also suggest useful starting points for conceiving roles for educators in experiential learning. Rather than limiting their focus to planning experiential occasions and assessing the learning produced in experiences, educators might think of themselves, their classroom activities and texts, and learners as part of experiential activity systems. These intersect simultaneously with each other's and many other sub- and suprasystems, influencing and being influenced by one another, in learning that is ongoing and expansive, at biologic, psychic, social, and political levels.

TERMS FOR READERS

Cartesian—Referring to ideas of Rene Descartes, 1596–1650, who proposed in his long-influential *Principles of Philosophy* that material substances (bodies) and mental substances (thought) both exist, but do so separately as quite distinct entities.

Critical (or emancipatory) pedagogy—An approach to teaching and learning, rooted in critical social theory, that aims toward social transformation by helping individuals develop awareness of social injustice through analyzing their own problems, tracing their connections to historical social forces, then developing reflective action for change.

Complex adaptive system—An open system of human and nonhuman elements, such as a forest, an immune system, a market system, etc., that is characterized by internal diversity among its agents, redundancy among agents (sufficient commonality to ensure communication), interaction, simple rules, decentralized control, a self-organizing tendency, and feedback loops.

Co-emergence—A term associated with complexity theory and increasingly with cognitive science, referring to the simultaneous emergence of beings, environment, and cognition through the ongoing actions and interactions among elements in a complex adaptive system.

SUGGESTED READING

Davis, B., Sumara, D. J., and Luce-Kapler, R. (2000). *Engaging Minds: Learning and Teaching in a Complex World*. Mahwah, NJ: Erlbaum.

Michelson, E. (1996). Usual suspects: experience, reflection, and the (en)gendering of knowledge. *International Journal of Lifelong Education*, 15(6), 438–454.

Usher, R., Bryant, I., and Johnston, R. (1997). *Adult Education and the Postmodern Challenge: Learning Beyond the Limits*. London: Routledge.

Varela, F. J., Thompson, E., and Rosch, E. (1991). *The Embodied Mind: Cognitive Science and Human Experience*. Cambridge, MA: MIT Press.

CHAPTER 64

Workplace Learning, Work-Based Education, and the Challenges to Educational Psychology

HUGH MUNBY, NANCY L. HUTCHINSON,
AND PETER CHIN

This chapter focuses on how the differences between learning in schools and learning in the workplace shape our view of the learner and prompt a rethinking of teaching, learning, and knowledge within authentic settings. The approach shows how concepts like communities of practice, situated cognition, and workplace learning influence views about the nature of school learning and about the relationship between school and work.

DIFFERENT KINDS OF KNOWLEDGE

Many of us who can ride a bike are unable to describe the complex laws of physics that explain how a bike stays upright when ridden. When we begin to fall to the right, we compensate by turning the wheel to the right. A physicist would explain that we are accelerating along the curve and balancing against the gravitational pull to the right. But that is not the knowledge we draw on when we ride a bike. This example was used by Michael Polanyi, in his *Personal Knowledge: Towards a Post-Critical Philosophy* (1957), to make a point about skilled performance and knowledge of natural laws, like the laws of physics. A flute player can perform skillfully without knowing the details of the physical laws governing harmonics, overtones, and lengths of vibrating columns of air. One can perform skillfully without knowing that one is following these laws, yet there is a form of knowing here. When we do something, we use an intriguing kind of knowledge, a kind of knowledge that is not easily put into words. Declarative knowledge, which is expressed in words, is familiar to us: the disciplines that make up most school subjects are like stockpiles of declarative knowledge. We can teach this kind of knowledge by saying or declaring it, and we can show that we know it by doing the same. But knowledge that cannot be put into words is different: how we ride a bicycle, how we recognize the face of a friend in a crowd, how we "bend" a soccer ball, how we carry out a dental procedure on a tense patient. All these activities use knowledge, and this chapter is about this kind of knowledge: how it differs from declarative knowledge, how it has been researched, how it is valued in society, and how we can help people acquire it. Ultimately, we show how a better understanding of the knowledge of action (sometimes called procedural knowledge) can lead to improvements in learning in school, and can help us recognize the importance of learning in authentic situations, like workplaces, which offer tasks and problems that represent everyday practice and that are within contexts outside schools.

Polanyi's important book argued against the dominant view at the time that scientific knowledge was objective—free from the distortions of human thought. In his book, Polanyi acknowledged the importance of Heidegger's concept of "in-living," which draws attention to the intimate relationship between ourselves as knowers and the world that we want to know and learn about. Our difficulty is that we live within our shared social system, and we cannot get outside it to inspect it objectively. This understanding severely damages the idea of objectivity in knowledge. The idea of objective knowledge is further dashed when we recognize that the social system we live within provides us with a language we then use to describe our world. So our knowledge is inseparable from our living within a social system. We can illustrate by showing the differences in descriptions of major events: if you studied U.S. history in a school in the United States of America, you would have learned about the War of Independence; but if you studied that same period in a school in England you would have learned about the American Revolution. The names convey quite different political stances toward the events, differences that illustrate how humans are socially engaged in their own declarative knowledge.

Before the idea of objective knowledge was questioned, theoretical knowledge was held in high esteem simply because it was separate from practical concerns. It was free from the appetites of experience: in a word, it was ideal. The philosopher John Dewey, in his *Democracy and Education* (1916), attempted to restore the balance by urging that significantly more attention be paid to experience and to "practical studies" in the school curriculum. We can see that modern classrooms do not reflect Dewey's views. And we can see the overwhelming influence of theoretical knowledge when we look at modern textbooks on educational psychology. These textbooks are dominated by research that assumes that all learning and all education of value occur in classrooms; only students who fail in this important learning are offered an alternative. Unlike successful students, failing students and at-risk students are encouraged to engage in low-status learning through action in authentic situations; they can participate in workplace learning, often called co-operative (co-op) education or work-based learning. The low status of knowledge gained in action presents problems for schools, for workplaces, and for psychologists interested in understanding how we acquire such knowledge. In this chapter, we argue that to advance the field of educational psychology, we must challenge the importance placed on theoretical knowledge and acknowledge the value of knowledge gained in action for all learners.

HOW DO WE LEARN TO DO THINGS?

Early accounts of human action leaned heavily on ideas about declarative knowledge and argument. For example, Aristotle distinguished between theoretical reasoning and practical reasoning. Theoretical reasoning ends in statements of declarative knowledge: all swans are white; this is a swan; therefore it is white. Practical reasoning ends in action: rain is forecast and I do not wish to get wet; therefore I take my umbrella. Practical reasoning sounds straightforward, but it is by no means the only kind of practical or action knowledge, and it certainly fails to tell us much about how such knowledge is acquired.

Interest in the nature of knowledge in action and its acquisition is a comparatively recent phenomenon in the psychological literature. This can be explained in part by the social status of declarative knowledge. In contemporary Western society, the careers that enjoy higher status are closely associated with declarative knowledge. Careers in law and in medicine, for example, are achieved after success in school and in university subjects that are largely repositories of declarative knowledge. To be sure, the professions themselves involve knowing in action just as most employment positions do. But candidacy for high-status professions results from success at examinations involving declarative knowledge.

Another reason for the comparative recency of interest in how we acquire knowledge in action may be a function of where research on learning has traditionally taken place. Research on learning, like most psychological research, has traditionally been conducted in psychology departments on university campuses, where it is relatively easy to find an abundance of potential research subjects and many examples of learning. Research on learning has also been conducted in schools, which aspire for their students to succeed in university, and thus teach the declarative knowledge that universities value. Not surprisingly, research on learning tended to reflect the available participants and material. So the high status of academic knowledge appears to have distracted us from asking questions about how the knowledge of action might be acquired.

Many writers have challenged the high status of academic knowledge. John Dewey argued strongly for the inclusion of vocational subjects in the education of all high school students. More recently, Donald Schön championed the cause of action knowledge. In *The Reflective Practitioner: How Professionals Think in Action* (1983), Schön demonstrated the complexity of knowledge-in-action and showed how successful practice depends on two different kinds of reflection. Reflection-on-action is the more usual form of reflection in which we think about our actions and their consequences after the event. This is to be contrasted with reflection-in-action in which there is a "conversation" between the knower and the action, a kind of conversation in which unusual events in practice are processed without deliberation but with a reflection within the action itself. Schön expands on this in his second book, *Educating the Reflective Practitioner* (1987), in which examples of complex performance are used to show how reflection-in-action contributes to competence, as in piano playing and architectural drawing.

At about the same time that Schön was demonstrating the demands and complexity of knowing-in-action, other researchers were becoming intrigued with a rather different form of action knowledge that has become known as situated cognition. The research emphasis in situated cognition is jointly on the role cognition plays in authentic and complex learning and on the role that the context or situation plays. Learning is assumed to go on in the interplay between the learner and the context, with the context being an integral part of what is learned. Vygotsky in his *Mind in Society* (1978) described how human activities take place in cultural settings and cannot be understood apart from those settings. In this perspective learning is fundamentally experiential and fundamentally social. Thus research on situated cognition takes us into realistic settings that are quite different from studies of learning in schools and universities. Many of the settings studied are workplaces.

In situated cognition, the interest is the complex relationships between the knower or learner and the relevant elements of the environment, sometimes called affordances. For example, in *Communities of Practice: Learning, Meaning and Identity* (1998), Etienne Wenger (1998) reported on his ethnographic fieldwork in the medical-claims–processing center of a large U.S. insurance company. He uses his accounts of the way people interact with one another and with the shared knowledge of the workplace to develop a social theory of learning. This way of understanding learning rests on the dual concepts of practice (especially a community of practice) and of identity. In Wenger's study, a group of claims processors were observed struggling with a complex worksheet that the company called the COB worksheet and that the processors called "the C, F, and J thing." The processors knew the steps to complete the worksheet and described it as "self-explanatory," while they professed no understanding of the reasons that the calculation was the way it was. The processors gave up on making sense of what they did, acknowledging that perhaps the company didn't want them to understand, and they put their effort into creating a work atmosphere in which that bit of ignorance would not be a liability. In practice, understanding is the art of choosing what to know and what to ignore in order to get on with our lives, and learning shapes who we are and how we see ourselves.

The practices for completing "the C, F, and J" worksheet and for understanding the process were the property of a kind of community and were created over time by people in a shared enterprise with shared ways of doing things. A community of practice can help a newcomer to acquire knowledge, and identity as a community member, by designing social structures that foster learning. Or a community of practice can keep newcomers on the margin or the periphery, forcing newcomers to make their own sense guided by their personal experiences. Learning belongs to the realm of experience and practice. Learning happens, whether by design or on its own terms, although it may be much more effective when systematic and planned.

The later part of the twentieth century witnessed growth in research and scholarship on forms of learning and knowing that departed from the more traditional experimental studies of learning. Many of these studies, like Wenger's work, were conducted in workplaces. It is probably not sheer chance that psychological research into action knowledge, situated cognition, and workplace learning coincided with increasing acceptance of descriptive and ethnographic studies alongside experimental studies. Detailed observational studies of, and interview studies with, workers are necessary precursors to identifying the research that needs to be undertaken in order to understand and then improve authentic learning in complex contexts like workplaces.

In his book, *Learning in the Workplace* (2001), Stephen Billett of Australia reported strategies for effective practice based on observation and interview studies in a wide range of workplaces. For example, workplaces can tacitly structure learners' experiences so they engage in increasingly more accountable tasks. More experienced workers can provide guidance so that novices can move to more independent responsibilities, whether they are miners, hairdressers, or chefs. Common or routine tasks in the workplace are a key source of learning about practice. They reinforce what the worker already knows, help the worker to make sense of what has been learned, and enable the worker to be vigilant for the nonroutine. The nonroutine may represent the breakdown of the routine or may represent wholly or partly novel tasks. Billett emphasized that many complex tasks in everyday experience in workplaces have combinations of routineness, resulting in many kinds of learning with varied implications for competence and identity. Authentic contexts like workplaces can contribute to rich learning in three ways. First, the particular situation provides activities to engage in, problems to solve, and goals to achieve. Second, direct guidance available in the workplace enables collaborative learning between novice and experienced workers. Third, the workplace provides indirect guidance both in opportunities to observe other workers, and in the affordances of the physical workplace setting and its tools. Because the context is part of what is learned, learning *in* the workplace, when socially structured, is particularly effective learning *for* the workplace. As we shall see, the effectiveness of work-based learning poses two challenges to long-held assumptions about school-based learning.

AN ENDURING TENSION: PROBLEMS FOR SCHOOLS

The functions of school, indeed the purposes of public education, have long been debated. Before the invention of public education, the early school curriculums consisted of classical subjects—declarative knowledge—that were deemed appropriate to the preparation of clergymen, doctors, lawyers, and teachers. The advent of public education, and then compulsory public education, saw attention given to educational purposes relevant to vocations other than middle-class ones. Vocational education thus became part of public education but, at the same time, it did so in a nonintegrated fashion because educational discourse soon became the ground for the now familiar distinction between academic and vocational courses, classes, streams, programs, and even students.

In the early part of the twentieth century, John Dewey railed against this distinction on several counts. For example, he found it socially divisive because it appeared to demean nonacademic knowledge while promoting academic knowledge and pursuits. More important, he found it miseducational because it seemed to ignore the need for schools to prepare youth for the world of work. Thus Dewey in *Democracy and Education* argued for the inclusion of vocational education in the curriculum for all high school students. Nearly 100 years after the publication of *Democracy and Education*, calls for some compulsory vocational education are still being made, under the heading of "New Vocationalism."

Among the curriculum challenges faced by schools are "What should be taught?" and "What are schools for?" A look at typical high school curricula over the last 100 years would lead one to suspect that the curricula are directed at preparing students for college and university entrance, and that little account seems to have been taken that as many as 75% of high school graduates will be in the workforce one year following graduation from high school. The assumption that the academic curriculum appropriately prepares high school students for "life after school" could well be erroneous, even though attempts are made to create instruction around tasks that mirror the context outside school.

It can be argued that preparing high school graduates to function in the workplace is the responsibility of the workplace itself, and that all schools should do is to prepare graduates to learn in the workplace. But there are striking differences in how schools and workplaces operate, and these differences suggest that schools may not be well suited to preparing students for how to learn in the workplace. These differences become evident when we adopt a curriculum perspective and ask questions about how information is organized, about who teaches, and even about the purposes of school and the workplace. In schools, information is organized and presented incrementally. But this is not necessarily the case in the workplace, where many tasks must by their nature be presented completely. As Billett observed, a learning task often involves observing a more experienced worker and then participating in the complete task.

In much of the school curriculum, the teacher stands, as it were, as mediator between the knowledge and the learner. This form of mediation is generally absent in the workplace, with the knowledge of action confronting the worker learner without the mediation of a person educated to teach. A third difference of note is the overall purpose of the enterprise. Schools, we know, ultimately exist to promote student learning, and one may presume that the activities of school are all designed to facilitate and promote that learning. The same cannot be said of the workplace. While it benefits workplaces to enhance the learning of novice learners, ultimately, in the private sector, the aim of the workplace is to make profit so that the enterprise thrives. In the service sector, this translates into serving clients. It is not that workplace learning is unimportant in these situations; rather workplace learning is subservient to these ends. It is not the prime motivator as it is in schools.

All these differences contrive to make the culture of workplace learning very different from the culture of school learning. As a result, we would expect that efforts to prepare high school students for the world of work would include ways to introduce students to the cultural differences. Work-based education (WBE) programs, like co-op education offer a route to this. These programs involve students for extended periods of time at a workplace while they are enrolled in school. Typically, students also engage in classroom orientation to the workplace and in reflective seminars. WBE programs usually are intended to forge relationships between school subjects and the workplace. But they can do more: they allow students to explore possible employment and careers, and they enable schools to provide credit courses that are closely aligned to the workplace.

WBE programs are places for helping high school students to make the most of workplace learning. However, these programs are raising questions that must be answered before schools can prepare adolescents well for learning in the workplace. First, if the workplace demands both declarative and practical knowledge of every worker, shouldn't schools be affording every student opportunities for both school-based and workplace-based learning, regardless of the student's goals for life after school? Second, if recent research on workplace learning rests on notions of situated learning in which the context is part of what is learned, how can we ensure that learning in one workplace is generalizable to other contexts? In other words, how can we be confident about what learning might be transferable and what is clearly not transferable, so high school students can be optimally prepared to learn from workplace settings?

Before we rush to place every high school student in a workplace, in response to the first question, we require an answer to the second question. In a recent paper, the Co-operative Education and Workplace Learning (CEWL) group at Queen's University in Canada showed that recent research in metacognition can inform instructional theories that may be helpful. When students are taught about commonalities among workplaces' demands for practical knowledge, while developing knowledge in action in a specific workplace, the students can then use that practical understanding of knowledge in action. With it, they can monitor and regulate (metacognition) their own performance in the current workplace, and analyze the demands of other workplaces. Routines illustrate this well. Most work consists of common demands or routines (and subroutines). For example, our observations of workplaces revealed "opening routines" such as the routine followed by a gardening center employee when he arrived for work at the beginning of the day: putting up "Open" signs, setting out lawn equipment, removing plastic from shrubs and plants, watering, etc. We noted "opening routines" at other workplaces, but they differed according to the workplace. Although individual routines are different, all routines have common features: something initiates them, they run until a defined end point is reached, they can get off-track, and they can be improved. These general features could be taught so that novice learners in the workplace monitor their own learning about the work they perform. As Billett argued, recognizing the routine reinforces the familiar, encourages increased understanding, and frees the worker to anticipate the nonroutine. Pushing work-based learning to encompass an understanding of the shape and characteristics of knowing in action within contexts, while acquiring knowing in action in one context, may surmount the challenges posed by the threat of context-bound learning.

In a recent case study, CEWL demonstrated the applicability of David Hung's (1999) notion of epistemological appropriation for understanding how work-based learning might be made effective for high school students. A high school senior, in a co-op education placement, was observed regularly over a six-week period during which she moved from an awkward novice who nearly fainted while watching a procedure to a competent dental assistant. By the end of the observation period, Denise, the high school senior, had appropriated the social aspects of the role, joining the community of practice by modeling her uniform and language on those of the preventative dental assistant (PDA) who mentored her. She had also engaged in cognitive appropriation and was able to aid the dentist unprompted, anticipating his need for tools and materials just as the PDA did. Extensive observational data that showed the PDA's regulatory behaviors of scaffolding, modeling, and coaching and the novice's corresponding regulatory behaviors of submitting, mirroring, and constructing contributed to Denise's learning in action. Unlike the sequential progression suggested by Hung's theory, the supervisor's and novice's regulatory behaviors continued for the duration of the term. Even during one day, there would be examples of all regulatory behaviors. This finding suggests that sequential progression occurs for each instance of significant new learning, and that new learning is constantly being introduced. Hung's regulatory behaviors focus attention on how supervisors can improve opportunities for novices' learning, and on how novices can become more engaged in both social and epistemological appropriation in work-based learning.

The second challenge to schools runs deeper. If high school seniors like Denise can appropriate knowledge in action and join complex communities of practice within one school term, can schools ignore the possibility that their emphasis on declarative, decontextualized knowledge in the classrooms of school is misplaced? The thrust of emerging frameworks like situated cognition is that learning ultimately belongs to the realm of experience and practice and follows the negotiation of meaning. Learning happens by design, and when we neglect to create the social infrastructures that foster learning, learning happens without design. But it may not be learning that we value or wish to encourage. And it may not be learning that enables individuals to negotiate successfully unfamiliar contexts and to join communities of practice by knowing in action, anticipating the nonroutine, and developing understanding. Our understanding of workplace learning challenges the school curriculum, and it also challenges the axiom "theory first, then practice." This axiom seems to have guided public schooling for over a century. Oddly, it seems absent from the unwritten rules of procedure that govern the 1000-year-old traditional relationship between master and apprentice. Recent research on workplace learning invites educational psychology to inspect this social tradition carefully.

The perspectives we bring to our encounters matter because they color our perceptions and our actions. If concepts like knowing in action, communities of practice, identity, and epistemological appropriation apply to the learning that goes on in workplaces, they are most likely applicable to the learning that goes on in other social contexts, including schools and classrooms. The social perspective on learning is relevant even when we don't intend to learn, because all meaning making eventually gains its significance in the kind of person we become. Like those claims processors observed by Wenger, how we negotiate—what we will know, what we will stop trying to understand, and who we will become—is the project of each of us. Thus situated cognition challenges educational psychology to shift from framing learning as essentially static and declarative to understanding learning as socially mediated, dynamic, and significant to who we are.

TERMS FOR READERS

Communities of practice—Informal social structures in which each individual is involved in joint or similar tasks, usually within a workplace. Wenger uses "communities of practice" to illustrate how learning is encouraged and acquired within authentic settings like workplaces. For Wenger, communities of practice have ownership of their knowledge.

Epistemological appropriation—Hung's term for the complex cognitive learning by novices. Hung's theory of epistemological appropriation was inspired by Polanyi's notion of the apprentice learning with the experienced practitioner, and it takes account of the regulation of learning afforded by the social relationship and by the situation itself.

Knowing-in-action—Schön's term for the knowledge of action or practice. Schön used the term to emphasize that this form of knowing resides in the action, as in tying a shoelace. As the laces are being tied, our knowledge is cued by each successive part of the complex action; it does not lie outside the action.

Metacognition—Knowledge about one's own thinking and problem solving. We use metacognitive processes when we plan and monitor our thinking in problem solving, decision-making, etc.

Situated cognition—The term comes from Vygotsky's view that learning is both social and contextual, or within the situation. Situated cognition has come to refer to the knowledge one uses in settings outside school, or the authentic settings of everyday practice.

SUGGESTED READING

Billett, S. R. (2001). *Learning in the Workplace: Strategies for Effective Practice.* Sydney, Australia: Allen Unwin.

Hung, D. W. L. (1999). Activity, apprenticeship, and epistemological appropriation: Implications from the writings of Michael Polanyi. *Educational Psychologist,* 34, 193–205.

Munby, H. (Ed.). (2003). What does it mean to learn in the workplace? Differing theoretical perspectives [Special Issue]. *Journal of Workplace Learning,* 15(3).

Wenger, E. (1998). *Communities of Practice: Learning, Meaning, and Identity.* London, UK: Cambridge University Press.

CHAPTER 65

Dialogic Learning: A Communicative Approach to Teaching and Learning

SANDRA RACIONERO AND ROSA VALLS

Dialogic learning is the result of the interactions produced in an egalitarian dialogue that is oriented to the creation and acquisition of new knowledge, which is the fruit of consensus. Dialogic learning depends basically on the interactions with others and it requires the maximization of the use of communicative abilities in any context—from home to the community, work, etc., and a more active, reflexive, and critical participation in society. In experiences grounded in dialogic learning, people are cognitive subjects of acting on the basis of a dialectic relation between thought and action. In this sense, dialogic learning is not another theoretical conception of learning but it implies a series of organizational and participative measures that favor learning, especially in contexts where other conceptions have only brought partial solutions.

Dialogic learning depends much more on the interrelation of the interactions that each individual has beyond those that take place in the educational context (the neighborhood, home, store, at work) or with the teachers. Dialogic learning is useful not only in educational centers, but also in the many spaces in which students relate, learn, and develop with others. In fact, dialogic learning does not refer exclusively to the instrumental teaching–learning relationship, but also occurs in the relations among educational agents in the school and the community.

Dialogic learning does not occur in power relations. It takes place in dialogic relations in which people contribute their knowledge from their experience and skills, on an egalitarian basis, with the intention of understanding, based on shared agreements, collectively creating learning through solidarist interactions, which would not have been possible in solitude. The result is learning with a deeper instrumental dimension and steeped in meaning as a result of the characteristics of the very interactive learning process.

This chapter explains dialogic learning on the basis of the communicative conception of teaching and learning, its theoretical bases and principles. First, we discuss the differences between dialogic learning and other learning conceptions: traditional and significative. Second, we present the seven principles of dialogic learning: *egalitarian dialogue, cultural intelligence, transformation, instrumental dimension, creation of meaning, solidarity,* and *the equality of differences.*

FROM SUBJECTIVITY TO INTERSUBJECTIVITY

From the industrial society until today, the understanding of learning has been enlivened integrating every time more aspects that surrounds it. The development of different understandings of learning is parallel to the series of changes that have affected all of the social spheres as a result of the shift from the industrial society to the information society. The technological revolution has permeated the very core of companies and we have gone from an industry-based economy to a globalized one based on information. The forms of work are changing: new labor sectors, an increase in the options available, and communication goes beyond the traditional boundaries of space and time. These changes have also transformed the educational and psychological sciences, which are currently evolving toward new perspectives in coherence with the centrality of information and dialogue in today's societies.

Teaching and learning processes are not maintained at the margins of these profound changes. In the information society, learning transcends the individual, as universal communicative skills become essential. From the earlier conceptions of teaching and learning, the focus in developmental psychology and education has moved from looking at the individual in isolation to looking at the subject in relation to their social and cultural context, where "the others," but especially the communicative interaction with "the others," is the main object of interest. In this context, within the psychology perspectives with a dialogic orientation, the communicative conception of teaching and learning emphasizes the importance of coordinating interactions among different educational agents and the learning contexts with the objective of obtaining the maximum results. This process has also determined the disciplines that have been integrated in the study of learning: from pedagogy to psychology and sociology, ending up with the need to recognize all of them. In the process of different understandings of learning, we could identify three basic conceptions in learning: the objectivist conception, the constructivist conception, and the communicative/dialogic conception.

Objectivist Conception

Learning in the objective conception was based on the idea that the students are passive subjects who receive information from a subject agent, the teacher, who posseses expert knowledge on the topic and transmits it. This learning is in consonance with the objectivist conception in psychology, for which reality exists independently of people's perception of it.

Learning is conceived of as the transmission of knowledge, in which the girl or boy's role is to assimilate the information. The teacher possesses the knowledge the student must grasp, the objective reality that must be assimilated by rote. Pedagogy, in this case, places the focus on the teacher as the fundamental element in teaching and learning, given that it is the teacher who has the knowledge to transmit. On the other hand, the psychology of traditional teaching emphasized the importance of the individual characteristics, such as memory, in order to favor an increase of learning, given that this was measured by the quantity of knowledge accumulated. This implies a learning that is fundamentally based on memory, largely absent of meaning, and highly dependent on the message relayed by the teacher.

The tradition of filling up the mind with information is no longer useful in the information society. Today information is available on the Internet, continually updated and much greater in quantity than what the human memory can store. If we want our students to be successful in the information society, we have to focus learning on the development of skills for processing and selecting information. Traditional exams that test the knowledge a person memorized without consulting any resource have lost their utility.

In the objectivist conception, teaching is homogenizing. The same things are taught without taking into account differences in context and culture. It is, therefore, an equality that also produces inequalities, given that it does not contemplate difference. The theme of multiculturalism would be dealt with from an approach of assimilation. School culture corresponds with the hegemonic culture, making it impossible for girls and boys from minority cultures to feel identified with the school if they do not abandon their ethnic and cultural identity in order to take on the dominant culture interpreted as superior. From this relationship of superiority–inferiority, the rest of the cultures are considered to be inferior, worse, and underdeveloped.

Constructivist Conception

In the eighties, there was a shift from the hegemony of the objectivist conception to the constructivist conception. The idea behind constructivism is that people construct social reality, and this construction is different because the meanings that each person gives to this construction are different. The constructivist conception sees learning as a cognitive process of construction and creation of meaning that takes place between two individuals. This occurs when a student is capable of relating what they already know, their prior knowledge, with what they are taught, the new forms of knowledge. When this happens, it is referred to as significative learning.

According to the constructivist conception, each process of knowledge construction is different for each person. Therefore, degrees in learning are referred to, and processes of learning or "not learning." Prior knowledge is the factor on which these degrees of learning depend. In this way, maximum learning is made to depend on the quantity and quality of prior knowledge of the student. The different learning results are justified by the level with which the student begins. The constructivist conception of teaching and learning, in consonance with Ausubel's significative learning does not highlight the objectives that must be attained at each level, the point each girl and boy must reach in learning within a given educational area or stage, but instead it stresses what they already know at the onset of learning. In the constructivist conception, the most decisive element in the teaching program is to know these different points of departure and to attend to them in a diversified way. That is to say, they teach different contents: a higher level for girls and boys who have more prior knowledge, and lower level for those with less prior knowledge.

Therefore, prior knowledge and how the girl or boy has this knowledge structured on a cognitive level, the knowledge schema, are the most important factors in learning. Further on, we will see how Vygotsky explains that teaching directed to levels of cognitive development that have already been reached (prior knowledge) is inefficient from the learning point of view. Teaching that is adapted to the deficits, to a low entry level, is not a form of teaching that provokes an improvement in learning and positively challenges the learner to move forward. The constructivist conception, by centering on the subject who learns, implies a step forward from the oversight in the traditional objectivist conception of learning, which is focused on the teacher as the unique agent of the process. The constructivist conception of teaching and learning recognizes the contribution of the student in the teaching–learning process, but they are seen as individual processes that do not take sufficiently the pedagogical and sociological aspects into account.

Communicative Conception

The communicative conception is grounded in everyone's capacity for dialogue. It is through dialogue and interaction with others that learning happens. It implies a form of learning that is based on the egalitarian dialogue of girls and boys with the teachers families, all equal, the community, etc., with *validity claims*. That is to say, everyone that interacts with the students has the same objectives of fostering learning; their claims are for truth. In all of these interactions, the aim of the people who relate to the girls and boys is for them to learn and there are no other personal interests whatsoever, such as gaining protagonism, involved in their relationships. From this conception, reality is seen as created by people, who depend on the meanings that they have constructed through interaction. Object reality is reached through the intersubjective process.

Psychologists like Vygotsky, Bruner, and Mead have stressed this idea from the sociocultural perspective and from symbolic interactionism. Freire says that people are dialogic by nature, and tend toward dialogue and relating with others. Chomsky explains how people are gifted with a cognitive structure for language. Habermas, in his theory of communicative action, develops the conception of communicative competency, with which he demonstrates that we are all subjects capable of language and action. Dialogism is part of the very nature of the person, they dialogue with others, with the norms, with themselves, with their emotions, norms and memories. Learning cannot be limited to a mechanism of grasping reality and its assimilation in line with Piaget; instead, it is a process that is much more complex, which includes an ongoing intersubjective dialogue that is later internalized and taken ownership of. In accordance with symbolic interactionism and sociocultural psychology, everything that is individual was first social.

The meanings that are created and the meaning that is produced with respect to school learning depend on the interactions that students have with other persons in different spaces. The most influential factor in learning is the interactions. Therefore, learning from the communicative or dialogic conception is the product of a process of collective construction of meaning through interaction. The interactions are aimed at reaching higher levels of learning. These higher levels of development are the focus of dialogic learning.

In dialogic learning, teachers, families and other adults facilitate dialogue, overcoming the limits of their own cultural borders that only allow them to see others through the lens of their own culture. From the communicative perspective, teachers have to know how to develop interactions with the context and processes of meaning construction that take place within them, emphasizing the egalitarian and the communitarian, in a series of actions in which education is not restricted to the teacher–student relationship but, instead, includes the entire social context in a global and unified activity. If the students learn in the interactions with a variety of adults besides the teacher, their education will have positive benefits with a greater richness of adult–student interactions from the learning point of view. Dialogic learning is valid on any educational level; it can be applied from early childhood education till adult education.

Conception	Objectivist	Constructivist	Communicative
Bases	Reality is independent of the individuals that know it and use it.	Reality is a social construction that depends on the meanings that individuals attribute to it.	Reality is a human construction. Meanings depend on the human interactions.
Example	The paper is paper regardless of how we see it.	The paper is a paper because we see it as an object that is appropriate for writing on.	The paper is paper because we agree to use it to write on.
	Traditional Teaching	**Significative**	**Dialogic**
Learning	One learns from the message that is emitted by the teacher.	One learns through relating new knowledge that is incorporated in the cognitive structure on the basis of prior knowledge.	One learns through interactions between equals, teachers, family members, friends, etc. who produce egalitarian dialogue.

(Continued)

Conception	Objectivist	Constructivist	Communicative
	of Teachers	of Teachers	of Teachers, Family Members, and Community
Education	The contents transmitted and methodologies used to do it	Knowledge of the learning processes of the actors and their form of constructing meanings	Knowledge of the learning processes of individuals and groups through the interactive construction of meanings.
Discipline	Pedagogical orientation that does not sufficiently take psychological and sociological aspects into account	Psychological orientation that does not sufficiently take pedagogical and sociological aspects into account	Interdisciplinary orientation: pedagogical, psychological, sociological, and epistemological
Consequences	The imposition of a homogenous culture generates and reproduces inequalities.	The adaptation of diversity without taking into account the inequality of the context generates an increase of inequalities.	With the transformation of the context, respect for differences is included as one of the dimensions of egalitarian education.

PRINCIPLES OF DIALOGIC LEARNING

In the following, we present seven basic principles that aim to provide a guide for reflection and implementation of the practice of dialogic learning. The principles of dialogic learning are expressed in different ways in each situation. All of them take into account psychological, educational, and social theories, as well as cultural knowledge, feelings, and academic aspects.

Egalitarian Dialogue

Dialogue is egalitarian when the different contributions are considered in terms of the validity of the arguments, instead of being valued on the basis of the position of power of the speaker, or on criteria like the imposition of culturally hegemonic knowledge. The educational process can be understood as a dialogic act. Through egalitarian dialogue students, teachers, family members, and others learn, given that they all construct their interpretations on the basis of arguments made by the others. Each person makes his or her own contributions to the dialogue; this equality approaches the ideal speech act of Habermas. Their relation is, at once, real and ideal. Real because the greater influence of certain voices is a reminder that the conversation is taking place in an unequal context, and ideal because they are on the road toward overcoming these inequalities. Dialogue becomes an instrument for learning. Everyone is capable of language and action as affirmed by Habermas; there is a universal capacity for language as Chomsky contends; and for Vygotsky, mind and society are inseparable—these contributions indicate to us that everyone can participate in dialogue on egalitarian terms, in which each person contributes his or her knowledge and experience to a process in which reaching the best agreement is sought.

Egalitarian dialogue transported to the educational center implies a profound change in the school culture, which is traditionally based in hierarchical relations where teachers determine what must be learned, how, and when. To reach egalitarian dialogue in the school, educational professionals should overcome certain conceptions of the families and especially those who are nonacademic. Furthermore, families should also be open in relation to the teachers, who have an image of them that distances them from a dialogic relation, an image that reflects institutionalized relations of power between them. Egalitarian dialogue in school is made possible when the community and school interact from bases they share: the maximum learning for girls and boys, and work jointly to reach it. In some schools this is manifested with mixed work commissions (family members, adults from the community, teachers, students) who are dedicated exclusively to working together to attain specific educational, social, and cultural objectives expressed by all of the agents for improving the school.

Cultural Intelligence

In the educational context, theories based on deficit have generated many low expectations with respect to students' capacities, as well as compensatory policies that have not been able to respond to the demand for quality education for all. Dialogic learning is contrary to the idea of "compensation" of deficits. It is about parting from the capacities of the students, their families, the teachers, and all of the people who interact with the boy and girl in order to accelerate his or her learning, especially those boys and girls from disadvantaged contexts.

Certain conceptions of intelligence tend to focus on certain abilities but to ignore others. Academic intelligence has been the most valued by privileged groups, designing standardized intelligence tests in which these groups turned up as intelligent and those who did not belong to them as deficient. An illustrative example is the Weschler intelligence scale, which places a high percentage of girls and boys "below the median," which leads them to receive an education of the minimum and very low results, which is fruit of this label.

Today we know that intelligence is not defined only by the concept of academic intelligence, and many studies (Cattel's fluid and crystallized intelligence, Gardner's Multiple Intelligences, Sternberg's Triarquic Theory) have presented evidence of it. The concept of cultural intelligence includes academic intelligence and other types of it. The three subareas of cultural intelligence are the following:

- *Academic intelligence:* Which we develop in academic settings and which is not alone in defining the intelligence of a person. In relation to the tests mentioned earlier, these are simply based on measuring what the boy or girl is able to do, but, considering Vygotsky, does not measure what he or she is able to do with the help of others.

- *Practical intelligence:* The differentiation between practical (which is used, and learning in the daily context) and academic intelligence is fruit of more recent research, thanks to the recuperation of the works of Vygotsky and Luria in the field of cultural psychology. One of the most important works about practical intelligence is by Silvia Scribner, who explains how we develop the same mental schema when we work with our minds, a theory that questions Piaget's homogeneity in the description of intellectual evolution.

- *Communicative intelligence:* This intelligence refers to the communicative and other skills that are useful for resolving situations to which a person in solitude would not be able to find a solution only with academic or practical intelligence. With communicative intelligence, strategies for shared resolution are proposed, which are based on communicative action taken on by participants in the learning processes. People can understand each other and act by using our communicative skills for everyone's success. On the basis of the idea that we all have capacities for language, as Chomsky defends, we are gifted with communication and through this the capacity to resolve any kind of situation on a day-to-day basis, and in the case of education, concrete learning situations. In a dialogic relation, a girl might have greater explicative strategies than a teacher to explain to her peers the process of resolving a problem, while she too is consolidating what she already knows or has just learned.

Dialogic learning is based on the recognition of the three types of intelligences in everyone, and the same capacities for participating in an egalitarian dialogue. Academic intelligence is only a consequence of school experience. In today's information society, increasingly, cultural and communicative intelligence take precedence over the academic. Dialogic learning promotes the development of these three types of intelligence, but, by parting from the recognition of the three, it does not obstruct anyone's participation in the teaching and learning processes in school.

Transformation

All of the educational projects that pursue transformation need utopia. Dialogic learning requires high expectations from all those involved in the interactive learning processes, trust in all of the students, and an orientation toward maximum results because without all these elements it is impossible to have teaching that is directed toward transformation of the entry levels. The transformative content that is proposed by this learning conception, in coherence with the rest of the principles, advocates for transformation of reality instead of adaptation to it. We are beings of transformation and not accommodation as Freire said.

In dialogic learning transformation transcends the classroom and the school, reaching the very context. The schools have to be another space in which students increase their interactions; that is why schools should open their doors to the whole community so that this transformation can be extendable. At the same time, the learning experience is extended for all participants; education for family members becomes a key element. In that moment family members and boys and girls share a learning space in the home that until then did not exist, transforming the boys' and girls' reference points.

Instrumental Dimension

Too often curricular contents have been adapted to the boys' and girls' context, parting from the idea of the importance of prior knowledge, instead of offering the necessary learning contents for them to move beyond their initial points. This curricular adaptation has been manifested in placing boys and girls from underprivileged contexts in groups, on levels, where the instrumental learning required for the information society is not guaranteed. This ends up making these schools parts of a system that instead of breaking down social exclusion contributes to reproduce it.

Dialogic learning is contrary to any reduction of learning, as many times is wrongly understood. Dialogue serves to increase and improve instrumental knowledge acquisition. The instrumental dimension ensures that dialogue is used for learning everything that is needed to live with dignity in the information society. In this way, prioritizing the learning of values to the detriment of instrumental learning is avoided, which was the fruit of proposals from decades past like the "pedagogy of happiness."

The effects on boys' and girls' academic self-concept when working in inclusionary situations, where the maximum learning is offered, is to increase their expectations in their capacities. School education must promote the instrumental dimension of learning for all boys and girls. There are many activities and initiatives that schools can adopt to guarantee this. One way is by opening learning spaces in the school beyond the school hours for its use and management by the community, where adults interact with boys and girls for learning comprehension (tutored libraries), for improving the use of ICTs (authorized digital rooms), etc. Dialogic learning is also produced in these spaces. Similarly, education of family members has an important influence on improving the instrumental learning of boys and girls.

Creation of Meaning

The danger of the absence of creation of meaning is extended to many spheres of our lives, beyond the school, and related with the risk and the plurality of options that characterizes our societies. Meaning resurges when people become protagonists of their own existence, or when they participate in joint projects through which they can transform their lives and society. The educational projects that generate the most motivation in today's information society are those that are promoting the creation of meaning. Meaning arises when interaction between people is guided by them, and when they are directly involved in the resolution of concrete problems or situations.

We must take into account that meaning is created in family members and students when the educational center offers learning that will make possible for them to be successful. In this sense, educational projects based on dialogic learning foster the creation of meaning in all educational agents. In terms of teaching–learning processes in the classroom, the student creates meaning in learning when he or she feels like they are learning something that is socially valued. The creation of meaning is related with motivation, but does not depend on it. The creation of meaning also increases motivation. In any case, motivation to bring meaning to learning does not depend on intraindividual factors, but instead it is a fundamentally social process. Motivation, just like meaning, is created in social interaction. This perspective dismisses the conceptions that attribute a lack of motivation in learning to the student, and justify low learning, pointing to little motivation and interest.

Solidarity

Dialogic learning is inclusionary and solidarist. Any educational project that aims to be egalitarian and to offer quality education must be based on solidarity. This solidarity does not only have to be present between boys and girls, but, especially between teachers toward boys and girls. Solidarity is based on offering the same learning and results to all students, regardless of their social, economic, or cultural background. The objective of maximum learning for all girls and boys, just like we would want for our own children or loved ones, means solidarity. This objective will not be attained in solitude, but in solidarity with the other agents that interact with the boys and girls. For this it is necessary to be grounded in the idea of not excluding any boy or girl from the classroom, or placing them in groups by level. Solidarity signifies work with all boys and girls within the classroom, attaining successful learning for all.

Solidarity ensures shared values, for which discourses on coexistence and pacifism are lived as something coherent with what is lived at home, the street, school and in the classroom. In integrated groups where students with different backgrounds and levels receive the same opportunities and instrumental learning is ensured for all, values like solidarity and respect for diversity, on the one hand, and social skills like teamwork, initiative, self-esteem, and even communicative skills, on the other, are more easily attained.

Equality of Differences

Beyond a homogenizing equality and the defense of diversity without contemplating equity among people, education based on the equality of differences is oriented toward real equality, where everyone has a place on egalitarian terms but from a respect for their differences. For people from the most excluded collectives, and disadvantaged situations with respect to other groups, it is not enough to have the same resources as their peers, or to offer them education "that compensates" their deficits; they need more than the rest, they need to accelerate their learning in order to be able to attain the same learning their peers with more advantaged personal situations have.

The idea that we are different has always existed and is tied in education to the need for different learning. But the reality that we are fundamentally equal does not mean we need homogenizing education, but instead respect for diversity with the pursuit for the same results. Dialogic learning takes into account diversity and equality. Beyond a homogenizing equality that is based on assimilation of ethnic minorities and cultural groups within the dominant model, and a defense of diversity that does not contemplate equity between people, the egalitarian education considering differences is oriented toward real equality, where everyone has the same right to live in a different way.

DIALOGIC LEARNING IN EDUCATIONAL PRACTICE

Dialogic learning can be found in educational practices for all ages, and academic levels. An example of the ways that dialogic learning is carried out in educational practice is through *interactive groups*, which are reduced and heterogeneous groups of students, dynamized by a volunteer. In these groups the students help each other in the joint resolution of activities parting from the premise that everyone has the capacities for resolving the activity. There are no differences between who knows more or less on that topic. As a result of this intersubjective dialogue the learning results are better, in terms of elaboration and because all of the students learn. Egalitarian and reflexive dialogue develops capacities with more depth than the usual forms of teaching. When a student explains to another how to resolve an activity, he or she reinforces what they know and consolidates it, at the same time as contributing to complex cognitive processes, strategies, and skills, which make understanding possible. The organization of classrooms in interactive groups promotes students to help each other in learning, and specific and individualized follow-up is attained for each learner. *Interactive groups* in the classroom favor instrumental learning in all participants.

In contrast to segregationist measures that separate learners by their levels such as tracking or special education units, it is important to point out the heterogeneity present in this practice. This is an essential factor, since the interactions that improve instrumental learning are the interactions that are produced through heterogeneity. *Interactive groups* augment instrumental learning in an environment of solidarity where everyone learns. All of the entry learning levels benefit from this form of learning.

Dialogic learning can be a way to attend to the new educational demands generated in the information society. Traditional proposals of teaching and learning centered on the boy or girl are no longer useful and do not promote equality of results in today's classroom. Dialogic learning is a communicative and interactionist alternative to reaching egalitarian education by means of *egalitarian dialogue* between all educational agents, *transformation* of the context and learning, the recognition of *cultural intelligence*, the *creation of meaning* through interaction, by prioritizing the *instrumental dimension* of learning along with *solidarity*, from the *equality of differences*; in this way success is possible regardless of any cultural or socioeconomic difference.

TERMS FOR READERS

Intersubjective dialogue—It refers to interaction oriented to reaching consensus and mutual agreement that takes place among people who, despite being different, agree to the aims and conditions of the interaction that make it possible to consider each other on equal terms.

Maximum learning—It refers to the provision of a high quality of learning that prepares each learner to face the challenges posed by the current society. This means that he or she will be prepared to access higher education or any job that he or she decides. It can be understood as the learning that provides the maximum opportunities to everybody.

Power relations—Those direct or indirect interactions in which, given an existing individual or structural inequality, the person or group holding the privileged position takes advantage of in order to impose their perspective. In power relations, interactions are based on the force of the power attributed to the privileged position, and not the force of the arguments themselves.

Validity claim—A term used by Habermas to refer to the situation of dialogue in which agreements are reached on the basis of the force of the arguments used by the speaker rather than the status of the position they hold.

SUGGESTED READING

Flecha, R. (2000). *Sharing Words. Theory and Practice of Dialogic Learning*. Lanham: Rowman & Littlefield Publishers, Inc.

Freire, P. (2003). *Pedagogy of the Oppressed*. New York: Continuum.

Chomsky, N. (2000). *Chomsky on Miseducation*. Lanham, MD: Rowman & Littlefield Publishers.

CHAPTER 66

John Dewey's Theory of Learning: A Holistic Perspective

DOUGLAS J. SIMPSON AND XIAOMING LIU

When examining Dewey's theory of learning, it is informative to begin with two essays—"Curriculum Problems" and "New Methods"—that he wrote in 1937 for a book titled *Educational Adaptations in a Changing Society*, which was edited by E. G. Malherbe. In the former essay, later renamed "What Is Learning?" he sketches several ideas that form important parts of the core of his learning theory, a viewpoint that he labels "the natural processes of learning" (LW 11:240). Consequently, he sketches his thinking about the child's "impulses," "needs," "hungers," and "purposes." He also gives attention to the child's "achievement," "growth," "satisfaction," and "elation" that come with learning as well as the teacher's responsibilities for "finding the occasions" and "creating the situations" that provide the means for "realizing [the child's] impulses" as she or he is led gradually from the early years of physical and social learning to more symbolic learning (LW 11:238–242). He emphasizes that "a well-balanced curriculum" provides for learning and growth of *all the elements of personality*, for [1] the manual and overtly constructive powers, [2] for the imaginative and emotional tendencies that later take form in artistic expression, and [3] for the factors that respond to symbolic statement and that prepare the way for distinctly abstract intellectual pursuits. (italics and numbers added)

He immediately asserts: A genuine school of learning is a community in which special aptitudes are gradually disclosed and the transition is made to later careers, in which individuals find happiness and society is richly and nobly served because individuals have learned to know and use their powers. (LW 11:242)

In these two comments several notable Deweyan ideas are manifest. First, learning involves the whole person or personality. Second, the scope of the student's abilities and interests are important. Third, learning is best achieved in a learning community, not as an isolated individual. Finally, learning is for both personal and societal development, not just for individual enhancement.

In the second essay, later renamed "Growth in Activity," Dewey provides insight into child and adolescent development and its relationship to learning and, thereby, amplifies his theory of learning. He claims that there are "three main stages" of a child's natural development (LW 11:243). These are as follows: (1) activity that is sufficient within itself, (2) activity that is controlled by its outcomes, and (3) activity that is focused on symbols (LW 11:243–246). We might refer to these three stages as the evolving periods of play, work, and symbols. But we should be careful to note what he means by these terms: *stages*, *play*, *work*, and *symbols*. For Dewey, these stages are not fixed by age or necessarily sequential because "individuals differ enormously." For instance, the symbols stage, in one sense the highest of the three because it becomes more dominant later in life, may start before the work stage does. Teachers, therefore, need to "guard against forcing square pegs into round holes" (LW 11:246). With these cautions, therefore, Dewey avoids the pitfalls of most developmental stage and structural theorists. The notion of a play stage in this context merely suggests that the young child—and the adolescent and adult, too—often engages in an activity for its intrinsic value or the satisfaction it provides. Personal satisfaction in the activity itself, therefore, is the dominant reason for play. The alleged second or work stage emerges gradually and is commingled with the play stage. As the child becomes more capable of and characterized by work, it is because she or he is interested more and more in an end, aim, or goal. That is to say, the child is interested in using her or his activities to reach a destination or to create an object. Or, as Dewey states, "Play tends to develop into games with certain objective conditions to be observed" (LW 11:245). This doesn't mean, of course, that there isn't intrinsic pleasure in the activity. Ideally, there is both intrinsic and extrinsic or goal-oriented pleasure in the learning process and outcome. The symbols or so-called third stage begins early in life but reaches its fruition in the "latter stages of schooling." Dewey cautions, however, that "the curriculum should be sufficiently differentiated for the child to be able to learn only what is intrinsically congenial to him [or her]" (LW 11:246). Thus, intrinsic pleasure should be part of the play, work, and symbols stages.

As the student develops in the stages of play, work, and symbols, her or his learning is actively occurring and may be analyzed, as we noted earlier, from two different perspectives, the micro and macro. Neither perspective is viewed by Dewey as always being prior to the other in time or development. Both often occur simultaneously, and each is dependent on the other. Neither exists without the other. Both are seen as complementary depictions of an overall personal, natural, and social learning experience. While both aspects of Dewey's learning theory focus on the child or adolescent, the micro-perspective delimits its field of inquiry radically to the learner, pushing the environment far into the background. The macro-perspective draws the learner to the forefront as she or he interactions with the physical, social, emotional, and intellectual environment.

A MICRO-PERSPECTIVE OF LEARNING

Dewey begins his learning theory with a reference to the child's native appetites, instincts, or impulses, which are always active and seeking ways to express themselves (LW 17:214). So images of the teacher pounding or pouring in information or leading or drawing out the developed abilities of the learner are essentially misleading from his perspective. Instead, the child's impulses overflow with activity, making learning a natural byproduct of being human. Thus, there is a sense in which "learning by doing" is an appropriate way to gain an understanding of aspects of his learning theory. Children don't learn and then do something with what they have learned. They learn by doing something. But the child's learning activities are not automatically and necessarily productive. Misbehavior and miseducative involvements are as probable as productive and educative ones if the child is left to herself or himself. Learning by doing, then, can be counterproductive, antisocial, and miseducative. As a result, parents and teachers—and other adults and older children who are informal educators in a community—need to guide children into worthwhile and educative activities. To ignore and withhold the guidance children and youth need isn't showing respect for their personal autonomy according to Dewey. Instead, it is "really stupid," for independent thinking does not emerge because students are left either to themselves or environmental influences. They grow as they are cultivated by respecting and caring educators, teachers and others (LW 2:59).

Table 66.1
Philosophical Assumptions and Classroom Practices

Natural Learning Theory	Natural Depravity Theory
A classroom is characterized by pleasantness and student alertness and activity.	A classroom is characterized by inhibition of impulses and teacher-instigated activities.
The teacher recognizes that there are learning impulses and seeks to use them.	The teacher doesn't think there are natural interests in learning and believes she must initiate it.
The teacher guides natural learning tendencies by means of external conditions and materials.	The teacher attempts to motivate learning by using external stimuli.
The teacher builds up natural learning tendencies via interaction with the classroom and school environments.	The teacher attempts to pour or drill facts and information into students because the student is not naturally interested in learning.
The student learns to express or apply what she or he is learning with others.	The student learns to repeat or reproduce what she or he is memorizing or learning by herself or himself or with others.

Since the activities of the child are for the most part exhibited through the body, the child is constantly using her or his hands, feet, ears, mouth, eyes, and nose. She or he is constantly engaged, doing something in and with the environment. As a result, impulses force the child to "investigate, inquire, experiment" (LW 17:215). Two points, then, are critical in understanding Dewey's learning theory at this juncture: children have native instincts and they will express themselves in nearly any environment, including those settings that are not designed to provide freedom for them to do so. Accordingly, the child

is looking for experiences, and in every moment of his waking life, he shows this original and spontaneous eagerness to get more experience, and become acquainted with the world of things and of people about him. The parent or teacher does not therefore have to *originate* these activities, does not have to *implant* them, they are already implanted in the child's makeup. What the teacher or parent has to do, is just to *supply* proper objects and surroundings upon which these impulses may assert themselves, so that the child may get the most out of them. (LW 17:215; italics added)

In this context, Dewey asks several questions about learning: Are there less apparent but intellectual appetites that are "awake, alive, alert, and looking for their food" during the school years? Are there key differences between school classrooms that are aware of these appetites and those that aren't? How are the answers to these two questions related to learning in schools (LW 17:216–217)? His own answers to these questions follow. To begin with, he claims that there are intellectual appetites that are discernible, that teachers need to recognize them, and that they must provide "the intellectual and spiritual food for these tendencies to feed upon" (LW 17:216). In addition, he argues that classrooms developed on a natural learning theory (children are naturally active and, therefore, inquisitive) do differ sharply from those that are based on a natural depravity theory (children are naturally active and, therefore, bad). Thus his answer to the third question, rooted in the times and places of his life, is partially illustrated in Table 66.1. The depth and range of Dewey's ideas on this specific point extend far beyond the content of this table, however.

Dewey's next step in explaining his micro-perspective of learning is to note that natural impulses usually express themselves through the muscles and movement. Similarly, the child's mental activity reveals itself in her or his physical activity. As a result, physical movement is as much "a vital part of the very process of learning" as sensation is. Sensation is one-half of the learning circle; movement is the other half. The circle or process is one, nevertheless. In the midst of sensations and movements, however, the mind is not passive; it is active just as the physical person is active. Physical movement, in particular, indicates that the mind is active and selective, for "the loving eye, the inclined head, the caressing hand, are all signs" of its activity and selection (LW 17:217). Therefore, mental and physical activity occurs when sensations are experienced. In turn, it is clear that sensation isn't isolated from mental and physical activity. Mental activity, sensation, and movement are a triad in that sensation "is the beginning of a movement which would investigate, would explore, and find out more about the thing producing the sensation" (LW 17:217). Even young children, because their minds are active and they are learning, make decisions or selections in different ways that influence further learning: (1) by attending to some sensations and not others and (2) by facilitating movement in some directions and not others. Instead of sensation and movements alone determining the learning process, the triad is involved: mind, sensation, and movement. Plus there is the influence of impulses and the purposing of the learner. Hence, neither mechanistic nor deterministic forces *cause* learning. They merely influence it. Learning is an ongoing, active, and selective process, not an unusual, passive, or stimulus–response outcome.

As a person matures, she or he learns to be more selective of responses to sensations (LW 17:218). The active, developing mind influences the learning process in the youth and adult in ways that it usually doesn't in a young child. On the other hand, this is not to say that the young child is "mindless" or doesn't use her or his mind. The opposite is the case even though greater maturity provides greater control of learning opportunities for older children and adults. As the learner develops as a complete person, selection is more conscious and made in the light of moral development. Throughout the learning process, then, the gradually developing but active mind initiates learning, selects stimuli, and responses to environmental realities. There is sensation and movement, impression and expression, mental income and mental outcome, instruction and construction, and ideas and applications. Collectively, they constitute the micro-perspective learning process (LW 17:218–221). The inseparable triad—the mind, sensations, and movements—are all involved in learning but, ultimately, "learning becomes part of ourselves only through the medium of conduct, and so leads to character" (LW 17:222). Conduct involves stopping to think of consequences, learning to select options that allow for present and future growth, and controlling one's impulses and desires until they are converted and transformed into "a more comprehensive and coherent plan of activity" (LW 13:41).

When Dewey's micro-perspective of learning is situated in a broader context, it is more clearly and correctly understood. His macro-perspective of learning provides this broader human, physical, material, intellectual, and interpretative context for understanding the activity and the learning of the maturing student.

A MACRO-PERSPECTIVE ON LEARNING

Dewey's broader approach to learning continues to focus on the learner, but he adds several critical elements that his micro-perspective forces to the background or largely ignores, exempli gratia, the teacher, other students, and the pedagogical and physical environment. The dynamic nature of the student, of course, remains important. Yet, the teacher (as a professional and as a person), environment (social, physical, and intellectual), and pedagogy (specific and general) move more to the foreground. The student's interaction, from a critical frame of reference, is with her or his environment, because it includes, among other things, her or his teacher and the teacher's pedagogy.

The interaction of the learner and the environment involves a possible but not necessary linear flow of experiences that begins with (1) the instinctive reaching out of the student and her or his (2) ensuing actions. Following these activities, the learner (3) encounters barriers in the environment, which, in turn, (4) causes tension and (5) disequilibrium and results later in (6) problem-solving experiences, (7) adaptation to the barriers, (8) reinstatement of personal harmony, and (9) reestablishment of personal equilibrium. This learning scenario, as described, may be interpreted as a somewhat standard but not necessarily ideal one if—and this is an important qualifier—the cycle is always believed to be completed in an expeditious fashion. But not all learning experiences even complete the cycle, much less complete it without interruptions and reconfigurations. In fact, the cycle of interactions may deteriorate and collapse at any point in time for a variety of reasons. Also, the phases of the cycle are not necessarily discrete, separated from one another but overlap and commingle. This rather untidy depiction of learning is supported by observation and experience, Dewey believes, and, consequently, is important for the educator to remember. In his theory, Dewey sees the learner entering, exiting, wandering, and reentering the learning cycle as she or he prefers or as she or he is drawn into specific aspects of the environment again.

The complete learning cycle or, we could say, whole learning experience includes the energizing influence of the instincts, purposes, and interests of the learner as she or he enters into an activity and encounters obstacles and disequilibrium as well as success in solving problems and returning to inner harmony. Learning, then, occurs at the micro and macro levels concurrently. The energy, activity, thinking, and selection of the learner cannot be discretely separated into just one of the spheres. Learning, therefore, may occur as impulses urge the learner to act as well as during her or his initial action, meeting barriers, undergoing of stress and imbalance, but particularly as she or he thinks through, analyzes, and solves problems. Likewise, learning may occur as the person adapts to her or his environment or the barriers encountered and, to a lesser degree, the ensuing harmony and balance enjoyed. The student's attention throughout the interaction and learning is on personal matters at first and, if she or he grows socially and morally, others' interests later. Learning, then, is primarily a social event or experience from Dewey's perspective, not essentially an individual activity. Inclusively, it is a natural, personal, social, and moral experience that changes the individual and promotes individual and societal growth in the future.

Learning from micro- and macro-perspectives, therefore, involves the whole person in her or his complete environment. Figure 66.1 depicts this complete interactive learning experience. Dewey's holistic learning theory, therefore, ultimately includes both the elements and ideas noted in the micro-perspective as well as the elements and ideas discussed in connection with the macro-perspective. Of course, the depicted "boundaries" that separate the micro and macro spheres do not actually exist in Dewey's mind and shouldn't in ours.

Dewey believes that, ideally, the person or student is active in her or his physical environment as well as social environment. As the child pursues her or his purposes through activities that the teacher has created, she or he regularly encounters barriers or problems and these produce, among other things, personal stress. The tension, if amply robust, may result in an inner imbalance or disequilibrium for the student. Since it is somewhat natural to like order in one's life, the student may then begin to think through the problem or attempt to address it. When the thinking is both reflective and fruitful, it provides the student with options to consider as she or he adjusts. Ordinarily, then, a person is stimulated to surmount an obstacle so that she or he can achieve her or his consciously selected purposes. Eventually, when the process and outcome yield a successful conclusion, internal balance returns and the person enjoys another state of equilibrium. Shortly, however, the student reenters the cycle as she or he focuses on a new purpose and pursues it.

In reality, learning is probably a great deal more complex—not to mention chaotic—than described for at least two reasons. First of all, it seems likely that the learner is often

Figure 66.1
A Holistic Interactive Learning Experience

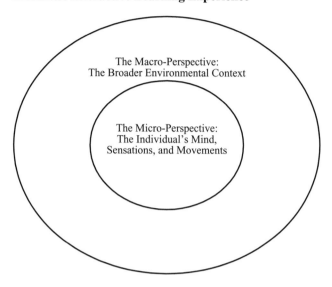

The Macro-Perspective:
The Broader Environmental Context

The Micro-Perspective:
The Individual's Mind,
Sensations, and Movements

multi-purposing as she or he learns and that one of her or his purposes may reduce the efficiency of pursuing other goals. The learner also is probably prone to enter, exit, and reenter the cycle at different times and after encounters with more than one obstacle. She or he might, for instance, encounter tension with one purpose and retreat to another school task or abandon the first task permanently. Or her or his disequilibrium may fade during class and return in another class or during the evening. The problem solving desired in one course or experience may actually occur later in the day in another class or on the way to school the next morning. As a result, the student may return to school the next day, then, not with an obstacle, tension, or disequilibrium but with satisfaction and explanations about how to adapt to the obstacle and move on to other challenges.

Second, the description given does not convey the complexity of the classroom that has twenty-five to thirty students. When thirty students are interacting with one another in activities, the factors that influence learning are exponentially increased and, thereby, the possibility of educative and miseducative experiences increases. Only a sophisticated, experienced teacher can take advantage of these diverse variables and students and turn them into desirable learning situations for each person. With pedagogical experts, "learning is controlled by two great principles: one is participation in something inherently worth while, or undertaken on its own account, [and] the other is perception of the relationship of means to consequences" (LW 2:56). Consequently, teachers spend a great deal of their time planning for participatory learning activities that enable students to understand the relationship and means of what they are doing to the learning outcomes.

CONCLUSION

Learning, for Dewey, is obviously a complex and, often, chaotic activity. The person is active in learning from her or his moments. Impulses and selections are a part of the process. But this micro-perspective understanding of learning needs to be merged with the macro-perspective, including the environmental sphere of others in the classroom and school. When combined, these two perspectives of learning create a personal, natural, social, and moral learning process in which a person is consistently looking for experiences and becoming more and more familiar with the world of things, people, and ideas. In this process, the teacher's job is not to attempt to pour information into the learner. Rather, she or he should "supply proper objects and surroundings" in order that "the child may get the most out of them." This learning process also results in part from the learner's activity that results in encountering obstacles, tension, and disequilibrium. Likewise, she or he thinks through problems, adapts to new environments, and experiences personal harmony and equilibrium. Dewey's holistic learning theory, therefore, provides a framework that may enable the educator to think more clearly and comprehensively as she or he builds educational environments that entice and guide learners to become independent thinkers, problem solvers, and community builders. So, we return to where we started: a well-conceived curriculum provides learning experiences that involve the whole person interacting with a community of learners, including the teacher.

SUGGESTED READING

Boydston, J. A. (Ed.). (1967/1972). *The Early Works of John Dewey, 1882–1898* (Vols. 1–5). Carbondale: Southern Illinois University Press.

Boydston, J. A. (Ed.). (1976/1983). *The Middle Works of John Dewey, 1899–1924* (Vols. 1–15). Carbondale: Southern Illinois University Press.

Boydston, J. A. (Ed.). (1981/1991). *The Later Works of John Dewey, 1925–1953* (Vols. 1–17). Carbondale: Southern Illinois University Press.

CHAPTER 67

Crash or Crash Through[1]: Part 1—Learning from Enacted Curricula

KENNETH TOBIN

Amira[2]: I'm going to be a doctor. Oh, I'm going to be a doctor. Ain't nobody going to stop me from being a doctor.

When I first met Amira she was a thirteen-year-old, Grade 9, biology student. She loved biology and was by far the best science student in her class. No problem appeared too challenging for her, she made an effort to respond to most questions asked by her teacher, and frequently her oral contributions overlapped with her teacher's talk. Especially in biology, Amira was a leader in the classroom, an active participant in lectures, small groups, and labs. She did her homework and was on the lookout to learn at every opportunity.

Amira lived with her mother and siblings in inner-city Philadelphia and attended a neighborhood high school in which most students were African American, living in circumstances of economic poverty. The school, referred to as City High, had an enrollment of more than two thousand students and, in an endeavor to create safer, more personalized environments, the school administrators created ten Academies, or schools within a school. Amira was in the Health Academy, which had five teachers and about two hundred students, mostly females. The Academy had one teacher for each subject area, Mr. Kendall being the science teacher.

Amira was a motivated learner and accepted responsibility for maintaining a productive learning environment during science classes. During a lesson on genetics, in which I was a researcher and coteacher with Ms. Stein, a prospective biology teacher, Kendall, and another researcher, there was insufficient time for the final planned activity. Rather than start a hands-on activity and be unable to finish, the coteachers decided not to begin. Fifteen minutes remained and, without further planning, Stein didn't have the experience to maintain a central teaching role. She looked fatigued as she announced to the students that Kendall would teach them about the dihybrid cross. Although he appeared startled by the announcement Kendall nodded his head in agreement and confidently strode toward the overhead projector, his mind feverishly reconstructing how he typically taught the topic.

"It's 9, 3, 3, 1," he said as he switched on the overhead projector and sketched a four-by-four matrix. However, despite 30 years of experience of teaching biology, as he considered what to teach he did not recall the salient starting points to get to the final solution. Left with no viable alternatives he tried to recall the pathway to a solution as he taught, frequently back-tracking as he searched for the right place to start.

A videotape of Kendall teaching at the overhead projector shows me at the side, interacting with students and on occasion talking animatedly to Stein. At one time I suggest quietly to Kendall that he let the students work out the phenotypic ratios associated with a dihybrid cross. However, Kendall was resolved to teach in an expository way from the front of the room and he never seriously considered an alternative division of labor among the participants (especially student-centered problem solving). He taught "off the cuff" and inadvertently made errors from which he was unable to recover. His confusion was apparent in repeated attempts to fill in the cells of his Punnett Square, nonverbal signals of frustration when his attempts failed, and his use of expressions such as "sorry," "can't remember," and "I got it wrong."

With the exception of Amira, the students quickly lost interest and ceased to participate. Amira knew how to solve problems like this and had well-developed ideas on how they should be taught. She had a strong sense of what Kendall was trying to teach, enjoyed genetics ("the dihybrid cross is fun") and her aptitude in math afforded an intuitive sense of how to proceed ("Yeah. I love math"). Unlike her peers she assumed collective responsibility for maintaining the flow of the lesson, and her efforts to make sense of the problem, ask questions, and solve the dihybrid cross were pronounced, helpful, and unique. Amira noticed Kendall's errors and offered suggestions in a continuous flow of dialogue. Toward the end of the lesson she worked on her own solution while Kendall continued to address the whole class, focusing intently on the overhead transparency on which he was creating his solution. However, his attempts were futile and the lesson ended with Kendall trying different permutations on the sides of his matrix and the students filing out of the room, headed to their next class.

WHAT IS AN APPROPRIATE LEARNING ENVIRONMENT?

In this section I place the vignette of the dihybrid cross in a historical context of the goals of science education, examining the relative emphases on concepts and inquiry skills. In opting for a perspective on science education that is grounded in cultural sociology I explore the salience of knowing and doing in ways that are both aware and unaware to learners and of the importance of being able to use what is known in anticipatory, appropriate, and timely ways.

Concepts or Skills

Historically science learning has been considered in terms of a conceptual perspective on science (i.e., facts, concepts, principles and big ideas) and then dichotomously as conceptual and inquiry skills (often referred to as process skills). During the curriculum revolution of the 1960s some of the teachers' guides and textbooks took polar positions, emphasizing either conceptual science or inquiry skills. However, as curriculum development proceeded into the 1970s and beyond there was growing awareness that the goals of science education should incorporate a balance of concepts, inquiry, and attitudes and values. Instructional models were developed and infused into resource materials such as textbooks and teachers' guides so that in science activities students were actively involved and had opportunities to construct their own knowledge through engagement, exploration, explanation, elaboration and evaluation (Bybee et al., 1989). This approach aimed to ensure that students used inquiry skills to create conceptual models for their experiences with science.

Constructivism, in its many forms, focused attention on the necessity for individuals to have rich sensory experiences with phenomena and opportunities for social collaboration with peers and the teacher as they made sense of their experiences in terms of what they already knew. Prior knowledge, negotiation, consensus building, and increased understandings of canonical science became hallmarks of learning science. In many science programs, emphases on learning science by doing science assumed a central position as did small-group and whole-class discussions in which students had opportunities to collaborate with peers and use the language of science.

Ways to Know and Do Science

A key goal in science education, which extends beyond constructivism and its emphasis on conceptual change, is to be fluent in using science to attain success in different fields. One way to address this goal is to regard science as a form of culture (Sewell, 1999), a system of schema (i.e., the conceptual side of science), and associated practices (i.e., patterns of action) that are enacted within fields (bounded by space and time), which are structured by resources (i.e., material, human, and schematic). Hence, opportunities to enact and learn science, in a field such as a classroom, depend on the resources available and the extent to which they can be used to meet the participants' goals. I use agency (Sewell, 1992) to refer to an individual's power to act in a field and use its resources to meet particular goals (i.e., appropriate the field's structures). As participants act, their actions are resources for themselves and others to pursue learning and other goals they might have (e.g., to earn respect of peers). Hence, as Kendall spoke and wrote on the overhead transparency, his actions were resources that participants could access and appropriate through attentive listening and other forms of participation. Kendall assumed a central role in which he expected everybody else to listen, observe, and silently work along with him, thereby restricting legitimate opportunities for participation. In spite of Kendall's implicit expectations, Amira created opportunities for participation. Her talk often overlapped with Kendall's and became a resource for the learning of all participants—for Amira, to clarify her thinking—for Kendall, a flow of suggestions on how to proceed—and for peers, ideas to evaluate and possibly remember.

Considering science education as culture focuses on processes that reproduce and transform the canons of science, not only as schema, but also as associated practices, some of which are unconscious. Like constructivism the concern is to ascertain what learners know and can do and structure learning environments accordingly. What does it mean to take into account the knowledge of the learner and teach him or her accordingly? What participants can do refers to their interactions with the structures of a field—the extent to which they appropriate resources, through successful interactions with materials, other persons, and schema (e.g., ideas, attitudes, values, rules, conventions). Part of doing involves participants' being aware of what can be and is being done. However, perhaps most culture is enacted without awareness. When particular resources are available, participants can anticipate their use and then deploy them in routines built from prior experiences of being in places like this one using resources like these. For example, if students have had prior experiences in a science classroom they may have developed dispositions to act appropriately in similar circumstances in anticipatory and timely ways.

Because the practices of individuals are part of a dynamic structure, a critical focus for science educators is to find ways to expand agency and ensure that all individuals can use their cultural resources fully to reproduce and transform the culture of science. As well as drawing attention to the salience to learning of the resources that can be appropriated, a cultural perspective draws attention to the fluency of enactment and reminds educators that when culture is enacted flow is often an important criterion in being able to use resources in anticipatory, timely, and appropriate ways to produce successful interactions. Hence, it is a goal for Amira to learn science in ways that would allow her to act scientifically in her lifeworld without having to be conscious of what she is doing and why she is going to do it.

The unusual circumstances associated with Kendall's having to teach without being fully prepared provides insights into some very central issues associated with learning. My sense is that Amira would have solved the problem if she had been asked to do so in an individualized task. She had the necessary prior knowledge and the motivation to formulate a solution. Amira was determined and this was exactly what she wanted from education—interest, challenge, and relevance. As we learned six months later, she remembered the solution was 9, 3, 3, 1 as Kendall stated from the outset, but she did not appear to learn from his subsequent efforts to obtain a solution in class time. His efforts to teach through exposition did not provide a structure to allow Amira or others in the class to solve the problem. However, his teaching did allow Amira to be actively involved as she interacted verbally with Kendall, attempted solutions in her notebook, and continuously made public suggestions on what to try next. However, there appeared to be few others in the class who were motivated or prepared to work alone in the structural environment that unfolded.

Structures can limit opportunities for some participants to successfully interact and learn, in which case their agency is truncated. From this perspective Kendall's practices during his teaching of the dihybrid cross may have truncated the agency of most students by limiting their possibilities for action and thereby minimizing both the number and types of resources available for appropriation. Kendall struggled and was not fluent while attempting to solve the dihybrid cross problem and his efforts were characterized by starts, stops, and changes in direction. However, even though most students lost focus as the lesson progressed it cannot be assumed that they learned nothing of science. Each student experienced a seasoned teacher struggling to solve a problem, persevering when he could not generate the correct solution, and continuously talking science as he thought aloud in successive attempts. The students were aware that the teacher knew the correct solution was 9, 3, 3, 1 and observed his serious efforts to show why this was correct. It is possible that by being in the classroom with Kendall as he endeavored to solve the problem of the dihybrid cross, the participants (students and coteachers) learned something about science even though they might not be aware of what they learned.

Looking back at what happened in the vignette leads me to suggest that the optimal learning environment is one in which students are active in producing structures to expand the agency of others in the class. Hence, setting up an environment in which participants interact overtly with material resources and others has the potential to enhance learning. Although I would have preferred more active and sustained forms of involvement, the students' experiences of the dihybrid cross allowed for their peripheral participation in problem solving and opportunities to hear and remember facts about genetics, witness how mathematics is used in explicating key ideas in science, and see how the big ideas of science are built on complex interrelationships among other science concepts. However, had Kendall followed my suggestion to allow the students to figure out the dihybrid cross for themselves, they could have been organized into small groups, a different array of human resources and actions would have structured their experiences, and the additional resources might have expanded their agency and hence their opportunities to learn. If the students were assigned the task of verifying that the solution to the dihybrid cross was 9, 3, 3, 1 it is probable that peers in Amira's group would have solved the problem, with Amira providing the structure necessary for them to succeed. In other groups the students would probably have required more structure, which in this case was available because of the presence of four coteachers. If only one teacher was available, then he or she could have provided each group with appropriate structure by moving from group to group, providing verbal and nonverbal assistance as desirable.

COGENERATIVE DIALOGUING

As a part of our research in urban schools we have instituted a form of activity in which the classroom (co)teachers, researchers, and two to three students meet as soon as possible after a lesson to review what happened, consider changes to the roles of participants, and negotiate consensus on what would happen in subsequent lessons (Roth and Tobin, 2002). The activities are called cogenerative dialogues, because their goal is to "cogenerate" collective agreements through dialogues in which all participants are encouraged to represent their perspectives truthfully, forcefully, and respectfully. Active listening of all participants is central to effective cogenerative dialogues. Our research suggests that participation in cogenerative dialogues allows students and teachers to communicate effectively across the boundaries of ethnicity, class, and age (Tobin et al., 2005).

Amira was selected and agreed to participate in a cogenerative dialogue concerning the lesson described above. Because of the way the lesson finished we entered the cogenerative dialogue abuzz with chatter about what could and perhaps should have happened in the last segment involving the dihybrid cross. As we approached the table around which we would be seated, the two researchers argued over different ways to set up the axes on the Punnett Square, Stein explained how she preferred to teach dihybrid crosses, and Kendall expressed frustration at losing the thread of how to teach it. Amira contended that she had just about figured it out and then she focused on the way that Kendall taught the final activity. In her analyses, Amira demonstrated a keen sense of how to be an effective learner and how teachers could best mediate the learning of students like her. Her advice to the coteachers, especially Kendall, included the following incisive comment.

Make an example to himself before he shows it to us. You understand what I'm saying? Like if I was to write a book, I would write it myself, read it myself to make sure that I didn't make any mistakes. And if I did I'd correct them right there before I make a good copy of it . . . a rough draft. He would have to make a preplan before he goes over it with us. That's the only thing I would think he would have to change to get a little more control because some of them kids is out of control.

Amira's analyses of teaching were not confined only to weaknesses in teaching nor to planning and organizing the class. In a good-humored way she chided Kendall on his tendency to tell stories and thereby lose focus. Also, Amira made the following comments about Stein:

Ms. Stein had a lot of control. Ms. Stein always got what she want whether we got what we wanted or not. Majority of the class passes, and she . . . mainly what she wanted is to get at least 80% of that class to pass, and you could just tell that by the way she taught. She wanted to get the majority of the class to pass. She got everybody except for like three or four people passing that class. And that is because either they didn't come to school or just didn't turn their work in.

Amira also commented on the extent to which Stein always used materials and equipment in her classes and supported her oral presentations with charts and well-constructed teaching aids. That is, she embraced the value of teachers using materials to structure learning in ways that expanded students' agency by increasing the number and variety of resources to access and appropriate. Amira's comments also recognized the value of having high expectations and the energy to reach out to all learners, even if their levels of motivation were not high initially. That is, Amira recognized the importance of teaching practices that led students to active participation and, in so doing, produce positive emotional energy.

Embedded within the remark about Stein having adequate control is the issue of how she was able to maintain appropriate participation and shared responsibility for learning. Stein did not always have quiet and well-ordered classrooms. In a one-year field experience she never gave up on her students. Every day she was well prepared to an extent that was obvious to her students, a sign that she was a teacher who cared for them. She got them actively involved, made strenuous efforts to create social capital, and never backed down when students needed firm discipline. Despite her slight build and cultural otherness (i.e., blond hair and white skin), Stein broke up fights and quieted students when they were boisterous. These practices earned the respect of students, who regarded Stein as very cool, caring, and anxious to better their education.

Amira was sensitive to the need for teachers to prevent students from disrupting the learning of others. Consistently, she connected this to the level of planning, the consistency of effort in class, and the demonstration of care for learning and welfare of students. Amira was concerned for the well-being of not only the students, but also the teachers. For example, she wondered how her mathematics teacher could stand the stress of teaching without more control of disruptive student practices. In an excerpt of an interview with me, Amira made the following comments about her mathematics class.

You don't get nothin' done in Ms. Smith's class. Ms. Smith has no control. She has no strategy. She has nothin'. I'm like how have you been a teacher for as long as you've been a teacher if you have no control, no organization? She loses everything. I'm like I don't understand how you've been a teacher for as long as you've been. And I be like Ms. Smith, come here. And I tell her to watch what I'm watchin'. I be like don't say nothin', just watch. This one turned around. This one talkin'. This one eatin'. This one playin' with the calculators. I'm like, what is this? This make no sense.

The above comments are salient because it is unusual, a contradiction, for students to explicitly evaluate and provide a teacher with feedback on her teaching performance. They show how Amira's participation in cogenerative dialogues equipped her to speak with her teacher about the quality of teaching and learning in the mathematics class. This seems especially important since Amira enjoys mathematics yet was failing in the class. Adopting shared responsibility for the teaching and learning in the class is consistent with our goals for cogenerative dialogues, in which Amira participated in her science class. However, Smith had not participated in cogenerative dialogues and may not have welcomed unsolicited feedback on her teaching. Hence Amira's comments to Smith may have been detrimental to subsequent interactions between them and the teacher's constructions of Amira as a mathematics learner. Educators should take care to protect students who, having expanded their roles to support their own learning, could end up in hot water with their teachers.

Students can experience identity problems if in one subject area they participate in collective bargaining about the roles of teachers and students and in other subject areas they do not. Similarly, teachers who have not participated in cogenerative dialogues can be threatened by the changing roles of students and efforts on their part to assume more power in relation to what happens in classrooms. Amira's initiative in adopting the role of critic and teacher educator was against the grain since the roles of students traditionally have been crafted as less powerful than those of the teacher and usually it is regarded as disrespectful for students to advise a teacher on how to improve her teaching.[3] If cogenerative dialogues are to reach their potential it will be important for teachers and students within a community to accept the expanded roles that inevitably unfold.

Although Amira is willing to assume responsibility for collective actions for agreed-upon goals, it is important to acknowledge that her perspective is just one of many to be considered. Amira knew what student practices should be eliminated and made suggestions on how to redirect students and enact a curriculum to minimize disruptions. Her arguments were rational and reflected a student perspective that is very much needed in urban schools. Even so, it is by no means certain that her suggestions would lead to sustainable learning environments that support the learning of science, and they do not take account of those practices that are unintended and beyond conscious awareness. Vigorous debate, preferably supported by video vignettes of what happens in classrooms, is necessary to illuminate roles and practices from a variety of theoretical perspectives. Accordingly, there is some benefit in having outsiders from time to time participate in coteaching of a class and associated cogenerative dialogues (e.g., university researchers, school administrators). What seems most important is for the teacher and his or her students to adopt a spirit of inquiry about teaching and learning and build a sense of community associated with collective goals and expanded roles for the different types of participants. It seems likely that through collective responsibility students, teachers, and other stakeholders could pull together with the intention of increasing learning through active participation in science.

DID SHE KNOW THE SCIENCE?

Some six months after the lesson on genetics I asked Amira what she remembered about the dihybrid cross and how it was taught. The following three vignettes capture some glimpses of her knowledge and the key steps involved in arriving at an understanding of the dihybrid cross.

Off to a Good Start

Amira sat down and stared alternately at the blank writing pad and her lunch. "I remember that it is 9, 3, 3, 1 but I'm mad at myself. I can't remember what it stands for." With that Amira began to eat her lunch and I started to draw the 16 cells of the 4 × 4 matrix. I did not get far before Amira reached out for my pen. "You do the monohybrid for father and mother first," she said as she drew and labeled two 2 × 2 Punnett squares. "What will we have?" queried Amira. "Let's have hair and eye color," I suggested. Amira labeled the matrix for the father as E, e for eye color and H, h for hair color. For the mother she selected recessive alleles for both traits (i.e., e, e and h, h). Skillfully Amira set up the 4 × 4 Punnett square with the four possible alleles for the father across the top (HE, He, hE, he) and for the mother down the left-hand side (he, he, he, he). "This is not 9, 3, 3, 1," she said immediately. "What is it?" I asked. "It's 4, 4, 4, 4." Amira responded intuitively. Without having to work all of the combinations she knew. However, she methodically worked all combinations and then described each phenotypically. Within a short time she had solved the problem and listed the solution as 4 Hh, ee brown, blue; 4 Hh, Ee brown, brown; 4 hh, ee blond, blue; 4 hh, Ee blond, brown.

Getting Closer

Amira smiled as she crunched into a mouthful of her sandwich. She seemed pleased with her success. Lately she was not experiencing too much success at school. Just today she was tossed out of French for failing to participate actively and her grades in English and computing were much lower than she wanted. But Amira was good at mathematics and genetics was a love of hers. She was enjoying herself. Once again Amira selected the alleles for hair and eye color for the father (H, h; E, E) and mother (H, h; e, e). Quickly she created the four possible gametes for the father (HE, HE, he, he) and mother (He, He, he, he). "It's 4, 4, 4, 4 again," she declared. "But it is different this time." Amira recorded the genotypes and alongside of each wrote the frequency and the phenotype. Then she combined those that had the same phenotype to obtain 8 brown, brown; 4 brown, blue; and 4 blond, blue.

They're Both Heterozygous!

"I know. I know. They will both be heterozygous on each trait." With a look of triumph on her face Amira created the 2×2 crosses for the mother and father. She then entered the possible gametes for father and mother as she had done before. Inadvertently she made a mistake in entering the possible gametes for the father (HE, hE, HE, he), but neither she nor I noticed. Accordingly, when Amira followed her routine she arrived at a frequency distribution of genotypes and associated phenotypes that she knew to be incorrect. Carefully she inspected the data in the matrix and admonished herself for making a careless error. "You've got to be careful," she announced as she changed the columns for the father to read (HE, hE, He, he). She corrected the information in the cells and turned her attention to her lunch. There was no need to finish the details—Amira knew she had it. "9, 3, 3, 1," she declared with a broad smile. "It has got to be the phenotypes."

IMPLICATIONS FOR LEARNING

The example of the dihybrid cross illustrates that, even though the full solution was never taught explicitly, and Amira did not seek the full solution either from books, the Internet, or other sources, six months after the lesson she had the resources to fully solve the problem, explain it discursively, and quickly identify and remediate flaws in her logic. The structure I provide in drawing the matrix and responding to her queries and suggestions is sufficient to support her agency and deeper learning. In this example, several important factors align. Amira is intensely interested in genetics and despite her failure to thrive in school mathematics she loves to solve puzzles involving pattern recognition and generation, combinations, and probability. Her prior knowledge and drive to know more are central to her deep learning and problem-solving success in this example. Also central is the provision of sufficient time for her to work out solutions, test them, and self-evaluate the adequacy of her final solution.

What is not clear from this example is the importance of Amira remembering that the solution is 9, 3, 3, 1. Could she have solved the problem without that knowledge and without me drawing the 4×4 matrix? Possibly she would have created these structures if I had not been present—we cannot know for sure. What is interesting though is that Kendall had similar structures, but under the pressure of having to teach others he could not proceed to a solution. I am not implying that Kendall could not solve the problem, just that in the context of having to teach others he needed additional structures to produce a solution.

The vignette about learning the dihybrid cross is salient because it highlights several advantages of thinking of learning as cultural production, thereby advancing beyond the mechanistic ways in which educational psychology often frames learning in terms of the cognitive processes of individuals. An examination of Amira's participation in a science classroom shows how her power to act, that is to access and appropriate resources, is dynamic and constantly unfolding. Her agency is mediated not only by her own beliefs, values, and goals, but also by the schema and practices of all others in a community. Hence, the material and human resources of a setting and schema such as rules, conventions, and ideology are central parts of the dialectical relationship between agency and structure, a relationship that mediates learning in a classroom. Amira's interest in biology and mathematics and her desire to become a doctor and hence do well at school are schematic resources that mediate the ways in which she accesses the somewhat limited resources to support her learning. Even though her teacher's practices appear to truncate the agency of most students in the class, Amira acts and thereby creates structures to support her own learning and the teaching and learning of others.

A key advantage of exploring teaching and learning in terms of the agency–structure dialectic is that efforts to improve learning do not focus only on individuals. Here the focus is on creating collective agreements and responsibilities for the quality of teaching and all learning within a community. Because agency is recursively related to structure, cultural production is always contextualized, involving interactions with material, human, and symbolic resources. If interactions are to be successful, participants in a community must have effective social networks and, within a particular field, those with the respect of others can use their social capital to access resources and enact culture in ways that reproduce and transform the culture of science.

CRASH OR CRASH THROUGH

Will Amira crash through or will she crash? Of course the metaphor of crashing connotes many images, from sleeping to meeting a grisly end in a motor vehicle accident. The vignettes about the dihybrid cross are evidence of an adolescent female with the power to coordinate mathematical and abstract thinking with science concepts such as genotype, phenotype, heterozygous alleles, and dominant and recessive genes. Amira could work out the details of the dihybrid cross despite her teacher having struggled to present the ideas in a whole-class activity. Although she was unsuccessful in completing the task in class, she was clearly on the right track. Even though the topic was not taught in subsequent lessons, in an interview six months later Amira worked out the details of the phenotypic ratios for a dihybrid cross when both alleles are heterozygous. In so doing she demonstrated an impressive knowledge of the culture of science and reiterated her confidence in being a successful scientist. Amira had an identity of being interested in and good at science. But how is her ability to solve problems that she has not previously been taught evidence of agency that can be transferred into fields not associated with learning introductory biology? Can Amira appropriate the culture of science to meet her own goals, especially those pertaining to academic success and life outside of school? If only success depended on Amira's determination to succeed. However, her agency is interconnected with the structures of the many fields in which she participates. Accordingly, whether or not Amira meets her goals is dialectically interconnected with the practices of others and schema such as expectations and rules, at least some of which are potentially hegemonic. In the next of this two-part series of chapters I examine contextual factors that structure and mediate Amira's achievement in school and progress toward her goal of becoming a doctor.

ACKNOWLEDGMENT

The research in this chapter is supported by the National Science Foundation under Grant No. REC-0107022. Any opinions, findings, and conclusions or recommendations expressed in this chapter are those of the author and do not necessarily reflect the views of the National Science Foundation.

NOTES

1. The philosophy of Edward Gough Whitlam, the former labor prime minister of Australia for three years, Dec 1972 to November 1975, was to crash through or crash. In the end Whitlam was to crash when Sir John Kerr, the Queen's appointed representative in Australia, removed him from office. The act of removing an elected national leader was highly controversial.

2. Pseudonyms are used throughout this paper.

3. There is a hint of disrespect in the interview that is not evident when Amira approaches teachers with suggestions for help.

REFERENCES

Bybee, R., Buchwald, C. E., Crissman, S., Heil, D., Kuerbis, P., Matsumoto, C. and McInerney W. (1989). *Science and Technology Education for Elementary Years: Frameworks for Curriculum and Instruction*. Washington, DC: The National Center for Improving Science Education.

Roth, W-M., and Tobin, K. (2002). *At the Elbows of Another: Learning to Teach Through Coteaching*. New York, NY: Peter Lang Publishing.

Sewell, W. H. (1992). A theory of structure: Duality, agency, and transformation. *American Journal of Sociology*, 98, 1–29.

Sewell, W. H. (1999). The concept(s) of culture. In V. E. Bonnell and L. Hunt (Eds.), *Beyond the Cultural Turn: New Directions in the Study of Society and Culture* (pp. 35–61). Berkeley, CA: University of California Press.

Tobin, K., Elmesky, R., and Seiler, G. (Eds). (2005). *Improving Urban Science Education: New Roles for Teachers, Students and Researchers*. New York: Rowman & Littlefield.

CHAPTER 68

Crash or Crash Through: Part 2—Structures That Inhibit Learning

KENNETH TOBIN

Based on what we know of Amira from the previous chapter, her future looks bright. Amira's goal of becoming a doctor seems within her grasp and her connections with our research team will open the door to opportunities for her to study advanced-level science while still at high school. However, there are worrying signs that her academic performance is slipping, especially in English and mathematics. Also, Amira's lifestyle is changing for the worse. During a meeting with her, after the dihybrid cross interview, Amira was not her bright self and looked downcast. Events in her home had changed appreciably and the impacts on Amira's identity, participation at school, and achievement were significant. In the following section Amira describes some issues from home and school that mediate her participation in science and other school subjects.

Slowly But Surely I'm Losing It

Amira: Every now and then for a long period of time I'll get really bad headaches everyday. Like last year from about the midsection of the year, just before changing classes and right after changing classes, that whole period of time, I had really, really bad headache at the end of the school day, right after lunch. And like this year ever since the beginning of the school year for like a week at a time, I have a really, really bad headaches where my eyes would water, my eyes would be red, my head would dry up for like a week, and then it'll go away. I'll be fine for like two weeks and then I'll get another headache.

My Aunt Tracey got evicted ... something happened with her house, and they kicked her out. My big sister was living with my Aunt Tracey. My brother started being at home more. And his daughter and his baby's mom moved in. Only two people clean up in the house. Every now and then my brother would help, but only me and my older sister clean up in the house. There's other people supposed to be helping, but don't nobody else do it. And I get really bad headaches.

I can't be in a house everyday all day and then have my mom nagging me about gaining weight. I'm like, "Mom, I'm normally out running about. I'm normally on my feet." And then she will nag me. "You look like you gaining weight. You need to start doing more stuff...." As soon as summer hit I'll be outside all day if I'm not baby-sitting my niece. If I'm not baby-sitting, I'm never in the house during the summer except ... I don't come in the house until 2:00 in the morning during the summer. Nine times out of ten, I'm on the steps from like 10 to 2 just sitting there. But during the day, I'm on my bike, I'm on my skates, I'm at a skating party, or I'm at a party at the swimming pool. I'm doing everything. I'm at the movies. I'm walking around South Street. I'm doing everything during the day. So I don't have time to sit and gain weight. I'm so active during the summer and now I'm in the house. I get really bored and I get headaches.

I want to move out of my mom's house, but for real I don't want to leave my mom. I don't want to move to my father's 'cause we don't get along. I don't want to move in with my grandmother 'cause we don't get along. I really do want to stay living with my mom, but I can't be where she's going to just put all the chores on me. If I'm not there, she can't put them on me. Then I'm going to feel bad for my older sister, because that's who it's going to fall back on 'cause there ain't nobody else going to do it, but I can't do it no more.

Yesterday I came this close from cussing out my mom, and I really do not appreciate that. It's not right. I have all the respect in the world for my mom, and even just thinking about cussing at her really, really irritates me.

I don't have the control . . . I'm slowly losing it, and I really don't want to. I'm trying to hold on to it as much as I can, but it's not working. It's just been little stuff just been irking me. And I guess it's because there's so much big stuff around me really, really messing with my head. The little stuff really irks me. Like the knuckleheads in my Academy. Every time I get a little mad I won't do anything . . . and then on top of everything, the grade.

I got a F in English because I didn't turn the work in. I found out about that the day before yesterday. Man, I cried from the minute I found out until I went to bed last night.

I was shocked at the unfolding story that began at home and bled into Amira's practices at school. Within the home there was an interest in Amira doing well and a determination on her mother's part to administer punishments if the report card did not measure up to expectations. The support took the form of dealing with deficits and there were no efforts to identify and change contradictions arising from home life and academic performance, especially the impact on school performance of an expectation that Amira and her sister would attend to cleaning, cooking, and child care on an as needs basis. Fortunately, Amira had a small group of friends who supported her, and that included watching out for her academic performance. Amira noted that,

the thing is the crowd I run with, they won't let you do stuff that's not going to let you achieve what you want to achieve. Like Sherida and Felicia, those are my friends; those are my heart. And they won't let me do anything that's going to keep me from . . . like when Sherida heard that I had got an F she said, "How you get an F?" She would actually make sure that I did my work cause the first report period I didn't do my English work. That's how I got a C. But she would make me do my work. Sherida would actually sit there until I would finish my work. And she did her work while she was making sure I was doing my work in English class.

Although it is reassuring that Amira has friends who encourage her to reach her academic potential, it is evident that there are many issues associated with home and school that are mediating her health and participation in academic work. Above all, Amira needs to create social networks with adults in the school and thereby gain access to structures she needs to help resolve the difficulties she has identified and create a program of study that leads to high school graduation and entrance into a pre-med program. However, it is evident in the following interview that Amira is unlikely to build the social networks she needs without the proactive intervention of others.

Somethin' About Me Has Changed
The following dialogue between Amira (A) and me (K) is an excerpt from an interview between the two of us.

A: I personally do not feel that I deserve that F. C or D, but I do not feel I deserve that F in no way, shape, or form.
K: It's probably a combination of what you did and what you didn't do.

A: But I didn't even really get bad grades and stuff like that. I do not appreciate that at all.

K: Have you talked to your teacher about it?

A: I don't want to say nothin' to her.

K: Given that it doesn't affect her at all, and it affects you a lot, doesn't it make sense to get together all your stuff in English and say, "Can we have a talk about that F?" You know grades can always be adjusted and changed.

A: I don't know what to do about that F. The reason I really don't want to talk to her is because I don't know what I'm going to say to her. I told you I lost a lot of my self-control. I don't know what I'm going to say to her. Something about me has changed so rapidly that I don't know ... I'm very unpredictable to myself, let alone to other people. I don't know. I guess I'm more unpredictable to myself than other people because people sell me short for what ... like first of all, a lot of these ninth-graders don't think I'll punch them in their mouth for saying something dumb. Because the dumb stuff that happened last year, people don't know what to expect ... they think that I'm not going to react in the way that I would. But they only know from what I didn't react to last year.

K: These kids you're talking about? Are they ninth-graders?

A: Some of them. But now, I'm actually talking about the tenth-, eleventh- and twelfth-graders. Like last year was a lot of stuff that I didn't retaliate, that I would retaliate to this year. Like ... I didn't retaliate because then I had the self-control that I don't have now. Like last year you could say whatever you want to me, and I would ignore you. You could still do that sometimes. It depends upon who you are. But if you're like Shawanda or somebody, you'll get punched in the mouth by me as bad as that sounds.... There's this one girl, she try to keep testing me and testing me. So far I haven't hit her yet. It all started from something dumb that happened around my way. And she keep thinkin' I'm a chump because I won't retaliate to an argument ... and right now I don't have the time or patience for anybody. I really, really don't. There's so much stuff goin' on and I got so much built-in anger I don't have the time for it. I don't have the energy. I don't have anything to deal with the stuff I deal with.

Amira is clear in her appraisal of her present circumstances that physical violence is likely to be inflicted on some of her peers and she avoids contact with one of her teachers, just in case. Presently there are many pressures and Amira does not have the resources to cope with them. She needs assistance, not only from among her closest friends and family, but also from within the school. Many of Amira's dispositions to act are framed by street code (Anderson, 1999), and she is chillingly aware of the likelihood and consequences of enacting those strategies either at school or at home. Urban youth, according to the code of the street, often seek to earn the respect of peers by physical aggression, including taunting and beating those they consider physically weaker. These codes seep into the school field, and Amira explains as almost inevitable the necessity for her to inflict violence on a group of peers she describes as knuckleheads. The consequences of not engaging in physical aggression will not stop at school life and there is an air of inevitability that Amira will probably have to fight and suffer the consequences of being suspended or expelled from school. More optimistically, and in contrast to those who seek to divert Amira from her goal of school success is a group of peers, Amira's *homies*, who look after her interests and provide structural support for her participation in activities that will ensure her success. According to Boykin (1986), communality is a disposition shared among African American youth. Hence, some of Amira's peers will assist her to navigate the conflict she anticipates and overcome the difficult structural problems of her home life, especially those that prevent her from studying and doing homework. However, as is evident in the next section, Amira's interactions with adults are not successful; significantly, she is not developing necessary social networks with her teachers, and is even avoiding essential conversations about her academic progress. The skills she developed in cogenerative dialogues are not being used to her advantage and her opportunities to learn are suffering accordingly.

STRUCTURES FROM THE HOME MEDIATE LEARNING

Events at home mediate Amira's practices at school (I think my home life affects a lot of my school work). Many problems seem to originate from an increase in the number of people living in her house from two to seven, including a child in need of care. Amira believes that she and her sister had to do all of the household chores, and she notes that the additional people reduce the space for study to such a degree that there is no longer room nor quiet space for her to do homework. Not only that, there is constant noise in the home and it is no longer conducive to life as Amira once knew it. Amira has gained weight and constant reminders from her mother increase her self-consciousness and she yearns for the summer when she dreams of life returning to normal. Even if it is desirable to do so, Amira cannot leave events from home at the front door to the school. When she comes in with a headache and bad feelings about her treatment at home, it is difficult for her to be enthusiastic about her classes and tolerant of her peers. In classes, the highly interactive target student of just one year ago is likely to put her head down and sleep or appear to sleep. Amira has headaches that probably are stress induced and efforts of a teacher or peers to get her to lift her head might be met with verbal or physical aggression.

I was aware that Amira's life was changing. To begin with, her hair changed color. First it was bleached, then dyed purple, and then red; finally she shaved her hair off. One year after the genetics class, Amira's participation in the classroom was different too. I observed her in social studies, was alarmed at her lack of participation, and discussed the changes in her practices with a concerned social studies teacher. However, when I saw her in a physical science class I decided to intervene on her behalf. Head down Amira seemed unmotivated and unchallenged. She slept through the class I observed and I then requested time to meet with her.

I had many concerns, not the least of which was that Amira did not have an advocate for her educational progress. Her relationship with her mother was close to dysfunctional, and her schedule at school was seemingly unrelated to the courses she took as a freshman and her career goals. I found it ironical and more than a little sad that Amira was attracted to the Health Academy because of her interests in becoming a doctor, yet the Academy had modest academic goals for the youth, whom they regarded as most suited for positions in the health field that did not require degree-level studies. Fortunately there was a small honors-level biochemistry class being taught by two graduate students from my university and I suggested to Amira that the challenge would be just what she needed. Her initial response might have been anticipated.

I don't need a more challenging curriculum . . . I need organization right now. Not so much as me personally organizing my books and stuff. No organization in my life. It might sound like I'm just blowing everything out of proportion. But I'm not. I need to get organized first. All I need is a break right now, and then I can decide what I want to do, where I want to go.

Amira's priority was to focus on the burden of events in the home and interpersonal conflicts with some of her peers. However, as I talked more about the biochemistry class in relation to her interest and strength in genetics and her goal of becoming a doctor she brightened up and showed enthusiasm for making a shift to the biochemistry class (For real? For real? I want to start . . . a lot of my friends, well, not a lot, like three of my friends have Saturday college classes). Not only that, a change to biochemistry would necessitate rescheduling of other classes too, leading to a fresh start in mathematics and French.

To my relief, Amira showed enthusiasm for the plan and because of the social capital I built over a period of five years of being a researcher and an occasional teacher at City High, I could act on her behalf, speak to the principal about Amira's problems at home, and convince the

Academy coordinator to change her schedule so that she could take the biochemistry class and thereby change her assignment to French and mathematics. Not only did she get a new science class, but also new French and mathematics classes and teachers. These changes breathed new life into Amira's academic life at school. However, the deep problems were not resolved. Amira's problems extend beyond school boundaries and it is clear that others must be involved in resolving them.

SCHOOL STRUCTURES ARE INADEQUATE

Amira's problems need the input of adults if they are to be resolved. However, Amira does not have trusting relationships with adults in the building. She likes her science teacher and respects her social studies teacher. However, she does not regard any adults as having the resources to assist her to solve her present academic and social problems. Furthermore, she perceives the counselor for the Academy as ineffective.

Ms. Wise is the counselor. I don't like her because she is more of a talk person. She's more of You listen, I talk. No matter what your problem is this has to be the solution to it. I'm like Ms. Wise, not everybody's problem is the same. She say, "Well, this will help." It won't. She just don't listen . . . she makes me so mad.

Apart from having a counselor with a reputation for not listening and suggesting one solution for all problems, there are no structures to identify and assist students in the Academy whose learning is hampered by factors outside of the classroom. I am curious about the structures that might emerge to take into account that most students in the Health Academy were African American, female, and living with economic poverty. My inscriptions of ethnicity, gender, and poverty are not intended to catalyze deficit remedies but to examine the strengths of these students and identify structures they can access to support their learning. Rather than planning and acting to control and truncate the students' agency, is it possible to provide structures to expand their agency, affording greater opportunities for them to act in pursuit of their own interests?

Although Amira's academic performance and classroom practices have plummeted in the last year there are few signs of awareness among the faculty and no steps from within the Academy to reverse the trend. The signs of decline are apparent to me as an outsider, yet from the inside they seem to be accepted as normal for some fifteen-year-old females. Perhaps this is a problem of having so many students with similar ethnic and economic histories. To be fair to the teachers and other adults in the Academy, there are 200 students with needs and providing personalized attention for each of them can be difficult. However, this was a primary reason for creating Academies in the first place: to allow for greater levels of personalization between smaller numbers of students and faculty and for enduring relationships to form over the four years of high school.

How is the Academy structured to identify students having problems and to resolve them? Regular weekly faculty meetings occur and students regarded by faculty as problems are identified and Academy-wide solutions are sought. Rather than diagnosing learning problems and taking appropriate actions, most time is given to resolving problems associated with student misbehavior, sporadic attendance, and late arrival to class. Ironically the focus is on management and control of students rather than curriculum, learning, and building a community. It is as if students have to make the changes needed for the Academy to function as a learning community. Furthermore issues such as fighting and sexual orientation are creating factions among the students and there is a growing necessity for dialogues about the different forms of diversity in the Academy and ways to deal with difference.

At the beginning of each day there is a homeroom class. Although Amira admires her homeroom teacher, the following vignette illuminates some major contradictions.

Druger's a good teacher. He's my advisory teacher. Like one day, I wasn't here. Somebody tacked his chair in computer class. And when I came back we couldn't do nothin' in advisory except we just had to go by the book. Like usually he would let us out of advisory. And all he had to do was see us to mark us in. And we didn't have to sit there like any other advisory teacher would make us do. And when he got his chair tacked, he made us sit in the class. We couldn't go out the class, couldn't nobody come in the class that didn't belong in our advisory, and if you were more than five minutes late you were late. And if you went back out, you were marked late. And it was like we was on punishment. That's what he called it. And he said, until I find out who tacked my chair, you all not going nowhere.

Neither Amira nor Druger see the potential of the homeroom period for communicating across boundaries such as those I identified above. Many teachers regard it as an imposition and not part of their professional duties. A problem throughout the school is that faculty arrive late for the homeroom period and students wander the hallways and use the time to socialize with peers, often from other homeroom designations. Amira prefers to socialize with peers outside of the confines of the classroom and she does not consider the opportunities that homeroom can provide her to build social capital with an adult and learn to communicate successfully across such boundaries as class, gender, and age.

The role of Druger as an advisory teacher must be questioned. The homeroom period is an ideal place for him to build rapport with students in a nonacademic context. Druger might have learned about the difficulties of Amira's home life, thereafter assisting her to achieve her goals at school. For example, it is an opportunity for Druger to learn about conflicts associated with heterosexual and lesbian youth in the Academy. Even if Druger does not have the personal resources to resolve issues like this as they unfold, he might bring them forward as discussion topics for all participants in the Academy. Arguably the homeroom period is a seedbed for the creation of culture that is essential to the Academy's mission, especially since the social and cultural histories of the teachers and students are so dramatically different.

BREACHING THE INEVITABLE

Will Amira become a doctor? Will she graduate from high school? The likelihood of either or both responses being affirmative is contingent on the extent to which Amira breaches or succumbs to the forces of social reproduction (Bourdieu and Passeron, 1990). She has a brilliant mind and is determined to succeed. If there is a way for her to break out of the mold in which she has been cast I am sure she will find a way to do it. Presently the forces of social reproduction appear to be moving Amira adrift of the course toward medical school. However, school structures allow her to redress some of the failures on her academic record. Having failed English, Amira went to summer school and passed the subject with ease, thereby expunging the failing grade from her academic transcript.

Now, as a junior Amira is once more on course to graduate from high school. However, the active and extroverted individual we observed in her freshman year is not actively involved in her present chemistry class. Yes, a chemistry class. Even though Amira took an advanced biochemistry class she was assigned to an introductory chemistry class, well below her level of attainment. This is a problem faced by many students in a school committed to maintaining the advantages of an Academy structure in which a small number of students and teachers comprise a community, thereby limiting the variety of science courses offered in a given year. It is easiest for the school to schedule students for the course that suits most of them and aligns with the preferences and qualifications of the Academy's science teacher. However, taking an introductory chemistry course is not in Amira's interests and will likely diminish her already plummeting interest in school. If City High is to address the problem of scheduling classes that better fit with the educational goals and career aspirations of students, there is a need for more input from the students and a greater degree of local control over the schedule. It is probable too that the Academy structure would have to be modified to allow advanced classes to be offered on a schoolwide basis so that such classes could contain viable numbers of students, be taught by well-qualified teachers, and be supported by appropriate material resources.

If teachers are to make a difference in the lives of their students, it is imperative that they are thoughtful and responsive to what students know, can do, and are experiencing in their lives. I regard it as important for teachers to be researchers of their own practices and the ways in which those practices afford the education of their students. A thoughtful teacher would not just look for patterns of coherence in the culture enacted by his or her students but would also probe to identify contradictions and make sense of them. Too often the language of teachers in and out of the classroom is replete with statements about patterns regarding classroom life, with little attention to the extent that these patterns are robust and whether or not there are contradictions that could be removed or perhaps strengthened to create new patterns of coherence. Unless we take significant steps to change the nature of urban schools, addressing the oppression of students and teachers and imagining how they might be differently construed, the futures of many students like Amira will be bleak indeed. Who will prevent Amira from reaching the goal she so desperately seeks—or dare I ask, who will step forward to help her on her way?

BEYOND STATIC MODELS OF LEARNING

"Girl, you got three strikes against you. You're Black, you're poor, and you're a woman. You've got to rise up. Take this chance and use it well." The Black, female principal of City High was an advocate for her students. She saw the potential in every one of them and refused to take deficit perspectives on what they could accomplish. I was confident that she would support my suggestions to provide greater challenge in Amira's academic program. Her support, a political act, was grounded in her short history as a principal at City High, where almost all of the students were Black and poor. Her approach was to be highly energetic and hands on. If there was litter on the floor, she picked it up, if students were out of line, she let them know about it. When she saw things she liked she was expressive in her support and encouraging to do more things like that. The principal wanted to offer more advanced placement courses and took every opportunity to get her students out of the building to learn in the community, especially on the campuses of nearby universities so that the students of City High would have images of themselves on college campuses, learning at a university. The principal realized that learning had to do with goal setting and being able to imagine possibilities that were related to experience. She knew only too well that the students of City High constituted an underclass, most of whom had never experienced the fruits of middle-class upbringing and adults who were college graduates. Accordingly, my requests to provide Amira with a new program were at first met with derision and then unwavering support. "Dr. Tobin! We got more than two thousand kids in this school. We cannot save them one at a time!" she chided me. Then without a moment of reflection she announced, "Let's do it Tobin. Bring Amira to see me"

In a principal's office, far from Amira and her peers, structures were created to support her agency. Those changes did not propel Amira in a deterministic way toward a pre-med program at College, but they did make it possible for her to stay on course with her vision of becoming a doctor. Amira's opportunities to learn were structured by others acting on her behalf and the new structures expanded Amira's agency, such that her cultural production, reflected in her learning of science, was now aligned with the political necessities of having to pass four science courses to graduate from high school and to know some science so that success was possible in college science courses.

In this chapter learning has been situated far beyond what is customary in standard education psychology, which often explores learning in ways that are decontextualized, individualistic, transhistorical, and politically neutral. Amira's life is complicated by society's inscriptions of her as a teenager with ethnicity, gender, class, and sexual orientation as especially salient. These inscriptions mediate her own dispositions, values, interests, beliefs, and talents, coming together in an identity that is fluid, changing as Amira crosses the boundaries of the fields that constitute her social life. Amira is not entirely free to inscribe her own identity because others interact in the fields she inhabits; thereby constantly changing the structure to which Amira's agency is dialectically interconnected. Because agency and structure are dialectically related within a field, and because the boundaries of fields are porous, the conditions of Amira's home life frame her experiences with peers in the streets, and then when she enters school, the stress of social life, as it is experienced macroscopically (across time and space), mediate Amira's readiness to access resources and her physical well-being.

The theoretical perspectives I have adopted in this chapter situate learning in historical, political, and social contexts that illuminate Amira's struggles against social reproduction. Part of Amira's struggle is against hegemonies that favor inscriptions that are masculine, upper- and middle-class, White, and heterosexual. However, my theoretical model is not deterministic and there are pathways to academic success and social transformation. Nonetheless, it is apparent that Amira cannot succeed solely through her own efforts. Others, especially those within the school, must intervene to create structures to expand the agency of students like Amira. Of considerable promise in this regard are structures that lead to the emergence of communities of learners, in which collective agreements about rules, roles, and goals can evolve and be negotiated.

CONCLUSIONS

Social life is enacted in multiple fields, each of which has porous boundaries. Accordingly, culture that originates in one field can be enacted in others. Enacted culture is experienced as patterns of coherence and associated contradictions and, depending on the specifics, culture may appear as related to learning or resistant to it. Many of Amira's practices described in this chapter might be regarded as structures that would not support or signify academic progress and its associated successful interactions. Unlike those practices described in the dihybrid cross vignette, which so evidently were associated with deep learning, those described in this chapter point to failure and lack of motivation to succeed. I have endeavored to point out that there are other ways to make sense of Amira's practices and schema rather than through the pervasive deficit lenses often used by adults to explain what they experience of urban youth in urban schools. The struggles that faced Amira in her lifeworld, many associated with her ethnicity and class, were overwhelming for her and she did not have human networks outside of the school to resolve her problems. Unfortunately the adults within the school were not responsive to Amira's changing patterns of participation. Although it is possible to point to my interventions and argue that the rest should be up to her, I argue that many others like Amira did not have an adult to advocate for them and presumably they failed to meet their goals.

The evidence I present in this chapter suggests that schools adopt perspectives that assume that individual students are on their own and will either crash through or crash depending on their personal efforts, including what must be done away from school. Hence structures associated with ethnicity and class, for example, might be regarded through deficit lenses and efforts might not be made to structure the school environment to allow students to use what they know and can do from their lifeworlds as foundations on which to build successful interactions and deep learning. An essential and all too rare focus might be on building solidarity within communities, such that social networks extend across the boundaries of ethnicity, social class, and age.

Schema that appear to be hegemonic for urban youth are beliefs that they are not university bound, do not enter professions such as medicine, and must overcome deficits associated with their ethnicity and social class through individual efforts, talent, and hard work. Schema such as these are counter to those that highlight the centrality of successfully accessing and appropriating resources in successful interactions, thereby generating positive emotional energy and solidarity within a community of learners. If efforts can be directed to the creation of collective commitments throughout a community and across boundaries such as those previously identified, then the success of students like Amira is more likely.

CODA

Amira graduated from high school after what was a roller-coaster ride replete with contradictions. In her senior year she left home and struggled to support herself with a variety of minimum-wage jobs. Even though she is presently in her freshman year of college, participating in a pre-med program, her grades are precarious and her eventual success remains dubious. Even so, I do not count her out. Amira remains committed to becoming a doctor and struggles against the forces that steer her off course. That agency is dialectically constituted with structure does not preclude Amira from becoming a doctor and fulfilling her dreams. Rather, through her agency, Amira can appropriate structures to navigate chosen pathways successfully, ignoring temptations to appropriate structures in pursuit of other goals, and identifying and crashing through hegemony, thereby resisting oppression and its reproductive cycles.

ACKNOWLEDGMENT

The research in this chapter is supported by the National Science Foundation under Grant No. REC-0107022. Any opinions, findings, and conclusions or recommendations expressed in this chapter are those of the author and do not necessarily reflect the views of the National Science Foundation.

REFERENCES

Anderson, E. (1999). Code of the street: Decency, violence, and the moral life of the inner city. New York: W.W. Norton.

Bourdieu, P., and Passeron, J-C. (1990). *Reproduction in Education, Society and Culture* (2nd ed.). London: Sage.

Boykin, A. W. (1986). The triple quandary and the schooling of Afro-American children. In U. Neisser (Ed.), *The School Achievement of Minority Children: New Perspectives* (pp. 57–92). Hillsdale, NJ: Lawrence Erlbaum Associates.

Memory

CHAPTER 69

Memory: Counter-memory and Re-memory-ing for Social Action

KATHLEEN S. BERRY

FOCUS OF THE CHAPTER

Memory as constructed by educational psychology to suit dominant features of modern life has particular flaws that need to be addressed. Critical theorists and pedagogues challenge educational psychology's traditional construction of memory. Furthermore, to rethink what memory is has implications for what counts as teaching and learning in a postmodern age. Why and how to transform modern notions of memory and a host of educational practices is the focus of the discussion that follows.

WHAT IS MEMORY?

This question requires a tracking of the changing faces of memory. How and why have constructions of memory changed over time and place? The significance of this question leads us to an examination of different modern theories, definitions, and practices that involves how knowledge and beliefs about memory were constructed. An examination of the history of memory can be tracked from everyday, informal existence to how and why it entered into the formalized structures of knowledge such as a discipline like educational psychology and the mainstream, formalized policies, discourse and practices of disciplines, institutions and daily activities in educational circles. For our purposes, educators need to ask how the theories and practices of memory entered the mainstream in a manner that speaks with authority and as if the knowledge and truth is absolute, generalizable, correct, natural, and normal. In other words, why have teachers and others consented to the constructs of educational psychology as having the dominant say on what is memory?

In Western civilization, memory has its roots in the origin of the word from the Latin *memor*, "to be mindful." The mind, body, and spirit could not be separated as the center of knowing and thus memory. This placed ideas of what memory is into a more bodily, spiritual dimension not simply as materially located and thus less visible, measurable, and controllable. The discourse surrounding what memory is also influenced what counts as teaching and learning. Teaching and learning in a fashion that enhanced and stored information in/as memory would be treated as a holistic dimension with no specific locale. In addition, the knowledge, values, beliefs, and histories of society and institutions would be constructed around an oral society, existing in the storytellers' renderings of truth, fact, events, and so forth. Memory informed mainly by oral knowledge, value, and history was dependent on immediacy, spontaneity, and playful structures. Each telling had a different twist, a different carryover from the first telling to each subsequent telling. This premodern information and storage of memory was context-specific. Societal knowledge and values of Self and Others was carried in the oral language of the storyteller. Although specific to the time and space, memory in pre-modern contexts was shifting and elusive, difficult to measure and control. What, of course, is missing from this earlier definition is memory as mindful of who, what, where, when, and how—which will be addressed later.

As society and technologies changed, so did the meaning and practices of memory work. Two major events occurred in Western civilization that affected the original interpretation of memory as mindful and the uses of the word. The first turning point was a philosophical revolution known as the Enlightenment. A major philosopher of this period, and the first to set the future theories and practices of Western psychology still in use today, was Descartes. He created the mind–body dualism that shifted memory into the mind as pure thought. "I think, therefore I am" (cogito ergo sum) became the catch phrase that captured the power of memory as mind separated from body and spirit. According to his philosophy, the latter two were not reliable as sources of knowledge. Memory became attached to cognition, to thinking, to a biological matter called the brain. This perspective set the foundation for scientific rationality (follow a method and you'll be rational), objectivity (subjective, personal, experiential knowledge does not give truth so cannot be used) and logical positivism (eliminate the human variables and that's logical). Cartesian philosophy legitimized treating memory as an object. Since that time, memory as a site for objectivity entered the theories and practices of modern education. In fact, memory today is constructed as a function of the brain thus producing, circulating, and sustaining the knowledge, belief, and value that memory can be rational and logical only if it is "objective"; that is, as an object separated from the body and spirit. With this theory as dominant, educators can control, manipulate, and test memory as cognitive knowledge, truth, and value. Other memories such as those produced and sustained by the body and spirit have limited to nil value in current modern, institutional policies and practices. One discipline in particular, educational psychology, used this Western, modern objectification of memory to produce and legitimize teaching and learning theories and practices that still dominate the field of education today.

A second major influence on how memory has been constructed by current academic disciplines such as educational psychology was the invention of the printing press. This may seem a strange connection—memory and the printing press. The intent here is to briefly track how Cartesian (Descartes) dualism moved from an initial position of power and reached the status it still holds today, especially in several areas including teaching, learning, and memory. Approximately within one hundred years of each other, the printing press, European colonization, and Cartesianism brought together the theories and practices of dualism—worldwide. There was barely a part of the world that was immune to the philosophical, intellectual, cultural, linguistic, political, and economic changes brought by the European colonizers. The authoritative power of Cartesian thinking was spread across the world by European colonizers and the powerful communication technology of the printed word. Print as the dominant communication technology of the modern era, along with other societal and institutional practices, enabled the circulation and legitimization of memory as objectified cognition.

Today, textbooks such as educational psychology's constructions of memory and other culturally constructed artifacts organize knowledge, truth, and practices that speak with a voice of authority that needs to be challenged. Historical changes in what memory is, as previously discussed, is compatible with the rise to power of scientific rationality, objectivity, and logical positivism, the most powerful intellectual and political forces in circulation today. The hegemonic forces used throughout the history of memory have led to consent by the masses (hegemony) of what memory is. In addition, practices that carry out the theories of memory enter the field of education, mainly through the discourses of educational psychology, and become accepted by policy makers, researchers, and practitioners all as naturalized, normalized, generalizable, and universalized. Memory remains an object; individualistic, singular, controllable, manipulable, testable, and measurable. Finally, and dangerously so, an object that can be controlled socially, historically, intellectually, and for political purposes. For critical pedagogues, this construction of memory, although dominant, is very problematic.

PROBLEMATIZING EDUCATIONAL PSYCHOLOGY'S CONSTRUCTION OF MEMORY

Critical pedagogues ask several types of questions about power; to name a few—intellectual, economic, social, cultural, historical, linguistic, gendered, racial, classed, spiritual power, and so on. Is the power equitable, inclusive, diverse, plural, and socially just for all? Who has the power and who doesn't? Why do some have it and not others? How did some get it and not others? What and whose knowledge, beliefs, truths, values, and practices count and don't count? And for the focus of this chapter, what counts as memory? Whose memories count and whose don't count? What other constructions of memory need to be included in theories and practices of teaching and learning? These are only a few of the questions asked by critical pedagogues for the purpose of problematizing texts, structures, policies, and discourses. In other words, critical pedagogues make everything and everyone problematic. That being said, it is not the same as making the world a problem, or positive and negative (a binary logic that is problematic), and then seeking a final solution. It is about examining and critiquing the world for locations of inequities, exclusiveness, and so forth. It is about making informed decisions but not for all people, all times and all places. It is about rethinking and changing the structures, policies, and practices that challenge the status quo, taken for grantedness of everyday practices such as, in this case, memory.

The brief history of memory presented previously is made problematic by the fact that critical pedagogues work with a host of theories about constructions of the postmodern world. Theories and their discourses that challenge, put into question educational psychology's dominance in the field of studies on memory come from areas such as postmodernism, postcolonialism, and post-structuralism; studies about delineated cultures such as by gender, race, class, religion, sexuality, age, nationality, ethnicity, and a host of other intellectual activities too vast to include here. Memory in traditional educational psychology is dominated by theories and discourse of cognition, brain studies, and scientific rationality, thus making it possible in educational circles to easily measure by quantitative means and treat memory as an object removed from human experience and the body. In addition, memory as object ignores the responsibility of society, institutions, and Western civilization to produce practices and spaces for personal and collective memories to be included in curriculum policies, classroom practices of teaching, and evaluation. Educational practices that support this dominant construction of what constitutes memory are legitimized and hegemonically enter teacher education, professional development, classroom activities, teaching methods, testing, learning, and administrative and curriculum policies. Furthermore, memory, as constructed by educational psychology, sets up a continuous interrelated system of marginalization (of other ways of knowing and being and remembering), erasure (selective forgetfulness), colonization (of the Other's memory and memories, imperialist's superiority), exploitation (of memories that are silenced, assimilated, or misrepresented), and violence (brainwashing by the dominant).

Memory as constructed by critical theorists and pedagogues is counter-memory and re-memory-ing. Memory is a location, neither subjective nor objective, neither concrete nor abstract, where a world of pain and struggle, joy and success, exists in time and space. Although contained in the phenomenological body through "lived experience," memory is connected to the world through intertextuality. Texts that construct memory range from oral to print texts, from family to civilizational texts, from ancestral to future times and spaces, and from texts that create totalitarism, oppression, fear, and silence to those that ask for freedom, social justice, agency, equity, and inclusion. Without memory as counter-memory to the discourses and practices of totalitarism and without the education of memory for social action, the dominance of educational psychology's notion of what counts as memory strangles the hope for freedom, social justice, and participatory democracy.

Traditional educational psychology works with scientific rationality and logical positivism in construction of memory. These approaches construct knowledge and knowledge processing as neutral and biological. Memory is seen as an information processing cycle of encoding, storage, and retrieval. Teaching and learning practices take on particular content, structures, and methods that sustain the cycle even to the point of testing and evaluating. Educational Ministries at the state and national levels decide on what knowledge is to be encoded and how. The knowledge usually is that which supports the culturally and intellectually dominant—enculturalization of the subjects, so to speak. How to encode is stated in curriculum documents and textbooks on teaching and learning such as those produced by the disciplinary paradigms of educational psychology and its fraternal disciplines, counseling and human development. Storage is seen to be in the brain; the cognitive mind that knows; a mind [not the human, just their mind?] is a terrible thing to waste. Retrieval lies in methodologies of measurement: recall, recognition, and relearning. In recall, the subject must produce the correct response given very limited cues (mnemonic devices). Recognition is a method of testing retrieval in which the subject is required to choose the correct answer from a group of choices. Finally, relearning, a method of testing retrieval in which students learn material and then relearn the same material after an interval of time and trials (Kaplan, 1990). And we know what happens to those learners who question the knowledge sources and producers. We know from experience, history, and research what happens to those who can't accept the knowledge; to those who store memories in other places like the body and the spirit; and we know that those who can't retrieve correctly and accurately the second, third, and tenth time are failures, bored, drop-outs, and deviants. Many of these learners are labeled learning disabled, intellectually deficient; learners with *poor* short-term, long-term memories. Dollars, time, and effort are spent on these learners to increase/improve their cognitive abilities, thus their memory. Programs are developed and professionals trained accordingly to provide remedial materials and sessions to correct, cure, reform, restore, and rehabilitate a learner's memory ability and capacity. The usual method is repetition of the very practices that the learner encountered in the first stage of encoding, storing, and retrieving knowledge. These approaches to memory and the methods used by traditional educational psychology are very problematic if contextualized in the theories, discourse, and practices of critical theorists and pedagogues.

Knowledge is not neutral; thus memory is not neutral. In other words, memory is a marker of power. Yet in most educational disciplines, policies, and practices, memory is considered as a neutral object. In critical studies, memory is located in the body, mind, and spirit at the individual level, a reclaiming of the original meaning of memory as mindful. Memory in critical studies is also constructed by societal, institutional, and civilizational policies and practices. This broadened arena of memory offers a multitude of locations and possibilities compared to the reductionist model of traditional educational psychology. It also necessitates the excavation (archeological examination) of what constructions of memory exist at certain spatial and temporal points that reproduces or resists the mainstream constructions of memory and its knowledge stored. Critical pedagogues also examine the connections (genealogy) between the different discourses on memory and critique the ways in which certain memories are supported by particular intellectual, economic, social, and historical contexts.

The examination and critiques are not meant to be mere exercises in academic logic. Foucault's analysis of discourse/text/practices, in this case of memory, called archeological genealogy, is concerned with the relationships between power and knowledge. In addition, archeological genealogy investigates how the relationships of power operate as conceptual frameworks that privilege particular modes of thinking and certain practices about memory and excludes others. Since symbolic systems of thought are the way humans organize and construct these frameworks, critical theorists and pedagogues find the competing discourses and practices about memory the site of unequal power relations and practices. "Moreover, power should not be thought of as a negative force, something which denies, represses, negates: power is productive . . . in fact power produces reality . . . domains of [knowledge, truth, belief and value]" (Storey, 1993). It is in these competing domains that critical pedagogues find inspiration to teach using counter-memory and re-memory-ing for social action.

Previously, I mentioned how and why modern constructions of memory were tied to scientific rationality and the printing press. It is now time to elaborate on how critical studies and pedagogues consider the role of postmodern technologies. Needless to say the most influential technology that redefines what memory is and how a reconstruction of what and whose memory counts is the computer. What the book was to the modern era, the computer is to the postmodern age. Even in terms of encoding, storage and retrieval, the computer has changed, not only how we think and act through memory but how we teach and learn. Without a doubt, it is the technology of the future and when it comes to knowledge is power, it is the computer that offers the power. On the one hand, we know it is the major source of knowledge for those who (individuals, societies, institutions, etc.) own and control computer technologies. An even greater power, as with book technologies, is for those who produce and control with the click of the mouse the multiple memories encoded, stored, and retrievable in a computer. Just because this technology can store and retrieve more varieties of knowledge and faster than books, what memories and whose memories count are still major questions for critical theorists and pedagogues.

I'm reminded of several undergraduate students who were asked to do a library search on a specific topic. We were in a 300-year-old university setting with books and documents dating back to the 1700s. Of the twenty-nine students given the task to do a research project, everyone of them headed to the computers. As a pedagogue of 40 years' experience, I was alerted very dramatically to the fact that the major source of knowledge for these postmodern students was the computer. Indeed they also use the technologies of television, film, and music as sources and occasionally parents, teachers, and books. However, the students still accepted these prosthetic memories (Landsberg, 2000); memories we have without having lived the experience it represents. For several reasons this is still problematic for critical theorists.

Memories, whether from body/mind/spirit experiences or second hand sources such as books, computers, and film, still remain individualistic possessions and reproduced those of the dominant group. The knowledge and values were researched and assumed to be the authorities as memory and memories were being constructed by the text's technologies. The way the students read the texts and reproduced the knowledge in essays and assignments remained unchallenged. Without alternative ways and the institutional spaces to challenge the knowledge, values, and structuring of memories, identities, and content, they had succumbed to the Enlightenment's philosophy of scientific rationality, objectivity, and logical positivism. Moreover, they accepted the knowledge and truth as essential (natural), stable, and for all people, for all times and spaces (universalizing). The knowledge is stored in memory for retrieval on exams or decision making in the future. If we accept educational psychology's traditional theory of memory, the above example presents no difficulty for teachers and learners. For critical theorists it does.

When teachers and learners accept the traditional theory of memory as produced by academic disciplines such as educational psychology; when this dominant construction of memory enters society and institutions as natural, normal, and universal; when memory is encoded with singular truths; when memory is stored as homogenous, authoritative knowledge; and when memory is retrieved as individualistic yet universal, the fundamental promises of a postmodern democratic society are being corroded. This takes us back to the questions asked by critical pedagogues: What counts as memory and what doesn't? Whose memories count and whose don't? What happens when dominant status quo memories are challenged (counter-memory)? What happens when one person's, one cultural group's, one nation's, one civilization's memories are in conflict with the dominant's? In what contexts were the memories constructed? By whom? How? How does context influence what and whose memories count? Why those and not others? What does it mean to have a "good" memory or a "bad" memory? These are just a few of the possible questions that can be and should be asked when the postmodern principles of democratic societies, institutions, and nations are at stake. Theories and practices of plurality, diversity, inclusiveness, equity, and social justice are just a few of the principles used when examining and critiquing, excavating and connecting, articulating memory and memories. Without these principles and freedom to ask the questions, memories are no more than objects of totalitarianism and brainwashing made to appear natural, neutral, and normal.

RETHINKING TEACHING AND LEARNING PRACTICES

A theoretical rethinking of what counts as memory produces a change in practices. Postmodern memory and counter-memory do recognize the practices of modern constructions of memory and uses their frameworks sometimes. They do so, however, with a different set of questions similar to those listed in previous paragraphs. To rethink our teaching and learning practices, what seems the best and, dare I say, logical place to start is with particular questions; questions that situate memory and memories in larger contexts than those of cognition as an activity of the mind/brain and beyond the responsibility of but not separate from individual memory. Practices that involve supplying memories works mainly through the symbolic (oral, print, visual, audio, concrete, abstract, etc.) ordering of thoughts. For these reasons, we also have to rethink how symbolic ordering of memories also has to change. The following is a partial list of ways that educators (teachers, administrators, parents, community, television and film producers) might begin to rethink their practices for the inclusion of postmodern memories and counter-memories.

1. Examine the practices you use to teach that has students learn in particular ways. Are they what you would consider complicit with, in conflict with, contradictory to, resistant to, negotiated with those of traditional modern ways of teaching and learning? In what ways? Why so?

2. Examine how other teachers, parents, educational administrators, institutional policies, disciplinary text-books on teaching and learning think you should teach. In what ways do they support differences from or confirmation of the dominant ways of scientific rationality and logical positivism as discussed above? Are practices that include different teaching/learning styles, multiple intelligences, and multiple mnemonic strategies encoded with messages of objectivity and methodological homogeneity that reproduces or challenges scientific rationality? In what ways do you teach that prevents the reduction of individual memories to objectification and instrumentalism?

3. Examine the materials (oral, books, film, TV, computer, etc) that store knowledge, beliefs, values, rep-resentations, etc. that become memories. Whose memories? Are they those of the dominant, negotiated, or marginalized? What memories are excluded? How does the knowledge and the structure of the

material/textbook order/encode memories? Are the memories individually retrievable or a group's collective memories? Whether individual or collective, how does the text/material privilege and legitimize their memories and silence or misrepresent the Other's memories? How and why does one set of memories deny the authenticity of the Other's memories? How and why do one set of memories constructed by one culture/nation/gender/race etc. minimize or trivialize the memories of the Other?

4. Examine the academic disciplines that produce certain memories. What boundaries exist between the memories on one discipline and another? In what ways do the disciplinary boundaries heirarchize certain memories such as those belonging to the highest form of knowledge according to Aristotle's theology, mathematics and physics, or the lowest in the hierarchy, which included fine arts, poetics, and engineering? How and why are the values, knowledge, and the memories stored considered universal? How can you teach that disciplinary memories can be challenged? What creative memories are produced when interdisciplinary studies are integrated into the teaching/learning difficulties? In what ways might creative memories point to the problematic claim of scientific objectivity and neutrality?

5. Locate yourself and your students in the memories of your teaching/learning contexts. What memories were/are produced by your ancestors? What gender, race, class, religion, history, nationality etc. shaped those memories? Those of your community? The institutions you teach and learn in? Whose memories are they? How did they become the official memories to teach/learn? Why? How are you/students positioned in the memories? Which positionings are privileged and which aren't? Why?

6. Contextualize your practices. What time and place were/are the memories generated from? What was/is the historical, cultural, economic, social, intellectual, and political contexts in which the memories were generated? What made certain memories generated in the different contexts have staying power? Why? What was going on in the different contexts that produced dominant memories and continue to reproduce exclusions, inequities, and social injustices? What memories are planted that are connected to other contexts that produces power and powerlessness? What memories produce and legitimize practices of violence, direct and symbolic?

7. Challenge assumptions carried in unexamined memories. What types of teaching and evaluation can be used that teach students to challenge truths, knowledge, beliefs in memories that are passed off as absolute, stable, neutral, and official? How can a variety of texts (oral, film, etc.) on the same topic, issue, content, and history act as counter-memories? How can you teach readers to disrupt the stability and authority of canons (texts considered classics), thus disrupt established canons of memories? ? What intertextual readings (how the memories generated in one text are dependent on memories borrowed from other texts) of a text can reveal contradictory memories that challenge dominant/authoritative visions of society and human relations?

These are only a few possible questions to initiate a change in pedagogical thinking and practices that are mind-full, about Self, Others, and relationships of power at the individual, societal, institutional, and civilizational levels. Articulation of these and many other questions challenges and expands the traditional constructions and practices of memory developed by disciplines such as educational psychology and modern educational policies and structures.

ACKNOWLEDGMENT

I would like to thank Scott Powell, undergraduate student at UNB, for his insights and research assistance during the writing of this chapter. He has a postmodern memory that is always mindful of the past, present, and future of the Other.

REFERENCES

Kaplan, P. S. (1990). *Educational Psychology for Tomorrow's Teacher*. New York: West Publishing Company.

Landsberg, A. (2000). Prosthetic Memory: Total Recall and Blade Runner. In Bell, D., and Kennedy, B. M. (Eds.), *The Cybercultures Reader*. New York: Routledge.

Storey, J. (1993). *An Introductory Guide to Cultural Theory and Popular Culture*. New York: Harvester/Wheatsheaf.

SUGGESTED READING

Cavallaro, D. (1997). *The Body for Beginners*. New York: Writers and Readers Publishing Inc.

Foucault, M. (1977). *Language, Counter-Memory, Practice: Selected Essays and Interviews*. USA: Cornell University.

Gur-Ze'ev, I. (2003). *Destroying the Other's Collective Memory*. New York: Peter Lang.

Kincheloe, J L., and Steinberg, S., and Villaverde, L. (1999). *Rethinking Intelligence: Confronting Psychological Assumptions about Teaching and Learning*. New York: Routledge.

Macey, D. (2000). *The Penguin Dictionary of Critical Theory*. London: Penguin Books.

CHAPTER 70

Memory and Educational Psychology

LEILA E. VILLAVERDE

Memory as cultural phenomena is regarded with romanticism and nostalgia most times. Memory as educational phenomena is considered as the quintessential storage space of intelligence. Memory as psychological phenomena becomes the marker of true reality orientation and normality. We tend not to think about memory unless we are loosing it or can't remember an important date, somebody's name, where we placed something, or a password. Therefore remembering and remembrance are both performances that mark our history or signal our emptiness. As the chapter unfolds I will discuss memory in cultural, educational, and psychological contexts in addition to elaborating on the performances of memory (remembering and remembrance). Last but not least I will discuss public memory and its effect on our pedagogical practices. The chapter will start with a brief history of memory, how it has been defined, how its use has changed through time, and how it affects our use of it in pedagogical contexts.

HISTORY OF MEMORY

The creation of the printing press changed the use of our memory forever. Print culture privileges isolated practices such as reading and writing as opposed to the more communal practices of storytelling, folklore, and shared social learning. Prior to printing or other documenting practices (i.e., writing), oral traditions and narratives were the main sources of knowledge construction and transmission. Jeremy Rifkin believes print detaches people from each other, therefore allowing words to be privatized and commodified. Dialogue, conversations, and other communicative interactions exercise our cognitive processes employing information stored, applied, and enacted. The use of memory to record history and pass it down from generation to generation was integral to many cultures. The success of philosophers, poets, theologians, politicians, and other leaders or orators relied heavily on the use and quality of their memory. Their intellect, creativity, and imagination are the products of rich and extensive processes. Memory was considered the great portal to history, morals, ethics, and culture. Different techniques were developed to sharpen memory and improve the use of language, as well as to increase what was known and how. In the ancient times of Greece and Rome memory was regarded as an intellectual/emotional space of boundless potential and human transformation.

As the premodern era gave way to the modern one, a paradigm shift occurred in how knowledge, learning, and cognition were constructed and studied. A more pronounced emphasis was placed on the sciences to explain any phenomena. The world and human beings were believed to mimic machines and the object was to focus on the discrete parts of the larger operating system. This was the age of reason, and cognition would be the source of scientific and industrial progress. Learning became mechanical, a process of rote memorization, recall, and skills. In fact the brain was often likened to a computer as it processes data, particularly the ways it encodes, stores, and retrieves information. Much attention has been given in educational psychology to the ways in which the brain sorts input, creating schemes to categorize unfamiliar information and therefore make it familiar and accessible. Piaget has discussed this through his concept of accommodation. Using the computer as an analogy for the way our memory works positions the learning process as a linear venture of give and take, of replication with limits and parameters. It subsequently assumes information remains intact through the input and output process. The more we mechanize this process, the higher the probability to assume control over it. Even when memory defies common retrieval strategies, experts are convinced the information can be accessed through hypnosis, medication, or drill practices. As a culture we have a difficult time accepting loss, or understanding that information as we knew it may not exist in the exact original form. Seldom does this mechanical approach to memory deal with understanding and application or transfer of skills from learned knowledge. The main concern is minimizing difference, increasing likeness, and restating what is known, not producing knowledge, learning, or insight, and much less focusing on the transformative potential of knowledge and how one knows it.

Human memory is a subjective entity and process. Memory cannot adequately be explained solely through the mechanics of a positivist paradigm. Another paradigm shift occurred, one that took us into the postmodern era, where subjectivity and multiple realities take precedence. This does not necessarily mean we have shifted our use of memory entirely, but rather we have come to recognize how past paradigms and inherent epistemologies produce a deskilling and deterioration of memory. As a result of the scientific and postmodern age many technological advances are widely accessible, from the proliferation of devices that will record and document important information, to the Internet, making all sorts of information available at one's fingertips, and finally the colossal increase of written texts. The largest task of memory in contemporary times is not to encapsulate cultural, individual, or collective history, but to remember where you wrote or typed the information. Memory is perhaps more heavily used to retrieve existing information whether it is our personal data or not. Intelligence (through a modern lens) is not about knowing the information, but where to get it, how to access it. This is yet another example of how the shifts in thinking overlap one another as time progresses. Even though chronologically we move forward in time, society and specifically institutions of learning use both static and dynamic/holistic approaches to cognitive studies. The postmodern shift allows for the rethinking of memory as it makes culture, place, location, and identity essential factors in how we process knowledge, emotions, and experiences. Educators can capitalize on this in order to bridge student lived experiences and school knowledge. Cognition is not a separate entity from emotion; on the contrary logic and emotion together forge the significance of what we perceive and experience. Understanding logic and emotion as integral to one another helps us process information for easier recall and application. In educational settings in particular, if we are able to relate students' meaning making process with how they feel and think about different disciplines and concepts we increase the quality of the learning experience. Postmodernism expands how we are able to see/perceive/internalize information to increase what and how it is possible to learn. The larger objective to rethinking educational psychology and, in particular, memory construction is to enrich the ways we learn, to learn more, and restructure who has access to learning in creative and meaningful ways. Understanding the complex process through which we remember, store, and know exposes the potential for negotiating the explicit, implicit, and null curriculum across disciplines.

Lets move into how memory and cognition work. According to the Atkinson–Shiffrin model of information processing there is an external stimulus, a sensory register, initial processing, rehearsal and coding, short-term memory, and long-term memory. The sensory register or memory contains the unprocessed information collected by all of our senses. The amount of information we can register through our senses is infinite; most of it happens while we are unconscious of it. During the sensory registration, information could be lost or forgotten if the individual is not told to organize it in some way. That is if the register does not beckon the stored images in long-term memory, what we sense will go unnoticed. Similarly during the rehearsal and coding process information could be lost or forgotten if the individual does not engage in means to retrieve or repeat the information that has been designated as important. Through this particular model the individual remains passive in the learning or recognition process, always reliant on somebody else—an implied external (outside the self) expert—to guide what he/she should retain or process as knowledge. The model also implies an unencumbered delivery from stimulus to memory. One of the major contributions of postmodernism and feminist theory is that emotion and logic are intricately connected in how knowledge is perceived, interpreted, and retained. How a stimulus is registered or processed can depend on the relationship (and what emotions are associated with it) one has to that stimulus or the time of day or any number of factors. The initial negotiation of stimulus occurs in working or short-term memory, which allegedly lasts only seconds and has an extremely limited capacity. These seconds can increase exponentially if the stimulus can find like information in long-term memory. The relationships or links in this process are important, as it is usually based on memories and emotions. Learning of new information can consequently become less difficult if educators and students can mobilize their memories and emotions in linking information. Through postmodernism these connections or rather relationships are more readily accessible, in fact necessary. The epistemology undergirding postmodernism regards phenomena through holism, not fragmentation. By understanding from the beginning how bits of information are part of a context, of something larger, we are more apt to search for meaning, not only in what we already know, but elsewhere in search for connections.

According to Slavin, long-term memory is a more complex entity with several components (episodic: stores images of personal experiences or events; semantic/factual: stores facts and general knowledge; procedural: stores how to do things; and flashbulb: stores visual and auditory clues). Often long-term memory is called permanent memory since information is believed to stay indefinitely and only ways of accessing it may become distorted or destroyed. The computer analogy again is commonly used to describe the way that information is stored, and sometimes inaccessible if the computer/mind cannot find the folder or file as a result of bit partitions or file renaming. The computer and memory are believed to be procedural entities following step-by-step programs. To approach the complex process of long-term memory in the same way (as a computer) again eliminates the human/subjective elements that affect the storing and retrieval of information.

Other information-processing models attempt to address the subjective nature of learning and memory. Craik and Lockhart developed the levels-of-processing theory, which brings to our attention the varying degrees of mental processing and the different levels in which stimuli are perceived. What makes something memorable according to Craik and Lockhart was the act of naming what we see. Naming then facilitates our ability to remember the object or experience and make sense of it. Similar to modern/positivistic epistemologies that seek to name and then classify and possibly control phenomena, this theory privileges naming as a practice, but in contrast equally privileges the context in which this naming occurs and the influence it may have over what meaning it creates or retains for us. There is greater possibility for political insight and critical awareness when credence is given to context, to the psychosocial factors that affect how we perceive and internalize knowledge. It is the theories that delve in these nuances that seem more fruitful to the call of the twenty-first century and seeing the individual not only as such, but as a social being historicized in a particular web of reality.

Dual code theory, developed by Paivio, explains long-term memory as processing information on two registers, visual and verbal. Not only are the visual and verbal recognized as important but as crucial, interdependent components in how and why we remember phenomena. Given our visually and textually saturated culture, the ways in which we code information would seem to resonate most with the structure of the surrounding environment. This coding makes most sense to the way in which information is organized in our society. Everywhere we look, everywhere we turn, we are bombarded with signs, directions, and logos. We navigate our world through color, symbols, images, and text. Dual code theory focuses our attention on the relationship between image and text, how together they enhance our understanding and learning. Image and text also create ample spaces for multiple literacies and narratives otherwise inaccessible with just visuals or just verbal cues/information. This theory offers great possibility in the classroom as well.

The parallel distributed processing model states that information is processed simultaneously in the sensory register, short-term memory, and long-term memory. This simultaneous process indicates that at the time in which we react or perceive to the external stimuli we engage in all sorts of connections through our senses and memory. This model also suggests that what catches our attention may be the result of what we expect to see through the familiarity of what we know, what we've known as stored/lived in long-term memory. This model leads us into discussing connectionism, theories that emphasize networks and associations through which knowledge is linked/weaved in our memory. These connections have significant implications for teaching and learning. Curriculum must be modified to deal with integration and not fragmentation. Rote memorization and recall would give way or would be complicated by inquiry-based projects and critical analysis. Questioning would anchor the core of knowledge production in order to maximize the connections between otherwise unrelated stimuli and increase the flexibility in thinking. Connectionism also refocuses our discussion to postmodernism as both theories stress the importance of relationships/connections/networks that create whole and dynamic systems, not static or linear structures.

These connections are also substantiated by the brain function; particularly the way neurons connect to one another through minute fibers (axons and dendrites) every time we engage in any mental activity. Rethinking educational psychology and the ways in which we approach the use of memory in educational experiences necessitates that educators reconceptualize curriculum, their ideology, and practice to suit students' growth and development in the twenty-first century.

MEMORY AS CULTURAL, EDUCATIONAL AND PSYCHOLOGICAL PHENOMENA

We use memories constantly. Anything we see, think, or experience acts as a catalyst to existing visual and textual information, whether we are conscious of this process or not. The memories activated create filters that interpret or classify potential or new memories. This is why many scientists believe that in large respect we only retain what to some extent we already know. Initially this may seem fatalistic or predetermined, only being able to know what you already know. I do not believe this is entirely true or prescriptive, but I do think it forces us to revisit the notion of "a priori knowledge." Many educational theorists strongly believe best practices of teaching rely on how well teachers can link to "a priori knowledge." The rationale being if we can access what we already know or what is familiar and position new knowledge in that light, then we are more likely to familiarize the unfamiliar, and thereby increase our wealth of knowledge and learning potential. This thinking also supports connectivism as a theory, focusing on the networks that link phenomena. A holistic perspective appropriately addresses the complexity of the brain, emotions, soul, entire self, and society. New pathways of learning can be created through the exposure and comprehension of difference between people, cultures, religions, generations, identities and so on through the relationships/connections forged in how we employ memory in print and narrative.

Langer refers to memory as the great organizer of consciousness, simplifying and composing our perceptions into units of personal knowledge. She further states that to remember an event is to experience it again, but not in the same way as the first time, because memory is a special kind of experience, composed of selected impressions. So even our personal history, she adds, as we conceive it, is then a construction of our own memories, reports of other people's memories, and assumptions of casual relations among the items, places, and people. Why aren't the teaching of history and the writing of "official" history regarded in the same way? Not only is memory a complicated process and entity for the individual, but even more so in magnitude for the public, culture, and society. Any cultural or public work has the potential to mediate memory, consciousness, and reality; therefore looking closer at the ramifications of the pedagogical space can lend greater insight into both cognitive and identity construction. Public sites of memory may work on all three realms, cultural, educational, and psychological.

Culture not only provides information on how we relate to one another in a given locale, but how to prioritize or discard information or experiences. Culture also provides filters and lenses through which to sift external stimuli and experiences. Culture creates historical scripts that forge communal and individual identities, consequently shaping memory. The cultural phenomena we negotiate on a daily basis and those that are embedded in our consciousness since early childhood form particular expectations, standards, and values. Cultural memory not only produces, but regulates how we define a collective, even national identity and ourselves. Culture is a way of knowing and being as it provides a buffer between self, truth, values, and possibilities. Popular culture also mediates pleasure, desire, and potential. Memory as a cultural phenomenon raises our awareness of the social influences on how we construct, internalize, and apply knowledge. In traditional educational contexts there is an attempt to eliminate social influences for fear of complicating students' success in standard courses of study. The misnomer here is the way in which social influences are regarded as obstacles not bridges. As we rethink educational psychology, culture is central to understanding memory as a social process and the social formation of the learner. Priority is given to the socio-cultural interaction of the self as it relates to the classroom context and learning. As educators validate and better comprehend cultural memory not only for their students but also for themselves, history, language arts, science, social studies, mathematics, the arts, and physical education become resourceful grounds for interdisciplinary curriculum. Where academic disciplines, students, teachers, and schooling intersect provides a cultural zone of contention, rediscovery, and production. As the editors stated this type of reconceptualization highlights the subtle dynamics of interpersonal interaction, and an individual's or a group's position in the cultural landscape.

Memory as educational phenomena focuses on how we learn, what understanding educators have of how we learn, and consequently how intelligence is defined. As stated earlier in this entry the most common analogy for the way our brain works is a computer. Unfortunately this analogy heavily limits the potential of the mind, soul, and body, that is of being. The analogy defines intelligence in terms of capacity, how much one is able to retain, catalog, and exhibit. There is an extreme reliance on hierarchies of intelligence, critical thinking, and high ordered thinking. The step-by-step, linear processes of cognition eliminate the importance of memory and its role in historical, social, and political practice. Education and schooling are deprived from rich intersections and encounters of deeper understanding and reconciliation. The use of memory in the classroom can unleash all sorts of curricular transformations. Giroux and Macedo discuss dangerous memories as those that contain perspectives disruptive to the masternarratives in history. The memories are classified as dangerous because they challenge mainstream documentation and historiography. They invite different ways of knowing and remembering by illustrating the political, cultural, social, and individual struggles that mark the history of place, power, identity, and community. Many steer away from such memories fearing the hardship and pain would be too much for students, particularly the young. We grossly underestimate youth and their abilities to critically negotiate knowledge, questions, and awareness. The too costly effect is the perpetuation of developing future generations of ahistorical, apolitical beings with incomplete consciousnesses. The rethinking of memory in educational psychology for the twenty-first century requires classroom practice and curriculum development not to neglect the difficult moments in history, the struggles and sacrifices of generations past committed to making the world a more just and equitable place to cohabit. The conflicts, the collisions in discourse, ideology, beliefs, ways of life are essential to who we are as human beings; it is fundamental to the human condition. If we continue to dilute or truncate history and knowledge in general this practice endangers the freedom of questioning the nature of knowledge, what counts as knowledge, what is of most worth, who does it privilege or disadvantage, how we can link knowledge to individual meaning making, and so on. These narratives also help to debunk the biological determinants of cognitive abilities. Too many students are labeled or made to feel unintelligent if they are unable to play the politics of "good, quiet, obedient student" who does his/ her work and does as expected on tests or performance outcomes. Unless students are able to adopt this formula for success schooling continues to be a task not an experience engaging the self and society.

Memory as psychological phenomena overlaps the educational realm to some extent, but also allows us to understand memory as an affective realm. Previously in the entry I discussed different theories that help explain how memory works in the cognitive process. These theories place emphasis on different cognitive processes to explain how we store and internalize knowledge, yet most underestimate the role of emotions. Emotions have a distinct impact on memory, recall, memorization, recognition, performance, and overall meaning production, however most cognitive theories discuss the effects of emotions as impediments to "true" or "effective" learning. The rethinking project in this encyclopedia compels us to view emotions in the landscape of memory and education as a basic nutrient to the sustenance of the holistic system (mind, body, soul, being). Emotional intelligence gained great popularity in the late 1980s placing importance on emotional development and behavior. In most regards emotional intelligence tests evaluate how individuals are able to identify their own and others' feelings to solve emotional issues. Many have questioned the research and tests that as a result prescribe "appropriate" behavior and displays of emotion. The attempt to standardize emotional response and understanding raises ethical questions in regards to differences in gender, culture, religion, and class, just to name a few of such important factors in determining the construction of subjectivity.

Memory as a psychological phenomenon has the potential to mobilize student engagement in curriculum and to increase the ability of students to become greater agents in their own life. If educators engage student desire, pleasure, interest, curiosity, creativity, and passion otherwise unfamiliar knowledge becomes familiar through new conduits. As educators expand their understanding of human relations theories, focusing much more on the cultivation of relationships in the classroom, the psychology of the classroom can be reframed from a competitive and sometimes punitive atmosphere to one of equitable inquiry, democratic access, mutual respect, and value of human life. Many educators may find it difficult to reconstruct the classroom environment because they have not had these types of reframed experiences before. The school is structured against a communitarian ideal; it is fragmented, competitive, and ordered for control. Knowledge is similarly structured and tiered into hierarchies of intelligence and social worth. This reality constructs particular defenses and expectations in behavior, attitudes, and dispositions most likely unbeknownst to most students and faculty or staff. If asked some would probably articulate their boredom, apathy, failure, pressure, lostness, or success and excitement. The more time students spend in such schools and classrooms the more these less than perfect environments seem natural and as they "should" be. An alternative is far from imaginable, courage to risk something different is nonexistent, and the cycle continues. The memories accumulated through the years (K–12) sediment the normativity of these experiences and the significance of school success or failure in a young person's life. When we delve into the psychology of school and schooling, not just cognitive psychology, we can focus on restructuring the psychological consequences of getting schooled. By understanding the psychology of memories, memories that are constructed through more than twelve years dictating how to know, then this awareness can produce proactive pedagogical reform, particularly of the learning environment. This perspective can not be reduced to pop psychology, but rather taken seriously as an opportunity to rethink, reconceptualize the artificial borders built between individual and community, self and other, and cognition and emotion as discussed by the book editors. The structure of schooling, schedules, curriculum, and the interactions with teachers, peers, or caretakers all contribute to the quality and intensity of memories. In closely examining the psychological dimensions of memories all of the above exert important influences in rethinking the connection between memory, educational psychology, and pedagogy. Educators in the twenty-first century must carefully attend to the nuances and possibilities unearthed by this reconceptualization.

REMEMBERING AND REMEMBRANCE

For learning to resonate with us, for us to retain it long enough to make meaning from it, and apply it to everyday living, there has to be a reason to remember. We tend to make remembering the linchpin to existing in a life of value. Think of the many individuals living with physical and psychological conditions that result in memory impairments or loss, which deem them unable to take care of themselves or classify them as a danger to themselves. Practices of control are implemented in the name of safety and the individual grows swiftly ill prepared to take care of the self. The apparent loss of memory should not impair or create a loss in connection, motivation, purpose, or identity. Sometimes individuals with impaired memory recall the past vividly but have trouble locating the present. Slowly, of course, the physical or psychological condition may deteriorate the past as well. But we become extremely upset when loved ones or we can't remember names or can't generate the appropriate emotions to display on cue. Anger or frustration results as the asynchronicity increases between the reality of the individual and the external/social world. As a society we rely on the use of our memory significantly to negotiate our identity on a daily basis and to connect to others, events, or things.

Huyssen defines remembrance as an essential human activity that shapes our connections to the past and the ways we remember shape us in the present. Remembrance, according to Huyssen, constructs and anchors our identity. Memories have a past, present, and future. Based on our experiences and our psychological and intellectual states at the moment of remembering, forgetting, and engaging we have the capacity to rewrite any given event for ourselves. Yet when we produce insight or learning the opportunity exists to rewrite/reembody our comprehension and engagement. Remembrance can be a pedagogical strategy to deter the repetition of unlearned lessons in history. Simon, Rosenberg, and Eppert assert that remembrance, inherently pedagogical, is implicated in the formation and regulation of meanings, feelings, perceptions, identifications, and the imaginative projection of human limits and possibilities. The use of memories in the classroom can transport you back in time, back in proximity to historical milestones, struggles, and definitive traumatic moments in the construction of public consciousness.

Conversely the censoring of memories, that is, the distinct regulation of which memories are crafted for public or collective consumption can also have great impact on the way identity is formed. In other words, remembering can be an individual and collective practice. Either way it may be arresting at times as the individual or culture continuously remember, recreating a past that many times was not lived by the person himself or herself but is significant to who she or he is and how she or he may see himself or herself. We tend to either romanticize or intensify the past through our vivid or hazy memories. The act of remembering coupled with critical reflection is an important pedagogical part of our human development. Remembering as a practice for a culture or society is often begrudgingly undertaken, yet incredible in repairing the present and future actions of members of the collective. Remembering will not in itself fix or undo the social inequities and injustices; nonetheless it offers youth, in particular, a wealth of information to envision a different present and future complicated by the responsibility of knowing and research. Remembering as a pedagogical practice dismantles the investments in vacuous traditions that continue to erode the democratic fabric and theoretical constructs the United States is based upon.

In carefully crafting pedagogy around remembrance a reconceptualized educational psychology allows for the intricate investigation of how memory has culturally and individually shaped memory, self, and identity as an individual negotiates the world. Forgetting also shapes the self and helps to question what is and what is not yet, and aids in developing a critical awareness about one's environment. The performance and experience of remembrance allows students and educators to get lost, lost in areas of history otherwise unexplored and taboo. This pedagogy contributes to the politicization of youth's identity connecting them to the significance of place, power, and time.

PUBLIC MEMORY AND PEDAGOGY

Public memory is constructed by landmarks, statues, historic places, museums, newspapers, television, folklore, celebrations and holidays, schools, curriculum, books, cultural artifacts, and any number of representational tangibles that mark national or local identity. These objects, people, places, or events mark our past, present, and future as they furnish a particular cultural script/landscape and collective experience that define what is American and what is not. Public memory attempts to unite a people and/or place and creates a sense of belonging for its members. Yet as it unites, public memory can also divide depending on the narrowness of the perspective or the meaning assigned to the signs and symbols of a society. Thus the connection between public memory and pedagogy creates a dynamic site for transformative curriculum. Revisiting the many ways in which collective consciousness and public memory are constructed facilitates a productive alienation from that which seems "natural," "normal," and "always been there." Investigating our landscape (background and foreground) through monuments, cultural artifacts, media and so on provide multiple contexts for curricular inquiry. Unfortunately students oftentimes are taught not to question their environment, not to comment on their experiences, not to research independently. History unless lived goes unknown and unproblematized, the consequence is more often than not apolitical and ahistorical individuals unprepared to exercise a critical citizenship. Nonetheless, school policy continues to focus on more standards and tests as quick remedies for a problem of knowledge definition, construction, and experience. These cultural artifacts educate the mass public about one version or a dominant rendition of history, human relations, civility, political correctness, and expected reactions/standards of life. As educators acknowledge and appreciate these resources in addition to the impact on cognitive processes, specifically memory, curriculum can transform into a living/dynamic system.

Other considerations for public memory and pedagogy are in the uses of technology. Media, television, and the Internet provide extensive access to knowledge, values, stereotypes, and assumptions about the self, other, and nation. These venues exert great power over public thought as well as contributing to how historical events are perceived and understood. Given the proliferation of images and saturation of the media in our lives, pedagogy has turned to the curricular riches inherent in the intersection of moving image, sound, and text. Cross-referencing these texts with traditional academic texts offers multiple intertextual readings for students and educators alike, exploring various perspectives and understandings of history, policy, customs, events, and politics. Documentaries can also reignite public memory and engage both questioning and dialogue in order to maximize the learning experience. Currently, many classrooms and schools are alienating places for youth instead of being exploratory places of knowledge, inquiry, and expression. Cognitive processes are not truly challenged or redefined, but rather just exercised in drill routines. Through the curricular use of technology, students can develop metacognitive abilities engaging in thinking about thinking and analyzing the ways in which they think and process information. Students discover greater agency in how they negotiate their learning experiences; these skills are also highly transferable to experiences out of traditional schooling structures.

The implications for the reconstruction of educational psychology are extremely powerful as it widens the possibilities for cognition and identity formation, expressly the social formation of the learner. Memory is a powerful tool in transforming places into living organisms with multiple perspectives of its history. A reconceptualized educational psychology helps understand how this works and how we might maximize the intersection of memory and educational psychology.

SUGGESTED READING

Huyssen, A. (1993). Monument and memory in a postmodern age. *The Yale Journal of Criticism*, 6 (2), 249–261.

Langer, S. K. (1953). *Feeling and Form: A Theory of Art*. New York: Charles Scribner's Sons.

Rifkin, J. (1991). *Biosphere Politics: A New Consciousness for a New Century*. New York: Crown Publishing.

Simon, R. I., Rosenberg, S., and Eppert, C. (Eds.). (2000). *Between Hope & Despair: Pedagogy and the Remembrance of Historical Trauma*. New York: Rowan & Littlefield.

Slavin, R. E. (2003). *Educational Psychology: Theory and Practice*. Boston, MA: Allyn and Bacon.

CHAPTER 71

Where Is the Mind Supposed to Be?

RICHARD S. PRAWAT

The notion that the mind can occupy various locations may seem strange at first. Nevertheless, this is an issue that has captured the attention of a number of educational psychologists recently. That said, it is also fair to point out that the majority of educational psychologists have *not* abandoned the time-honored notion that knowledge generation, the mind's most important function, takes place entirely within the head. This second group differs about what aspects of knowledge creation ought to be emphasized—coherent structures versus the processes that turn up the patterns or regularities known as concepts—but they are not much concerned with the issue of where those processes take place. Others, like good businessmen, argue that location is everything. They believe that knowledge generation, and thus mind, is an outside-the-head phenomenon. Those that embrace this notion, however, like their more traditional counterparts, evidence some interesting and important differences about the particulars.

Before elaborating on these differing views, and attempting to provide an historical context that will shed light on the origin of these disagreements, I will take up the issue of why the mind's location might matter to psychologists and educators (as opposed to philosophers, who cannot avoid dealing with the problem). The argument goes like this: If you seek to understand how the mind creates knowledge, or if you are interested in efforts to enhance the process, then you ought to know where the action takes place. Learning theorists and teachers who locate the action in the head, in the child's own experiential workspace as it were, have some ideas about where to begin the process of studying, or intervening in, the mind's work. Similarly, psychologists or educators who believe that this process takes place out in the open (e.g., in the apprenticeship-like relationship that connects novice to master) focus on a different set of variables thanks to this assumption. (Not all mind-in-the-world psychologists ignore individual sense making. Sociocultural theorists, in fact, argue that it is alright to focus on individuals as long as one uses the larger interpersonal and cultural context to interpret what they are doing; this is consistent with the notion that mind is "distributed" across both public and private domains.)

Not surprisingly, the mind location issue strongly influences the views that psychologists and educators are willing (or able) to entertain with regard to the process of knowledge acquisition. This is obvious when one focuses on those who believe that the mind is in the world. For all intents and purposes, they are limited to two overt or observable variables: routines or procedures that can be modeled and (hopefully) internalized, and language that can be appropriated or dispensed with depending upon the instructional agenda. Both can legitimately be viewed as knowledge acquisition processes that are *in* the world. It is not an accident, then, that the two groups of mind-in-the-world theorists have highlighted one or the other. Sociocultural theorists have opted for procedure or strategy, the most widely cited example of which might be "reciprocal teaching." Like master carpenters or tailors, master readers (i.e., teachers) work with novice readers, carefully modeling comprehension strategies when reading text like paraphrasing main ideas, asking questions about segments of text, speculating about the future content of passages— all with an eye toward gradually passing off responsibility for this activity from teacher to student.

Social constructivists have settled on language as the mechanism for acquiring knowledge. They cite postmodern philosophers like Richard Rorty and, before him, Ludwig Wittgenstein to support their contention that much is to be gained by viewing knowledge as language, and the knowledge acquisition process as akin to participating in a kind of "language game." According to this perspective, knowledge claims, in the form of propositions and assertions, represent moves in the language game. Whether or not a particular move is allowed to stand depends upon a number of things, including who has made the move and why. Ultimately, however, the fate of any new way of talking is decided on pragmatic grounds: Does the new way of talking—using nonsexist language, for example—increase the likelihood that those making this move will get what they want? Following this argument, use of the expression "mental illness" to describe aberrant behavior won out in the language game because its use came to be associated, at least in many people's minds, with kinder and gentler ways of responding to what hitherto had been referred to as "mad" or "disturbed" people.

In the classroom, social constructivist pedagogy involves negotiating understandings through discourse. The teacher, by modeling disciplinary talk and guiding students in the use of that talk, seeks to reach a consensus with the class about how it, as a surrogate disciplinary community, will talk about certain shared activities and processes (e.g., using the term *refraction* to describe the bent appearance of a straw in a glass of water). The focus here is on the uses and misuses of discourse within a discipline: How does one go about questioning knowledge claims in a discipline like science? What constitutes a persuasive argument for and against such claims? Who participates in the discourse? Who remains silent?

The in-the-head theorists show a similar level of disagreement, equally polite, about process. At the risk of oversimplification, three differing schools of thought are in evidence here. There are the radical constructivists, with their close ties to the great Swiss psychologist Jean Piaget. There is the cognitive science or information processing school, which is a fairly diverse group. And, third, there is a group, mostly in mathematics, which has been heavily influenced by the work of George Herbert Mead and Herbert Blumer. Drawing on the theory known as symbolic interactionalism, they share with social constructivists the belief that meanings are socially negotiated while still maintaining a firm focus on individual sense making. The latter takes place in the head but is shaped and influenced by the social interaction one has with others. In fact, this approach assumes that there is a dynamic tension between self and society. Meaning is owned by the individual but produced through social interaction.

Radical constructivism and information processing both have deep roots in philosophy. The former, as indicated, is based on the work of Jean Piaget. Piaget was quite explicit about the debt he owed to the rationalists. Similarly, information processing theory is based on empiricism. These philosophical connections are important because they help explain how adherents of the two approaches view knowledge and its acquisition. Rationalists and empiricists, historically, have taken different stances on the issue of the relationship between sense and intellect. Rationalists like Descartes drew a sharp distinction between these two domains. The first, which plays a passive role, yields at best impressionistic data. It takes active intervention by the mind to turn this information into the clear and distinct ideas that he most associated with the intellect. Piaget built on these ideas in the key distinction he drew between what he called "figurative" (sensory) and "operative" (logical) knowledge. The latter consists of logical rules like the ability to look at something from more than one perspective—to realize that one can simultaneously be a brother to one member of the family and a son to another. Individuals use their logic, which becomes more sophisticated with age, to create knowledge structures; the latter, reflecting the development of logic, become more coherent or integrated over time.

Empiricists take a different stance toward the relationship between sense and intellect, viewing the two processes as distinct but more equal than the rationalists. Sensory input helps define particular objects—particular dogs or trees, for example. The role of the intellect is to sort through this particular data to find patterns, ways that one particular object resembles another. The basis for this resemblance is tested against promising additional candidates. If it is a key attribute, like having paws as opposed to brown-ness for a dog, it will continue to discriminate between members and nonmembers of the category. The rules that define like things become our concepts, the basic building blocks of knowledge. Concepts, in turn, are related through propositions. Cognitive scientists accept the most important premise of empiricism, the notion that information processing is inductive in nature. Mental activity flows internally from specific input to more general structures (schemas or frames). The process of identifying regularity in the environment, they believe, is made easier by the fact that information is packaged in ways that make this identification easier. Being about the size of a hand and having feathers are two attributes of bird-ness that covary with some regularity.

One assumption that information processors share with radical constructivists is that the internal processes that produce knowledge are deliberate; they cannot be turned on or off by someone else. This is not to say that the processes are not responsive to environment conditions. On the contrary, our minds become more active when we encounter difficulty or impasse, especially if our current ways of construing the situation appear not to be helpful. Problems that get in the way of things we want to accomplish become the impetus for restructuring or repatterning our experience. While radical constructivists and information processors view the process of restructuring or repatterning as primarily an individual event, sociocultural and symbolic interactionalists do not. They do, however, buy into the notion that knowledge is instrumental—that it helps us overcome difficulties or, stated minimally, that it allows us to more effectively or efficiently reach our goals—but they reject the notion that there is such a thing as individual problems or even goals. The latter are culturally defined, even to the extent that there are fundamental differences between "school" mathematical problems and "out of school" mathematical problems.

The knowledge that allows us to solve these kinds of problems is also culturally defined and, more important, socially acquired. Furthermore, this knowledge is often less "taught" than "caught" as we work alongside more knowledgeable others in an effort to overcome difficulty or reach a goal (e.g., being able to go to recess in the case of school mathematical problems). Social constructivists, though they focus more on language than procedure, share the premise that teaching is "enculturation" and that knowledge plays an instrumental role in this regard. One learns to talk about phenomena in science or mathematics in disciplinarily acceptable ways, they argue, because it is associated with good things—good grades, good interactions with teachers, and more facile talk about related phenomena.

What is remarkable about these various constructivisms is not how they *differ* but what they share in *common*. In all cases, the teacher's role is more the proverbial "guide on the side" as opposed to the traditional "sage on the stage." In all cases, knowledge is seen as instrumental, as a means to an end. In all cases, the way to get students to engage with knowledge is to make sure that they see it as instrumental. This, in turn, means that the teacher must get students, individually or as a "learning community," to engage with personally meaningful problems. Given the notion that learning is enculturation, some theorists believe fervently that these problems must be more than personally meaningful—they must also be "authentic." Unlike word problems in mathematics, for example, where students learn to apply algorithms in response to key words like "how much," authentic problems are considered more challenging and more likely to lead to the acquisition of transferable knowledge and skills because they approximate the kinds of problems dealt with by people within the disciplines.

From an educational standpoint, it does not matter much which of the five alternative perspectives a teacher embraces. In fact, it may make sense to "mix and match." If a teacher is intent on students' acquiring a generic cognitive strategy or procedure, the sociocultural model provides the most explicit guidance about how the teacher can *facilitate* this process. If the intent is to challenge the way individual children make sense of their own experience—an example might be the commonsense notion that weight alone determines whether objects sink or float—then radical constructivism offers explicit ideas about how a teacher can *facilitate* this process. If the goal is to get students to appropriate certain modes of discourse in advancing and defending claims in a science or mathematics class, then social constructivism has some helpful ideas about how teachers can *facilitate* this process. If follows from this, of course, that the issue of whether or not the mind is inside or outside the head matters very little to teachers. If true, this interesting fact gives rise to two important questions: The first asks why the mind's location is such an important issue for psychologists; the second asks why the four main views outlined are more alike than different in their application to education, at least as regards the all-important issue of the teacher's role in the instructional process. The answer to both questions lies in the distant past—in fact, in the far distant past, the fourteenth century to be exact.

It was in the fourteenth century that the common ancestor to all of the philosophical "isms" mentioned above was born (i.e., rationalism, empiricism, postmodernism). The name of the common ancestor, philosophically speaking, was another "ism," *nominalism*. Many, if not most, philosophers regard the triumph of nominalism in the fourteenth century as a signal event in the transition to modern times. Nominalism, a number of scholars have declared, is the philosophical basis for all of Western thought and culture. I have told the story elsewhere of how this set of beliefs came to prevail in the great philosophical debates being waged in the high middle ages (a time, by the way, that is being positively reevaluated by recent historians). These debates were so heated that many exchanges of views ended up being exchanges of threats and even of fists. The story is worth recapping here because it bears on the two questions raised above.

Many things were at issue in the great philosophical debate in the fourteenth century. The main bone of contention between William of Ockham, who developed nominalism, and John Duns Scotus, his predecessor, and main rival as the originator of scholastic realism, was the status of universals. Ockham insisted that all commonality between objects (i.e., horses, men) and events (the attraction and repulsion of magnetic poles) represents a mental creation, the mind's detection of a resemblance or similarity between different, particular objects and events. Duns Scotus insisted that commonality actually exists, independent of our thoughts. What makes an object or event unique (e.g., this dog), he argued, is intertwined with what makes it an example of something more general (e.g., a dog). At issue, then, was the question of whether regularity is a word (e.g., a "concept"), a perceived and named similarly derived from one's own particular experience, or whether it actually exists in nature. This argument may seem arcane but its resolution in favor of the nominalist position has had far-reaching effects on philosophy, both modern and postmodern.

One far-reaching effect is that nominalism led to a walling-off of mind or, in the case of postmodern nominalism, its encasement in language, thus eliminating the possibility that mind can have any direct relationship with the world. This last claim may seem strange, especially in light of postmodern efforts to locate mind in language and language in the world. Focusing on this issue first, it is true that language is in the world and does, in a sense, "operate" on that world in a tool-like manner; this is not unlike how a shovel operates on the soil it moves. What language cannot do is mesh or join with that world. To do that, two things are required: ideas must originate in the senses, and the world has to be an equal partner in the enterprise. Nominalists limit the world's role to offering up particular objects. The mind is the star in this scenario; it is the mind that acts on particulars in the process known as "induction" to create the generality or regularity that is associated with understanding.

Duns Scotus, writing some twenty years before Ockham, may have been the first to put mind and world on equal footing. Regularity or universality, like rationality in humans or, in later centuries, gravity or photosynthesis, is present in nature. Furthermore, the role it plays in making itself known is as active as that of the human mind. Scotus was the first to posit a relationship of true reciprocity between mind and world. This last point requires some elaboration. The middle ages were dominated by religion; both Scotus and Ockham, in fact, were members of a religious order as well as academicians. The vexing philosophical issues that Scotus struggled with was how to respond to Aristotle, whose newly discovered writings, lost to the West for a thousand years, were wreaking havoc with the Catholic church. Scotus, and before him, Aquinas, tried to square Aristotle's notion of natural law with divine power, evidenced by God's spontaneous will. Contrary to Aristotle's teachings, the scholastics thought that God could, if he so willed, change a human embryo into a tree. Contingency rather than necessity was the order of the day. Scotus's solution to this vexing problem was to view *in*determinacy in positive rather than negative terms. Contingency does not represent nature falling short in some way. Rather, it represents the wide-ranging nature and creativity of God's thought. At the moment of creation, God sees all the possibilities open to him, now and in the future. In a sense, the alternatives are all spelled out ahead of time. It is the function of God's will, when the proper time comes, to determine which, if any, of the possibilities he actualizes.

Scotus's decision to put possibility on the same continuum with necessity humbled intellect at the same time that it elevated will. It is will, at both the divine and the human level, that converts imperfectly understood possibilities into fully realized facts. Confused knowledge, grasped qualitatively (e.g., metaphorically), is the first step in the acquisition of more certain knowledge. The brilliance of Scotus's solution was to allow for a type of knowing that could put the mind in direct relationship to the object or event the inquirer is attempting to know. Individual objects are an amalgam of particular and general attributes. The mind *discovers* generality; it does not, as Ockham would argue, *create* it. The discovery process is a joint one. Both "object and author," to use Scotus's language, play active roles. It surfaces as mere possibility and is grasped by the mind as a sign (e.g., called a "phantasm" by Scotus). Charles Sanders Peirce, who built on Scotus's ideas in the nineteenth century, would liken this imaginative rendering of generality to that of a metaphor; a modern-day example might be seeing the plant as a "food factory." When the object is viewed through the lens of the sign, it contributes to the discovery process by allowing certain features to emerge in sharp relief while blocking other, presumably irrelevant features.

The term Scotus used to describe this hybrid sign-object was, appropriately, that of the "physical universal." Drawing on our modern-day example, this means that during the qualitative first stage of coming to understand, the individual can truly see the plant as a factory that produces food—see that there is a production process going on within the confines of the leaf, that these products are warehoused, that a waste product is given off, and so forth. Two points are worth noting here: Scotus's scholastic realism allowed for the mind to mesh or interrelate with the world in the early stages of understanding; concepts are immediately obtained from objects. (This understanding, of course, must be reformulated as a proposition.) Second, Scotus's view of God (and nature) is an intellectually friendly one. By building essence into being, God all but ensures that our experience with nature will be a conceptual as well as a sensory one. Furthermore, although God does not tip his hand in advance, he does make choices that follow a logically consistent pattern. This is a direct outgrowth of the notion of possible worlds. God can decide, to use a non–middle-ages example, to allow or not to allow life forms to develop on earth; once that decision is made, other decisions, like what role to assign intelligence, follow from it.

Ockham rejected Scotus's view, and did it in a way that must be considered radical from our current-day perspective. Scotus's assumptions, Ockham argued, limit God's power and thus must be rejected. While Scotus sought a balance between will and intellect for both God and man, Ockham insisted that God's will must always reign supreme. The idea that God, in the exercise of that will, is somehow bound by the set of possibilities that he was initially willing to entertain, made no sense to Ockham. God need only please himself. With one stroke of his famous Razor, Ockham eliminated the notion that God set out to create an articulate world, one that man could grasp and appreciate. Gone with the same decisive blow was the ancient distinction between substance and accident, the particular and the universal. This last distinction was also viewed as an unnecessary obstacle to God's infinite power. Nothing "essential" to an object can preexist in God's mind because that also would serve as a constraint on God's power. God cannot be subordinate to either nature or reason.

God thus created a relation-less world, which is to say, a world filled with particular things. Those particular things may resemble one another in various ways, but that resemblance resides entirely in the things themselves, not in some third construct that might be termed a "relation" or a "commonality." This is a fine point but one that is extremely significant. It moved the all-important task of identifying regularity or pattern into the head—thus cutting off at the knees the promising notion, proposed by Scotus, that mind and object play reciprocal roles in the identification of lawfulness. Furthermore, because nominalism prevailed over scholastic realism, Ockham's encasement of mind in head (or in language in the present, postmodern era) set the tone in philosophy for virtually its entire existence. A logical consequence of this stance is that there is no way for individuals to *directly* (if qualitatively) test the validity of the regularity they create in their minds. According to nominalism, we have no direct access to objects—to "things in themselves"; we have access only to our representations of those objects.

In Ockham's theory, this problem was compounded by the fact that he ruled *out* the possibility that the concepts—the "names"—that result from identifying similarity can be represented by composite images (i.e., a general dog image). Concepts are represented by individual things in keeping with his notion that there are no generals or universals in either the world or in thought. This is the opening wedge in the nominalist distinction between input and output, content and process. The nominalist wedge between content and process was widened further by Ockham's insistence that concepts are, at best, intermediate products. The final products of knowledge are the propositions that relate one or more concepts to another. The important point to keep in mind is that Ockham introduced a clear demarcation between the senses and the intellect. Scotus, on the other hand, argued that sense and intellect are on a continuum. The midpoint on this continuum is marked by a construct, the "concrete universal," that he (and Peirce much later in the nineteenth century) defined as a hybrid of the physical and the mental (i.e., a metaphor, schematized and applied to the object).

Descartes, the first of the modern philosophers, was to widen the sense–intellect divide even further. As a number of recent scholars have pointed out, Descartes picked up on Ockham's notion that an all-powerful God is under no compulsion to play it straight with man. God has the power to deceive as well as to illuminate. He can, if he chooses, make one see things that do not exist or overlook things that really are present. The lesson that Descartes was to draw from this is that the senses are not to be trusted. With or without God's help, Descartes decided, sense is an unreliable partner in the process of knowledge acquisition: the stick that appears to be bent in water, the sun that seems small in comparison with objects on earth are two instances that testify to this fact. Descartes' skepticism called into question the whole idea of knowledge, as he himself understood. The notion that the senses can deceive gave rise to the profound doubt that led Descartes to search for the one thing about which he could be absolutely certain. That turned out to be, to Descartes' satisfaction at least, his famous principle, "I think, therefore I am." The soul searching that resulted in the discovery of this fundamental principle led to the discovery of another, which, while implicit in Ockham's theory, was to be made explicit by Descartes: Trust the power of the intellect to overcome the shortcomings of the senses. The key to true knowledge lies in the inner sanctum of the human mind. This notion was to become a staple of all rationalist thinking in the future. Richard Rorty describes the rationalist approach as that of turning the "Eye of Mind" away from the confused representations derived from sense to the clear and distinct ones created by intuition and logic.

Descartes argued that intuition is the starting point in the creation of certain knowledge. Mathematics points the way in this regard. One can mentally intuit the fact that triangles are bounded by three lines; that spheres are bounded by a single surface; or that one can, through the power of indefinite addition, create infinity large numbers. Simple, necessary truths like these become the basis for deductive reasoning. The way to arrive at certain truth as regards *particular* instances (e.g., "I think therefore I am"; "This square is a rectangle"), Descartes insisted, is to start with a *general* principle about which there can be no doubt (e.g., "Whatever thinks is," "All squares are rectangles"). The particular instance is always deduced from the more general principle in the process known as analytic reasoning. Descartes allowed for two other ways of knowing: impulse, which is where we take information provided by the senses at face value (e.g., agreeing that the stick in the water is bent), and conjecture, which is based on general principles that we believe to be true but about which we lack certainty. Propositions like the notion that we have a body and that various other bodies exist in the vicinity of that body are included in this second category. The highest honor, though, goes to analytic thinking.

John Locke, who was born in 1632, eighteen years before Descartes' death, took issue with two of the latter's key ideas and did so in a way that tied them together. In so doing, he laid the groundwork for empiricism, a variant on nominalist philosophy that served as the intellectual rationale for seventeenth-century inductionist science. Whether or not the senses are untrustworthy is a moot point, Locke argued; the senses are our *only* source of knowledge. Even mathematical or fantastic objects (e.g., leprechauns) that cannot be directly experienced are constructed from concepts derived from experience. As the last statement implies, Locke also rejects Descartes' notion of innate ideas. Locke's approach more clearly hued to the nominalist line laid down 300 years earlier by William of Ockham, with some important exceptions.

According to Locke, we process sensory input in a two-stage fashion. The first stage, if that is the correct term, is composed of what Locke terms "simple" sensory ideas (Locke used the term "idea" in a generic way to refer to the mental contents of both perceptions and thoughts). Some simple sensory ideas "resemble" their objects (e.g., size, shape, number). Others, like sound, do not. (We do not hear the vibration that produces sound; we detect its *effect* on our hearing apparatus.) Simple ideas, according to Locke, are the building blocks of sensory experience. The mind draws on these to construct "complex" sensory ideas that capture the richness of objects like dogs and trees, a process that invariably involves selection. One cannot possibly include all of the sensory elements associated with a pet dog, for example; one must home in on those—a distinctive sound, smell, type of movement—that offer the greatest opportunity of identifying the dog as one's own.

The act of "compounding" simple ideas to construct complex ones sets the stage for the act of abstraction, a process that yields the "collection of common sensations" known as concepts. Fortunately, nature colludes in this. There is a relationship between attributes that prove useful in identifying particular objects (e.g., a distinctive type of bark in the case of my pet dog) and those that prove useful in identifying a category of objects (e.g., barking as opposed to meowing sounds). Because Locke is more explicit than Ockham about how sense connects to concept, it is not surprising that he is also more explicit about the role that words play in the process. Words do not stand for things; they stand for our ideas about things. Most of the words we use in communication are general terms. The ideas that they stand for must therefore also be general. His compositional approach to complex sensory ideas—which accepts the premise that they are never as complete as they could be—allows for the creation of abstract ideas that nevertheless consist of concrete content. This is achieved by simply stripping away irrelevant particular attributes.

The problem with this approach, which the other great eighteenth-century empiricist, David Hume, was to build on, is that it involves an enormous amount of compounding or "synthesis." Furthermore, despite nature's help in bundling sensory elements, the process seems extraordinarily burdensome from a mental processing perspective. This was Kant's concern. Immanuel Kant is the third great modern philosopher who deserves some brief discussion. Before delving into his solution to the problems raised by the two groups of nominalist philosophers, the rationalists and the empiricists, it might be helpful to once again pick up the threads of the initial argument about the location of the mind. Both rationalists and empiricists, it should be obvious, locate mind in the head. Furthermore, because both draw a sharp distinction between the sensory input that constitutes the raw material for knowledge, and the intellectual output–concepts and propositions—that represents the content of knowledge, they share a common problem: How does one test the validity of knowledge created in the recesses of an individual's mind? The only answer either can provide is to say, "Closely monitor the internal process."

Rationalists like Descartes, who put their faith in deductive logic, use internal coherence as the test of the rightness or truthfulness of one's beliefs. True beliefs hang together; they "fit" or cohere. Empiricists face a tougher task. The two aspects over which they have some influence are sensory input and language output. Thus, early empiricists like Locke emphasized the importance of reforming language. He complained that "vague and insignificant" forms of language pass for the "mysteries of science." Francis Bacon, one of the pioneers of empiricism, called for a special kind of language in science that more closely approximates the "primitive purity" of things. Prior to Bacon and Locke, rhetoric—the art of persuasion—was the process of choice in the attempt to separate truth from falsehood. The problem with rhetoric, the empiricists thought, is that it is as much an art as a science. In skillful hands, even a bad argument can be made persuasive (the core of the word "suadere" shares a root with "suavis," which means "sweet" in Latin). Science needs to cultivate discourse that stays as close as possible to its experiential roots.

As indicated, early empiricists also emphasized how important it is to carefully monitor the sensory input. This meant one thing: adhering to method. Method is everything. At the core of method was what might best be termed "disciplined seeing." The would-be scientist had to train his (or, less the norm, her) eyes to make sure that the sensory input represented, as far as possible, genuine, "indubitable" fact. All things come to us in the particular but that must not be taken to mean that they come to us in a muddle; aspects of the particular can be noted and referred back to during the pattern finding and naming stage (in the process known as induction). It soon became evident to the empiricists that one need not rely on nature to present its particulars—it is possible to "tweak" these particulars in a more controlled way in the effort to discern pattern, especially a cause-and-effect pattern, which is science's highest ambition. These experimental manipulations, the prime example of which is Boyle's famous seventeenth-century air pump demonstrations, were taken to stand for how things actually work in nature.

As suggested above, one can map truth conditions developed by the early rationalists and early empiricists directly onto those developed 300 years later by their psychological counterparts—the so-called radical constructivists (neo-Piagetians), and the information processors. Radical constructivists like Ernst von Glasersfeld have adopted the internal coherence criterion developed by

Rene Descartes in his famous "structures of thought" argument. Similarly, information processors seek to track the flow of data from input, through abstraction, to propositional knowledge. A machine unimaginable in Locke's time, the high-speed computer, has been appropriated for this task. The argument goes like this: When a computer program, designed to mimic processes used by humans, produces behavior that parallels that observed in a real-life situation, the result is said to constitute a "sufficiency proof," which validates the information processing model.

The other two learning theories talked about earlier—the sociocultural and social constructivist approaches—might appear to have an advantage over the head encased views just described when it comes to knowledge validation because the processes they emphasize are overt rather than covert. This is possible, I submit, because socioculturalists and social constructivists have made a virtue out of what Scotus and Peirce would consider a great weakness in current approaches to learning: This is the distinction, nominalist in origin, between content and process. As has been shown, this distinction is a key feature of rationalism, empiricism, and even of Kant's valiant attempt to meld the two (see below). Thus, sociocultural theorists argue that mental activity, like the physical activity involved in tailoring or weaving, can be externalized and modeled because it is content free. The comprehension-monitoring activity taught during reciprocal teaching, activities such as summarizing and question asking, while intended for reading, can be applied to oral-language situations as well. Social constructivists make a similar point about "language-ing." They reject what they consider to be the outdated, modernist view of language as a container or holder of knowledge and meaning. The function of language is to manage or coordinate human relationships. Both sets of theorists, then, build on the notion that there is process without content.

History, including intellectual history, is filled with "what ifs." One of the major what ifs relates to Peirce's effort in the late nineteenth century to resurrect Scotus's unique version of what, from the present-day perspective, could only be called "realist constructivism." Peirce argued forcefully that Scotus's view did not get a fair hearing in the fourteenth century. It lost out to Ockham's nominalism on political and not philosophical grounds. Scotus's belief that generals or universals actually exist in individuals was viewed with suspicion by the humanists, who joined forces with the nominalists to defeat this notion. They equated this idea with a more conservative stance toward authority, the subtext for them apparently being that it takes extraordinary expertise to tease out the regularity posited by Scotus. In that sense, the aversion nominalists and humanists felt toward Scotus's realism is not unlike the aversion social constructivists feel toward scientific realists—a major factor in the ongoing "science wars."

Peirce did not just base his realist constructivism on Scotus's five centuries old work. He had a more recent model, Immanuel Kant, who Peirce termed "his revered master." Kant is best known for his attempt in the late eighteenth century to reconcile the dramatically different stances taken by rationalists and empiricists. In the first approach, reason runs roughshod over the senses, while in the second the converse often appears to be the case. Kant's well-known solution to these problems was twofold: he argued that our perceptual apparatus is structured in such a way as to compel us to compound or synthesize sensory input to produce "bundles" of spatially located and temporally ordered sensation. Similarly, our cognitive apparatus all but mandates that we conceptualize experience in certain predetermined ways. Thus, we always attend to the number of objects in the experience, the intensity or "realness" of the experience, the scope of time of the experience—whether, for example, we are dealing with things that are happening now or that will happen in the future. Finally, we take note, again in a general sense, of the nature of the relation we are coming to terms with—whether, for example, it is an object–attribute or cause–effect relationship.

Less well known but of equal importance to Peirce was Kant's insistence that what we come to know about objects is their form or essence. Kant was the first modern philosopher to resurrect the notion that both commonness (i.e., universals) and particularity coexist in individual things.

Like Scotus, he believed that the former tells us more about the object than the latter. Cognition requires concepts, Kant insisted, and concepts are always universals that take the form of rules. The rules, not surprisingly, are constructed by the mind but—and it is this "but" that causes several recent interpreters of Kant to label him a "realist"—they are based on *real* universals. In Kant's theory, these universals are not experienced directly, as they are in Scotus's approach. The universals are embedded in sensory experience and pulled out, in the form of "schemas," by the imagination. The mind then represents this generality in the form of a rule.

Peirce used Kant's theory as a starting point for his own version of Scotus's realism. After many false starts, Peirce rejected the Kantian approach—where the universal is grounded in fact but made by the mind—as too weak. He opted for a much stronger version of realist constructivism. Like Scotus, Peirce argued that, through a process of creative perception facilitated by metaphor (e.g., seeing the regularity known as photosynthesis as akin to manufacturing a product), we directly and reciprocally interact with the regularity or universality that we are trying to understand.

The important point to ponder, especially by those interested in reconceptualizing educational psychology, is what would happen if psychologists and educators suddenly adopted a nonnominalist version of constructivism, one that does not assume that process and content are distinct, or that the test of knowledge is always instrumental. More to the point, what would happen if we adopted what, for a lack of a better term, might be labeled "realist constructivism." The set of advocates for this approach, giants of philosophy like Duns Scotus, Immanuel Kant, Charles Sanders Peirce, and, somewhat arguably, John Dewey in the second half of his life, is every bit as impressive as that belonging to the nominalist camp. To this illustrious group one must add the voices of virtually all current scientists and philosophers of science who agree that induction pales in comparison with the role that insight or illumination plays in teasing out important regularities in science like atomism (the metaphor for which was a tiny solar system), or natural selection (the metaphor for which was man selecting to create new animal species). This last fact alone has huge implications for teachers and students, suggesting an approach that differs dramatically from that described earlier.

Teachers in the realist constructivist classroom certainly would not play the traditional "sage on the stage" role. Nor, interestingly enough, would they assume the more passive "guide on the side" stance described earlier. Teachers in the realist constructivist classroom would adopt a role that differs in important ways from these other two roles. They would function like expert tour guides—those at least who manage not to upstage the phenomena it is their responsibility to bring to their charges. The expression that best captures this third role is that of "sage on the side," a person who works hard to get his or her students to see the wondrous regularity that those in the disciplines have worked so hard to turn up—not just in science but in mathematics, if that is the teacher's subject, or history or literature. The teachers, in this approach, would embrace the insight provided by Scotus and Peirce: All understanding has its roots in qualitative thought. The implication of this notion for teaching is that teachers must rely on tools like metaphor, physical enactment, technology-mediated simulation, and the like, to tease out and concretize the most salient aspects of the important regularities the are trying to get their students to understand.

TERMS FOR READERS

Empiricism—A "trust your senses" philosophical theory that played a pivotal role in the development of experimentally based science.

Nominalism—The theory that holds that generality is created in the human mind from particular sensory experiences.

Postmodernism—This theory takes the nominalist content–process distinction to a new level, downplaying the role of language as a carrier of content in favor of the notion of language as a tool.

Rationalism—An approach to knowledge that equates truth with the mental integrativeness or coherence that results when one applies logic to fact

Realist constructivism—The philosophical view that maintains that human beings, through a creative act of intelligence, can directly access the regularity or lawfulness present *in* the world.

FURTHER READING

Haack, S. (1998). "We pragmatists. . .": Peirce and Rorty in conversation. In S. Haack (Ed.), *Manifesto of a Passionate Moderate* (pp. 31–47). Chicago: University of Chicago Press.

Miller, A. I. (2000). *Insights of Genius. Imagery and Creativity in Science and Art*. Cambridge, MA: MIT Press.

Prawat, R. S. (1999). Cognitive theory at the crossroads: Head fitting, head splitting, or somewhere in between? *Human Development* 42, 59–77.

CHAPTER 72

Neuropolitics: Neuroscience and the Struggles over the Brain

JOHN WEAVER

Neuroscience is the latest interdisciplinary field that is producing impressive results in the quest to understand and map the brain. It combines cognitive psychology, neurophilosophy, computer programming, and medicine. Neuroscience also is a sign of the times as it seeks to unveil and reduce the mysteries of the brain to a principle of transparency. Transparency is a hallmark characteristic of our postmodern world as the Visible Human Project in anatomy and Physiology, "reality" television, online shopping, virtual architecture, and surveillance cameras suggest. In our transparent world, we work from the assumption that everything can and should be opened in front of our eyes so we can peruse, investigate, lurk, and pry into the interworkings of all facets of life. Neuroscience is no different than voyeuristic television in this regard. Neuroscience offers us fresh insights into such issues as the mind/body dichotomy, the stale nature/nurture debate, diversity, and creativity. Yet, it also threatens to open up frightful issues dealing with the minds of criminals, unborn fetuses, and life or death issues. In spite of what many of the advocates of neuroscience proclaim, this new field of study has ushered in a new era of neuropolitics in which the mind/brain is a new site of political struggles. In this essay, I want to explain the basics of neuroscience, delve into some of the interesting issues neuroscience reinvigorates, and remind my readers that neuroscience has the dangerous potential to become a new form of eugenics where purist's nightmares are put into action.

NEUROSCIENCE BASICS

Neuroscientists estimate that there are one hundred billion neurons in the brain with each neuron containing thousands of synaptic connections. Each synaptic connection symbolizes a weight or a strength that the neuron can use to connect to other neurons to create a network for sight, taste, touch, smell, or the many other functions the brain performs. The potential strengths and weaknesses of the connections are virtually infinite given that the potential neuron networks can choose from scenarios that contain one hundred billion neurons connected to one hundred trillion synapses. For example with sight, the neuron connections can range from legal blindness (poor neuron connections) to a life time of 20/20 vision or better (very strong connections) with millions of possible levels of strengths in between this continuum.

This land of infinite possibilities is only the beginning of the neuro-odyssey into the brain. Given these possibilities for connections each brain is unique with different neural connections shaping each brain differently even for identical twins who might experience the same things throughout their lives. There should be little wonder why the brain has remained a mystery for centuries. How could anyone draw generalizations about the brain when every brain is different in terms of neural networks and synaptic connections? To make the understanding of the potential connections more daunting is the reality that the brain is always active, losing neurons here and making new connections there.

These staggering numbers have not stopped neuroscientists from understanding the brain because like so many other fields in science, neuroscience has benefited greatly from the development of computers. Specifically, neuroscientists have learned to utilize parallel processing computers to understand the brain. Whereas Descartes, Leibniz and other early speculators of the mind and brain did not have the benefit of computers, neuroscientists do, and they are using it to their advantage to advance numerous theories about the brain.

The use of parallel computers is called Parallel Distribution Processing. It works from the assumption that the brain with its one hundred trillion synaptic connections has different layers of neuron networks with each neuron and its synaptic connection aiding in a function of the brain. For example, the neuro-philosopher Paul Churchland points out that humans have only four taste receptors in their mouth. Yet, of course, there are more than four types of tastes. Our taste receptors overcome this simple problem by having different levels of activation for each kind of taste. As Churchland points out if there were only ten activation levels on our four receptors that would still mean we could distinguish between 10,000 different kinds of tastes. We remember these tastes by moving through different layers of neurons creating different paths within the brain in which each neuron in the path represents a small part of the experience and remembrance of taste. Like a parallel processing computer, if we were to lose a few of the neurons within our connections to recognize say the taste of a lemon, we would not lose that ability to recognize a lemon nor would we have to relearn the taste of a lemon each time we tasted one. The same holds for parallel computers. If there is a glitch in one or two areas of a program, a parallel computer would not lose its ability to process a program. It would only find a new way around the program error. Given that the brain works on a parallel distribution process, it is able to continue to function with a loss of 10 percent of its neurons without major damage to our ability to function. This does not mean that the brain's ability to function on a parallel distribution basis prevents any permanent loss of function. When the brain loses too many of the neuron layers as a result of a lesion that disrupts the normal network pathways we lose that function and the result can be major long-term brain dysfunction.

This ability to create neuron patterns permits neuroscientists to speculate how the brain creates its own concepts and categories to remember and house different experiences such as specific tastes, the recognition of faces, or the recognition of similar words. Humans are able to remember different tastes, faces, or words because the neuron pathways not only work in a forward moving motion from the world to the sensory-motor apparatuses of our bodies to the numerous neuron layers within our brain, they also work backward. This ability is called feedbackward or recurrent pathways. Recurrent pathways permit the brain to remember experiences such as tastes, faces, or words that are similar and the brain is able to construct prototypes or categories in which similar experiences or concepts can be placed, remembered, and stored until they are needed the next time the brain experiences the taste of a lemon, sees a familiar face, or reads/hears a new word. This ability to create and maintain recurrent pathways permit the brain to work in an efficient manner so it need not create new neural pathways each time it comes upon something that is similar but slightly different from something else.

If this was all that neuroscientists knew about the brain it would not be much. The key to this theory about neural pathways is the ability to know what part of the brain is activated when say the brain is creating neural pathways to categorize and create a prototype to remember what a lemon tastes like. It is here that parallel processing computers along with Magnetic Resonance Imagings (MRI) and Positron Emission Tomography (PET) scans have been vital. What neuroscientists have discovered/created is a Baudrillardian example of a simulation creating an understanding of reality. Through the use of parallel processing computers, neuroscientists have been able to create artificial neural networks that provide clues as to how actual neural networks function. For example, neuroscientists have created computer programs using activation patterns, parallel distribution processing, and a method called backpropagation (a method to discover the various weights of synaptic connections) to produce a computer program that can recognize faces in a manner just as effective as humans. This program created by Garrison Cottrell and his laboratory group with its backpropagated synaptic connections acted similar to the way the human brain does. It created prototypes of male and female faces and from this was able to recognize familiar faces introduced to it in a training set.

Taking this knowledge of how parallel processing and activation patterns function in computers, neuroscientists with the assistance of MRI and PET scans are trying to understanding what part of the brain performs what functions when dealing with activities such as recognizing familiar faces. PET scans provide neuroscientists with the ability to watch which part of the brain and which neurons are activated causing an increase of blood to that area of the brain. MRIs provide the computer images of the brain that can be dissected and exposed to the cubic millimeter. The output from these three computer-generated images—artificial neural networks, PET scans, and the images of the brain garnered from MRIs—have given neuroscientists much to speculate about.

THE HOPE OF NEUROSCIENCE

The successes of neuroscience in the last twenty years have lead to the rethinking of basic psychological debates that have existed since the inception of the discipline in the late 1800s. One of those debates is the stale nature/nurture debate. This debate is prominent in the debate over the intelligence of a child: is the child born intelligent or is the child a product of its environment? The debate has become a dreadful way to justify inequalities in places such as United States and England where political officials and policy makers pay lip service to notions of equality. Neuroscience weighs in on this debate and suggests that when it comes to the development of the brain it is both nature and nurture but once the child is born it is nurturing that is most important. Each neuron is "predisposed" to perform a certain function within the brain (nature), however, when a child is born all neurons are fair game and can be used to perform any function no matter what its destiny was. After a child is born and neural networks are constructed, the first networks to be created are not the last. The human continues to develop neural networks that help them understand the world around them. The old adage one cannot teach an old dog new tricks fits perfectly in a world where certain ideological policy makers want to limit the support governments give to certain social groups. However, the reality of the brain is that all brains from those of a child to that of a senior citizen are constantly growing, and if given a chance all brains can be nurtured to accomplish things psychologists thought impossible.

This ability to create new neural networks in the lifespan of the brain leads us into the issue of multiculturalism. The neurophilosopher Paul Churchland believes that those people who are able to create numerous neural pathways in order to see and understand moral dilemmas in the world will be those people who are better adapted for a diverse world. Given this assumption about the need and ability to create more than one neural pathway for moral reasoning, and given the growth of diverse cultures within the United States and other nations, it is an imperative that schools begin to nurture in the minds of children alternative ways to see the world. Those children who are sheltered from alternative views of the world and alternative approaches to moral issues will find their brains have stopped growing and as a result their conflicts with the world around them have grown.

We can take the same notion of promoting neural pathways to understand creativity as well. If the solution to various problems depends on how well we create alternative neural pathways to see and understand the world around us, then we can use this same reasoning in regards to creativity. In order to promote the creativity of young people schools need to provide students alternatives to approach a problem or subject from as many different angles as possible. The creative student will be the person who can see that there is a humanities solution to a scientific problem or understand that there are numerous ways to represent the world without proclaiming one has the Truth. Unfortunately, while neuroscience is taking us in these interesting directions, schools are moving toward standardization and the stifling of the creative mind. Even more tragic is when schools are not trying to stifle the creativity of students through standardization, they are trying to normalize and pacify students through psychoactive drugs in the name of classroom management and high performing (test taking) schools.

Neuro-philosophers such as Patricia Churchland are suggesting that the research in neuroscience is providing new insights into the centuries old debate about the mind and body. Patricia Churchland along with her colleagues Antonia Damasio and Paul Churchland have argued that neural networks and their abilities to represent the world and induce moral reasoning within human brains demonstrates that there is no dichotomy between the mind and the brain. The brain is the mind and the mind is part of the body. There is no mysterious substance or even a spirit. Take away the brain and one takes away the mind. Neither one can function without the other. Such an approach obviously opens up not only philosophical questions but questions about deeply embedded theological questions that are the hallmark of many dimensions of Western civilization.

IS FRANKENSTEIN'S CREATION AROUND THE CORNER?

The notion that the mind is the physical brain not only broaches serious theological issues but also raises potentially dangerous cultural and social concerns that neuro-philosophers seem to be either ignorant of or ambivalent toward. It is the answers (or the neural networks we create) to these moral debates that will determine the type of society we will live in and whether Frankenstein's monster is just around the corner.

It is the neuro-philosopher Paul Churchland who broaches many of these issues in his path-breaking book *The Engine of Reason, the Seat of the Soul: A Philosophical Journey into the Brain*. He offers suggestions and insights into many of the social issues that concern us. For instance in regards to the death penalty, Churchland implies that there is an alternative. One of the things Churchland suggests is that we could learn many things using a comparative brain approach. He advocates the pooling of all the PET and CAT scans and MRIs into one system so we can compare all the brains within the system. Image you have been experiencing a persistent tingling in your limbs and some times a loss of feeling in your digits. You go to your doctor, she scans your brain, places your brain images into a database, the database compares it with all the people who have suffered strokes and the program prints out a diagnosis that suggests you are on course for a stroke. How relieved would you be to know that you just averted a major health crisis? This is the potential of Churchland's suggestions.

Unfortunately he does not stop at helping doctors with diagnoses. Churchland suggests that this database can be used to see what it is within the brains of some to be recidivist criminals. If doctors could locate a commonality in the brains of recidivists would society be tempted to use it to "control" criminals? Would this be our version of a frontal lobotomy? Here everything that we have gained in the name of nurturing from neuroscientists, society will lose if Churchland's scheme is adopted. To suggest that there is a neural pathway within repeat criminals ignores all the environmental dimensions such as poverty and free market Darwinian social policies that reward wealthy corporations and punish poor individuals. Such schemes and ideas cannot be left up to drifting neuro-philosophers who fail to see any problem with their visions of utopia constructed through the lens of a MRI computer screen. There needs to be a vigorous public debate and vigorous standards protecting the minds of individuals no matter how dangerous the people may be. It is only public debate, public action, and public vigilance that will prevent neuropolitics from becoming Mary Shelley's nightmare.

The politics do not end with criminals. Churchland offers insights into other social matters. If we work from the premise that neuroscience has demonstrated that everything we have contributed to such nonmaterial things as the mind or the spirit is actually the physical brain at work, then we can conclude that the brain is the meaning and the source of life. If the brain is dead, then so is the rest of the body. This has major implications for the whole life cycle. If the brain is the determining characteristic for what is a living thing, then the abortion standards of the United States need to be changed. The brain in a fetus is not developed until the third trimester; therefore the fetus is not a human being conceived at birth and abortion is legal up to the full development of the brain. Anything before full development is not a taking of a life. No matter where one stands on the issue of abortion, this matter has to meet the same standard as that of the treatment of recidivists. If there is no public debate over these issues and only scientific proclamation, then we have abandoned our dreams of a democracy and ceded our rights to a handful of scientists.

This matter concerns the elderly too. Should individuals who have suffered a mild or even extreme loss in their brainpower be allowed to end their life because their quality of brain activity and function has decreased? The Neuro-reduction of life to the brain suggests yes. What about the adults who have been in an accident and are labeled brain dead but their heart, lungs, and other vital organs are still functioning? Are these persons dead, should they be permitted to die, and should we be able to "harvest" their organs to give to someone who might have a failing heart but a sound brain? Neuro-philosophers would suggest yes to these issues. How ever you might respond to these questions is a matter of your conscience or how many neural networks you have developed to understand these moral dilemmas. But respond we must. Our responses will dictate the directions neuroscience research will go and how it will be used in our society. Our democracy depends on how we respond to these issues, and we can rest uncomfortably knowing that pharmaceuticals, medical companies, and other high-stake groups are hoping we abdicate our democratic rights and responsibilities because there are billions of dollars to be made in this new research.

A final dimension of neuropolitics is the manner in which science is conceptualized within the realm of neuroscience. Neuro-philosophers such as Paul and Patricia Churchland construct an image of science that is based more in the ideals of science—fantasies of science—and less in the reality and politics of science. The Churchlands often construct science as a fallible endeavor but always self-correcting. Their works are filled with pre-Kuhnian ideals that treat science as a rational endeavor, and free of any interpolitical maneuvers. If emotions enter into neuroscience, they are held in check with the sound principles of science. The construction of science as something above human endeavors is a centuries old strategy to place acts of scientists above critical questioning. The Churchlands continue this tradition.

The work of sociologists, anthropologists, and philosophers of science such as Bruno Latour, Peter Galison, N. Katherine Hayles, Arkady Plotnitsky, Alan Gross, Steve Shapin, and Evelyn Fox Keller have demonstrated that science cannot avoid politics, and neuroscience is no different. No matter what neuroscience accomplishes, it will be caught up in the political struggles of representing data, competing for funding, constructing myths of who discovered what, and controlling the flow of knowledge to determine what will enjoy the label of truth. When developing theories of the brain and how neuroscience can assist us in developing public policy, it is dangerous to stake out such a naïve claim of science that one finds in the work of the Churchlands. To work from the assumption that science is self-correcting, rationale, and apolitical will set the stage for the creation of public policy that will eventually do more harm than good.

A more fruitful approach to science is found in the work of Martin Heidegger, Giles Deleuze, and Felix Guattari. These philosophers have established the principle that it is philosophy not science that is the most important endeavor when thinking and creating. Science enframes, observes, and categorizes the real, thereby limiting and unsuccessfully trying to control it. Philosophy on the other hand creates concepts to think about the real, which includes science. Rather than enclosing debate over matters of the real, philosophy opens up possibilities to think about it. Neuroscience in all its brilliance will serve the needs of the world best if science is not idealized so as to make it immune from critical questioning. Debating the politics of this new field is the place to start in order to make sure we as citizens of the world have an opportunity to shape the course of neuroscience and how the discoveries/ theories of this new field will be utilized in our name.

FURTHER READING

On Neuroscience

Churchland, Patricia (2001). *Brian-Wise: Studies in Neuro-philosophy*. Cambridge, MA: MIT.

Churchland, Paul (1996). *The Engine of Reason, the Seat of the Soul: A Philosophical Journey into the Brain*. Cambridge, MA: MIT.

Damasio, Antonio (1994). *Descartes' Error: Emotion, Reason, and the Human Brain*. New York: Quill.

———. (1999). *The Feeling of What Happens: Body and Emotion in the Making of Consciousness*. San Diego: Harcourt.

———. (2003). *Looking for Spinoza: Joy, Sorrow, and the Feeling Brain*. San Diego: Harcourt.

Ramachandran, V. S., and Blakeslee, Sandra (1998). *Phantoms in the Brain*. New York: Quill.

On the Philosophy and Critique of Science

Connelly, William (2002). *Neuropolitics: Thinking, Culture, Speed*. Minneapolis, MN: Minnesota.

Deleuze, Gilles, and Guattari, Felix (1994). *What is Philosophy?* New York: Columbia.

Galison, Peter (1997). *Image and Logic: A Material Culture of Microphysics*. Cambridge, MA: Harvard.

Gross, Alan (1996). *The Rhetoric of Science*. Cambridge, MA: Harvard.

Hayles, N. Katherine (1999). *How We Became Posthuman: Virtual Bodies in Cybernetics, Literature, and Informatics*. Chicago: Chicago.

Heidegger, Martin. (1977). *The Question Concerning Technology and Other Essays*. New York: Harper Torchbooks.

Keller, Evelyn Fox (2002). *Making Sense of Life: Explaining Biological Development with Models, Metaphors, and Machines*. Cambridge, MA: Harvard.

Latour, Bruno (1988). *Science in Action: How to follow Scientists and Engineers through Society*. Cambridge, MA: Harvard.

Plotnitsky, Arkady (2002). *The Knowable and Unknowable: Modern Science, Non-Classical thought, and the "Two Cultures."* Ann Arbor, MI: Michigan.

Shapin, Steve (1994). *A Social History of Truth: Civility and Science in the Seventeenth Century*. Chicago: Chicago.

CHAPTER 73

Desperately Seeking Psyche I: The Lost Soul of Psychology and Mental Disorder of Education

MOLLY QUINN

> What lies behind us and what lies before us are tiny matters compared to what lies within us.
>
> Emerson

> A mind too active is no mind at all.
>
> Roethke

> Long ago, in a kingdom far away, there lived a king and queen who had three daughters. The royal couple was most fortunate in that the gods had endowed each maiden with the gift of beauty. Still, while the eldest two possessed wit and charm and intelligence, it was the third and youngest daughter who was by far the fairest of them all. The light of her countenance, her gentle radiance, her ethereal beauty, inspired all who met her. Her name was Psyche . . .
>
> Introductory Re-telling, Myth of Psyche

The study of educational psychology rarely, if ever, incites the inspiration of poets, introduces the insight of philosophers, or includes the illumination of myths. Yet, such is at the heart of understanding what it means to be human, of gleaning knowledge of the human mind, of glimpsing the nature of the human condition—and through such, grasping truths about human growth and action, and how these might be most fruitfully fostered in this work we call education. But why, then, doesn't this field of study reach, more than not, this heart of things? And must it—is that its proper work and address? If not, what is? And what does it, in fact, or what should it, incite? Herein we raise questions both about the problems and possibilities inherent to this enterprise we call educational psychology. Here, let us seek its promise of insight and illumination by first exploring and addressing some of its fundamental problems.

EDUCATIONAL PSYCHOLOGY

The term is rigid and dry, cerebral and serious, its work subject to and structured by legitimization but principally through the cold calibrations of a hard science in what appears to be its most linear, logical, empirical, and positive (or instrumental) sense. At least, we think, its contributions are sound; we can rely upon them. The hard, objective, unengaging edges of this field of inquiry constitute, in fact, its strength, its rigor, and its virtue—the very ground of our confidence in it and its discoveries. Still, that which educational psychology connotes hardly inspires us to contemplate or marvel at the profound human mysteries and motivations subsumed in its study, as the subject—and object—of its study, and referenced in its very name. At best, it seems, we call to mind Piaget and his insights into different developmental stages for learning, Montessori and the implications of her work for a child-centered pedagogy, or Gardner and his theory of multiple intelligences capable of broadening in some measure our concept of intelligence, and mind. Or practically speaking, we enjoy, perhaps, the validity of scientific research to support certain beliefs—even if often somewhat obvious—and practices issuing from them, such as: students learn more effectively with support and encouragement, hungry children have difficulty concentrating in school, or reading with children at home positively impacts academic learning. And we attend, in the name of this science and its findings about human learning, to things like time-on-task, wait-time, positive feedback, and scope and sequence in instruction. Conceivably at worst, we model our educational practices after Skinner's discoveries about manipulating human behavior, approach learning through the reductive lens of Bloom's taxonomy of knowledge, or initiate teaching in some formulaic presentation of Tyler's Rationale or "Teacher Effectiveness." However, in most of these cases, we build, however unwittingly, on the history of predictive and prescriptive education, bolstered by educational psychology, that turns texts into tests and students into statistics—all too often in the service of educational inequality, of social regulation and reproduction—by IQ testing and ability grouping, via psychological labels and deficit models. In addition, this kind of education, and the psychological study that supports it, with its dehumanizing effects, escapes scrutiny because it is cloaked in the guise of scientific objectivity, the language of neutrality. It also undermines and diminishes the powers of the human mind, often trivializing and de-intellectualizing the work of education, paradoxically at odds with the aim of educational excellence. Alas, this portrait appears to paint, as well, the dominant and enduring legacy of educational psychology. This legacy, and the problems it perpetuates, is certainly, of course, something we need to investigate further—hopefully toward transforming it in ways that cultivate our humanity, rather than diminish it, through the work of this field of study and the work of education itself.

"DESPERATELY SEEKING PSYCHE"

The problems that plague the field of educational psychology have indeed seriously hindered the realization of its immense potential for understanding the human mind and assisting the realization of its highest powers. In fact, the field has been "troubled" from the beginning, it seems, and the target of criticism, with its predecessor psychology since its inception as a discipline of study in the latter part of the nineteenth century. The judgment to which it has been subjected, however, has not abated its power—making it all the more critical to address what is at issue in its work. In truth, educational psychology is laden with the concerns with which the fields of education and psychology themselves are laden, especially given their histories. We can further posit that our very selves and our very societies—how we conceive of and construct them, are essentially fraught with these problems, as well. Basically, educational psychology—largely symptomatic of the ills of modern times—looks enthusiastic and [rigorously], at that which lies behind us and before us and about us, and fixated upon externals, misses the all-important "within" us—fails to genuinely see *us*. With its overly active mind, inquiring into mind, the field misses *mind* itself, having lost *its* mind, we could say. Desperately seeking Psyche, educational psychology does so in all the wrong places; or worse, it seems to have forgotten exactly who it is that it seeks to find, and to know.

According to the philosopher John Locke, the images and ideas within our minds are the invisible forces that govern us, that to these we ever readily—and mostly unconsciously—submit.

The "mind"—paradigm, worldview, and framework—of educational psychology remains largely itself unexamined, and thus there is little realization that it suffers from an unacknowledged and unaddressed impoverishment of the imagination. The images and ideas directing the work of the field have let Psyche herself slip from view. What this means is that a central problem facing the field of educational psychology at present is its focus, and view—its conception of the object of its study, and thus of itself as well. Its psyche—including her education—lacks depth, fullness, and its essential humanness—as merely seen through the ideas of the self or the subject or the conscious mind. Absent is Psyche—a metaphor for the human mind in all its mystery from ancient Greece, an image of the soul in search of the divine from medieval times—etymologically defined in relation to the principle of life, the spirit or breath of life, the mind, the soul and source of consciousness. Absent is her story, as well, her journey of transformation, her ephemeral beauty, her discovery of love. Instead, with respect to educational thought, Psyche is imprisoned in corseted constructs like intelligence, cognition, and learning. Yet, how, why, has educational psychology forgotten so much of Psyche in its quest for her? We need to understand, perhaps, this failure of the imagination in a more substantial way in order to overcome it.

The academic psychologist Couze Venn (1984) raises important questions about what has been the dominant project of psychology, and thus also operative in educational psychology, from its beginnings—calibrating the human subject: Does psychology have this measure? And what of its instruments, that which is regulated by them? What does psychology actually construct, and undertake? In the name of what, and to what effect? Venn relates a history defined by charting pathologies, drawing up taxonomies, and setting norms of human conduct that are inscribed in institutional practices. As a social science, psychology, it seems, has understood its part in the complex of activities constituting society, yet has failed to appreciate how such a context has directed its own discourse and activity. Mapping out a preliminary genealogy of psychology as a discipline, he establishes not only the historical character of psychology's "subject" but also critiques this very subject—which is, in fact, the object of psychology's study. In short, this thinker has offered us a provocative interpretation of the problems we must address with respect to the work of educational psychology through a historical look at the field upon which it is founded—psychology, critically analyzing its central images and ideas.

From its development in the nineteenth and twentieth centuries, psychology first defines itself against philosophy, seeking answers to the mysteries of the Psyche primarily through the model of science. In this way, at its conception the field itself significantly limits not only its ability to question its own assumptions, to inquire into the ground of its own work, but also its view of Psyche—the subject of its work. Venn highlights for us two unexamined, and troubling, constructs upon which psychology is founded: (1) the notion of the human subject and (2) the science of positivism. Who/What is the subject? The subject is a historically mediated synonym or substitute for Psyche—psyche. A product of seventeenth century thought, this notion sets forth an understanding of humanity via the image of the unitary, rational individual. Psychology, thus, positions itself as the science of the individual, the human subject taken up as its specific scientific object of study. The new discipline of study, built on the foundation of positivism, supports the development of a positive science of society—the idea conceived in the early 1800s that society concedes to scientific analysis, is subject to the rules of natural science—and affirms the possibility of its rational planning. Its contribution in this endeavor is then this science of the mind wherein the mind—materialized, naturalized, and constrained within the rational—is viewed as an object of science whose processes can be empirically identified, observed, measured, predicted, and thus ultimately acted upon as well.

Many, and yet somewhat monological in effect, have been the historical influences brought to bear in psychology's birth and development as a discipline—built largely upon ideas established in the seventeenth century. From Descartes' philosophical certainty—"I think, therefore I am"— the individual comes not only to be taken as primary, but also to be conceived abstractly and empirically as the human subject—both of law and politics, as well as of science and reason. From the Copernican Revolution, and its mechanical metaphors grounded in mathematics, science is embraced as the most solid foundation for understanding the world, and human conduct therein— with an emphasis on the material and measurable. Reason, in fact, particularly as directed via science, is deemed to be the source of truth—knowledge gleaned through it superior to any other competing knowledge claims. From Bacon, by the conceptual split between mind and body and the primacy afforded the human subject, knowledge is increasingly viewed as power to dominate, to act upon or discipline nature (and the body) technically and practically to serve human ends. Once psychology addresses its subject, the mind—given material status with the body—has lost much of its grandeur as seen through ancient tradition. Rather, trapped in images like the logical machine or information processor, the mind—Psyche—is also easily subjected to this rule by the power of knowledge.

From the Enlightenment project, the triumph of the new explanatory structure of science and reason over myth and religion, nature is desocialized and the world disenchanted. The centrality of the human subject is strengthened, to which Psyche and her mythological depths are reduced. Despite its marks of progress, the Enlightenment, in absorbing the whole of human imagination under the rubric of reason—featuring science and the individual, cultivates, in fact, its impoverishment. Myth is discredited, and all the realms of meaning not subsumed by science. From this view, madness, once inextricably linked to genius, suddenly endangers the whole of reason—and thus also the whole of humanity, increasingly defined by the principle of reason. The most-dreaded disease, a threat to the social order, madness is that which must be silenced, isolated, tamed, eradicated. This "dark side" of reason, by which reason itself is almost exclusively measured, is contained then, and "mad" individuals possessed of it, via institutionalization or some other established technology of control. The medical model is brought to bear on matters of the mind. Such ideas clearly find expression in psychology's origins, as a field, its foundational concerns with pathology and prescription, its concerted efforts at mental measurement, its clinical underpinnings.

From Darwin and evolutionary theory, the idea of a science of the mind actually becomes possible, reason naturalized and subject to empirical study, and the focus on deviations and norms fortified as well. Reflecting Darwin's classification of biological organisms and his idea of the fixity of types, Piaget positions psychology as a science of cognition, the biological model taking on greater importance, through scientific child study and the establishment of developmental stages of learning. The historical notions of rationality and normality are made natural, assumed as a given by the field. In addition, from the mid-nineteenth century ideal of utility, psychology, as the science of the mind, further aims excessively at its behavioral manifestations. In concert with the utilitarian principle that makes "the good" defined as "useful" natural law, the field of study—motivated by disciplining and amplifying the powers of the human mind, maximizing its utility—instrumentalizes the mind, subjecting it to these growing social technologies of control.

Clearly, Psyche cannot be captured by cognition alone, nor reduced solely to reason—even the human "subject" is not ever wholly subject to technological control. Yet, work in the field focusing on the mind's powers of intuition and self-reflection, for example, is marginalized nonetheless. Freud—and those that follow him—works to articulate a science for Psyche that attends also to her secret, even unconscious, desires—her ways of resistance that defy reason and sense. Yet, Freud seeks still the systematization of science, insufficient before Psyche's dark mysteries. In addition, born as psychoanalysis, his work presents itself as a competing science that is met with disdain by psychology proper. In the conceptual omission of feelings and desires from reason, psychology separates itself almost wholly from psychoanalysis, which is relegated to unreason's realm. The "subject" of psychology is partial, in this way, neither complete nor whole. And this is the subject educational psychology takes up, as well.

In analyzing the historical ideas and images at work in psychology's birth as a field, Venn indicts psychology of a certain ahistoricism: conceived through the birth of "modern man" and his new rationality in the idea of the human subject, psychology ignores the historical character of its object of study. As the science of the mind, postulating its rational and objective foundation apart from philosophy, the psyche it seeks is not exactly worthy of the name. This subject of psychology as the subject-of-science conforms well to strategies of administrative regulation as generated by research in the social sciences. Absent the impact of social context, consistent with positivistic science, this psyche, he suggests, is the rationalizing subject of capitalist economic exchange. An implicit individualism upon which it is built, that even humanistic perspectives in psychology—critical of scientism and positivism—usually assume, further undermines the power of culture, context, and community in Psyche's constitution.

An ongoing issue for psychology, and educational psychology in turn, is then that its central focus, the taken-for-granted, normative idea of the human subject, is still largely unquestioned, neither seen through its historicity nor in its exclusivity—despite abounding criticism aimed at this very concern. Not only has contemporary scholarship raised questions about the possibility of understanding the subject apart from social context, but also about the subject itself, as the object of psychology's study—positing rather *subjectivities* (in the plural), shifting identities that are culturally constituted without center or certainty. A constitutional feature of modern society, it seems, while we may not be able to exceed the limited idea of the individual, it is clear that we need, at least, to recognize that it is neither natural nor normal. As we interrogate this idea and ground of psychology, and individualism—the worldview which is its friend, we realize that the subject, the individual, is in fact male, rational, middle-class, white, of European descent: an unexamined norm that works socially to reproduce the status quo, and its inequities; to silence the psyches of the excluded others. Such work, as well, within the framework of positivistic science is legitimated in claims of neutrality and objectivity.

In this way, educational psychology, especially as drawn upon via the work of education, has provided instruments and mechanisms for perpetuating social norms, and pathologizing psyches who do not embody them. The philosopher Michel Foucault has posited further that such institutional practices have power in constituting individuals, actually shaping our own identities and self-perceptions, according to norms that benefit the economic order and well-being of the state. How, for example, are children from more communally based or less achievement-oriented—even less consumer-driven—cultures than that assumed by educational psychology assessed and addressed by it? The conclusion is: not well. Educational psychology, grounded in these central constructs of psychology, is additionally, in large measure, the brainchild of behavioral psychology specifically—with its tendencies to reduce Psyche even further and sometimes nearly fully to behavior—the external activity of the human subject ("I do/I act, therefore I am.") its primary concern. Such practices, of course, reflect a larger worldview—particularly Western—that is inordinately oriented around the extroverted, material, scientific, and individual, at the expense of the inner life—that which is immaterial, interpretive, poetic, (inter)connected, and whole—Psyche's very substance.

In *The Lure of the Transcendent* (1999), the educational scholar Dwayne Huebner articulates this concern further in pointing out that the practices we engage, as well as the language we use, are drawn from the images in which we have chosen to dwell. Thus, since in educational psychology, we have a troubled imagination, we also seem to have problems with the language we use to understand the Psyche and her education, as well as with the practices we advocate and initiate through such study. His critique of the field of education, and the psychological research that informs it, is that the language of "learning," of "student and teacher," trivializes and simplifies the educational endeavor, the pedagogical relationship, and their part in the journey that is life. In fact, teacher and student share the human condition, constituted by possibilities beyond realization, in a world both infinite and mysterious. The framework educational psychology provides, defining also discourse and activity, hides, and in many ways denies, this truth. What we are striving to uncover here is the way in which educational psychology, via its history, tends to be totalizing (as its parent, psychology) in its view—it psychologizes human life, and the work of education, which is to say that it operates under the assumption that all can be reduced to psychological analysis and explanation. Nestled within the authority of science and research, it not only claims to articulate reality/what is real but also dismisses understandings of Psyche and her education provided through other ways of knowing like poetry, myth, and philosophy—or reinterprets them through its own narrow lens. The result, according to Bernie Neville (1992), is indeed a language for education, via educational psychology, which is without a soul—that is, Psyche (Psyche means "soul") has actually been left out of the conversation. What this effectively means, as well, is that we have an education system that is without soul, as well—what we do in schools, based on the "research-based" recommendations educational psychology delivers, undermines the Psyche, and thus our humanity, and greatest human ideals, as well.

The inspiration to return to Psyche here in our thoughts about the work of educational psychology has come largely from the work of Neville. In his *Educating Psyche: Emotion, Imagination and the Unconscious in Learning* (1992), he returns to myth, that which historically predates philosophy and psychology in addressing the ultimate questions that concern human life and growth. He builds his examination of educational psychology and the schooling it supports upon the premises that the unconscious mind within us directs us far more powerfully than does the conscious, and that the image is still our original and preferred way of knowing—in fact perhaps its ground, abstract conceptualization a later evolutionary development in human thought. From this perspective, he looks at the problems of educational psychology through the images and stories of ancient mythology, and situates himself as an advocate for Psyche. Educational psychology, he suggests, has pledged allegiance to Apollo, the sun god. This divinity celebrates the clear light of consciousness in manifesting what is. In modern terms, grounded in the European ideals of the Enlightenment from the seventeenth century, the hero is logic, rationality, and science. This ruler has, as well, endured perpetual challenges from what he calls romantics in the field from the nineteenth century, who align themselves with the mythic figure of Dionysos, the god of ecstasy, impulse, and the irrational. Another mythic character more successfully, however, competes with Apollo: Prometheus. Known as the god of technology, Prometheus brought fire to humans for which he was severely punished. Gaining strength in the industrial age, this spirit allures via the force of action, as the engineer and instrumentalist. However, while consciousness is perhaps divine, and agency in the material world as powerful, the rule of either is one-sided, partial, and problematic. Neither is able to touch the life and depth of Psyche. Through her story, as well, we know that neither Apollo nor Prometheus does she love. Her kindred is another god: Eros—to whom we will turn in the next chapter in our attempts to re-mind our education, and its psychology, to embrace soul—Psyche herself—in its work.

What this portrait reveals, in addition to raising questions about how narrow and lifeless is the language educational psychology uses to articulate its subject, is that the educational practices this field sanctions are actually detrimental to the full and free growth of the human psyche. Education as informed by this discipline, particularly via schooling, in homage to Apollo and Prometheus, overlooks the depths of the learner, even in reducing the person to "learner," obsessed rather with intellect and utility—compulsively caught up in the cerebral. Conventional teaching, as well, via its grounding in educational psychology, works diligently at, what Neville calls, "cultivating incomplete people." Psyche is little acknowledged—reduced to intellect alone. The disciplines of study, which in their truest embodiment are foundations for nourishing the mind and heart, are rather stripped of this power in an emphasis on things like outcomes, assessments, or performance indicators. Even study, once a soulful endeavor engaging the inner life, is reduced to the amassing of "factoids" or the finding of answers to questions students have not asked, nor about which they care. Subjects not readily subsumed under the rubric of science or subject to systematization tend to be undervalued in the educational system—increasingly so as students progress through their schooling. In addition, the important role of the imagination in science is unacknowledged, as well as the use of metaphor in the presentation of its findings. Left out of the equation in mathematics is its core, which involves the provocative and inspired search for a language to express the invisible and infinite, its part in the cosmic design. Science becomes facts, math becomes measures, and psyche becomes known solely through productions prescribed by others.

Educational psychology, in this way, cultivates educational thought and practice that is one-sided, narrow, and ultimately ineffectual. Having utterly lost sight of Psyche, it by in large sets forth a perspective and pedagogy that has very little to do with understanding or educating Psyche at all, that actively and unwittingly works to exclude her and hide her from view. In our heart of hearts, and mind of minds, however, we feel and know it might be otherwise, that Psyche may in fact be sought and actually found—a *fairest-of-all* treasure without measure. We must, then, remind ourselves thus, and turn to this promise and possibility, as well, in our seeking.

REFERENCES

Huebner, D. (1999). The Lure of the Transcendent. Mahwah, NJ: Lawrence Erlbaum.

Neville, B. (1992). Educating Psyche: Emotion, Imagination and the Unconscious in Learning. North Blackburn, Victoria: Collins Dove.

Venn, C. (1984). The Subject of Psychology. In J. Henriques, W. Holloway, C. Ururin, C. Venn., and V. Walkerdine (Eds.), *Changing the Subject: Psychology, Social Regulation and Subjectivity*. London: Methuen.

CHAPTER 74

Desperately Seeking Psyche II: Re-Minding Ourselves, Our Societies, Our Psychologies, to Educate with Soul

MOLLY QUINN

What lies behind us and what lies before us are tiny matters compared to what lies within us.

Emerson

A mind too active is no mind at all.

Roethke

Long ago, in a kingdom far away, there lived a king and queen who had three daughters. The royal couple was most fortunate in that the gods had endowed each maiden with the gift of beauty. Still, while the eldest two possessed wit and charm and intelligence, it was the third and youngest daughter who was by far the fairest of them all. The light of her countenance, her gentle radiance, her ethereal beauty, inspired all who met her. Her name was Psyche . . .

Introductory Re-telling, Myth of Psyche

Educational Psychology—this field of study indeed does not generally summon adventures in exploring the great "within us" of human consciousness, or the great "beyond" transcending mind, or the dark albeit lovely journey of Psyche in her pursuit of love. We tend in this terrain to rough it through the rigid, dry, cerebral, and serious matter of "mind" rather than revel in the wisdom and wit of philosophy, poetry, or myth. In short, we fail in some fatal way to get to the heart of the human—mind, motivation, movement, and moment. Psyche, or some aspect of her, is perhaps sought—but in all the wrong places. And if we really seek in this inquiry to understand human growth and action, and how to foster their highest expressions via the work of education, we are at present somewhat desperate. But the formula we fall to in educational psychology is not final. Just as we can be transformed by the renewing of our minds, so too can the field be re-minded. For at the heart of educational psychology there is a heart for seeking Psyche—despite what it presently connotes, its foundational impulse denotes much that speaks of its promise and possibility for knowing this "fairest of them all" within us all and illuminating an education to cultivate her highest potential.

Let us also consider, then, what this formulation—*Educational Psychology*—denotes, for therein may lie its deeper signification, and animation, that which may draw us compellingly into its work, and even perhaps to a more fruitful employment of it for the purposes of education: its possibilities. There we may find poetry, philosophy, and mythology, as well, and their revelations to be part and parcel of the study of educational psychology, and its understandings. *Psychology*, as literally defined, for example, undertakes the study of (*-ology*) the *psyche*—concerned with articulating, presenting, listening to, and understanding its *logos*: its reason, or word. Psyche is its subject; unearthing the word—*raison d'etre*, reason for being, purpose and path, logic and way—of psyche, its task. Psychology is, in short, the science of the psyche. But how do we define *psyche*? What is the psyche? Psyche, as we generally think about it, refers essentially to that which is human: the self, the subject, or—more directly, perhaps, for the concerns of education—the mind. Even as defined thus, we get the sense that psychology—as the systematic study or science of the human subject or self, the intellectual endeavor that strives to understand the intellect itself—is an intrinsically enticing and profoundly important discipline of study. At its heart, it seeks the *heart* of "you" and of "me," the innermost being of the individual, whether approached via the path of mind or emotion or will or behavior. The object of its inquiry is each of "us" at our most intimate, personal, and profound center.

Psychology seeks, in this way, the truth of the inner life that directs the outer one—whether viewed as "the ghost in the machine," the immortal soul, the socially constructed self, or the "pinnacle" of biological evolution. Sometimes, admittedly, it primarily seeks this understanding in order to *redirect* human thought, emotion, and action to certain preestablished ends, toward particular social ideals—a practice that more often than not perhaps, ironically serves to diminish and distort the very knowledge of the psyche it seeks to uncover. Still, when the human "I" turns to inquire into itself, its very "I," as psychology essentially aims to do, an awesome undertaking is at work, through which we all are made subjects of this study and implicated in its findings. We may have erred here, then, in asking "What is psyche?" instead of "Who is Psyche?"—indeed, for each of us, surely the "fairest of them all." Psychology, as well, may have erred in its own identity construction and self-reflection: clearly, the question to which it addresses itself intersects powerfully with the work of philosophy, religion, art, and culture. Perhaps, instead of a separate discipline of study, it is in fact an inter-, multi-, trans-disciplinary field of inquiry—the most comprehensive and truest portrait of Psyche, its aim.

If this aspiration were not grand enough in scope and purpose, educational psychology takes on an even grander challenge still: it strives to engage the work of psychology *educationally*, to draw upon this truest understanding of Psyche in order to cultivate—or at least gain insight into—her highest education. But what does this mean exactly—to educate Psyche, through a knowledge of her nature and way? Educational psychology, in fact, seeks to address this very question. And if we but consider some of the origins of our notions of education, we begin to get a glimpse of the enormous promise the field of educational psychology holds for us in understanding, and in cultivating, our humanity. For, education—the word itself drawn from the Latin *educere* meaning "to bring forth" or "to draw out" and *educare* meaning "to rear" or "to nurture"—is fundamentally concerned with the "bringing forth" of human life, with drawing out "the fairest of them all" in us, with nurturing *Psyche's* growth and vitality. This is no small task, nor is such simply "cerebral and serious." In fact, our opening descriptors—"dry" and "rigid"—are antithetical, it would seem, to the expressed aim and address of education, of psychology, and of educational psychology. For the sake of Psyche—and her word, for the sake of education—and its work, even for the sake of science itself perhaps, we must surely, then, continue to explore additional ways to rethink and reconceive educational psychology—as a source of inspiration, insight, and illumination—to mine its virtually infinite potential for embracing all that is true and good and beautiful in human life.

RE-MINDING OUR SELVES, OUR SOCIETIES, OUR PSYCHOLOGIES

Yet, educational psychology may indeed find Psyche in *re-minding* itself, or at least seek her more faithfully and educate her more fully in taking this way. What, though, does re-minding educational psychology mean exactly? It concerns a great deal more than reconceptualizing a particular specialization in the academic field of psychology; it concerns embracing a new understanding of ourselves and our societies, as well as our psychologies—one that heeds the call to educate with soul, with Psyche in mind. This understanding does not take Psyche, or education, its own understanding even, for granted, but rather asks and asks again and continues to ask who Psyche—soul—is, how to truly know her, and what educating her actually means. Additionally, while this may appear to be a daunting—perhaps even impossible—task, though essential, to revive Psyche, to let her live again, to return her to her rightful place at the—*as the*—heart of psychological inquiry, it helps to realize that this transformation is already at work culturally, our very psyches as yet striving to be heard. This call to *re-mind*, as well, is also a call *reminding* us of our possibilities, the inherent albeit hidden treasure psychology and education offer in their deepest significations and foundational impulses.

In seeking change, indeed, we are returning—in society and culture at large—to our origins and roots, to the wisdom traditions from whence emerged the inquiry of science, the study of psyche, and the dream of education. In large measure, new age thought is attending old age philosophy and alternative medicine is grounded in ancient healing practice. In varied and sundry cultural domains and academic disciplines, we are working to integrate East and West, body and mind, past and present—even science, art and religion—in our ways of thinking and being, or at least benefit from making connections between them, and looking at intersections of what before had been seen as necessarily separate and even conflicting. The rise of philosophical counseling (as well as life coaching and wellness counseling) as an alternative to traditional psychotherapy or psychoanalysis speaks more directly with respect to the field of psychology in evidencing this shift at work. The idea, pithily expressed—*Plato, not prozac*, is that the clinical and medical model adopted by psychology, directed by notions of the normative and pathological, is insufficient— that its deficit/deficiency orientation is, in fact, misoriented, along with its tendency to reduce human being to human behavior. Philosophical counseling, and other offerings like it, intimates this return to Psyche as soul in that from this framework the challenges we face are seen as part and parcel of the human condition, addressed with an eye to the larger contexts in which we find ourselves; the insights of philosophy or other ways of knowing like spirituality and art, in addition to science and psychology proper, are drawn upon for understanding.

As is often the case, however, the very discipline of study initiated to learn of Psyche, psychology, has resisted this cultural and intellectual critique, and thus internal examination and transformation. Education, because institutionalized via schooling and strongly shaped by the field of educational psychology, also reflects this cultural lag in consciousness, as it were. Still, there are signs of openings in the educational and psychological imagination; still, educational psychology can be re-minded, and reminded of Psyche: her story and her word (logos)—that is, her way.

The story of Psyche comes to us through an ancient Greek legend. Bernie Neville (1992), in *Educating Psyche: Emotion, Imagination and the Unconscious in Learning*, relates how the Greeks, great respecters of reason, understood that reason itself is but a small light within a much grander surrounding darkness, and that to light upon it alone is to obscure our view of reality and of the human mind. From this perspective, the human mind, or soul, partakes in the mystery of creation; she—Psyche—walks in beauty, no doubt, but she also dwells much in darkness, living in the shadows perhaps even more than the light. This is part of the wisdom, in fact, that Psyche's story implicitly communicates to us. For, Carl Jung, James Hillman and other scholars of psychology have recognized the archetypal power of myths and metaphors like these in articulating truths about the human condition, and the cosmic design of which we are a part. Entertain us, they may, but these stories also set forth intriguing portraits of the world, nature, culture, society, and the "self" for us to contemplate, and from which to gain insight into ourselves—our own psyche's story, in this case. Let us look, then, a little closer at Psyche's story, what it speaks, and who it is educational psychology might more faithfully seek to know.

From ancient lore, we know that Psyche is the third and fairest daughter of an earthly king. This maiden is so honored for her beauty that Aphrodite (or Venus) herself, the goddess of beauty, grows jealous of her, and sends her son Eros (or Cupid) to cast his arrows at Psyche to have her fall in love with a monster. The king is compelled by Apollo, the god of light, to leave his daughter alone on the rocky mountaintop where her husband, a winged serpent, will come to her. Eros, smitten himself with love for Psyche, takes her instead through a grassy fragrant meadow where she finds rest beside shining waters. She is brought to dwell in a glorious mansion and Eros becomes her love, but only in darkness, coming to her by night. Psyche embraces this union with joy, and knows her kind mate can be no monster. Yet, she is filled with doubts when her jealous sisters raise questions about the man or monster she can never see. Finally, one night, she shines a lamp upon his sleeping form to find that he is indeed her handsome beloved. He awakes, though, and flees: Psyche loses her love for lack of trust. Tormented, she spends her life searching for him. She pleads with Aphrodite herself who, with no intention of honoring her promise to reunite Psyche and Eros, gives her many dark and humanly impossible tasks to perform. Yet, in each of them, Psyche is helped by nature's creatures. Returning from her journey to Hades (hell) to bring back the beauty of Persephone (death) for Aphrodite, she opens the box of Persephone's dark beauty in her curiosity and falls into a deep sleep. By now, Eros is healed of his heart wounds and is himself in search of Psyche. He awakens her and enlists the help of Jupiter against Aphrodite's fury. Psyche herself is given immortality and the pair are joyously reunited for all eternity.

What does this story say—about Psyche, about her education, her mind, and the way of knowledge? In concert with Socratic wisdom, this myth tells us that things are not as they appear to be, that insight is often realized in the experience of darkness, that the light of truth is but one facet of understanding. When we reach the limits of our own knowing, become aware of our own ignorance, it is then and there, perhaps, that we actually approach wisdom. Knowing itself is elusive and enigmatic, the process of learning nonlinear, even surprising and unpredictable—in the moment, unique, experiential. Education is constituted by irreplaceable "Aha" moments we are incapable of manipulating or regulating, and these are usually preceded by periods of intense questioning, difficult confusion, and rigorous inquiry. Genuine understanding, as well, emerges from authentic questions that involve the heart as well as the mind.

This story tells us, especially, that Eros is a central figure in understanding the path of Psyche, her passions and purposes. It is her heart for Eros that engenders her education and growth. Eros, also known as Cupid, is amour's messenger, the god of love. The son of Aries (or Mars) the god of war and Aphrodite (or Venus) the goddess of beauty and sexual love, he is known in lore also as one who often creates confusion, shooting arrows into the hearts of mortals and gods, compelling them to love. A handsome man in Psyche's myth, he is also the forerunner to the baroque baby angels of Christianity—guided as well by love for Psyche. In either case, the figure speaks of Psyche's binding relationship with the divine, that which is sacred and immortal. She must, perhaps, know him only in darkness, and through great difficulty, but her journey with him—and unbreakable union—is ultimately one of great joy and blessing. In traversing this path, she also comes into her own fullness—of beauty, love, and glory. Knowledge is achieved via marriage with experience in the fullness of love. And confusion is not an enemy but a precursor to new understanding.

Freud, realizing the power of *eros* for psychological understanding, uses the term, in fact, to signify what he identified as the source of all human action—sexual energy or desire. Even here, he reduces the power of this image, for Eros is the life impulse itself—complex and even paradoxical. Psyche is drawn by all Eros embodies: creativity, evolution, process, passion, and transcendence. Eros is the man who leaves his mother, goddess of sex, to know love with another—to unite with Psyche, the soul—mutually, in relationship. In so doing, he smites himself, moves beyond himself, with his own arrow of love. Since there really is no story of Psyche without Eros, Freud is at least wise as a student of the psyche in seeking Psyche to keep in mind that which she herself seeks. Education is, then, a kind of lovemaking, as it were, in the realm of unknowing, wherein the psyche ventures beyond itself/herself to know the Other, experientially, relationally, dialogically—if even that strange and unknown other is a text or discourse or discipline of study. Through such, she also comes to know herself in a new way, changed, in fact, by the encounter. Psyche, the knower, ever seeks union with the "known"—that which she seeks to know.

Neville, in fact, concludes that knowing is like a religion for the psyche—it binds us to the god. Psyche's search of love takes her to the discovery of Love itself, in herself. The story sets forth an image of becoming, an image central to our depth psychologies, to humanistic and existentialist psychologies in and out of education. In this sense, there is a legacy contemporary educational psychology may look at and into, study seriously, for better understanding Psyche and her educational way, at least redress the present imbalance in its view. Neville highlights, for example, a few scholarly resources for such: Assagioli's concept of pychosynthesis involving integration and growth through thought and reflection, traversing the unconscious, personal, and transpersonal aspects of mind; Maslow's evolutionary idea that the psyche is compelled to move by design beyond itself, to transcend itself in working toward self-actualization; Jung's notion of the way of individuation engaging a collective unconscious; Rogers's tenet that a key dynamic in psyche's development is an actualizing propensity; Progoff's proposition of the organic psyche, inherently progressive, aimed at integrating the personality, and helped through archetypal images; and the work of Adler and Rank who suggest that the psyche is drawn by meaning inherent within its unique existence, forces neither wholly conscious nor unconscious, by a will-to-integration. This is, in a way, education as lovemaking directed ultimately at union with oneself, as well as the Other, and perhaps all that is. It calls to mind the work of Viktor Frankl, philosopher and psychologist—as well as holocaust survivor, and his critique of Freud. Frankl (1946/1992), in *Man's Search For Meaning*, contends that the quest for meaning is what draws Psyche in the final analysis, and effectually compels her education. Indeed, this quest engages questions of ultimate concern—desire and pleasure, or love and *eros*, integral to this search, and yet the objects of such passion and what constitutes this meaning are unique to each person, and central to his or her own educational way—albeit not without socially and culturally directed aspects.

Psyche's story is indeed a myth of transformation, engaging heart as well as mind, impacting her identity and efficacy in the world. Educational psychology may do well to ground itself in this image of becoming and change that is education's work, one that powerfully impacts the whole person in a particular context, one that reaches beyond itself, humanity itself, in complex ways via society, culture, history, and such. As such, there may be posited rather educational psychologies in the plural; for, the myth of psyche teaches us, in fact, that no one field or theory can lay claim to reality—representing or manifesting it, that all understandings of Psyche in this case, are also metaphors, lights in a larger surrounding darkness. Neville calls them "fashionable lamps" the field of educational psychology has provided—whether constructivist or behaviorist or humanistic, each provide but a picture postulated as master portrait, the definitive view of Psyche's education. Psyche's tale speaks of monsters and gods, of darkness and death, of mystery and marriage, and more. If the field would seek Psyche indeed, it might attend the metaphorical, multiperspectival, multivocal, rather than the monolithic.

Seeking psyche, then, means listening to her, as well, and giving voice to her words. We re-mind ourselves, indeed, through language. Acknowledging the partial and insufficient language used in educational psychology to understand and articulate the subject of its inquiry, we might open our minds to the power of language in speaking and seeking Psyche anew.

Psyche, for instance, literally means "soul," yet such is a term with which we are generally uncomfortable—academically and educationally. Soul is not only referential of that which we conceive of as "unscientific" but actively "religious." It speaks of inexplicability, the possibility that there is a certain something that is ever and always mysterious at the heart of what is truly human, inescapably ungraspable in Psyche and in the human condition. Soul suggests that our source is somehow eternal, immaterial, and spiritual—that beyond the body, biology, and behavior may lie Psyche in truth, the animating principle of life and consciousness. This is the soul or psyche of Plato: first and foremost whole, the source of the good, it corresponds to the *real* person or mind—above matter, self-directed and director of the body. In Aristotle's language, the psyche is the functioning excellence, the form, of the living body; like vision to the eye is the soul to the body: we know psyche as embodied and inseparable from the body, through its rational and nonrational functions; that is, survival, sensation, volition, and reason. Heraclitus is reported to have said that no matter how far or deep one traveled, one could not reach the end of psyche's logos or words, hidden and unfathomable. Scholars of intellectual history posit that the soul, thus Psyche in truth, was discarded in the seventeenth century with the rise of science and empiricism—once a kind of bridge between body and spirit, and the source of feeling, imagination, sensitivity to beauty, and love from medieval times. It is interesting, as well, that later in the nineteenth century Freud, attempting a systematic study of Psyche, not only met Eros but found in the science and psychology of his day no language to speak of her, to truly conceptualize the mind. Despite his devotion to science and the light of Apollo, he is compelled to return to myth, metaphor and poetry in order to seek and speak Psyche.

Here is, then, something with which educational psychology might wrestle—its discomfort with the meaning and history of Psyche—her very name, its object of study—and work to stop excluding it from its voice and view. Even the sciences, which the field so faithfully seeks to imitate, acknowledge the mysterious and infinite in their contemporary work and way. Einstein, with other exemplars of scientific and mathematical genius in history, has explicitly suggested that being alive to his work requires being moved and enchanted by the awe-inspiring mysteries he explores, involving the heart and soul in contemplation. A dialogue between the languages of the sciences and humanities and analysis of their elucidations and limitations, common insights and points of contention, then, is important for the work of education and progress of psychology—to genuinely seek a more inclusive language(s) to explore and articulate Psyche and her education. The etymological histories of related concepts—that is, mind, education—are also sure to uncover rich linguistic terrain for more faithfully addressing the labyrinthian journey of Psyche that educational psychology seeks to know. Attentiveness to language might well mean reviving our listening capacities, as well—in the field, perhaps via a return to genuine "child study" (Van Manen, 1990) in cultivating a greater receptiveness to the heart and mind of Psyche herself. Additionally, conversing and collaborating with those in curriculum studies particularly working to explore the experience of education (i.e., via autobiography or phenomenological analysis), interrogate the language of education (i.e., via postcolonial theory or poststructuralism), and elaborate an education of liberation (i.e., via feminism or critical pedagogy) may elucidate new directions of promise for educational psychology to pursue. For, such scholarship, aimed at reconceptualizing education itself, implicitly if not explicitly seeks Psyche whom the project of education claims to serve, to offer her freedom of voice and fulfillment of agency—to understand and embrace her, her word, her way.

We may be so bold as to posit that education, in its native tongue, is indeed the way of Psyche. The human "self" or "subject" inherently seeks to know herself, "to draw out" or "bring forth" (from the etymological root of *to educate*) herself in all her vitality and truth—expressing, manifesting, and actualizing her extraordinary potentials, possibilities, powers, in the world in which she participates and finds herself, and of which she is part and parcel. In kinship with Keat's definition of life as the *vale of soul-making*, Psyche's way is constituted by this creative work—education, shepherding her "coming out," her debut. This is the education that attends and assists in the effort of the soul's nascence/ renaissance, making/remaking, minding/re-minding—as there is much the soul encounters in living that thwarts this call. From this perspective, we are all "teachers"—Socrates's midwives to birthing soul knowledge, and "learners" engaged in our own rebirthings; education is the way of re-minding ourselves, our societies, and our psychologies.

Educational psychology—attending its problematic ground and unearthing its rich promise, in remembering, and remembering itself, stands in a most powerful position to be that scholarship most intimately engaged in exploring Psyche and recommending an education that nurtures "the fairest of them all" within us all. Returning to the *heart* of its inquiry, the field—drawing upon the insights of the arts and sciences (philosophy and myth and math and art all gifts of psyche's making) and dialoging across its own internal disagreements (i.e., humanistic, behavioristic, pscyhoanalytic)—may then be one that *aesthetizes* rather than anaesthetizes, wakes us up to ourselves and to our educational possibilities in the world. Through this discipline of study, Psyche, in fact, may formally and fully think and rethink herself and her highest education, the call of the human condition in a living cosmos of immense mystery and beauty.

REFERENCES

Frankl, V. (1992). *Man's Search for Meaning*. Boston: Beacon. (Original work published 1946)

Neville, B. (1992). *Educating Psyche: Emotion, Imagination and the Unconscious in Learning*. North Blackburn, Victoria: Collins Dove.

Van Manen, M. (1990). *Researching Lived Experience: Human Science for an Action Sensitive Pedagogy*. Ontario, Canada: The Althouse Press, University of Western Ontario.

CHAPTER 75

What Educational Psychology Can Learn from Psychoanalysis

MARLA MORRIS

Psychoanalysis is the study of the psyche in the context of social relations. Founder Sigmund Freud argued that psychoanalysis could help one uncover repressed emotions so as to free one of all sorts of psychological resistances that keep one from fully developing as a human being. Some of these resistances, further teased out by Freud's daughter Anna Freud (1966/1993), are these: reaction formation, reversal, turning against the self, introjection, projection, transference, regression undoing, and more. Educators might begin to better understand students who are resistant to learning if they understand the ways in which the psyche protects itself from what is new and threatening. If a student acts out in class, it usually has to do with some deeper repressed feeling the student transfers onto the teacher or the texts being studied.

Employing psychoanalysis educational psychologists are able to dig deeper into the most basic and primordial dimensions of the mind. Traditionally concerned with the forces of irrationality and the ways they shape thinking, consciousness, and one's everyday actions, psychoanalysis moves educational psychologists to explore new dimensions of the learning process. Any dynamic that shapes student action in a way that is contradictory to the manner in which traditional educational psychology frames the learning process is very important. Indeed, it is psychoanalysis that allows educational psychology to view the formation of identity from unique vistas not attainable in the mainstream of the discipline.

In such a process psychoanalysts often discern the unconscious processes that create resistance to progressive change and induce self-destructive student (and teacher) behavior. Psychoanalysis offers hope to progressive educational psychologists concerned with social justice and the related effort to transform the elitism of cognitive studies. When psychoanalysts take into account the Deweyan, Vygotskian, and more recently the poststructuralist rejection of Freud's separation of the psychic form the social realm, psychoanalysis becomes a powerful tool in educational psychology.

Psychoanalysis is helpful to teachers especially so that they do not project their prejudgments onto their students. If they work through their unconscious repressions with the help of an analyst, they probably would become better teachers because they become more aware of their psychic formations and tendencies toward projection. Psychoanalysis is particularly helpful in the face of conflict in the classroom. How to psychologically manage students' outburst or refusals to learn are issues with which psychoanalysis grapples. For example, if a student acts out by throwing paper airplanes or falling asleep in class, or says negative things to the teacher, more than likely these forms of acting out have little to do with the material at hand or with the teacher. The student may be reminded, perhaps unconsciously, of his or her father or mother with whom she has a difficult relation and simply transfers those negative feelings onto the teacher. If the teacher has undergone analysis and understands the complexity of students' resistances, she might be more understanding of student misbehavior and even perhaps more forgiving.

Sigmund Freud suggested that the psyche is made up of three overlapping parts. These parts are metaphors, not literal places in the brain. Freud suggested that the id, ego, and superego are all interrelated and yet serve different purposes in psychic life. The ego is what Freud called the reality principle. The purpose of the ego is to allow the psyche to be in touch with reality. That is, one is aware of the world via the ego. The ego allows one to function, to make distinctions between this and that, to understand differences between the self and the world. The superego is one's conscience. The conscience, Freud tells us, is what we inherit from our parents. We internalize the commands, the "oughts and shoulds" we hear from our parents into our psyche and integrate these into our personalities. Morality is the superego. The superego tells us when something is wrong, when not to do things. The id, on the other hand, is related to one's sexuality. The id is also the site of the unconscious, where repressed memories are housed and where dreams occur. Again, in Freud's later thinking all three of these cites are interrelated and metaphorical. The goal of psychoanalysis is, according to Freud, to make one's unconscious repressed conscious. The goal is to get rid of repressed materials so that one can live more freely with less transference. The goal is to act out (acting without remembering why one is doing what one is doing) less and make more free choices.

In order to become more free to act in the public world, one must, however, pay close attention to one's psychic life. Here, Freud especially focuses on the dream life and inner reality. In fact, one of Freud's well-known books is devoted to dreaming (*The Dream Book 1900*). However, even if one pays attention to the messages in dreams there will still be left over content with which to deal. Dreams do not clarify, but they point to certain clues that might help one better understand why one acts in certain ways. Freud, therefore, did not think that psychoanalysis could get at the truth of one's being; in fact, toward the end of his career he felt that psychoanalysis was limited in what it could do. Freud felt that because of repression (memories which are buried), one only touches on the iceberg of psychic life. Here, like cognitive science, Freud would agree that very little can be known about the ways in which humans operate psychically. But unlike cognitive science, Freud argued that the reason for this is primarily due to repression. The notion of repression does not play much if any role in cognitive science.

Freud was mainly interested in intrapsychic phenomena. One of the main themes of Freudian psychoanalysis is what he termed the Oedipus Complex. Here the child at around the age of five, struggles with at least one of his parents. The child feels drawn toward one parent and repulsed by the other. Freud believes that male children are drawn sexually toward their mothers and want to kill their fathers. These ideas Freud takes from the Greek myth of Oedipus Rex. The child has to work through these struggles in order to realize that he cannot be sexually drawn to his mother nor can he commit patricide. Once he resolves this complex he can then grow into a fully mature human being. If the child, on the other hand, gets stuck inside the Oedipus conflict and acts this conflict out in life, he will transfer these feelings onto others and marry someone who reminds him of his mother, while avoiding persons who remind him of his father. Some analysts claim that the Oedipus conflict can be enacted by girls as well as boys and call this the Electra Complex. Here, the girl child will want to marry her father and kill her mother (figuratively). Thus, in later life, if she hasn't worked through this and resolved it, she will marry someone who is like her father and avoid people who are like her mother. All these later life experiences are guided by the psychological term *transference*. Freud argues that the more one acts out of transference the less one has resolved repressed memories. Again, the point of psychoanalysis is to come to terms with these struggles so that one may be free NOT to marry one's parents, as it were. Freud believed that negative transferences were driven by what he called the death instinct or thanatos. Thanatos, he suggests, is older than Eros, or the life instinct or love. Both of these instincts operated in our psyches throughout our entire lifetime. Some people have more death instinct tendencies and therefore are more self-destructive, others have more life instinct and tend to grow psychically. Toward the end of Freud's life he began to incorporate more and more discussion around the death drive in his work against the backdrop of the Nazi accession to power in Austria.

Psychoanalysis as a movement began to split apart and grow with the development of what is termed object relations theory. The founder of this movement was Melanie Klein. Klein, unlike Freud, argued that the Oedipus conflict occurs much earlier than Freud did and that the superego is well developed in young infants, something to which Freud disagreed. Klein, like Freud, thought that there is a death instinct that drives the child toward destructive impulses. Freud is thought to focus mostly on the phallus and the relation of the male to his own psychic workings, even though the majority of Freud's patients were women. Without Freud's women, there would be no psychoanalysis. Many of his patients went on to become well-known analysts themselves.

Klein's contribution to psychoanalysis revolves around several themes. One of them is the term *phantasy*. Here "ph" designates phantasy that is unconscious. Children at the preverbal stage, according to Klein, engage in wild phantasies about their mother. Primarily these phantasies are sadistic. The child fears for his life. He fears that the mother will annihilate him. In what Klein called the paranoid-schizoid position, the child phantasizes biting, sucking, and robing the mother of her inner contents so as to control her. If the child can move toward the next phase, called the depressive position, he can begin to feel guilty about feeling such negative things about his mother and start the process of reparation with the mother. If the child cannot do this, if he becomes fixated at the level of the paranoid-schizoid position in later life he might develop paranoid schizophrenia or other mental illnesses. Unlike Piaget, Klein's two positions are not stages, but rather movements that one goes through, throughout one's lifetime. Klein believed that children's play reflected inner psychic worlds of phantasy and she was perturbed by the violence of these phantasies. She concluded that children make up bad things about their mothers, whether or not the mother really does something bad to the child. She believed, in other words, that evil comes from within. Children tend to polarize thinking into good and bad, what Klein called the good and bad breast. Polarized thinking, then, for Klein is considered childish. The mechanism that causes one to see in black and white is called splitting. Klein believed that mental health could be gained by limiting splitting tendencies and integrating the personality. Here Freud's aims were the same. The more integrated a personality, the healthier that person would be mentally. Klein's main focus is, therefore, on the relations between the child and her mother. Her focus is also mainly on the preverbal, or pre-Oedipal.

Other object relations theorists include W. D. Winnicott, W. R. Bion, R. D. Fairbairn, and Michael Eigen. Not all these theorists wholeheartedly agree with Klein's position. In fact, Fairbairn (1954) and Winnicott believed, unlike Klein, that children become bad because they were treated badly by their mothers. Thus, environmental harm makes people bad. Klein, on the contrary, felt exactly opposite. Fairbairn's name even means, fair child, or innocent child. He believed that children are innocent until their mothers destroy them in some way. According to Psychoanalyst Naomi Rucker (1998), there are many ways to destroy children: kill their self-esteem, kill their ambitions, destroy their dreams, and destroy their abilities. The thrust of object relations is to intrapsychic. That is, object relations theorists feel that it is not enough to simply talk about interpsychic phenomena as Sigmund Freud did. Rather, object relations theorists talk about the child's psychic relation to her mother and her world. Now here, the difficulty is that psychic relations are mostly unconscious. And so, object relations is mainly about how one unconscious relates to another. Object relations theorists argue that children develop internal objects, which are impressions and phantasises of their mothers and other important people. These ghostly representations housed in the unconscious then get projected onto the real mother and others. So what is real and what is psychically created gets confused. The idea for object relations theorists is mostly that one untangles these internal objects so that one can relate more freely with others, and not get trapped in the tangles of transferred objects.

The gist of these main schools of psychoanalysis suggests that what is important in our lives is thinking about what is unthinkable, what is unconscious. One can only do this with an analyst because it is difficult to undo repressed memories and internal objects. One tends to be blind to one's inner workings. Psychoanalysis is very helpful in the educative realm for the reasons I have mentioned previously. But it is also helpful to the scholar who tries to figure out what to write about and what to think about. Autobiography in educative sites, then, becomes important both for teachers and students. The main lesson of psychoanalysis is to know thyself.

Educational psychology could be reconceptualized if it turned back to the work of Sigmund Freud. Most educational psychologists, however, dismiss Freud as a fraud. I think this dismissal comes out of a certain resistance to Freud's work on dreams and the unconscious because these are NOT quantifiable. But what child is quantifiable? What life is reducible to numbers, to prediction and control? Psychoanalysis is hardly about prediction and control, those old ideas that drive behaviorism. The goal of psychoanalysis is to foster free expression in children and adults via uncovered repressions, which fixate persons in traumas of their youth. School violence could be greatly reduced if teachers would pay more attention to the psychic life of children. Students would not act out as much as do violently if they could talk through their problems with analysts. In fact, psychoanalysis has been called the "talking cure" because through talking one finds out about oneself. But until our psyches are decolonized by buried memories and repressed feeling, we can never be free to act as we choose. We will always be slaves to the masters of our unconscious and the Oedipal drama.

SUGGESTED READINGS

Fairbairn, R. D. (1954). *An Object-Relations Theory of Personality*. New York: Basic.

Freud, A. (1966/1993). *The Ego and the Mechanisms of Defense*. New York: International Universities Press.

Freud, S. (1900). *The Interpretation of Dreams*. (J. Strachey, trans.). London: Hogarth.

———. (1914–1916). *Instincts and Their Vicissitudes*. (J. Strachey, trans.) London: Hogarth.

———. (1915/2005). *The Unconscious*. (J. Strachey, trans.) New York: Penguin Books.

———. (1930/1961). *Civilization and Its Discontents*. New York: Norton.

Klein, M. (1940/1975). *Love, Guilt and Reparation*. New York: Delacourte Press.

———. (1950/1975). *Envy, Gratitude and Other Works*. New York: The Free Press.

Rucker, N. and Lombardi, K. (1998). *Subject Relations*. New York: Routledge.

CHAPTER 76

Using Critical Thinking to Understand a Black Woman's Identity: Expanding Consciousness in an Urban Education Classroom

ROCHELLE BROCK

Rochelle: Oshun is my alter ego. She is the power of my African past and my African American present that I call forth when I am attempting to write myself into understanding. For me Oshun is the manifestation of critical thinking. She provides educational psychology with a taste of non-Western cognition—a dimension sorely lacking in contemporary manifestations of the discipline. This chapter moves us to think about what Black women's ways of seeing (understanding there is diversity within the category) might offer psychologists working in the educational domain.

Many subjects touched my soul, many inspired thought, anger, concern for the future and growth. Looking back, the discussions and readings about language, oppression, interracial dating, the American Indian, the Chicana woman and the "place" of the African American woman influenced my being the most. My mood of the day was determined by how well our discussion went in class. If the discussion was frustrating, I was frustrated all day long. If I was enlightened by the class discussion, all day I felt a glow of newly discovered knowledge (*Racism and Sexism*, p. 103).

Oshun: What to you is critical thinking?

Rochelle: The ability to deconstruct and reconstruct your world?

Oshun: How is it accomplished?

Rochelle: It's never completely accomplished. It's really more of a process, something to be constantly worked at. Accomplished denotes an end point or finished product and critical thought is a constantly changing entity.

Oshun: How does it relate to you as a teacher?

Rochelle: I begin and end with it. It's central to my being and therefore my pedagogy.

Oshun: How does that centrality manifest itself in your teaching?

Rochelle: It means that the most important thing I can give my students is the skill to critically analyze all and everything in their life. If, in my pedagogy, I provide my students with the tools to politicize their world, then I'm happy.

Oshun: Politicize?

Rochelle: Yes, understand the social, historical, political, and economic realities of a situation. I want to instill in them a new way of thinking, a new mode of cognition—the knowledge to both read the word and the world. I want to bring them to a "consciousness of self." And, the knowledge that all human interaction is politically inscribed should and must inform that consciousness of self. For example, when I deconstruct my existence as a Black woman it both informs my understanding of self and reframes my pedagogy. I am Black, female, and a teacher. Those three identities are intricately connected; it is impossible to separate them from each other.

Oshun: Separating them is not an option if you want to become/remain a complete person. Tell me, how do you negotiate between your identity as Black and as a woman? Do you feel torn as to which struggle you align yourself with? And what is the connection between Rochelle as teacher and Rochelle as Black woman?

Rochelle: Wow, too many questions at once. Haven't you heard about the correct method of inquiry for a teacher?

Oshun: Girl, I don't pay much attention to the traditional "best practices" methodology. See, I want you to struggle with articulating an answer that simultaneously addresses all the questions. Remember you are writing about critical thinking, educational psychology, and teaching and you don't want to create false binaries. Use your critical thinking skills to figure it out.

Rochelle: Okay, let me situate myself in history: in my story. Critical thinking forces me to contextualize my existence. As such, I need to view myself through the lens of race, class, and gender. It's difficult as hell to negotiate all my identities, especially race and gender. I understand the need to fight in the war against racism as well as sexism and at the same time I also realize we are often forced to choose between the two. Black women's struggles have been framed within a false dichotomy of race and sex. Often forced to choose between the fight against race or gender oppression, we have to constantly reassert the need for a combined struggle. Black women encounter a triple jeopardy where they must constantly negotiate the intersection of race, class, and gender oppression which has forced us into a desperate struggle for existence and the search for a "space" where the freedom to exhale is possible.

We are talking about power. Picture three boxes, each distinctively smaller than the one it is within. The box which consumes and encapsulates the others is the large space of power where White men, and to a lesser degree White women, experience varying degrees of domination and control and is seen in the systems and structures of society. Sexism, an integral ingredient in understanding relations of power and privilege in America, determines that although White women function within this power discourse of men they are seen as powerless because of gender which becomes the bind of sexism. Within this space is a significantly smaller box; the place where Black people experience pain and isolation. But it is also the place where Black men live, and although controlled by racism, it still offers a degree of control and provides Black men with the tools to oppress Black women. Denied the power and the privileges of White women, White men, and Black men, Black women are imprisoned in a still smaller box that represents the narrow space of race and a dark enclosure of sex which has engendered a web of pain where Black women strive for the right to *be*. Of course the binds of class exists in the three boxes and its effects are experienced differently depending on race and gender. (Gloria Wade-Gayles, 1984)

It is difficult to separate race from class from sex oppression because in our lives they are most often experienced simultaneously. For example, I am not poor today, a woman tomorrow, and Black the following day, but a poor Black woman everyday I breathe. It would be foolish for me to think that all Black women are poor, and that's not what I mean to imply. Instead, I assert that regardless of class a Black woman's existence—how she understands her life—is framed within those three critical domains and to ignore one is to mystify all the others. That's what you meant about creating false binaries. In order to understand my existence as a Black woman I need to be aware of the myriad forms of power. The skills of critical thinking, of a critical form of cognition force me to constantly analyze my existence through the lens of race, class, and gender. And when I use this example in my classroom it provides a visual representation for students. I frame the entire discussion of Black women through the box analogy, which gives the student a picture to hold onto. I try to open the lid on that tiny box, expose and make sense of the realities of Black women. My consciousness as a teacher is framed by my consciousness as a Black woman. And my ability at critical thought forces my students and me to reflect on and delve deeper into an issue.

Oshun: Yes, but it's important to remember that critical thought is not some type of crystal ball, mystically providing the "right" answers to every question. Its magic is that it provides the space to deconstruct your world. It is in this space that we can begin to imagine and then develop strategies, which rupture all that we think we know. We question the nature of our own thinking and importantly that of others. We become conscious beings.

As conscious beings Black women realize that they are engulfed in a constant struggle between the structures of race, gender, and class causing us as Black women to wage an eternal war against a racist, capitalist, and patriarchal society. Clearly, groups are given or denied power based on race, sex, and class in America. Hence, Black women experience triple jeopardy in a white capitalist patriarchal society which requires racial oppression alongside sexual and class oppression. So, where does your critical consciousness lead you?

Rochelle: The trajectory of my life leads to self-awareness. Critical thinking allows us to see the multiplicity of oppressions. And through it we demystify the layers of oppression and begin to ask the questions that will lead to enlightenment. A critical consciousness of the forms of Black women's oppression is infused in my teaching, in my view of what is deemed higher-order cognition. They construct me as an educator ... my pedagogy and the content of all my classes. I have come to realize that the ability to think critically about our existence is paramount to our survival. As an African American woman in a society that devalues us at every turn, survival is often the main goal. From negative depictions on television to negative depictions in the ideology of America, African American women are under a constant siege, battling for survival. As a critical teacher, I try to force my students to understand the anger and also the pride I feel in my Black womanism. More importantly, I lead them to an understanding of the "culture of survival" that Black women have historically possessed. Because of this I frame my teaching within a Black feminist discourse, which fosters students' understandings of the forms ideology has assumed so as to construct the identity of Black women through images/stereotypes that work to control a Black woman's identity. One of those ideological forms emerges in educational psychology's testing industry that consistently fails to validate our ways of making sense of the world as cognitively worthy. Lives are devastated everyday because of this ideological sorting tool.

Oshun: Let me ask you a question to make your use of critical thinking a little clearer. I know that all human interaction is politically inscribed and earlier you spoke of situating yourself in history. Isn't the connection between politics and history commonly understood?

Rochelle: Unfortunately no. Noncritical education decontextualizes history and our positions in it. We are seldom taught how to critically view our place in history—how it has constructed our identity. The circuitousness of political discourse assumes a godlike, patriarchal position of "hide-and-seek" information whereas the "politics of history" necessitates critical insight into that which seems obvious.

Oshun: "Politics of history" or "politics of representation"?

Rochelle: The "politics of history" allows us to better understand the "politics of representation." For example, consider the sinister names we are called: bitch, ho, unwed mother, matriarch, emasculator of all men but especially Black men, slut, ugly, aggressive, strong/weak, and low-aptitude students. I could continue but why bother; we all know the names used to define Black femaleness I'm about to go to church here! You know people are always trying to define me even though they know nothing about my reality. I ask, no I demand, that my students unpack the names used to describe and explain Black women. The political "justifications" for those names are as sinister as the names themselves and through a critical understanding of the "politics of history" they (the students) begin to accept that these names are not innocent and trouble-free.

Oshun: Yes, but are we being too deterministic? Don't we, as Black women, have the choice to accept or reject their definitions?

Rochelle: Good questions. When I talk about the "politics of representation" my words are not meant to take the power of individual Black women away. I don't mean to trivialize or essentialize Black women's reality but the triple oppression of race, class, and gender intersect under the umbrella of patriarchy, which defines, shapes and constructs the forms of domination used against African Americans. There are powerful ideological justifications for the existence of those definitions that manifest themselves as stereotypical controlling images. Hegemony's ideological control has manifested itself in various forms including—but not limited to—images which chisel a Black woman's identity as mammy, matriarch, sapphire, Jezebel, and the welfare mother. These are the archetypes of Black female misrepresentation, impersonating an outside-imposed identity and are shaped by dominant society so as to make racism, sexism, and poverty appear as a natural, inevitable part of life.

Schooling has historically hidden this knowledge. Students may understand these stereotypes on a subconscious level, but seldom will they be able to articulate the reasons for their existence. Because critical thinking is a central piece of my pedagogy, students constantly challenge their prior assumptions leading them to a new way of thinking.

Oshun: Yes, and challenging those assumptions "helps" in the development of a liberated mind. Shouldn't that be the purpose of education?

Rochelle: I have devoted my life to destroying those assumptions in the minds of my students. Stereotypes of Black women are interrelated, socially constructed, controlling images, each reflecting the dominant group's interest in maintaining Black women's subordination. These cultural stereotypes are designed to legitimize the causes of and reasons for Black women's oppression. They help to maintain interlocking systems of race, class, and gender oppression and are tools that serve to mystify societal structures and psychological categories created to achieve the legitimization of oppression. Utilizing critical thinking, the ability to deconstruct, we can analyze these various ideologies and their many manifestations.

Oshun: Speak my sister! When Black women go through life not understanding or knowing the stereotypes exist they run the risk of becoming the image.

Rochelle: When we don't see what's there, when the vision is blurred or hidden, our choices become limited or nonexistent—we remain truncated beings. Instead, when we are *conscious beings*, we are not aware of what is "out" there and as such we at the very least possess the knowledge to seek further where the stereotypes of Black women live. This knowledge leads to an understanding of the ideological forces that play upon a Black women's identity.

Consider the representation of Black women in popular culture. The four areas through which ideology occurs—legitimization, reification, mystification, and acquiescence—can be seen in the object and subject relations of the various controlling images.

Oshun: Every time I watch a music video my spirit cries.

Rochelle: I know. To be attractive or sexy in many of those videos means a scantily clad Black women must degrade herself, shaking derriere and gyrating hips, in front of a (usually) fully clothed Black male. Black women are objectified and the more the viewing audience sees the objectification the more it becomes reified or "real." Of course in order for this objectification of Black women to work it must happen on numerous fronts—the multiplicity of oppression. The objectivity of Black women is therefore reinforced. The identities of Black women are shaped, in part, by and through these negative images of who they say they are. When I use critical thought as the goal in my class students begin to see where these depictions originate. They see the power behind their constructed definitions of self. I am pleased to say that they see the political forces that shaped and shape those constructions. They not only make superficial connections with historical stereotypes of Black womanhood they also are able to understand the social, political, and economic forces which acted upon the creation of those very images.

Oshun: Once when you were teaching a class on The African American Woman. I was there; did you feel me?

Rochelle: Yes, you're presence was everywhere—guiding me to understand. All that we have been speaking of was a central part of the class. My main purpose was to demystify those influences on Black women's identity. Twice a week, in *The African American Woman 102*, my students and I discussed the insidious ways Black women are constructed. The social, historical, political, and economic realities of being Black and female in this society were addressed. Many of the students entered class thinking it was going to be a simple history class and that the knowledge they would leave with were names, achievements, and dates—decontextualized "useless" information on Black women. Instead, I informed them that the class was grounded in understanding the construction of Black womanhood and that we would employ the concepts of ideology, epistemology, the *Other*, deconstruction, hegemony, devaluation, dichotomy, binary opposition, subjugated knowledge, and stereotypes to accomplish this very difficult feat. Through an understanding of these concepts they would begin to partially open the door in their realization of Black women. I provided a list of new words and concepts and insisted students struggle to understand the new. I dared them to whine! In other words, I asked them to use every critical thinking skill they could find!

I compelled my students to take their knowledge to the next level through a critical analysis of assigned and suggested readings. We spent time looking at the social constructions of the other, oppression, domination, the politics of epistemology, dichotomies between Black and White women, ideology, media representations, etc.

Through readings, documentaries, films, and class discussions we dissected the life/existence of African American women. This dissection allowed the students (Black and White, male and female) to understand the various ways ideology has historically attempted to control and dominate African American women. In addition, an understanding of Black womanist thought allowed the students to see the ways Black women not only deconstruct the race, class, and gender oppression, but also the connections between Black female activism and empowerment.

Oshun: That was one thing I loved about your class. You did not just set Black women up as victims. You told our real story and a large part of that story is activism. I always enjoyed your class discussions on the archetypes of Black female subjugation. As I said earlier, you know, how unaware most students are regarding the stereotypes. It was interesting how every semester most of the students were not aware of the stereotypes, but once they learned of them they begin to point them out in media today.

Rochelle: When we teach students to stop and really look closely at what surrounds them, they typically become angry about all the things they never noticed before. We begin this conversation with a journal entry from one of my students who wrote about the joy and pain of new knowledge. To this day, I think the best and most creative midterm I have ever given was when I had my students critically deconstruct the cover from a "gangsta rap" CD. Girl, the cover offended every feminist piece of my being. It was, in animated form, a modern version of Black women portrayed as Sapphire. When I close my eyes I can still see it—a street corner scene in the projects, Black women dressed as hoochies, hanging out of windows, wearing lots of gold, exaggerated features, big red lips, blonde hair, and huge breasts. The cover was bad enough, but when the Black fraternities and sororities used a version of it to advertise a party, it truly became a teachable moment.

Oshun: So what did you do?

Rochelle: Girl, I marched down to the record store, flipped through the rap CDs till I found the right one, made a color overhead and then started the hard part—the actual test.

Oshun: And . . .

Rochelle: For the last hour we have been talking about Black women, critical thinking, critical educational psychology, and identity—how they all come together. I wanted my students to use their knowledge to critically deconstruct the picture—how it all came together. The "artist" who created the picture did not just wake up one morning and say, "Hey, the perfect way to sell this compact disk is to have Black women dressed like whores." There is a long, painful history behind their decision: forces acting in society on that person to make the picture the obvious choice. I needed the students to understand that and importantly to recognize their place in allowing the picture to be used as advertisement. I wanted to show the student that we discussed in class was not something removed from their everyday life but instead constructed that very life. I wanted them to be aware.

Oshun: The midterm represented the intersection of your critical understanding of Black women and your pedagogy. But there is so much that went into the class and the picture—how did you narrow it to a three-hour midterm?

Rochelle: I asked the students to deconstruct the picture from a Black womanist perspective describing the picture in agonizing detail. They then needed to discuss the historical relationship of Black women's representations from a *social*, *political*, and *economic* standpoint, specifically utilizing the theories of key thinkers in Black Feminist thought. Importantly they needed to explain Black women's oppression, devaluation, and strength. Finally, they had to analytically discuss why the picture was allowed to be used, why its "negativity" went unnoticed and accepted, and why a Black organization used the image to promote a party.

Oshun: How did it turn out? Did you get the answers you were looking for?

Rochelle: It all came together. I mean I felt like a mother giving birth. They got it and they articulated what they got. Critical thinking allowed them to make the connections between Black women's oppression of the past and Black women's oppression today. They connected the historical controlling images with images used today of Black women. They understood their own acquiescence and collusion in the maintenance and manifestation of those images and I am glad to say they were angry—at society and themselves.

Oshun: It's getting late and I'm being called back to the queendom. Is there anything else you need?

Rochelle: Did I answer your question about my three identities and what I want to give my students? Did I make you see how interconnected those four things are? Did you feel my passion and anger when I spoke of Black women? Did you sense the anger my students felt once they acquired the critical thinking skills to deconstruct their world? Through my words, could you hear the screams of my Black female students once they realized the many injustices that were placed on them? Did you also hear their sounds of completeness once they finally realized what ideology has hidden from them for so long? Do you now understand that the greatest thing I can give my students and myself is the ability to question? Did I make it clear that we (Black women who teach) must learn to weave our own future, to create a tapestry of hope and teach students to utilize critical thinking skills as the seam to hold the tapestry together?

Oshun: Yes, you did my sister!

FURTHER READING

Hills-Collins, P. (1991). *Black Feminist Thought: Knowledge, Consciousness and the Politics of Empowerment*. New York: Routledge.

hooks, b. (1989). *Talking Back: Thinking Feminist, Thinking Black*. Boston: South End Press.

Wade-Gayles, G. (1984). *No Crystal Stair: Visions of Race and Sex in Black Women's Fiction*. New York: The Pilgrim Press.

CHAPTER 77

Pedagogies and Politics: Shifting Agendas within the Gendering of Childhood

ERICA BURMAN

This chapter aims to substantiate four claims. Firstly, dominant models of child development are inscribed with implicit norms that reflect (among others) particular gendered attributes. Secondly, these gendered attributes "fit" or coincide with particular forms of political subjectivity. Thirdly, contemporary shifts in the engendering of models of child development and education are indicative of broader changes of models of the subjects that correspond to current economic-political agendas. It follows from this that, fourthly, as with claims to childhood generally, we should be wary of the ways gender is deployed within educational and psychological debates since these are both informed by and in their turn culturally inform the wider political arena. I finish by indicating how and why critical educationalists and psychologists should be wary of new feminised models of the educational or psychological subject by suggesting that these may be pursuing old oppressive agendas in cuddlier forms, or even elaborating new equally insidious varieties.

Having identified these claims, a word here about their status. I am deliberately using rather indirect descriptions of influence or effect, such as "reflect," "inform," "inscribed within" etc., that rather blur the direction of causality and location of responsibility. This is because I am concerned here with relationships between patterns of cultural norms in circulation about gender and childhood and broader political-economic contexts, rather than with mapping the directionality of links between specific politicians or policies and shifts in models of childhood. This is not to say that such links cannot sometimes be made, and indeed I will offer some indicative examples as I go along. I leave exploration of more specific elaborations of relationships for another time, or another researcher, bearing in mind also the complexities of such an enterprise—that needs to steer a careful course between conspiracy theory on the one hand, and on the other a voluntarism that abstracts theorists from the historical, political, and cultural contexts that both enable their influence and structures the reception of their ideas. (Denise Riley's 1983 evaluation of the role of the psychoanalysts Bowlby and Winnicott within the trajectories of state-funded day care provision for children does just this kind of detailed historically located and conceptually elaborated work). Rather my concern here is focused on exploring a discernable cultural shift within the gendering of models of childhood. As should become clear, I see ambiguities and complexities around the shifting locus of "development" as precisely what obscures an easy answer to the question of determination.

Before I really begin, let me clarify some methodological presuppositions for this analysis. Firstly, I am going to be dealing with representations of childhood, or qualities accorded an ideal-typical model of the developing child. But this does not mean I am only discussing models of childhood. I am drawing on a broadly Foucauldian understanding of the structuring of cultural-political discourse such that—although I do not have space to say much about this here—every model of the child implies equivalent subject positions for others around him or her: for parents, teachers, other welfare professionals and, as I will endeavour to indicate, even the nation state. Some of these positions are more clearly specified than others. Prescribed positions for teachers and mothers, for example, are usually pretty unambiguously identifiable from any specific pedagogical approach (usually either as negligent or intrusive), while that for fathers is often more variable in the sense of discretionary (though ultimately also amenable to pathologization). It is the murky character of the role of the state and transnational economic-political processes that demands further analysis.

In pursuit of this theme, the discussion that follows traverses territory that may seem far from education. I will be juxtaposing economic and psychological models of development and making claims that connect political and psychodynamic notions of "investment." While such disciplinary border crossings may appear tenuous, my arguments precisely concern links between allocations of financial and emotional resources. Moreover, the cultural connections between children and emotionality speak to a set of culturally contingent but potent relations.

THE STATUS OF CHILDHOOD

The Western world is currently witnessing an explosion of concern about children—abused children, delinquent children, children as victims, and children as aggressors. These wildly contradictory concerns (with protecting children and protecting people *from* children) indicate the cultural burden carried by children and young people as the repository of identification for the human subject more generally. Steedman's (1995) historical analysis traces the emergence of the motif of the child as the personification of interiority, of a sense of unique selfhood or individuality that lies inside the body. The economic and cultural conditions for this motif alongside modernity implicate this model of childhood within the consolidation of the nation state and its imperialist/colonialist projects.

From this moment the bifurcation of childhood is confirmed. And these cultural motifs still circulate. Vulnerability, innocence, nostalgia for times past, or even nostalgia for times denied or withheld by the actual conditions of our past childhoods—all these qualities inform contemporary representations of childhood. In this way childhood becomes our past, beyond merely being a period of life that all adults have gone through, but rather this comes to be filled with imaginary investments that probably say more about the dissatisfactions with and insults of our current adult lives under late capitalism than any childhood we actually had, or wished for as children. "Remember that feeling of total control?" goes a car advertisement of the mid-1990s, interpellating the subjectivity of the owner-driver to that of a little boy depicted playing with his toy car. In this sense, there is danger in the sentimentality that surrounds representations of childhood. For it is so replete with adult emotional investment that we threaten to overlook the actual conditions and positions of contemporary embodied, acting children and young people.

Where these do impinge, the shattering of such ideal-typical representations can instigate bitter vengeance. Children who transgress models of childhood suffer stigmatisation and vilification to a degree that must tell us something about societal investments. Children who have sex, who work, who are violent—that is, children who behave like many adults—far from being included into the adult world are ejected from it. In Britain the public and policy response to the two child killers of two-year-old Jamie Bulger in 1993 was to render them monstrous, as outside humanity, rather than as departing from cultural norms of childhood.

There is now a significant literature on the history of childhood as largely a modern invention, with the contrasting modalities of modernity informing early educational philosophies. The romance of the child as natural, closer to nature, gives rise to particular problems when children act "unnaturally." Clearly an ideological notion of "nature" is at work that covers over the violence of its domestication and exploitation. And this is where educational and psychological models fit well with broader discourses of "development." For the discourse of development relies for its benign mask upon a model of the developing subject as passive, compliant, and grateful for its needs being attended to. While post-development theorists have amply highlighted how this model warrants the oppression and exploitation meted out by international aid and development policies, child activists have shown how Euro-US models of childhood at best fail to engage with the key issues facing most of the world's children and young people, and often in this process simply pathologize them further.

The naturalised, and so presumed universalised, status of childhood plays an important role within this dynamic, while such moves effect a harmonization between individual and national interest and well-being, as in the Human Development Index formulated by the United Nations Development Project in 1992 and used in its subsequent annual reports to measure disparities between more and less "developed" countries.

The concept of human development ... is a form of investment, not just a means of distributing income. Healthy and educated people can, through productive employment, contribute more to economic growth. (UNDP, 1992, p. 12)

This device not only commodifies individual development as a condition of national development, but also how this abstracts specific national economic trajectories from the ravages of the international and multinational market, thereby eschewing the latter's responsibilities for "underdevelopment" or impoverishment.

EDUCATING THE CHILD

So the abstraction structured into the call to, or for, childhood is inevitably disingenuous. It functions potently: to distract or displace attention from the actual child or children under scrutiny to some distant other, (mis)remembered place, and through this, to designate the current challenges surrounding children and childhood as deviations from this thereby naturalized condition. Indeed it has been claimed that the introduction of compulsory primary level education—occurring in the late nineteenth century across Europe—owed much to public concerns over threats to social order because of the rise of an economically active and politically engaged generation of working class young people. This is not of course to romanticise the kind of work (including its conditions and level of remuneration) that children and young people were (and are) engaged in, but rather to point to other motivations for the call to educate children. Indeed the very flexibility and in some respects social irrelevance of the definition of childhood has contributed to the difficulty of being able to interpret historical records for children and young people's political involvements, in the early factory strikes for example.

This is where we see the link between childhood as an origin state—whether of innocence or sin—and childhood as a signifier of process and potential. Pedagogies, theories of teaching and learning, subscribe to specific models of the student (and correspondingly also of the teacher). The schooled child, unlike the working child, was positioned as without knowledge (and so in need of teaching). The educational project then erased or pathologized the knowledge that children already possessed. Clearly behaviorist approaches epitomize this, but the other more nativist theories in circulation around the early twentieth century put forward equivalent projects to classify, and control by (at best) segregation and surveillance, potentially unruly or undesirable elements. (I say "at best" since the links between the early psychologists—especially those who developed the statistical apparatus of psychometric testing—and eugenics are now widely documented.

Here we see the convergence of political and educational projects. "Catching them young" clarifies the policing and custodial as well as social engineering agendas that have informed educational initiatives of all varieties. The modelling of the ideal citizen through educational practices was there from the inception of modern state-sponsored schooling, and given only a new liberal twist in the post-World-War II period with the emphasis on building democratic subjects through appropriate familial and schooling interventions. The rational unitary subject of the modern nation state was explicitly prefigured within educational philosophies. Piaget and Dewey were prepared to link their philosophies with their politics, and both saw in education a way of improving society. As the slogan goes, "our children are our future." By this we pin our fantasy of the future onto children as signifiers of futurity, of the world to come or what it could become, as well as of what is now lost—so highlighting the multiple and mobile character of the temporal significations effected by childhood. Either way, in so doing we run the risk of justifying deficits within children's present for a model of the future (or past)—whether national or environmental—that they have played no part in formulating, and may not ever be in a position to enjoy.

Now let me reiterate that I am not implying we should dispense with such agendas. Rather I am arguing precisely the reverse: that we cannot. Representations of childhood as we know them—and "we" here extends from Euro-U.S. contexts to all over the world through globalization and through international aid and development (especially child development) policies—are shot through with normative assumptions that tie individual to social development. It may well currently be impossible to disentangle them. But at least we can attend to *how* they are entangled, and with what effects. In particular we can look at how the state is configured within such subject formations—to counter the ways the abstraction of the child works to bolster the privatisation of the family and so occlude states' responsibility for constituting the very problems they then claim to address.

ENGENDERING THE DEVELOPING CHILD

So far I have been talking of "the child" and children in a gender-neutral way. Yet—notwithstanding the ways childhood functions precisely a warrant for abstraction from the social-gender and (all other aspects too—class, culture, attributed or assumed sexuality) in-fuse representations of childhood. This is not only a matter of grammatical pronoun attribution (although this is of course indicative not only of how the masculine pronoun "he" is taken as representative of humanity, but also of how this secures the mother/child "couple" safely and prefiguratively within the domain of heterosexual relations), but also less directly of cultural qualities that have gendered associations.

The rational unitary subject of psychology, like the model of the rational, autonomous, self-regulating, responsible citizen is—culturally speaking—masculine. Piaget's model of the child as mini-scientist, information-processing models of cognition and the like all reiterate the culturally dominant project of modernity: mastery. Learning as an individual, self-sustained process bolsters a gendered model of the rational, self-sufficient, autonomous, problem-solving subject. Various commentators have highlighted the covert as well as explicit ways in which educational and psychological models of the developing child privilege cultural masculinity (which in practice do not necessarily benefit boys any more than girls).

So, in terms of the dualisms surrounding childhood, these map onto a gendered division. The state of childhood seems a needy place: associated with dependency, irrationality, and vulnerability. These are of course qualities associated with femininity, and indeed this culturally sanctioned elision between women and children has many profound effects. These go beyond claims to special treatment or protection, alongside diminished responsibility and secondary civil status, to usher in a general infantilization of the condition of being a woman. Here it is useful to recall how such representations of femininity are not only profoundly classed but are also part of the ideology of colonialism, with claims to women's emancipation figuring within the rationale for imperialist ventures, as indicated also recently in the recent war against Afghanistan. Drawing on the wider influence of evolutionary theory, models of development were recapitulationist: ontogeny was understood to recapitulate phylogeny, with the child in its individual developmental trajectory recapitulating evolutionary process. In terms of early psychological theories, the child, the woman, and the native/savage (along with other rejects from the modern development project of productivity—the mental defective and degenerate) were all positioned at the bottom of progress' ladder. At the top was rational, white, Western, middle-class man, and the task of individual—as now international—development was to expedite the ascent. Thus prevailing models in their portrayal of development, as linear and singular, reproduce the gender and cultural chauvinisms of their times and places.

Further problems arise when considering the position of girls who encounter a double dose of this set of inscriptions—as both child and incipient woman. The invention of the new development category the "girl child" speaks to this conundrum, since she is neither quite a prototypical child nor woman; but invites further intervention precisely owing to her liminal position to both positions. The slogan "Educate a girl and you educate a nation" in circulation around the time of the launch of the UN Convention of the Rights of the Child has been taken up by many countries. Here we see how gendered agendas surrounding the connection between women and nation, with women as responsible for cultural as well as biological reproduction and so subject to particular social and sexual regulation become expressed through the intensification of intervention on (behalf of) girls and young women. Indeed "Education is the best contraception" was the slogan of the World Bank Poverty Report in 1986. The elision between woman as mother and girl as pupil effects a double move: not only are women primarily considered in terms of reproductive activities but childhood is so thoroughly gendered that "the girl child" is regarded as an incipient woman, and thus a future mother. On one hand within dominant Western psychological models the *invisibility* of gender, and correspondingly implicit celebration of culturally masculine qualities has worked to marginalize or pathologize girls. But outside this context, the *visibility* of gender functions to combine the oppressions of being a child and a woman for "the girl child." In contrast to the gender-free discourses of childhood and adolescence that have characterized Western literatures, and have offered some scope for maneuver for girls and young women, it seems that "girl children" of the (political as well as geographical) South are scarcely children: they are girls. Helpful as some of the measures for girls may be, putting gender on the agenda is not always or in all respects emancipatory.

FEMINIZING DEVELOPMENT?

So if the rational, autonomous problem-solving child fitted with the modern development project, what shifts attend postmodern (or late capitalist) shifts in labor and production processes? Alongside the general crisis of credibility of the project of social improvement, we have witnessed a general backlash against educational approaches that emphasized individual self-expression and exploration. Like many other modern aspirations, the liberal project of education as the route to social mobility has not delivered—in the sense that social stratifications have widened within and between nations. Worldwide and within each country the rich get richer while the poor get poorer. From the mid-1980s economic recession started to impact on educational horizons, with instrumentalist agendas coming to the fore, as well as general crises over "standards." There were of course continuities underlying these apparent shifts. For example, Avis (1991) analyses how the individualism of child-centered approaches was part of what made possible the apparent reversal of British educational agendas from progressive education to "back to basics" vocationalism.

Yet this changing context seems to have produced a new set of beneficiaries. Amid claims of falling standards, or perhaps as a response to this, girls are apparently doing well at school. Over the past five years British girls have achieved higher school-leaving examination results overall, and in almost all subject areas except Physics. Are we witnessing a change, even a reversal, in educational philosophy or models? Walkerdine and others (1990) had earlier documented how girls were "counted out" by teachers, with their diligence and good behavior working merely to confirm their status as "plodders" rather than as possessors of the "natural flair" that marked true cleverness (exhibited by the more unruly boys). In their follow-up study the trends indicated earlier are now exacerbated with those girls marked as succeeding continuing to succeed, while the others had "failed" further.

The educational "overachievement" of girls has generated much public and policy discussion in the United Kingdom, and the very terms of this discussion of course deny the ways girls were explicitly disadvantaged within the previous assessment system (with multiple-choice tests discriminating against girls, and even then the original test scores subject to alteration because of girls' better performance in order to ensure an equal balance in educational selection processes). Now with the move toward more, and more continuous, assessment girls' stereotypical qualities of docility and conscientiousness appear to be advantaging them (and boys' qualities of indifference and last minute flurries no longer delivering). The extension of the skills wrought in the domestic sphere to schooling seems to be paying off.

How does this shift mesh with more widespread societal changes? We are told that we live in a postfeminist era, with struggles for women's rights now fulfilled. It may be true that some women have benefited from the widespread cultural move away from traditional hard-nosed patriarchal approaches to management and business and the rise of a psychotherapeutically informed culture that emphasizes "people skills," including "emotional literacy" and "emotional intelligence"—all qualities associated with femininity. With the decline of manufacturing industries in most developed societies and the rise of the service sector as the major source of employment "emotional labor" has assumed an unprecedented significance (Hochschild, 1983). Certainly girls and women form an increasing target for such initiatives, and worldwide women have never before been so enlisted into development projects, while women form the ideal-typical labor force within the information technology sector as new cottage industry (giving rise to Haraway's, 1991, famous analysis in terms of cyborg subjectivity). But just as getting women through the "glass ceiling" does not necessarily change anything about the disproportionate dimensions and distributions of the institution (including even gender inequalities), so the recruitment of women and girls to the education and development process may be less in their interests than first appears.

Indeed when the public focus on gender in relation to educational achievement is displaced to attend to class and "race" we get a very different picture, while even those middle-class girls who appear to be succeeding in these times of increased pressure and competition are doing so at major personal cost to their mental health. So while the feminisation of development is in part illusory, insofar as such claims have some purchase we need to look again at how they work.

GENDER AND NEOLIBERALISM

There is something very powerful about current shifts in gendered imagery, even if these images are spurious. Current economic conditions seem to have detached processes of feminization from women, to extend them to men as well. So now men suffer conditions of part-time, casualised, and low-paid labor that were formerly associated only with women. The very notion of a continuous "career" that unfolds with one's own unique developmental trajectory as the apotheosis of cultural masculinity under modernity has suffered irreparable change. Within the public eye men now figure within public and mental health targets, as sufferers of undiagnosed depressions and as potential candidates for suicide or self-harm. In my locality (Manchester, UK) there are now special internet counselling services (such as CALM—the Campaign Against Living Miserably) specifically set up to address young white men who are considered likely to feel unable to access suitable support services in part because doing so would transgress their—now maladaptive—gender norms.

The current cultural preoccupation with men as vulnerable, rather than hegemonic, not only co-incides with other narcissistic insults to the modern gendered arrangement of man-as-breadwinner, but also with broader curtailments of the grandiosity of Western expansionism (the current invasion and occupation of Iraq being a reactive overcompensation for, rather than contradiction of, this). Androgyny, hailed since the 1970s as mentally healthy, now fits the flexibility required of the new world order.

It is in this context that a new model of the human subject could be said to have emerged. This model, recalls Steedman's (1995) discussion, in that it is gendered as female. But, as with her account, its very femininity does some significant additional work not possible with a culturally masculine model. A cultural example comes to mind as an illustration. The film *Amelie* (dir. J. P. Jeanet, France 2001) concerns a gamine young woman who finds gratification in helping others, and in so doing finds love. This film was a huge success (generating a uniform wave of "it's lovely" responses even from monolingual Anglophone audiences usually resistant to reading subtitles) and has been said to have revitalized the French film industry. Yet notwithstanding her good intentions (and how "good" are they really? For the film does interrogate her motivations...), she can be seen to impose developmental agendas upon the recipients of her good deeds, rather than engaging in consultation with them about what it is that they want (the blind man and the Moroccan men being significant examples here). This is exactly the problem of development policy and practice—whereby the beneficiaries are required to tailor their needs and desires to the agendas of their benefactors (and usually they have to pay for it too in loan guarantees and interest rates). Yet this recapitulation of old imperialist themes within the film's narrative escapes notice precisely because it is performed by a lovely, vulnerable young woman, whose neediness and beauty seductively distract us from this.

Are we now witnessing a feminisation of the neoliberal subject who can better realise traditional globalizing aims? Do shifts in models of gender indicate genuine changes in gendered power relations, or are they merely surface displacements whose novel aspects obscure the continuity of preexisting agendas? Jenson and Saint-Martin (2002) in their cross-national analysis of shifts in social policy, claim to have identified a new model of the subject that they call LEGO™ after the children's educational building blocks. This new social policy takes education and development as the key route to economic prosperity, aiming to maximize individual productivity through participation within the paid-labor force. Like the children's toy its key tenets focus, firstly, on "learning through play" (as a self-motivated, nongoal directed activity), with play becoming a practice that can become instrumentalized into a form of legitimized "work" through a commitment to "lifelong learning." Secondly, there is a future orientation to this approach, emphasizing activation of human potential for later benefit as the mode of social inclusion and protection from marginalization, rather than focusing on corrections to existing social inequities of distributions of goods and access to services. Thirdly, it links initiatives supporting individual development to community and national development. Lifelong learning becomes the route for individual protection and security from the instabilities of national economies and international labor market fluctuations.

Critical educationalists have long critiqued this idealisation of play, so in this context of the rise of the knowledge-based society it is interesting to see its reemergence. Its links with individualized, psychologized notions of skill development that have a long history coinciding with industrial development. The focus on individual activity and familial context is cast explicitly in terms of maximizing human capital, warranting policies of cutbacks in state support for the unemployed—including (the usually female) lone parents who are now to be offered increasing incentives to enter the labor market (and suffer increasing penalties and pressures if they do not). Parental employment becomes the route for solving child poverty, while there is an assumption that full employment is both possible and desirable—something that flies in the face of the structural unemployment that has been part and parcel of postindustrialization. The "activity" on which such measures rely therefore is generated by individuals, not the state.

The two ideas—that work is the route to maximizing individuals' well-being; and social cohesion that is the well-being of the collectivity, depends on such activity—lies at the heart of notions of activation as a social policy, and an "active society" as a policy goal. (Jenson and Saint-Martin, 2002, pp. 15–16)

Further, within this activity/activation model, individual and collective good collapse into each other, importing all the political problems of a voluntarism that makes individuals responsible for their social position. But now this is a feminised form of social participation, that exudes "family-friendliness" and "emotional literacy"—for the "activity" of this form of learning is not only rational problem-solving but now includes care—at home and at work. This is where neoliberalism meets pedagogy: and perhaps where, with the generalization of the condition of play and celebration of child-like qualities within contemporary culture, the longstanding infantilization of women through their association with—and with the status of—children has been extended into a more comprehensive strategy that enjoins us all as active learners.

How might educational practice attend to and respond to such analyses? Clearly there are few easy answers but some intermediate analytical and practical strategies can be indicated. Firstly, an interpretive vigilance is needed toward the interwoven and mutually legitimising models of individual and economic development. These typically enter educational discourse through a set of statements about societal needs and character. Some of these statements are presumed obvious; others indicate explicit shifts in social policy gaze. As Jenson and Saint-Martin indicate, currently there is attention to state investment in childcare and early education as a way of countering not only contemporary child poverty and disadvantage but also of warding off future sectors of social exclusion of marginalization. But these apparently benign measures function within a neoliberal model of the marketization of human potential that ties responsibilities for welfare and well-being to the economically productive individual and family.

Secondly, it is important to attend to the slipperiness of gender within educational discourses, both in terms of evaluating the new possibilities this presents and old problems this covers over. Current initiatives to mobilize women within the paid-labor market form a key priority for many advanced as well as developing countries. The extent to which this is emancipatory for women is debatable. Women and children's (low-paid and unpaid) labor have long been a key reserve resource for familial survival, and they are now undergoing ruthless exploitation across the world, albeit in different ways in richer and poorer countries. This explicit mobilization of women's labor potential and the focus on the active model of individual development that is epitomized by the educational dictum of "play as work" coincides with unprecedented retraction of state welfare provision, and therefore threatens to intensify women's responsibilities for both economic and child development.

Finally, we need to look to counter-examples that disrupt the kinds of mutual relationship or determination that I have highlighted here, to document how pedagogies can revolutionize rather than confirm the political arrangements they work within. In their analysis Jenson and Saint-Martin take pains to emphasize that identifying policy convergences, or even the emergence of new policy "blueprints," does not mean uniformity either of implementation. Feminist and postdevelopment critiques now argue that attending to the different agendas and interests of the various stakeholders or actors involved within any development intervention helps to identify the variety of its effects, including—at least potentially—counterhegemonic ones. So equipped, we may be able to notice if gendered fluctuations in and between models of the child, child carer, and worker give rise to any more useful pedagogical and political strategies.

SUGGESTED READING

Broughton, J. (Ed.) (1987). *Critical Theories of Psychological Development.* New York: Plenum Press.
Burman, E. (1994). *Deconstructing Developmental Psychology.* London and New York: Routledge.
———. (1995)Developing Differences: Gender, Childhood and Economic Development. *Children & Society*, 9(3), 121–141.
———. (1998). The Child, the Woman and the Cyborg: (Im)possibilities of Feminist Developmental Psychology. In K. Henwood, C. Griffin, and A. Phoenix (Eds.), *Standpoints and Differences: Essays in the Practice of Feminist Psychology*, pp. 210–232. London: Sage.
Francis, B. and Skelton, C. (Eds.) (2001). *Investigating Gender: Contemporary Perspectives in Education.* Buckingham: Open University Press.
Richards, G. (1997). *'Race', Racism and Psychology.* London: Routledge.
Sachs, W. (Ed.) (1992). *The Development Dictionary: A Guide to Knowledge As Power.* London: Zed.
Schlemmer, B. (Ed.) (2002). *The Exploited Child.* London: Zed.
Yuval-Davis, N. (1998). *Gender and Nation.* London: Sage.

REFERENCES

Avis, J. (1991). The Strange Fate of Progressive Education. In Education Group II, Cultural Studies, University of Birmingham, *Education Limited: Schooling, Training and the New Right in England since 1979*, pp. 114–142. London: Unwin Hyman Ltd.
Haraway, D. (1991). *Simians, Cyborgs and Women.* London: Verso.
Hochschild, A. (1983). *The Managed Heart.* Berkeley, CA: University of California Press.
Jenson, J. and Saint-Martin, D. (2002) Building blocks for a New Welfare Architecture: Is LEGO™ the Model for an Active Society? Paper prepared on August 20–September 1, 2002, from the delivery at the 2002 Annual Meeting of the American Political Science Association, Boston.
Riley, D. (1983). *War in the Nursery: Theories of Mother and Child.* London: Virago.
Steedman, C. (1995). *Strange Dislocations: Childhood and the Idea of Human Interiority 1789–1939.* London: Routledge.
United Nations Development Programme (1992). *Human Development Report.* Oxford and New York: Oxford University Press.
Walkerdine, V. and the Girls and Mathematics Unit (1990). *Counting Girls Out.* London: Virago.

CHAPTER 78

Knowledge or Multiple Knowings: Challenges and Possibilities of Indigenous Knowledges

GEORGE J. SEFA DEI AND STANLEY DOYLE-WOOD

We begin first by grounding our critique within the decolonizing space of the anticolonial framework. As pointed out elsewhere (Sefa Dei, 2000), the anticolonial discursive framework is an epistemology of the colonized, anchored in the indigenous sense of collective and the importance of developing a common colonial consciousness. Colonial in this sense is conceptualized not simply as foreign or alien but imposed and dominating (Sefa Dei and Asgharzadeh, 2001). The anticolonial framework allows us to engage educational problems through connections of knowledge, discourse, culture, and communicative practices of schooling. We understand education as realized within a historically developed and socially maintained space that is structured through interrelationships among the multiple sites of teaching/learning and the everyday practices of community and cultural life. To take into account these interrelationships means not only to understand how they shape the substance of schooling, but also how learning and pedagogy operate in our society on much broader levels to include critical decolonizing consciousness, agency, and spirituality. Our intellectual focus on indigenity, local indigenousness, and the power of knowledge to alter the encounter of the colonizer and the colonized (in ways that point to the instability and fluidity of the colonial relation), is to show the dynamic of the resistance inherent in colonial relations, as well as the ability of the colonized to manipulate the colonizer and his or her colonial practices. The ways in which local knowings confront colonizing practices that are continually reproduced and deeply embedded in everyday relations, represent powerful sources of knowledge that allow the daily resistance and the pursuit of effective political practice to subvert all forms of dominance to take place. We take the Euro-American school system and the experiences of different bodies within these schools as a means through which such relations can be examined. It is maintained that within schools there are material-structural, ideological-spiritual, and socio-cultural-political dynamic schooling practices that produce significant differential material consequences for both dominant and minoritized bodies. Smith (1999) has explored the relationship between knowledge, research, and imperialism, pointing to the ways such relations have come to structure our ways of knowing through the development of academic disciplines and through the education of colonial elites and indigenous/ "native" intellectuals. Critical education must therefore expose colonizing knowledges and social practices that have destroyed (and continue to destroy) human creativity in the context of our relations with our social and natural environments.

In colonial relations of power, hegemonic knowledges have allowed colonizers to secure their dominance through a fictional creation of sameness and commonality at the expense of difference and heterogeneity. To discuss therefore, the possibilities of educational change in North America we must first understand the power of discursive interruptions to conventional practices of schooling that fail to account for difference in relation to ethnicity, gender, class, religion, language, and culture. Such identities are inextricably linked to schooling and to knowledge production. To understand the nature and extent of colonial/colonized discourse and practice at school we must interrogate and hear the voices of different subjects as they speak about their schooling experiences. Colonialism when read as imposing and dominating never ceased with the return of political sovereignty to colonized peoples or nation states. Indeed, today colonialism and recolonizing projects are (re)produced in variegated ways. For example, within schools the manifestation of this process takes place in the different ways knowledges get produced and receive validation, and the particular experiences of students who are counted as (in)valid in contrast to the identities of those that receive recognition and response from school authorities and discursive curricular practice. Through an examination of the power dynamics implicit in the evocation of culture, histories, knowledges, and experiences of the diverse bodies represented in the school system, we see how colonialism and colonial relations can be masked under the conventional processes of knowledge production and validation. In other words we are speaking of questions that seek answers to who counts, what counts, and why, in terms of different knowledges, multiple ways of knowing, identities, and experiences.

EDUCATIONAL PSYCHOLOGY CRITIQUE AND BRIEF HISTORICAL OVERVIEW

Historically, the field of mainstream educational psychology has viewed teaching and learning through a cultural lens that is predominantly Eurocentric in nature. Consequently, its conceptualization of how people learn, think, and develop ways of knowing in relation to their natural/social world, rests largely on post Enlightenment notions of deductive reasoning, cause and effect, stimulus/ response, and sensory/cognitive definitions and understandings of intelligence and knowledge acquisition. Hermann Ebbinghaus (1850–1909), for example, argued that the cognitive connections a person makes between particular concepts is correlative to the frequency with which they are encountered (Driscoll, 1994). So for example the mental response a person may make to the stimulus of bread with the mental idea of butter will be governed by the number of times the person has experienced these two concepts in association with each other. In other words, learning and remembering is contingent upon frequency and repetition. Edward Thorndike (1874–1949)—the "father of educational psychology"—in pursuing the theory of stimulus/reflexive response, asserted that when a mental connection is made between a given situation and a response, the strength of the connection is increased as it is further used, practiced, or exercised (Joncich, 1962). Thus, the child who says "apple" at every sight of the fruit increases (according to Thorndike) his or her tendency to *think* and say apple at its every future appearance.

The notion of stimulus and reflexive response with regard to learning became associated in turn with the idea that within all animal organisms a basic learning mechanism exists that can be conditioned by socio-environmental factors. The most notable example of this theory to be studied under experimental conditions can be found in the work undertaken by Ivan Pavlov (1849–1946). In his experiments with dogs Pavlov observed that after several experiences of hearing a tone just before food was placed in its mouth, the dog would begin to salivate in response to the tone even before it received any food (Driscoll, 1994). From then on the dog began to expect food when it heard the tone and began watering at the mouth. These ideas of what came to be known as "classical conditioning" are still very much a part of schooling practices today. The school recess bell represents perhaps the most evocative contemporary example.

Basic learning mechanism theories have been particularly influential however, in studies related to infants. Possibly the most famous (or infamous) of all studies in this regard is that performed by Watson and Rayner (1920). Watson, an early member of the behaviorist school argued that if behavior is conditioned it could, as a consequence, be modified or changed by experience, either through punishment or rewards. In order to demonstrate their theory that children's fears of animals were not innate but were in fact shaped by their environment, they exposed a nine-month-old boy to several white-colored animals such as a rat, a rabbit, a dog etc. The baby at first proceeded to play with the animals with no apparent sense of fright. They then hit a steel bar with a hammer just behind the baby's head as he reached for the rabbit. The boy subsequently cried with fear at the loud noise. After several repetitions of the hammer hitting the bar, the baby proceeded to cry whenever he saw the rabbit. Watson and Rayner reported that the child's fear of the white rabbit extended to the many white, fuzzy objects he was also shown, including a dog, a fur coat, and even a Santa Claus mask. Fear of white rabbits, fur coats, and Santa Claus masks is not inherited, they argued, it is learned.

Despite the profound ethical issues raised here, the overall idea that behavior can be conditioning through rewards and punishment has become a staple of Western concepts of teaching and learning. We see this in the hierarchical allocation of rewards and punishments in the schools and specifically the operation of merit badges. One of the main proponents associated with this area of educational psychology is that of B. F. Skinner (1904–1990). According to Skinner, the process known as "operant conditioning" (that is to say, learning through rewards and punishments) "shapes behavior as a sculpture shapes clay" (Cole and Cole, 1993, p. 16). The implication here is that all students enter the schools as disembodied lumps of clay. As such, the teacher's role lies in shaping these mere lumps into a fixed, institutionally sanctioned, cultural entity of what counts as the norm. Where there is deviation from the norm it is to be hammered back into *normal* shape. But what does this mean for student subjectivities that do not conform to this preset (and pre-invented) cultural norm? What does this mean for students entering the schools and classrooms whose "shapes" are formed through the embodied knowledges of difference?

As Philip Corrigan (1990, p. 156) has rightly pointed out schools not only teach subjects they also teach, and *make* subjectivities. In this sense, hegemonic discourses of superiority/inferiority are invested and constituted in the racialized bodies of students through the epistemic and material violence of colonial knowledge and through the violent routines of normalization. Oppressive/repressive messages proclaiming what is culturally/racially legitimate and what is not are pervasive in discourses of normalization. They are structurally grounded in the hidden culture of the schooling institution itself. They become explicit/implicit in forms that project a "deep curriculum" (Sefa Dei et al., 1997, p. 144) that is to say, those formal and informal aspects of the school environment that intersect with both the cultural environment and the organizational life of the school. As a result White/Eurocentric neocolonial dominance is spoken loudly and unequivocally in the formations of normalizing routines that are institutionally supported. Minoritized students are constrained into disembodied silence and their capacities of expression and communication severely regulated by cultural/racially charged discourses of what is considered acceptable, appropriate, or what is approved and not approved. It is the educator and more accurately the "deep curriculum" that determines which bodies should speak and which should not. What is considered speech and what is not. What should be spoken, for how long, in what form, and in what language. As Corrigan (1990, p. 160) has noted, it is through this process that "we can begin to see how schooling hurts." We begin to see how normalizing routines are productive of "active wounds," that is to say wounds that are seared into the struggles of students who are institutionally discounted as "(ab)normal." Such wounds become active in their accumulative capacity to despiritualize, disempower, disengage, and shut out minoritized students from their schooling environment and community. Moreover, in their disregard for the asymmetrical power relations that shape the lives of students, Cartesian-Newtonian teaching approaches based on cause and effect, Western empiricism, and deductive reasoning sustain and (re)produce the epistemic and material violence that minoritized students face daily in their engagements with dominant systems of power. In *Rethinking Intelligence*, Joe Kincheloe has noted the dangerous implication of Western cognitive/educational psychology in schooling methodologies of this nature (Kincheloe, Steinberg, and Villaverde, 1999). Grounded on a culturally specific post Enlightenment theoretical foundation, Western educational psychology as a field "measures" and seeks out traits of intelligence with which it is culturally familiar. As a result "unknown attributes of intelligence" that cannot be measured by psychology are dismissed and ignored. Thus, the possibilities of engaging with the diversity of thought are stifled.

The "measuring" and testing of intelligence first emerged from the field of educational psychology in the late nineteenth century. Francis Galton initially attempted to measure the speed of human reactions and to devise psychological testing formats. G. Stanley Hall constructed questionnaires in his attempt to understand how children's minds worked. In addition, James Mckeen Cattell created "mental tests for students at the universities of Pennsylvania and Columbia." The individuals however, who have had the most impact are Alfred Binet and Theophile Simon. Originally the Binet scale that they created at the Sorbonne in Paris (first published in 1905–1908) was aimed at targeting mentally challenged children for specialized programming. The scale was later developed to produce the Stanford-Binet testing scheme from which emerged the use of IQ (intelligence quotient) testing. This testing format, which was adapted by Lewis M. Terman for use in America, is in common usage today in schools across North America in its purported capacity to measure intelligence and academic performance. The administering of such tests however, has engendered strong criticism in recent years (Brown et al., 2003; Cannella, 1999; Dei et al., 1997; McClendon and Weaver, 1999), particularly in terms of their propensity to only test certain fixed notions of intelligence, knowledge, and ways of knowing. Furthermore, as Kincheloe points out, in the political context of psychology's legitimizing practices, "those who deviate from the accepted norms . . . fail to gain the power of psychological validation so needed in any effort to gain socioeconomic mobility and status in contemporary Western societies" (Kincheloe, Steinberg, and Villaverde, 1999).

Within the socio/historical discourse of Western schooling practices, standardized testing continues to produce and sustain a colonial system of power relations in which "valid" knowledge constitutes a hegemonic cultural language (re)producing the histories, experiences, aspirations, subjectivities, and ambitions of colonizing peoples to the erasure and negation of the colonized. Forced into viewing their pasts, histories and embodied knowledges as a lack or deficit, minoritized students are thus coerced into the violent process of amputation. Moreover, colonial and colonizing knowledges not only reduces indigenous experiences, histories, and ways of knowing to insignificance, it actually appropriates its own violent colonizing history in seductive/subtle ways that suggests to the student that colonial violence is (has been) necessary in order for "progress" (in the Western Enlightenment sense) to take place (Zine, 2003). Thus, student "proficiency," "progress," "excellence," and "achievement" in this context are predicated on mastering uncritically the violent language/knowledge of colonial domination and oppression. Ngugi wa Thiong'o (1981), long ago noted the insidious power of colonial language in its knowledge productive form, citing it as the "most important vehicle through which . . . (European/colonial) power fascinated and held the soul prisoner. The bullet was the means of the physical subjugation, language was the means of the spiritual subjugation."

A major component of the insidious nature of hegemonic knowledge and one of the significant means through which colonial knowledge (re)produces itself, is the conceptualization of knowledge as racially neutral and apolitical. This in turn has strengthened the political ideology of merit or meritocracy that informs contemporary justification and support for standard achievement testing. Despite extensive evidence to the contrary, there is a persistent assumption that all students start from the same level playing field. Socioeconomic contexts, systemic social inequality, and social difference that afford some students with greater privilege and advantage over others are denied. As it has been argued elsewhere(Dei et al., 1997, p. 124), "meritocratic principles cannot be applied in a society where racial disparities exist, as they are in effect corrupted by social and cultural biases which can preclude the just determination of students abilities."

The invocation and conceptualization of knowledge and learning as apolitical and neutral is exemplified in the cognitive learning theory of the Swiss developmental psychologist Jean Piaget (1896–1980). Arguably the most influential figure in the field of educational psychology, Piaget held that development arises from children's own efforts to master their environment through a process he referred to as, "assimilation and accommodation" (Cole and Cole, 1993). *Assimilation* is defined by Piaget as a process in which the infant actively attempts to assimilate his or her existing experiences of his or her environment into what he or she already knows. If they are unable to do this they then must *accommodate* what they already know and assimilate it to the new information they have acquired. According to Piaget, when this is achieved they are said to be in a position of "equilibrium" or balance. However, in his perception of knowledge as neutral Piaget, eschews the notion that learning takes place within racial/cultural, social contexts of power relations. Knowledge, in Piaget's framework is viewed as raceless, classless, genderless and thus "universal." Moreover, the development of agency on the part of minoritized children in the face of dominant colonial discourses such as white privilege is ostensibly denied. This latter aspect becomes significant when we bear in mind that Piaget (1928, 1932) was also one of the first developmental theorists to look at the possibilities of teaching democratic and moral ideas through the vehicle of direct student participation. According to Piaget, if children are to understand the notion that people make rules to enable them to live with one another, they must then be able to participate in their own discussions and constructions of classroom rules. Rules become hegemonic however, when they arise from a knowledge base that not only negates the voices and experiences of marginalized peoples, but relies on that very negation to secure power and oppression. Consequently, the conceptualization of "moral teaching" within this paradigm is profoundly problematic.

Working within a similar paradigm and taking his cue from Piaget's stage theories of cognitive development Lawrence Kohlberg (1984), pursued further research to find identifiable and regular stages of moral development in children and adolescents. Kohlberg hypothesized that just as learners in Piaget's cognitive stages were seen to go through the same sequence of stages, the same could be applied for moral development. His theory saw moral development divided up into three main stages with two substages. The first main stage is that of the "pre-conventional" stage, characterized by a sense of morality that is based on adherence to rules backed up by rewards and punishment. In this stage children will display obedience to set rules simply to avoid punishment from the power of figures of authority. The second stage of "conventional" sees the child behaving in ways that conform to the expectations of his or her social world, that is, family, peer group, school etc., The final stage is that of the "post conventional" where the child judges his actions and those of others on the basis of reasoning other than simply abstract notions and morality. According to Kohlberg, the reason for doing "right" in this stage is the "rational belief and the validity of universal moral principles and a sense of personal commitment to them."

Theories of this nature continue to have a great influence on contemporary mainstream educational psychology particularly as it applies to teacher training, teaching methods, and the institutionalized Eurocentric learning process of students within Euro-North American educational settings. Taking his cue from both Kohlberg and Piaget for example, Thomas Lickona

(1993) has looked at the process of fostering moral development in children. Following on from Piaget's idea that elementary school children become increasingly capable of "decentering," that is to say, keeping more than one idea or concept in mind at a given time, Lickona argues that elementary school children cognitively develop an increasing capacity for taking into account consequences and alternatives when attempting to solve moral problems. In other words, they are able to place themselves in the shoes of another thereby moving from a position that is self-centered and egocentric to one that begins to consider the needs of not only another individual but also that of the group.

According to Lickona, as the cognitive side of moral development takes place the "self consciously rational aspect of character development" can be nurtured in such a way as to foster a union of cognition and affect so that children come to feel deeply about what they think and value (p. 55). Following on from this, elementary teachers are urged to encourage their students to participate in classroom discussions involving issues of possible moral dilemmas that may emerge in their learning experience. As Lickona argues, children need practice "both as moral psychologists who understand wrong doing and as moral philosophers who declare what is right" (p. 56). In addition, students should be guided toward what Lickona refers to as, a "true norm," that is to say, an "operative moral standard, one which children will hold themselves and others accountable." Norms such as this, according to Lickona, "create a support system that helps students live up to their moral standards. Through this process of putting belief into practice, a value becomes a virtue." (p. 56).

The notion of a "true norm" however, is extremely problematic. Moreover, the question must be asked, whose "moral" and ethical standards are we referring to? The question is not posed; rather it is taken for granted that the knowledge emanating from the curriculum, institution, and teacher is sacrosanct and not open to contestation. And yet who are these bodies in the classroom? Most definitely they are not the raceless, genderless, classless, disembodied students that they are purported to be. What if the "moral standards" and "true norms" disseminated by the knowledge base of the curriculum and teacher are in themselves "immoral" in terms of their hegemonic and colonial assumptions and values? Serious problematics arise when students in the classrooms described by Lickona live their daily social lives outside of school impacted by what Molefi Kete Asante (2003) has referred to as "potholes of racial hostility" only to find that within the school itself such hostility is naturalized within the language and culture of a Eurorocentric cognitive knowledge base. The major flaw in Lickona's thinking we would argue is reflective of the general problematics within mainstream educational psychology as a whole, both in historical and contemporary terms. With the exception of Lev Vygotski (1896–1934) who argued in the 1930s that learning takes place within social and cultural contexts, mainstream educational psychology and resulting teaching applications have failed to question the Eurocentric nature of the discipline (Vygotsky, 1978). Moreover (Ausubel, 1963; Bloom et al., 1956; Briggs, 1980; Gagne, 1968, 1985; Means and Knapp, 1993), they have failed to question the colonial dominance and racialized violence of what is taken for granted in dominant discourse as universal, "valid," "rational," or "legitimate" knowledge, and in doing so, they have become implicated in the asymmetrical power relations of colonial domination and student alienation as it relates to the academy.

INDIGENOUS KNOWLEDGE AS TRANSFORMATIVE PEDAGOGY

Our academic and political interest in writing this paper is to enunciate a counter-hegemonic, paradigm shift by placing the discussion in the broader context of rethinking the possibilities and limitations of schooling and education in pluralistic societies. In order to discuss the possibilities of indigenous knowledges we place our discursive politics within the anticolonial framework.

An anticolonial prism theorizes the nature and extent of social domination and particularly the multiple places power works to establish dominant-subordinate relations. This prism also scrutinizes and deconstructs dominant discourse and epistemologies while raising questions about its own. In our engagement of the anticolonial lens to assert indigenous knowledge therefore, our intellectual project is to highlight and analyze contexts and alternatives to colonial/imperial knowledges.

As argued elsewhere (Sefa Dei, 2004), anticolonial thought has its roots in the decolonizing movements of colonial states that fought for independence from European countries at the end of the Second World War. The revolutionary ideas of Frantz Fanon, Mohandas Gandhi, Albert Memmi, Aime Cesaire, Kwame Nkrumah (1963, 1965), and Che Guevara (1997), to name a few, were instrumental in fermenting anticolonial struggles. Most of these scholars were avowed nationalists who sought political liberation for all colonized peoples and communities using the power of knowledge. In particular, the writings of Fanon (1952, 1963, 1988/2000) and Gandhi (1967) on the violence of colonialism and the necessity for open resistance, and Albert Memmi's (1957/1965) discursive on the relations between the colonized and the colonizer, helped instill in the minds of colonized peoples the importance of engaging in acts of resistance to resist the violence of colonialism. In later years, and speaking particularly in the contexts of Africa, other scholars including Aime Cesaire (1972), Leopald Senghor (1996), and Cabral (1969, 1970) introduced questions of language, identity, and national culture into anticolonial debates for political and intellectual liberation.

Following independence a new body of "anticolonial" discourse emerged. This discourse appropriately labeled the postcolonial discursive framework, undeniably shows powerful links to ideas of earlier anticolonialists (Ashcroft et al., 1995; Gandhi, 1998) But the varying ideas of postcolonial theorists such as Suleri (1992), Shohat (1992), Slemon (1995), Bhabha (1990, 1994) and Spivak (1988, 1990, 1999) largely focused on the interconnections between imperial/colonial cultures, colonized cultural practices, and the constructions of hybridity and alterity. The strength of postcolonial theory lies in pointing to the complexities and disjunctures of colonial experiences and the aftermath of the colonial encounter. In fact, Bhabha (1990) has shown that the colonial encounter and discourse cannot be assumed to be unified and unidirectional. Spivak (1988) also emphasizes the possibility of counter knowledges that emerge or are constructed from marginal spaces and the power of such voices for the pursuit of resistance. As Shahjahan (2003) has further argued, in a more general sense, postcolonial theorizing demonstrates the shift of anticolonial thought from a focus on agency and nationalist/liberatory practice toward a discursive analysis and approach, that directs our attention to the intersection between "Western" knowledge production and the "Other," and Western colonial power (Shahjahan, 2003, p. 5).

But the world is about more than simply subjects and their identities. A contemporary emerging trend in understanding knowledge production is to focus on the interplay and exchange among and between cultures and communities, and, specifically, to look at how this process of interaction offers possibilities of understanding our world today. Our histories and cultures are interconnected and the politicized evocation of culture and history is useful if it allows for an interrogation of the asymmetrical power relations that characterize human interactions, as well as the ensuing contentions, contestations, and contradictions of everyday practices. Questions of politics, culture, identity, and materiality are intertwined. In this case schools become sites to understand how such contestations unfold daily in the lives of learners. It is within schools that one witnesses the complex, multiple, and intersecting social relations of learning and teaching in contemporary society and the possibilities of drawing on multiple knowledge forms.

There is a discursive, ethical, and political connection in the evocation of indigenous knowledge to affirm local history and cultural identities of indigenous peoples. Indeed, while culture may be negotiated, questions and issues of identity are not negotiable for indigenous peoples. It has been argued that local indigeneity emerges from long-term occupancy of a place (Brokensha, Warren, and Werner, 1980; Fals Borda, 1980; Fals Borda and Rahman, 1991; Sefa Dei, 2000; Warren et al., 1995). This standpoint bears testimony to the power of culture, history, and tradition of indigenous peoples. For, while there may not be the unity of experience, nor uniform response to colonization among subjugated groups, there has been a consistent approach to the affirmation of local knowings through identity and cultural politics. In fact, studies of indigenous knowledges affirm cultural histories and identities through a politics of representation. As a consequence, such discursive approaches call for critical methods of inquiry in order to evaluate the potential of indigenous knowledge forms to bring about social and educational change.

In arguing for Western curriculums to open up space to indigenous knowledges we are not simply seeking the replacement of one center over another, nor are we seeking to (re)create and sustain false dichotomies of conventional/colonial/external knowledge as bad and non-Western/marginalized/indigenous knowledges as good. Rather, what we are calling for are diverse ways of knowing that are dynamic, continuous, and represent a multiplicity of centers. Moreover, we view indigenous knowledges not as romantic, static/fixed entities but rather as collaborative, liberating, and fluid. As argued elsewhere (Sefa Dei et al., 2002), our conceptualization of indigenous knowledge refers to a body of knowledge derived from the long-term occupancy by a people (not necessarily indigenous) of a specific locale or place. From this situatedness in depth understandings/knowledges encompassing particular norms, traditions, and values are accrued. Mental constructs born from lived/learnt experiences serve as guides to regulate and organize ways in which people and communities live and make sense of their world. They become the means through which decisions are formed in the face of challenges that are familiar and unfamiliar (p. 6). We view indigenous knowledges as differing from conventional knowledges in the sense that colonial/imperial hegemonic impositions are absent.

In addition as noted elsewhere (Sefa Dei, 2000, forthcoming) speaking about indigenous knowledge does not, and should not necessarily commit one to a dichotomy between "indigenous" and "Western knowledge" (Agrawal, 1995a, pp. 413–439, 1995b). Indigenous knowledge does not reveal a conceptual divide with "Western knowledge," that is to say, indigenous is not strictly in opposition to "Western." "Indigenous" is to be thought of in relation to Western knowledge, and as a concept that simply alludes to the power relations within which local peoples struggle to define and assert their own representations of history, identity, culture, and place in the face of Western hegemonic ideologies. Implicit in the terminology of "indigenous(ness)" is a recognition of some philosophical, conceptual, and methodological differences between Western and non-Western knowledge systems. These differences are not absolutes but a matter of degree. The difference is seen more in terms of (cultural) logics and epistemologies, that is, differences in the making of sense (from an indigenous standpoint) as always dependent on context, history, politics, and place. There is however, a politics of affirmation of important differences that distinguish multiple knowledge forms by their unique philosophies and identities that must not be lost. The interactions of different cultures and cultural knowledges has always been part of human reality and existence and although what may emerge from an articulation of two or more disparate elements is often a new distinct form, it does not necessarily mean that the former disparate elements will not lose their character, logics, and identities. In a global context when dominant knowledge forms usually appropriate other knowings and claim universality in their interpretations of society, there is a politics of reclaiming the indigenous and local identities. This reclamation has a purpose in unmasking the process through which Western science knowledges, for example, become hegemonic ways of knowing by masquerading as universal knowledge.

We would argue therefore, that "indigenousness" is central to power relations, global knowledge, and ways of acting, feeling, and knowing. Indigenous knowledge acknowledges the multiple, collective, collaborative origins and dimensions of knowledge, with the belief that the interpretation or analysis of social reality is subject to different and oftentimes oppositional perspectives. We see indigenousness therefore as emerging from an indigenous knowledge system that is based on cognitive interpretations and understandings of the social, political, and physical/spiritual worlds. Indigenous knowledges include beliefs, perceptions, concepts, and experiences of local environments, both natural and social. To speak of "indigenousness" in African contexts for example, is to enunciate questions related to local culture and social identities (Sefa Dei et al., 2002, p. 72). It is to underscore the importance of decolonizing the "international development" project in Africa. Different forms of knowledge represent different points on a continuum. As such they are dynamic, building upon each other in accumulative forms that allow different ways for people to perceive and act upon their world. In the contexts of Western (mis)education systems, indigenous knowledges intersect with anticolonial agency to enable students to arrive at different ways of seeing and articulating both community and individual experiences of marginality and resistance within their space of learning.

The calling to mind of culture and indigenous knowledge as a form of classroom pedagogy is useful to the extent that it works with the power relations of knowledge as well as the social dynamics of change and the continuity of history. Culture is about ideas and practices. All ideas and social practices as forms of knowledge are constitutive of power relations. The ideational component of culture suggests the social relations of knowledge may include local myths, proverbs, songs, fables, and other forms of folkloric production as legitimate ways of knowing that have profound pedagogic, communicative, and instructional effects for learners. Leilani Holmes (2002) for example, in evoking Hawaiian indigenous philosophies of knowledge reveals a "grounded epistemology" in which the concept of *blood memory* plays a crucial and significant role. Within this indigenous framework Holmes is not referring to "blood quantum," the code of eugenics that has been used by colonial systems of power to define (by U.S. standards) who is Hawaiian and who is not for the primary purpose of dispossessing indigenous peoples from their lands and entitlements. Rather, "blood memory" is conceptualized and evoked in ways that speak back and challenge the destructiveness of these very same colonial discourses through cultural and spiritual connections made between Hawaiians to each other. As one of the parent generations (*makua*) reveals in an interview with Holmes, "it does not matter where Hawaiians live. They can live all over the world . . . when you say that you are Hawaiian, we never say 'how much Hawaiian do you have?' which is a total . . . alien concept, but the fact that you are Hawaiian and you are 'ohana' (family) and that we eat out of the same . . . bowl . . . And that we come from the same roots. And that's the connectedness that . . . brings all Hawaiians together, no matter how much Hawaiian they have by blood quantum" (Holmes, 2002, pp. 41–42).

Indigenous knowledge of this nature represents an immensely powerful and liberating source for spirituality and decolonizing agency. Where the sense of identity and of belonging is an experience of dislocation and alienation in marginalized bodies and communities, and where Western knowledge production reproduces and sustains such marginality and spiritual disconnect, indigenous knowledges of this nature speak to an anticolonial pedagogy that challenges the colonial hegemony of Western schooling practices and in doing so reveals possibilities for radical transformation (Sefa Dei, forthcoming). "Blood memory" points to a human connectedness that transcends Western notions of identity predicated on homogeneity and static/fixed racialized conceptions of culture and the nation-state. Caution however, should be exercised, when we speak of incorporating indigenous knowledges into the curriculum. Indigenous knowledges can never be evoked if they are simply to become part of an exotic tacked-on approach to an otherwise dominant colonial center. An understanding and respect of time, place, and political context is crucial. To decontextualize indigenous knowledges from issues of land, spirituality, cultural histories, and resistance to colonial hegemony serves only to reinscribe the colonial project.

The implications for the field of educational psychology that emerge from our discussion rest in part, we would argue, on two of the key tenets of indigenous knowledges and multiple knowings that consistently fail to be addressed to any significant extent in mainstream educational theorizing and practice. These are agency and spirituality. Both of these crucial elements represent a site of transformation which educational psychology can (and must) clearly benefit if it is to remain relevant to the lives of minoritized peoples and communities in their engagements with the academy.

Within the anticolonial discursive framework we conceptualize agency as a site of liberation and the practice/theorization of resistance by colonized and marginalized peoples to systemic oppression/repression. We view it as a site of empowerment and active resistance formed by the oppressed within specific social/spatial asymmetrical relations of political power. To borrow from Grossberg (1993) we define agency as the "articulation of subject positions into specific places (sites of investment) and spaces (fields of activity) on socially constructed territorialities. Agency is the empowerment enabled at particular sites and along particular vectors . . . it points to the existence of particular formations of practices as places on social maps, where such places are . . . potentially involved in the making of history. Agency as a site is . . . realized (when) specific investments are enabled and articulated." To speak of anticolonial agency then is to know our political self. It is to resist, rupture, and renounce dominance and oppression in counter hegemonic ways. It is to refuse the violation and despiritualization of our collective minds, bodies, and souls. It is to know and see colonialism for what it is, not for what it *claims* (Eurocentrically/universally) to be. Anticolonial agency arising from an anticolonial discourse (Sefa Dei et al., 2002, p. 7) places stress on power held and sustained through practice in local/social spaces to survive colonial and colonizing encounters. It argues that power and discourse are not the exclusive terrain of the colonizer. The power of resistance and discursive agency reside in and among colonized and marginalized groups. As argued elsewhere (Sefa Dei et al., 2002, p. 7), subordinated/colonized peoples had a (theoretical and practical) understanding of the colonizer that "functioned as a platform for engaging in political/social practice and relations." The notion of "colonial" is therefore grounded in power relations and inequities that are imposed and engendered by tradition, culture, history, and contact. Anticolonial agency/theorizing however, "rises out of alternative, oppositional paradigms, which are in turn based on indigenous concepts, analytical systems and cultural frames of reference" that are vital in reclaiming our sense of self and spirituality.

Our enunciation of anticolonial agency and indigenous knowledge as decolonizing educational practice constitutes, we would argue, a libratory form of spiritual resistance. When we speak of anticolonial agency and counter hegemonic epistemologies and practices as forms of spirituality however, we are speaking of an action-orientated, revolutionary spirituality and not simply one that is aesthetic. We are speaking of an inner spirituality that allows for the making of emotional and intellectual paradigmatic shifts. While recognizing that there are multiple articulations and readings of spirituality our understanding of spirituality here is not necessarily an ascription to a high religious/moral order, but rather an understanding of the self/personhood and culture as a starting point in our engagements with education and learning. As Dei has argued elsewhere (Sefa Dei, 2004), education is anchored in a broader definition that encompasses emotional/spiritual dimensions and cultural knowledge. An identification with the learning process that is personalized and subjective makes it possible for learners to become invested spiritually and emotionally in their education.

Spirituality and spiritual knowing can be pursued in schools as a valid body of knowledge to enhance learning outcomes. Spirituality encourages and engages in the sharing of collective and personal experiences of understanding and dealing with the self. A great deal of what is "universal" in spirituality is related to aspects of knowing and asserting who we are (in relation to dominant knowledges that tell us something else) what our cultures are, where we come from and the connections of the self to the other. Research by Dei (2004) has shown that spiritual knowledge and spirituality have important implications for reconceptualizing African education, and the education of the learner. Critical educators within Africa today are teaching youth to be spiritually informed and to think of themselves as both Africans and global citizens. Learning proceeds through the development of the African self and identity. Critical teaching allows the learner to stake out a position as African, a position that is outside and oppositional to the identity that has been, and continues to be, constructed in Euro-American ideology (Sefa Dei, 2004).

Spirituality in this respect therefore is an implicit antithesis to the Western concept that the learning of curriculum is ever solely "universal," where universal means neutral and common to all. We argue that spirituality as a form of resistance allows for identification with ourselves and the universal, which in turn provides an implicit means through which we can assert ourselves collectively and individually. In this form spirituality becomes a powerful tool for resisting mis-education, domination, and discriminatory forces. When spirituality is occluded in classrooms, school curriculums, and systems of education as a whole, the resulting assault can have destructive consequences, particularly for the development of self and identity in minoritized individual/community contexts If nurtured and respected, spirituality can be utilized to involve and energize both schools and local communities. The ways in which people have understood, understand, and seek to further understand their world necessarily includes, place, time, and many other critical aspects that include, among others, the world of the material, of the social, of ideas, and of the spiritual. This is the case regardless of how individual groups may perceive or define "spiritual" (Sefa Dei, 2004). The spiritual development of the learner is therefore a crucial dimension of learning and of education as a whole.

CONCLUSION

The question then is why do we call for the centering of indigenous knowledges and what do we see as its fundamental role in the academy? The strength of indigenous knowledges lies in their application to the lived realities of people. The relevance of indigenous knowledges is that they speak to the practical and mundane issues of social existence. In the face of entrenched hegemonic relations and global economic and ecological threat, knowledge is relevant only if it strengthens a people's capacity to live well. By being concerned first and foremost with questions of survival, indigenous knowledges offer insights into everyday lives and the challenges and desires that help shape human action and history. As others have noted indigenous knowledges are knowledges rested in "the livelihoods of people rather than with abstract ideas and philosophies" (Agrawal, 1995a, p. 422) But unlike Western science knowledge, indigenous knowledges cannot be simply understood in terms of its utilitarian purposes. Its existence signals the power of the intellectual agency of local peoples. It is symbolic (intellectually, politically, and emotionally) in the projection of others that local peoples can and do know about themselves and their societies. It is about culture, identity, and political survival. When articulated and positioned in the academy it gestures to the efficacy of local peoples' understanding of their own world, and from their own perspectives, as a starting point from which to interrogate, challenge, and subvert the dominance of particular forms of knowing.

Educators and spaces of educational theorizing such as mainstream educational psychology, must therefore take "critical discourse" seriously in terms of broadening our knowledge of what it means to "transform" (through activism and creativity) knowledge from the mundane to a more spiritual engagement/connection with the discursive practices so that we can move away from a preoccupation with "limitation" to "possibilities" of pedagogy. The possibilities of pedagogy include educators being bold to acknowledge and respond to difference and diversity within the schooling population. This means ensuring curriculum, pedagogy and texts reflect the diverse knowledges, experiences, and accounts of history, ideas, and lived experiences and struggles. Such possibilities require that the educator enacts and applies his or her agency in the classrooms. There must be accountability in terms of how educators can evoke power to address issues of minority schooling. In fact, in the contexts of schooling in North America there are multiple sites of power and accountability. Educators are urged to frame educational "praxis" in terms of agency and deliberation, as well as a constant confrontation of the varied forms of domination and subjugation in the schooling lives of youth. The implications of radical scholarship in Euro-American contexts today therefore are to theorize inclusive schooling work beyond the boundaries of adherence to the sacredness of educational activity. We must all develop an anticolonial awareness of how colonial relations are sustained and reproduced in schooling practices. To have a decolonized space requires a decolonized mind. Colonialism is situated in the psyche and we cannot create decolonized schools without decolonizing the minds that run them. We believe in political action for change. Consequently, there is power in working with resistant knowledge. Resistance starts by using received knowledges to ask critical questions about the nature of the social order. Resistance also means seeing "small acts" as cumulative and significant for social change (Abu-Lughod, 1990, pp. 41–55). It will for example require shifting away from Eurocentric/Western theorizing and discursive practices toward a radical lens that interrogates hegemonic discourses and centers the exigencies of the marginalized. It will mean embracing the epistemologies of anticolonial agency.

REFERENCE

Abu-Lughod, L. (1990). The Romance of Resistance: Tracing Transformations of Power Through Bedouin Women. *American Ethnologists*, 17(1), 41–55.

Agrawal, A. (1995a). Dismantling the Divide between Indigenous and Scientific Knowledge. *Development and Change*, 26, 413–439.

———. (1995b). Indigenous and Scientific Knowledge: Some Critical Comments. *Indigenous Knowledge and Development Monitor*, 3(3), 3–5.

Asante, M. K. (2003). *The Survival of the American Nation: Erasing Racism*. New York: Prometheus Books.

Ashcroft, B., Griffiths, G., and Tiffin, H., (Eds.). (1995). *The Post-colonial Reader*. New York: Routledge.

Ausubel, D. P. (1963). *The Psychology of Meaningful Verbal Learning*. New York: Grune & Stratton.

Bhabha, H. K. (Ed.). (1990). *Nation and Narration*. London: Routledge.

———. (1994). *The Location of Culture*. London Routledge.

Bloom, B. S., Engelhart, M. D., Furst, E. J., Hill, W. H., and Krathwohl, D. R. (1956). *Taxonomy of Educational Objectives, Handbook 1: Cognitive Domain*. New York: McKay.

Briggs, L. J. (1980, February). Thirty Years of Instructional Design: One Man's Experience. *Educational Technology*, 20, 45–50.

Brokensha, D., Warren, D. M., and Werner, O. (Eds.). (1980). *Indigenous Knowledge Systems and Development*. Boston: University Press of America.

Brown, M. K., Carnoy, M., Currie, E., Duster, T., Oppenheimer, D. B., Shultz, M. M., and Wellman, D. (2003). *White-Washing Race: The Myth of a Color-Blind Society*. Berkeley, CA: University of California Press.

Cabral, A. (1969). *Revolution In Guinea*. New York: Monthly Review Press.

———. (1970). National Liberation and Culture. The 1970 Eduardo Mondlane Lecture, Program of Eastern African Studies of the Maxwell School of Citizenship and Public Affairs, Syracuse University, February 20.

Cannella, G. (1999). Postformal Thought as Critique, Reconceptualization and Possibility for Teacher Education Reform. In J. L. Kincheloe, S. R. Steinberg, and L. E. Villaverde (Eds.), *Rethinking Intelligence: Confronting Psychological Assumptions about Teaching and Learning*. New York: Routledge.

Cesaire, A. (1972). *Discourse on Colonialism.* New York: Monthly Review Press.

Cole, M., and Cole, S. R. (1993). *The Development of Children* (Scientific America Books). New York: W. H. Freeman and Co.

Corrigan, P. (1990). *Social Forms/Human Capacities* (p. 156). London: Routledge.

Driscoll, M. P. (1994). *Psychology of Learning for Instruction.* Allyn and Bacon.

Fals Borda, O. (1980). *Science and the Common People.* Yugloslavia.

Fals Borda, O., and Rahman, A. M. (Eds.). (1991). *Action and Knowledge: Breaking the Monopoly with Participatory Action Research.* New York: Apex.

Fanon, F. (1952, translated 1967). *Black Skin, White Masks.* New York: Grove Press.

———. (1963). *The Wretched of the Earth.* New York: Grove Press

———. (1988/2000). Racism and Culture. In C. Eze (Ed.), *African Philosophy* (pp. 305–311). London: Blackwell Publishers.

Gagné, R. M. (1968). Learning Hierarchies. *Educational Psychologist,* 6, 1–9.

———. (1985). *The Conditions of Learning* (4th ed.). New York: Holt, Rinehart & Winston.

Gandhi, M. (1967). *Political and National Life and Affairs.* Ahmedabad: Navijivan Press.

Gandhi, L. (1998). *Postcolonial Theory: A Critical Introduction.* New York and Chichester, West Sussex: Columbia University Press.

Grossberg, L. (1993). Cultural Studies and/in New Worlds. In Cameron McCarthy and Warren Crichlow (Eds.), *Race Identity and Representation in Education* (pp. 100–101). Routledge.

Guevara, C. (1997). The Essence of Guerrilla Struggle. In David Deutchmann (Ed.), *Che Guevara Reader* (pp. 66–72). New York: Ocean Press.

Holmes, L. (2002). Heart Knowledge, Blood Memory, and the Voice of the Land: Implications of Research among Hawaiian Elders. In George J. Sefa Dei, Budd L. Hall, and Dorothy Goldin Rosenberg, (Ed.), *Indigenous Knowledges in Global Contexts: Multiple Readings of Our World.* Toronto, ON: University of Toronto Press.

Joncich, G. M. (1962). *Psychology and the Science of Education: Selected Writings of Edward L. Thorndike* (p. 14). New York: Teachers College-Columbia University.

Kincheloe, J. L., Steinberg, S. R., and Villaverde, L. E. (1999). *Rethinking Intelligence* (p. 2). London: Routledge.

Kohlberg, L. (1984). *The Psychology of Moral Development: The Nature and Validity of Moral Stages* (Vol. 2, p. 87). New York: Harper & Row.

Lickona, T. (1993). Four Strategies for Fostering Character Development in Children. In A. E. Woolfolk (Ed.), *Readings & Cases in Educational Psychology.* Allyn and Bacon.

McClendon, R. C., and Weaver J. A. (1999). Informally Speaking: A Continuing Dialogue on Postformal Thinking. In J. L. Kincheloe, S. R. Steinberg and L. E. Villaverde (Eds.). *Rethinking Intelligence: Confronting Psychological Assumptions about Teaching and Learning.* New York: Routledge.

Means, B. and Knapp, M. S. (1993). Cognitive Approaches to Teaching Advanced Skills to Educationally Disadvantaged Students. In A. E. Woolfolk, *Readings & Cases in Educational Psychology* (p. 214). Allyn and Bacon.

Memmi, A. (1957/1965). *The Colonizer and the Colonized.* Boston: Beacon Press.

Nkrumah, K. (1963). *Africa Must Unite* (pp. 9–49). London: Heinemann.

———. (1965). *Neo-colonialism: the Last Stage of Imperialism.* Edinburgh, England: Thomas Nelson and Sons.

Piaget, J. (1928). *Judgment and Reasoning in the Child.* London: Routledge & Kegan Paul.

———. (1932). *The Moral Judgment of the Child.* New York: Free Press 1965.

Sefa Dei, G. J., Mazzuca, J., McIssac, E., and Zine, J. (1997). *Reconstructing Dropout: A Critical Ethnography of The Dynamics of Black Students' Disengagement From School.* Toronto, ON: University of Toronto Press.

Sefa Dei, G. J. (2000). Recasting Anti-Racism and the Axis of Difference: Beyond the Question of Theory. *Race, Gender, Class,* 7(2), 39–56.

———. (2000). Rethinking the Role of Indigenous Knowledges in the Academy. *International Journal of Inclusive Education,* 4(2), 111–132.

Sefa Dei, G. J. and Asgharzadeh, A. (2001). The Power of Social Theory: the Anti-colonial Discursive Framework. *Journal of Educational Thought*, 35(3), 4.

Sefa Dei, G. J., Hall, Budd L., and Rosenberg, D. G. (Ed.) (2002). *Indigenous Knowledges in Global Contexts: Multiple Readings of Our World*. Toronto, ON: University of Toronto Press.

Sefa Dei, G. J. (2004). The Challenge of Inclusive Schooling in Africa: A Ghanaian Case Study. *Comparative Education,* Lawrenceville, NJ: Africa World Press.

Sefa Dei, G. J., and Doyle-Wood, S. ("in Press") . Is We Who Haffi Ride Di Staam: Critical Knowledge/Multiple Knowings: Possibilities, Challenges and Resistance in Curriculum/Cultural Contexts. In Yatta Kanu (Ed.), *Curriculum as Cultural Practice: Postcolonial Imaginations*.

Sefa Dei, G. J. (2004). *Schooling and Education in Africa: The Case of Ghana*. Trenton, NJ: Africa World Press.

Senghor, L. S. (1996). African Socialism. In Molefe Kete Asante and Abu S. Abarry (Eds.), *African Intellectual Heritage* (pp. 342–354). Philadelphia, PA: Temple University Press.

Shahjahan, R. (2003, May 28–30). Mapping the Field of Anti-colonial Discourse to Understand Issues of Indigenous Knowledges. Paper presented at the congress meeting of the Canadian Sociology and Anthropology Association. Dalhousie University, Halifax.

Shohat, E. (1992). Notes on the 'Post-Colonial'. *Social Text* 31/32, 99–113.

Slemon, S. (1995). The Scramble for Post-Colonialism. In B. Ashcroft, G. Griffiths, and H. Tiffin (Eds.), *The Post-colonial Reader*. New York: Routledge.

Smith, L. (1999). *Decolonizing Methodologies*. London: Zed Publishers.

Spivak, G. C. (1988). Can the Subaltern Speak? In C. Nelson, and L. Grossberg (Eds.), *Marxism and the Interpretation of Culture*. Basingstoke, Hampshire: Macmillan Education.

———. (1990). *The Post-Colonial Critic: Interviews, Strategies, Dialogues*, Sarah Harasym (Ed.). New York and London: Routledge.

———. (1999). *A Critique of Postcolonial Reason: Toward a History of the Vanishing Present*. Cambridge, MA and London: Harvard University Press.

Suleri, S. (1992). *The Rhetoric of English India*. Chicago: The University of Chicago Press.

Thiong'O, N. (2006). The language of African literature. In Ashcroft, B., Griffiths, G., and Tiffin, H. (Eds.), *The Post-colonial Studies Reader* (pp. 285–290). New York: Routledge.

Vygotsky, L. S. (1978). *Mind in Society*. Cambridge, MA: Harvard University Press.

Warren, D. M., Slikkerveer, L. J., and Brokensha, D. (Eds.). (1995). *The Cultural Dimension of Development: Indigenous Knowledge Systems*. Exeter, UK: Intermediate Technology Publications.

Watson, J. B., and Rayner, R. (1920). Conditioned Emotional Reactions. *Journal of Experimental Psychology*, 3, 1–14

Zine, H. (2003). *A People's History of the United States, 1492-Present* (p. 8). New York: Harper Collins.

CHAPTER 79

Making the "Familiar" Strange: Exploring Social Meaning in Context

DELIA D. DOUGLAS

The EveryDay

Where are You from?...
I'm Not a racist, but...
     I can't believe that there are Still People who Think like that....
...Perhaps You misunderstood?
     Well, it is kind of hard for People not to be racist....
...We are all racist aren't we?

CANADA ON MY MIND

Too often the increased visibility or success of a handful of racially diverse people in society is regarded as evidence of "social change" since it is assumed that a numerical shift signals the absence of racial hostility. We are far more familiar (and indeed comfortable) with allegations of racism that involve white supremacist and extremist groups. There has been far less attention given to the ways in which our daily lives are crucial sites through which practices and beliefs regarding white racial superiority/power/domination are produced. Indeed, part of the persistence and pervasiveness of racism lies in its very definition. That elements of the "everyday" are not seen as linked to the process and practice of racism is part of the prevailing racial logic which seeks to undermine all but the most overt, and hence well known, symbols and manifestations of racial animosity.

In the past two decades, critical race scholars from a variety of disciplines have furthered our understanding of the dynamic nature of racial meanings and their interconnectedness to other formations such as gender, sexuality, and geographic location. Much of this work argues that race is a social concept that is given meaning according to the historical, political, and social context in which it is located. Furthermore, these writings challenged the notion that race is only relevant to those typically deemed racial subjects, namely non-whites by identifying "whiteness" as a racial identity that shapes the lives of people within various systems of privilege and power. Additionally, some of this work has focused on the ways in which racial meanings, racial identities and expressions of racism are conveyed through "everyday" practices such as gesture, tone, thought, feeling, and gaze (Essed, 2002).

This essay draws upon this work by examining a number of social situations to explore the subtle, dynamic, and sophisticated ways in which social power is conceived and reproduced to maintain prevailing structures and relations of race and gender, power and inequality. In this sense the discussion seeks to disrupt dominant assumptions that have organized educational psychology by challenging the ways in which the discipline has conceived of race, processes of racism, and the social formation of the learner. I address a variety of social settings in order to illustrate the continuing significance of race and the persistence of racism at this historical juncture. The vignettes also reveal how manifestations of racism in one setting are linked to other settings; there is a pattern to the ways in which black Canadians are marginalized and socially excluded in their daily lives. The diverse situations also exemplify how individuals are part of larger contexts by suggesting how social events, and broader discourses of race and gender shape how we think and feel. In this regard they highlight the importance of taking into account the multidimensional nature of racial identity and expressions of racism. In this sense the paper challenges traditional curricula in educational psychology that has neglected or trivialized the complex ways in which the social formation of the learner is profoundly influenced by broader social processes. Our lives outside of the classroom inform our ways of thinking and being in the classroom. In addition, I am using these anecdotes as empirical examples that challenge a discourse of whiteness that has traditionally organized the field of educational psychology. The dominant theoretical frameworks in the discipline have tended to address race as though it were only relevant to non-whites. Building upon the insights of critical race scholars this discussion explores the ways in which race shapes all of our lives; whiteness is also a racial category and an ideology. Finally, the essay seeks to make visible the ways in which the key concepts and cultural values associated with educational psychology, embedded in terms like objectivity, neutrality, and universality are in fact part of the reproduction of a discourse of whiteness. That is the privileging of whiteness is achieved when those who are in positions of authority ignore the complex ways in which the lives of students and teachers are structured by sociocultural processes and relations of power that inform the way they interact in the classroom.

In sum, this discussion operates from and speaks to different levels of experience, interpretation, and analysis. On the one hand it offers illustrations of the importance of the *everyday*, to make explicit the often intangible but ever-present sociocultural meanings that are lived and felt in various social settings. In this regard taking these experiences of daily life into account offers an alternative conceptual and analytical model that challenges dominant frameworks in the discipline by placing sociocultural processes and systems at the center of inquiries involving educational practices and the social formation of the learner. The series of vignettes is meant to illustrate how our lives outside the classroom inform our interpretations and understanding of race and gender difference in the classroom environment. In pointing to the political and social struggles associated with blackness and whiteness it is my hope that we can advance our understanding of the relevance of cultural and social processes to the ways in which we think, learn, and teach about race and racism (as they interact with gender) in educational psychology.

WHO IS/CAN BE CANADIAN?

In this next section I offer a brief sketch of the historical and cultural background of Canada to introduce the context in which black Canadians conduct their daily lives. My interest in issues of identity, the everyday, and social meaning in context are borne out of my particular history as a black Canadian woman, born in Britain, raised in central Canada, and educated in both Canada and the United States. Canada is one of the locations to, and from which I write and speak. In Canada, blacks live in and through the shadow of the productivity and visibility of black American and black British scholars, writers, and cultural practitioners. The ensuing outline is meant to draw attention to the fact that students and teachers alike encounter and negotiate beliefs and representations about race (in addition to nation and gender) from a variety of sources (e.g., visual and print media, family, friends, school), which influence their sense of self and other. These varied perspectives regarding difference and identity are significant because they affect educational practices; they influence students' construction of their own identities and they structure their interaction in the classroom.

The meaning(s) of racial and ethnic identities in Canada as well as questions about belonging, are integrally tied to the cultural symbols, in addition to the economic and political formations that exist within the country. Thus, in order to understand Canadian configurations of black racial identity, it is necessary to identify some of this nation's distinct characteristics. Canada, the largest country in the Western Hemisphere, consists of ten provinces and three territories (i.e., the Yukon, Northwest, and Nunavut). The diverse terrain of the land (e.g., prairies, wilderness, arctic, Maritimes) constitutes unique geographic, economic, cultural, and political regions. Correspondingly, the structure and organization of this country is shaped by competing and contradictory ideologies about unity and our national identity. Here I am referring to the legacies of the history of European settlement which produced Canada, such as the indentured labor of Chinese workers who built the railroad and the enslavement and displacement of aboriginal peoples from their land. Moreover, in 1988 the federal government instituted the Multiculturalism Act as a way of acknowledging and embracing the diverse population of the nation. Accordingly, this policy says that all citizens have the right to equal participation in the building of the Canadian nation. In addition, the ongoing struggles between the competing voices of the two "founding" colonial powers, Britain and France, are key sources of national/regional/provincial/local tension. The fact that Canada is officially a multicultural and bilingual country also influences the manner in which racism is interpreted and lived.

The racial and ethnic composition of Canada also varies by region: the majority of the population lives in the eastern provinces of Quebec and Ontario. Although the genealogy of black settlement in Canada is diverse, extending from the west to the east coast, and dates back several centuries, the details of this history are largely absent from national discourses and curricula. The historical privileging of white ethnicities over other racial groups has contributed to the invisibility and silencing of the Canadian component of the African diaspora in both curricula and in the public imaginary. For example, few are aware of the fact that slavery and segregation were also practiced within the borders of Canada. The legacy that is oft repeated is that blacks who reside in Canada are the descendants of former slaves who traveled north to escape slavery. Part of the reason this particular connection between American and Canadian blacks is embraced is due to our geographical proximity to the United States and our susceptibility to American racial discourses. However, this narrative is troubling because it implies that Canadian blacks are ultimately a derivative of American blacks and the United States readily becomes the "home" of all things "black." Consequently, this narrative also strengthens the extant belief that racism in Canada is not as odious as that which is practiced in the United States. Depending upon the character of the experience that is being described one might hear "Well you would expect that in the United States, not here." In Canada, we engage in a kinder and gentler version of racism than that which is practiced south of border.

Furthermore, the ubiquity of black American culture suppresses our knowledge of the experiences of black Canadians who have emerged from different circumstances. For example, as a result of the end of World War II, and a change in Canadian immigration laws, the black population grew as many West Indians migrated to Canada. Nevertheless, despite their length of stay, black West Indians are still seen as "recent arrivals." One of the consequences of the lack of information regarding the diverse history of black settlement and participation in the building of Canada is the belief that black Canadians are from "elsewhere" (i.e., America or the West Indies). For example, the descendants of those who came in the 1950s are continually asked, "where are you from?" In sum, the lives and images of black Canadians are formed and understood in relation to broader historical, cultural conditions, and political frameworks. Specifically, issues of belonging and racial authenticity (i.e., "black is . . . black ain't") shapes attitudes regarding black entitlement, participation, and belonging to the Canadian nation. For example, if you are not seen as a member of society then your concerns and interests are deemed irrelevant.

The next section considers a number of empirical examples to make explicit the link between belief systems, lived experience, and social structures in order to reveal how the nature of the daily lives of black Canadians creates ways of thinking and being, which has consequences for how we think about and teach about race in educational psychology.

VIGNETTES

I: Forget me . . . Not!

Ben Johnson and the Social Production of "Blackness"

Given that one of the themes of this paper involves examining how meanings of race and gender are shaped by the sociocultural context in which they are located, the figure of Ben Johnson is instructive. Fifteen years on and the legacy of "black Ben" continues. . . . Seoul Korea, 1988: it was a September to remember . . . With his arm raised signaling number one as he crossed the finish line, Canadian Ben Johnson finished well ahead of his American rival Carl Lewis in the men's 100-meter Olympic final. Ben Johnson's moment of triumph was portrayed as significant because it "proved" that Canada could compete on the world stage with the athletic strongholds (most notably our neighbor, the United States). It was later revealed, however, that Ben Johnson had taken a banned substance and he became the first athlete to be stripped of a gold medal due to steroid use.

No longer a national hero, black Ben became a "Jamaican born" Canadian citizen who had brought shame upon the nation. The truth is, he was always "black Ben." Raised in a single parent home, the white media had previously played upon the familiar imagery of a young black male of humble beginnings who came to Canada hoping for a better life. Once he fell from grace he was re-racialized by the very racial ideology which tried to use him as the emblem of a multicultural Canada, and turned on him by identifying him as a *recent* Jamaican immigrant. When he was "good" he was Canadian, but when he was "bad" he was from "from foreign."

The impact of this "scandal" is noteworthy because it extends beyond the realm of sport to incorporate beliefs about West Indian immigrants, citizenship, and belonging. Particular racial and national ideologies were mobilized to undermine Ben Johnson's ties to Canada. Unable to drive him out of his "home," he has been symbolically expelled from membership in the Canadian nation. The continual evocation of the stereotypical figure of "black Ben" as a Jamaican man who disgraced "the nation," reinforces public discourses about "black" (i.e., Jamaican) men as the source of illegal immigration and crime in Canada. Thus, black Ben remains part of gender, racial, and national narratives about citizenship and belonging to the Canadian nation. Other positive tests come and go, but Ben's ignominy is forever. He endures his punishment in perpetuity. A pariah, his public marking serves a purpose; it reminds us that for many, belonging to the Canadian nation is conditional. Consider the pervasive drug use in predominantly white countries such as the former East Germany, and the former Soviet Union, competitors in the Tour de France, (along with black Americans Carl Lewis, CJ Hunter), and the hundreds of others worldwide who have yielded positive drugs tests since September 1988. Steroids, only in Canada, eh? Pity.

... Lest we forget ... Ben ... Black Ben. May he never rest in peace ...

II: In/Visibility Blues

... But you don't LOOK Canadian ... Where are you from?

Recollections ...

Are you from Kenya? My wife and I traveled there some time ago and you remind me of the "people" we met there ...

> When out alone or with another black girlfriend, this question inevitably appears: WHERE are you from? I/we say that I/we are Canadian. If my girlfriend happens to say that she was born and raised here in Vancouver, her response is met with silence and a look of confusion both of which are followed by the customary second question: WHERE are your parents from? If I/we say that one of our parents is from the West Indies then this reply is met with a look of satisfaction: ah, that explains "it". ....

> Once I asked the inquirer "oh you mean where did I get my 'color' from"? This of course produced silence and awkwardness. My suspicion was confirmed however—what the person really wanted to know is where does this/our "blackness" come from? (Apparently, from "elsewhere").

The idea that one cannot be black and Canadian has been confirmed through conversations with friends and family, as well as through the many experiments I have performed over the years when I have been asked where am I from? The fact that the conversation does not end when I/we say Canadian reveals the underlying assumption: surely we are from a country with a *recognized* black population. This question illustrates how a racial consciousness about blackness and belonging is produced; it suggests that black Canadians are not, or cannot be from *here*. This seemingly innocuous question conceals an ideology of white privilege, which reproduces a racial boundary. In this context, who is/can be Canadian? Who are the citizens of this multicultural nation? What are the criteria for membership? Country of birth? Length of stay? The question where are you from? is part of a pattern and practice of exclusion from the Canadian imagery. If we are considered "outsiders," then it is not surprising that we are not seen as entitled to the same rights and privileges as those who are considered "insiders." We find ourselves in the difficult position of being dislocated many times over, when we are not recognized as being members in the very location(s) in which we live. As a consequence, our presence is frequently seen as an anomaly or an "exception." In sum, this construction of the black "presence" in Canada is inexorably linked to a number of social formations, namely national discourses which position West Indians as recent immigrants, the increasing presence of black American cultural formations, and education systems which do not address the genealogy of black settlement in Canada.

Eye to Eye: The Politics of Misrecognition.   Vancouver, British Columbia

> At an annual party, a white woman approached me to tell me how much she had enjoyed my singing the previous year. I told the woman that she was "mistaken," it was not I, but "another black woman" who she was referring to (Serena, a girlfriend of mine, as it happened). She paused. "Well I KNOW that I have met you before" she then said with conviction ...

> Tia, a South Asian woman, works with my girlfriend Kara (who is black). On different occasions when I have gone to visit Kara, their white colleagues have mistaken me for both Tia and Kara. From talking with Tia, I learned that people have on occasion, also mistaken her for me. For the record, we are different heights, hair texture and style ... we are three different women "of color."

> On numerous occasions I have been approached on the street by white people I do not know who greet me as though I am a familiar friend. After several seconds, (because it takes them that long before they actually "see" me?) they stop talking because they realize that I am not the person they think I am. (I simply shake my head and move on.)

Once while sitting in a café in Toronto with a black female friend, a young white woman interrupted our conversation to tell me that I looked identical to a black female friend of hers whom she had just dropped off at the airport. I stared blankly at this woman and said nothing (what does one say?) When she left my friend said in an exasperated tone, "right and 'we' all look alike..."

Visual dissonance.   As the above anecdotes indicate, the practice of misidentification is not confined to a particular setting; these interactions are inherent to the society in which we live. Moreover, the recurrence of these situations suggests that they are neither aberrant, nor are they simply the actions of "strange" individuals. These encounters do not take place in a social vacuum; they are linked to broader belief systems and structures about "difference." In this context they reveal the taken for grantedness of whites consciousness of blackness. That is, these incidents are illustrative of the contradictory ways in which we are simultaneously *seen* and *not seen*. While the population distribution of each region undoubtedly informs and shapes the public's expectations regarding the existence of different racial groups, these anecdotes support white stereotypes of blackness which perceive black women (and other "women of color") as an undifferentiated category. These examples offer insight into established patterns of interaction between whites and black "others." The system of white racial power is operationalized through the act of misrecognition because the white gaze, which produces this consciousness, remains hidden from view.

III: Travel Tales

West Coast, U.S.A. Post-911 America: From domestic to terrorist in three short steps. The following incident took place in 2003. I was teaching at a University in the Pacific Northwest for one quarter and on one occasion I returned home to Vancouver, British Columbia for the weekend. I had driven directly to the airport following the completion of my second class of the day. At the first security check an elderly white gentleman looked at my passport and then back at me and asked, "are you sure you don't want to stay in town this weekend and wash my windows?" I declined his offer and I had managed to take three steps forward before I was confronted with the second wave of security. At this point a white woman in her thirties proceeded to go through my carry on luggage and then she searched me thoroughly. I asked why I was the only person being subjected to that kind of scrutiny (I had watched white women and men proceed unchallenged). Her response was that "she needed to look busy."

The Power to 'See ...'.   What does it mean for this white female security officer to "look busy with a black female body"? (In this instance being Canadian made no difference, I was simply racialized as a homogeneous black body). There were certainly other bodies available but they were white. Given that black bodies have historically been marked as a threat, if not threatening, this woman's interrogation of me makes it appear (to both the public and her colleagues) as though she is doing her job, rather than simply trying to "pass the time away," as she suggests.

Vancouver, British Columbia en route to Los Angeles, California. It was August 2003 the height of summer holiday travel. I was the only black amongst a sea of white American tourists returning "home" from their cruise to Alaska. A customs agent (an elderly white woman) singled me out. Did I have a return ticket? Yes, I reply, but it is an electronic ticket. Yes, I have a copy of the receipt on my computer. I am then asked to show this receipt. I boot up my computer, which of course takes a minute. I begin the process and before it is complete, she says to me skeptically, "Oh, it won't start up? "No" I said, "it just takes a minute." Once I showed her the receipt she granted me entry and I was able to travel another day.

Given that this is not the first time I have experienced this kind of attention (I had been a target of immigration and security agents well before September 2001), it is difficult to not see this as an occasion to exercise racism without the practice being named as such. We are all not equally under surveillance in this time of "heightened security"; the hyper-visibility of blackness takes on a whole new meaning under these conditions. There are increased opportunities and an accompanying rationalization for this kind of social surveillance. What about my vulnerability, at the hands of customs and immigration officials? It is inconceivable to either the officials or to onlookers that I am concerned about my own safety. The fact that I, the only black person in sight, am involved in an extended interrogation is confirmation to everyone in the vicinity that a black person is not trustworthy. So potent is the 911 narrative regarding the potential danger of air travel that this manner of treatment is performed under the guise of "safety," not as a strategy of white racism. In sum, this situation illustrates how a logic of white supremacy is reproduced and white subjectivity is performed through interaction with discourses of gender and nation. The scrutiny and response to my black female presence is unidirectional for only the view that whites have of me is deemed important. Again, the fact that neither the gaze, nor the actions of the agents are questioned is illustrative of how the process of white racial power sustains itself. The structures and ideologies of gender, race, and nation, which construct "whiteness" as non-threatening, are constitutive of the social atmosphere in which we conduct our daily lives. In this context, the privileging of whiteness remains invisible to "common sense" views of the world (Crenshaw, 1997).

> Recently I had to go to the dentist (I cracked a tooth while eating licorice!). Before my mouth was frozen the conversation turned to this project. When I described the difficulties I have experienced while trying to cross the border, my dentist (a frequent flier) acknowledged that traveling through Los Angeles is becoming "more weird" but added that I am being singled out because "there must be something in my file." I should add that he is a white male in his late 40s. On my next visit five days later, he told me that the evening following our conversation he had seen a television program about crossing the border and a "blonde woman" (his characterization) had talked about how she was being hassled when she went through customs . . .

This story illuminates several issues that frequently arise in discussions, which include issues of gender, race, and racism. First, it is assumed that I am the source of the "problem"—how can an institution (or its agents) be at fault? Second, my dentist grants my experience legitimacy (well sort of) because he has received confirmation from another (i.e., unbiased?) source, in this instance a white woman. After watching this television program my dentist concluded that it is simply "women" who are being harassed at the border. Regardless of our "visible" (i.e., racial) differences, the end result is the same (i.e., harassment). So influential is the belief that race makes no difference, the very power and privilege residing in his ability to "not see" race remains unquestioned. His initial identification of me as the source of the problem also denies the fact that whiteness is also a racialized position which designates members and outsiders. We were both stopped, this blonde and I, but was it for the same reasons? If a white woman is harassed does this mean that there is no difference when a black woman is harassed? Or is it not harassment at all? And given the different cultural positions which black and white (blonde) women hold in society, it is likely that her interrogation may be seen as unusual if not unjust, while mine would be expected. To what extent is surveillance (as a suspect) a part of her daily life? The fact that we occupy different positions in society owing to a racial hierarchy is not considered in my dentist's interpretation of these incidents. This denial of racial difference is significant because the ability to acknowledge or negate the relevance of race is part of prevailing strategies of white racial domination. That is, the assertion that our experiences were the same privileges his position of white (male) racial power, which imposes one definition of reality as *the* definition of reality.

> The other day, while working on this project my girlfriend Kara called me from the airport to relate a disturbing experience with an immigration officer (white, male, and in his late 40s). She was on her way to an American destination for the weekend. She had not traveled in over a year and she was unprepared for the aggression she encountered. The interrogation began with a question; there was

no effort at civility (apparently at this juncture, why bother?). At one point, the agent, frustrated with her answers, told her "I ask the questions here . . . and . . . I have the power to send your butt back." Indeed.

IV: The Academy

This section comprises my experiences both as a student and as a faculty member to draw attention to the experiences and meanings that emerge in different contexts.

As a Graduate Student

Ontario, Canada, the late 1980s. It was my first term in a doctoral program. I was the only non-white student in a required theory course in which there was only one male. Each week a graduate student had to prepare one of the course readings for the seminar. When it was my turn, the professor (white and male) spent the better part of the class trying to undermine my efforts to present the reading. Rather than direct the questions to the others, he continued to isolate me from the other students, directing his focus and attention toward me, asking me specific questions each time I tried to generate a class discussion. He redirected the seminar to topics which he deemed important, implying that the areas that I had chosen to explore were not the ones that should have been addressed. For the most part, the other students remained silent. After class a number of women approached me in the woman's washroom to let me know that they were uncomfortable with the way this professor had treated me. They felt that "something was wrong" (the students did not characterize what they had witnessed as a demonstration of white male racism). One student, acknowledged as one of the "brightest" students in the program, told me that she could not understand why this professor had treated me "that way." She admitted that had he asked her the same questions she too would have struggled to answer them. I later learned that another student was so disturbed by the events that had occurred, she had told another student that she had considered dropping out of graduate school (she was in the first year of her master's degree).

The public nature of this professor's actions is significant. Crossing social boundaries tends to reveal the boundaries. The classroom was his place of institutional and social power and thus it was the place where he could exert his racial and gender domination without it being read as such. Identified as an interloper to the social order, my presence could not go unchallenged. His attempts to silence me, literally and symbolically, also sent a message to the other students—that they were superior. They deserved to be in the classroom. It is important to add that his efforts to undermine me did not end there; they continued for the duration of the course. Other incidents took place in his office, in the margins of my papers, or in his final comments on my term paper which included remarks on my character, not the content of the essay.

Word leaked in the department about his conduct and one night I received a telephone call from a senior faculty member, (white and female) who asked me if I thought that I was being treated this way "because of my race or my gender?" That is, was it racism or sexism?

The above question is important because it points to a lack of understanding regarding the complex ways in which women's experiences and identities are simultaneously shaped by multiple axes of power. It also indicates how white subjectivities have the "privilege" of not seeing "race" as relevant to daily life. More often than not discourses on gender have examined the experiences of white women, and discourses of race, when dealing with "blackness," have focused on the experiences of men. The assumption that it is both possible and appropriate to separate elements of my identity marginalizes and distorts the nature of my experiences as a black woman. The term *sexual* harassment, for example, has made it difficult for women to identify and analyze the diverse ways in which women are harassed. I was the only person in the class who could be visibly identified a member of a racial group. No one else in the course was subjected to that kind of public humiliation. The nature of this interaction illustrates how strategies of racialization are able to effect material and ideological consequences. This professor's actions enforced the racial boundary by privileging whiteness, while simultaneously advancing a narrative of white racial superiority (Crenshaw, 1997). The lack of awareness of the racialized nature of sexual harassment prohibits a critical understanding of the ideologies and strategies, which inform this kind of discrimination. In turn, the inability to comprehend the nature of the interaction undermines subsequent efforts to respond to this kind of social domination.

The Rules of Racial Authenticity Revisited . . . The Sounds of Racism

California, U.S.A., the early 1990s. As a graduate student I had wanted to be a teaching assistant for a class–titled, "Women of Color in the United States." When I called the professor (black and female) she told me that given the nature of the material the position was reserved for women of color. I was dumbfounded, but I remained silent. I did not feel comfortable asserting my black female identity at that moment . . . the fact that my racial identity had been determined by my voice, signaled a great deal . . . I apparently didn't "sound black" . . .

The above example offers yet another illustration of the ways in which black racial identity is interpreted according to a limited (and limiting) set of parameters. In this instance the ascription of a particular style of speaking to racial difference is part of the stereotype of blackness. The fact that this exchange involved a black American female professor indicates how particular ways of seeing and living one's blackness are normalized to the detriment of us all.

As a Professor

I recently taught a course titled, "Race, Gender and Nation: Postcolonial Narratives of the Diaspora." It was a senior-level class and all the students were white women. One of the students was struggling in large part because she had no background in either women's studies or race scholarship. After several weeks, the student approached the director of women's studies to tell her that she was dropping the class. During their conversation the student asked the chair why I "hate *them*"? When the director relayed this conversation to me, she assured me that this student's comments had had nothing to do with race.

On the last day of class on field research I asked the students to discuss their thoughts on the course. One student, a white woman in her 30s announced that one of the things that stood out for her was that "we talked about race a lot."

These two examples are instructive because they point to how narratives of race and gender socialize us regarding ways of being and thinking about the social world. It is important to recognize that, for the most part, education does not produce these narratives, nor does it examine the issues that these anecdotes illustrate. For the majority of the students, my classes have been the first time that they have encountered material which examines the intersection of formations such as race, gender, sexuality, and class. Certainly in sport studies (one of my areas of specialization) courses on "race" are rarely part of the curriculum and courses on gender rarely consider race. I proposed a different way of examining ideologies and relations of race and gender power. This troubles those who have been exposed to conceptual and analytical frameworks which treat racism as the behavior of aberrant individuals or extremist groups and construct gender as a monolith. Race is not seen as relevant to their lives in and outside of the classroom. In this context, issues pertaining to race and the problems of racism, remain the property of those marked as racial "Others."

Returning to the first example, I disagree with the chair's interpretation; the student's comments had everything to do with race and gender. Are students openly hostile when they don't understand physics, or English literature? And if so, do they assume that the instructor "hates" them? Do they tell the chair of the department? Whiteness is not typically explored as a subjectivity and racial formation. Moreover, students' assumptions and experiences are mediated by racialized and gendered subject positions that are connected to broader social and historical frameworks.

Emotions and perspectives are shaped by race and gender power; in this student's imagination, I was the stereotypical "angry black woman." Her construction of me as the source of the problem privileges whiteness by evaluating me from an unmarked racialized position of white subjectivity. Her expressions of discomfort (and fear) illustrate how the manner in which knowledge is received is negotiated in relation to the racialized positions held by students. The practice of associating the material with me, the black female instructor, indicates how an ideology of whiteness generates a particular representation of the cultural politics of difference. The persistence of discourses of white supremacy is due to the fact that we are socialized to be oblivious to the ways in which our everyday lives are conducted within relations and structures of domination.

Of course to have issues pertaining to "race" taught by a woman who is recognized as member of a subordinate racial group presents particular dilemmas and concerns. Discussions of hierarchies of power and inequality often invite displeasure and hostility. The notion that race is only relevant to "non-whites" (i.e., those who are typically seen as raced) reproduces a racial logic, which renders whiteness invisible. This in turn reproduces the racial hierarchy whereby whites and whiteness are seen as natural or normal, and thus the standard against which "difference" is measured. More often than not race is only seen as relevant in a course in which race is in the title and then there may be an expectation that the course will be taught by a "raced" individual. Gender is often not seen as raced and sexualized. This consciousness and the interaction that it engenders are part of the taken for granted atmosphere in which we conduct our daily lives.

I was already a graduate student when, in my seventh year of university, I first had a teacher who was neither a white male nor a white female. This significant absence did not prompt me to pursue a career in higher education however it did make me painfully aware of those who are regarded as legitimate instructors. The lack of diversity has consequences for us all, as that which is unfamiliar soon becomes unrecognizable. The preponderance of white male and female teachers means that other racial groups are not conceived of as educators. Those who are frequently seen in the position are readily understood as authorities, and may well believe themselves to be best suited to the profession. It is not enough to say that the status quo is "normal" or "natural": visibility/presence conveys power and privilege. Over time what we *see* becomes what we understand and believe. The white racial privilege that accrues from this "common sense" construction of reality is rarely questioned and the white racial power that underlies it remains hidden. Surely we can comprehend the implications for all those who are absent? Where are the aboriginal, "asian," latino, chicano, and black teachers? Their/our absence indicates the resilience of racial and gender hierarchies and the belief systems which sustain relations of dominance and inequality.

CLOSING REMARKS: SCENES OF (RE)CONSTRUCTION

As I stated at the outset, one of the aims of this discussion is to interrogate our everyday lives as a key site and source of racial antagonism. I have described a number of events and anecdotes to illustrate the diverse ways in which social power is exercised through social relations and situations. These are not sensational tales, in that they do not involve encounters with groups commonly held as white supremacists. The prevalence of the various interactions gives the impression that these are "natural" events. In seeking to undermine the status quo I wanted to make explicit the ways in which deep-seated patterns of feeling, thought, and interaction reproduce social power in a manner that is rarely questioned. Because these particular stories illustrate the racial structuring of daily life they advance our understanding of the conditions under which racial injustice, racial inequality, and the privileging of whiteness occurs. In this regard the interrogation and inclusion of the taken-for-granted elements of our lives is crucial for these experiences and are sources of knowledge which need to be analyzed. For members of racially subordinated groups, their ways of being and thinking are shaped by structures and belief systems which position them as racial others. I had wanted to draw attention to this area of experience to challenge dominant ways of interpreting the cultural and political significance of race in educational psychology. I had wanted to acknowledge and address how the daily lives of black Canadians creates ways of knowing and being, which need to be incorporated into our educational practices so that we do not reproduce racism through the materials that we use in the classroom.

The persistence of racism also rests in the unquestioned standards and activities around which much of everyday life is structured. At present the logic of white racial superiority is reproduced through strategies which identify and position blacks as "the other" without revealing narratives of whiteness as a racial formation and subjectivity. The fact that the everyday world is organized around processes of racialization that are not made explicit is in part due to the ability of whiteness to be the unmarked position, which identities the "other" (Fiske, 1996). This operationalization of white racial (and gender) power sustains white supremacy because it is embedded in the very atmosphere that structures our daily lives. Similarly, the trivialization of the continuing significance of race and the marginalization of contemporary expressions of racism contribute to the reproduction of educational psychology as a white discourse since the ability to name when and where race is relevant is a privilege largely available to whites. These examples of everyday life are therefore an important pedagogical device for they challenge the view that learning, thinking, and teaching are not influenced by sociocultural processes.

Previously I mentioned that the prominence of U.S. discourses on race, as well as the institutionalization of multiculturalism and bilingualism, has contributed to a certain complacency regarding racism in Canada. In addition, Canadians receive versions of race relations in the United States, which strengthen the view that racism is less overt (i.e., not as offensive) in Canada. This belief is in fact its own form of racism and it is one factor which has hindered our ability to take seriously the cultural politics of difference and inequality as they are made manifest in Canada. The above vignettes offer insight into the complex ways in which the material and ideological elements of white racism have been normalized in the organization of our everyday lives both in and outside of the classroom. The challenge remains for us to acknowledge and address the ways in which the social and political significance of the constructs of race (and gender) is of profound importance to us all.

TERMS FOR READERS

Blackness/Whiteness—does not refer to skin color but to the fact that notions of "black" and "white" are social and political concepts whose cultural meanings have ideological and material consequences. In this context racial identities are lived and understood in relation to the historical, political, and social structures in which they are located.

Everyday Racism—refers to discrimination, which occurs daily. It is embedded in our patterns of communication and social interaction. It involves those elements of daily life which are often taken for granted such as attitudes, feelings, emotions, and relationships with coworkers, and friends.

Racial Authenticity—refers to the notion that there are particular criteria which identify a person as a member of a racial group. For example, at different historical moments, there are cultural struggles regarding the nature, dilemmas, issues that constitute blacks as political and social subjects.

Racialize—refers to the practice of assigning racial meanings to the social world (e.g., social relations, structures, and belief systems).

REFERENCES

Crenshaw, K. W. (1997). Color-blind Dreams and Racial Nightmares: Reconfiguring Racism in the Post-Civil Rights Era. In T. Morrison and C. Brodsky Lacour (Eds.), *Birth of a Nation 'hood: Gaze, Script, and Spectacle in the O. J. Simpson Case*, pp. 97–168. New York: Pantheon Books.

Essed, P. (2002). Everyday Racism. In D. T. Goldberg and J. Solomos (Eds.), *A Companion to Racial and Ethnic Studies*, pp. 202–216. Malden, MA: Blackwell Publishers, Inc.

Fiske, J. (1996). *Media Matters: Everyday Culture and Political Change*. Minneapolis, MN: University of Minnesota Press.

CHAPTER 80

Gender and Education

ELLEN ESSICK

What is gender? How does gender affect one's ability to learn as well as one's perspective on that learning? In our society the terms sex and gender are often used interchangeably. Sex refers to whether one is biologically female or male based on genetic or anatomical characteristics. Gender on the other hand entails much more and relates to masculinity and femininity and the expectations associated with one's biological sex designation. Gender, one's masculinity or femininity is determined by the society in which we live. In other words it is a social construction, set in motion at birth for most boys and girls. Messages about what it means to be male or female are sent to children from very early ages and continue to be channeled to them through adolescence and into adulthood. Schools often play a very significant role in the channeling of these messages and how educators choose to address them can be paramount in a child's life. While it is important not to essentialize all men or all women into these socially constructed positions, recognizing the various epistemologies or ways of knowing often attached to gender might provide a greater insight into helping men and women learn by targeting learning strategies directed toward specific epistemological stages. Educational psychology makes clear different students have various learning styles, yet these distinctions are often essentialized or generalized through several social factors such as race, class and/or gender Gender, in specific, may be a key determinant in the ways in which students process information and the particular learning strategies Employed in the transfer of knowledge. This chapter will discuss how gender, be it masculine or feminine, is a social construction and how operating with knowledge of this social construction may provide greater insight into developing more effective learning opportunities for all students, male and female. Even more specifically, it will examine how the schools could use this reconceptualized approach to educational psychology to change the way we look at the gender and learning in the educational system. Many researchers believe that males and females think and process information in different ways based on their gender. These "ways of knowing" are challenged and reconstructed in this chapter allowing for new approaches to identity, as well as cognitive development. While the assumed cognitive differences in gender affects both female and male students, pedagogical research suggests that the socially prescribed roles of femininity are more likely to have a negative impact on learning outcomes for females. Therefore, speaking primarily about the impact of traditional educational psychology on female intellectual development and the effects of feminine dispositions on learning may provide a better understanding of how to redefine the educational experience for both genders.

THE SOCIAL CONSTRUCTION OF GENDER

While the social definition of femininity as well as masculinity has changed over time, an emphasis on woman as caretaker, woman as passive bystander, and woman as physically and emotionally weak still exists. In contrast, men in American society are still expected to be strong, aggressive, and emotionless providers. The contexts in which men and women find themselves have changed over time but the meanings have remained largely the same. Socially constructed feminine identity requires that women relinquish much of their physical and emotional power and exhibit this lack of strength through passive physical, intellectual, and social interactions. Women are to be soft and demure taking up very little physical space. Femininity in this light requires a dependence on men for both physical and emotional strength. Men in turn are expected to remain strong both physically and emotionally serving as providers for females as well as for themselves. These ideas become a source of conflict for many women and men. They may feel quite ambivalent about society's ideas of femininity and masculinity but still feel trapped within them. Many women become so enmeshed within this social construct of femininity that often they have no concept of how to begin to move outside of this paradigm. And why should they? The schools, the institutions in which they have spent the majority of their time have, sometimes unknowingly, helped to shape this paradigm. Even some of today's most intelligent men and women are unable to recognize how they too have become co-opted into these socially constructed images. Not only do they fail to recognize the social construction of the images but also often fail to recognize the gendered ways in which knowledge is produced and constructed. Students are judged not only by what they know but also by the processes by which they come to this knowledge. In an educational setting the more a student deviates from the expected way of coming to knowledge based on gender, the more he or she stands to lose, particularly in an environment where intelligence is measured on an expected standard for coming to this knowledge. Academically aggressive males and females elicit very different responses in the academic environment. As a result, teachers in the classroom often fail to see how their own behaviors toward students are influenced by gender, both their own gender and that of their students. Since feminine behaviors considered acceptable in the classroom are often quite limiting to the learning process, it is helpful to specifically examine how this femininity is constructed both socially and academically. Through this understanding, today's educators have the opportunity to change the educational and psychological methods used to encourage or discourage young women and men alike.

FEMININITY

Biological differences exist between men and women at birth, but this is where biology ends and society takes over to construct the feminine presentation that is often detrimental physically, emotionally, and academically to women today. Simone de Beauvoir spoke of this notion over thirty years ago suggesting that one is not born, but rather becomes a woman and that feminine behavior and feminine existence is in fact determined by the entire civilization in which a woman lives.

From the moment a little girl is placed in a ruffled dress and instructed not to get dirty, her culture's idea of appropriate feminine behavior is becoming ingrained into her psyche. She quickly learns that different sets of behaviors both socially and in the academic setting are required of her by others including other females around her in order to remain feminine. Additionally, attached to these physical and behavioral requirements are moral imperatives providing reinforcement for "keeping women in line." Women are to remain thin, beautiful, and virginal at all costs. The guilt often attached to this suggestive morality insures that women will not only continue to strive for an unrealistic body ideal or sexual abstinence but will be guilt-ridden for not reaching what is also seen as a moral ideal. A woman will spend countless hours dieting, exercising, or subjecting her body to never ending cosmetic procedures in an attempt to reach this ideal. In addition, the implied assumption with regard to femininity is that all "feminine women" are also heterosexual women. A mandated heterosexual existence keeps women in line and terrified of "the other" or any other that may speak more accurately to their emotional as well as sexual feelings. Her sense of pride and self are destroyed as she attempts to attain these unrealistic moral standards. This heteronormative assumption applies not only to female behavior but also to reading and educational practices in the classroom. Teachers often fail to see how they too have become enmeshed into this notion and create their classrooms from this perspective. Activities, behaviors, and appearances as well as all educational processes are viewed through this heteronormative lens. In *Is there a Queer Pedagogy? or, Stop Reading Straight*, Deborah Britzman (1998) presents ways of understanding and discusses reading practices that look beyond gender to a more inclusive or queer view of the educational experience. This Queer view of education eliminates the need for gender-specific morality often imposed on females. Instead it allows for a broader view of morality that requires affirmation of the dignity of all students. If this is the case then obviously girls must also be part of this equation. Feminist theologist Carol Gilligan (1982) suggests that an ethic of caring can be positively associated with female behavior. While Gilligan sees this ethic as equally valuable to traits associated to male behavior, many individuals maintain the belief that this position of caring and nurturing is sociobiological and should be held at a lower level of esteem than the moral ethic of justice that Gilligan attributes most often to masculine behavior. Throughout history, American society has developed strict norms concerning acceptable appearance and behavior for women. Since the beginning of the Industrial Revolution there has existed a separation between the public and private lives of the family. The public life, usually the responsibility of the male adult of the household, required a strong assertive life void of feeling and emotion. The man received pay for his work and along with this pay came a position of hierarchy in the family. The man lived in a bottom-line culture of competition, drive, and motivation that took on a very formal appearance. At home the female of the household directed the private, domestic life of the family. The shift toward male dominance came and continued throughout the advent of the Industrial Revolution and the assignment of monetary value to the jobs typically held by men. With money came status and power for men but a devaluing of the jobs and positions of women. Also attached to this status came an emphasis on education for males in the household. Given this patriarchal foundation of American culture, men typically developed and perpetuated the standards of physical beauty, social position, and education inscribed to women. This belief system translates into today's society in the form of disparity of pay between jobs encompassing nurturing or emotional care and technological or industrial professions. In the school setting boys are encouraged to take courses founded in the sciences that will directly affect their abilities to attend certain colleges and universities as well as follow particular career paths. Girls are often encouraged, sometimes indirectly not to take those same educational directions. Teaching, childcare, and other "human service" careers that show care, concern, and compassion for individuals are considered not worthy of compensation reflected in most technical and industrial types of jobs. The task for society in general and specifically through the schools is to combine what Gilligan calls the justice perspective on moral thought usually attributed only to males by the culture and the caring ethic of moral thought attributed to females into a belief that both males and females are of equal value and of equal cognitive ability. Sensitivity to others does not have to be seen as a moral weakness and inferior to competition and success. Rather both sensitivity to others and assertiveness can be seen as positive traits for women and men alike.

Men and women who fail to reach the appropriate social standards of masculinity and femininity often subject themselves to what the society views as negative labels. Soft, pleasing, polite, quiet, dainty, and nice are words that represent the standard for acceptable behavior among young women. Anything different earns her any number of perceived negative labels from masculine or aggressive, to lesbian to slut. If she is very young and refuses to follow the expected norms she gets a slight reprieve and is labeled a "tomboy" by those around her. Once she reaches puberty this is no longer considered acceptable behavior. Women are taught from very early ages to maintain an expression of difference. When meeting a male they are to avert their eyes downward and avoid direct eye contact and confrontation. A bold, strong, or aggressive woman may not produce and convey the appropriate image. This behavior is carried into the classroom as girls apologize for interrupting to ask a question or censor themselves in order not to appear as a "know it all" in the classroom. In *School Girls*, Peggy Orienstein describes her experiences observing middle-schoolgirls in the classroom. She interviewed girls who routinely knew the correct answer to questions asked by the teacher but never raised their hands to answer the question. Many of the girls felt that to answer would jeopardize their social position with the boys in the classroom.

Conversely, Men are awarded privileges, not only with their own bodies but also with their behaviors that would be at best inappropriate and at worst insubordinate if practiced in the same fashion by women. Boys are rarely reprimanded for yelling out answers in the classroom but rather commended for their knowledge and understanding. They are encouraged to take assertiveness to the point of aggression. By participating in theses behaviors they do not compromise masculinity; rather, they often confirm it. Women on the other hand are expected to control these behaviors at all costs and failing to do so compromises their femininity. Men receive very little reprieve if they fail to meet socially constructed masculine standards and are also labeled with terms ranging from prissy to sissy or passive to fag for failing to meet socially constructed norms for masculinity. Boys who fail to portray the appropriate image in school are labeled and often carry those labels throughout their educational careers.

The conflicting messages heard by many women students become overwhelming and it becomes an impossible task for many adolescents to know where they fit into this confusing picture. They want to be seen as feminine yet in order to be successful in many arenas they must behave in direct opposition to this "feminine standard."

This femininity, while not a given, is quite widely accepted in American culture. This is not to say that women would not like this feminine "ideal" to be different or have the freedom to rebel against its physical and political constraints. But the nature of social construction is such that often women not only accept this "way of being" but also become part of the system that creates and perpetuates it. It is also understandable that in a society that has become so enmeshed with this construction of femininity as well as masculinity, the culture itself loses site of its stifling impact on females and males alike. While social construction affects both males and females, the negative impact of the construction of femininity on females physically, emotionally, and academically cannot be ignored.

PERFORMING FEMININITY

So why have women become so enmeshed with this socially constructed notion of femininity? Many women understand and even embrace the need to look more critically at the many culturally prescribed roles women are expected to fulfill in our society, yet must constantly be aware of the inconsistencies in their behavior as they struggle to excel in areas which are antithetical to the "feminine." This performance begins at very early ages and nowhere is this more evident than in the academic environment of the classroom. Valerie Walkerdine (1997) examined the expected performance of females as they enter the mathematics classroom. Those young women who excel in math are said to be "hard workers" while the boys who excelled are labeled intelligent. The young women take on this performance as the hard worker and fail to see their own potential as bright, intelligent young women. Many young women are even discouraged from taking math class altogether because to do so would not be the correct performance of femininity. Changing this performance challenges male domination and superiority.

Walkerdine goes on to discuss the threat that women present to a patriarchal society by exhibiting their power in a pedagogical setting. Women often live in very contradictory terms with an intense fear of stepping over the gender divide. The classic response then is the performance of femininity.

This fear of stepping over the gender divide may be a key determinant in the perpetuation of social and emotional problems such as eating disorders among women. Many young women struggle to be as perfect as they can be in the classroom but at the same time recognize the social and intellectual expectations of society. Women are kept in line via the performance of femininity. It is much easier and acceptable to see a woman as a frail, sick anorexic than as a strong, assertive, and competent woman not only for those around her but for herself as well. Since the day she chose not to answer a question in math class for fear of appearing "too smart" she has been performing femininity. The struggle between performing academically and the performance of femininity becomes overpowering as women negotiate the decisions to sacrifice one role for the other.

Ultimately this performance affects how women see themselves physically and emotionally as well as academically. The continual messages of how one is to perform begin to affect the self-esteem of young women, which in turn creates and perpetuates a vicious cycle reflecting weak, incapable women. Again, the problem becomes that of the young women rather than the culture, which created her. Peggy Orenstein (1994) describes observations with young women in a school setting and the social and pedagogical practices that prevent women from taking full advantage of their educational experiences. Orienstein reasons that we do girls a disservice when we encourage young girls to feel good about themselves without addressing the culture and its construction of femininity that originally perpetuated this low self-esteem.

Young women quickly learn that it is not only more acceptable in society to "perform femininity" but it also protects them against the terrifying idea of confronting the overwhelmingly misogynist ideal perpetuated by the patriarchal cultural. She has no notion that she has become so enmeshed in this culture that she not only performs femininity outwardly to the rest of the culture but inwardly within her own personal concept of herself as well. What started in the classroom with young boys and girls infiltrates the personal lives of women as they move toward adulthood and women begin to lose the innate power that exists within them. Attributed to this notion of performance of femininity, and often masculinity, is the idea that men and women, or more specifically masculinity and femininity bring with them specific epistemologies or "ways of knowing."

WAYS OF KNOWING

Epistemology can be defined as the process or route by which a person comes to know what he or she knows. What is one's epistemology? Where and by what means do individuals come to know what they know. Do we know things as women, as men, as children, from the heart or is each individual born into a culture that determines his or her epistemology? While some individuals may have a true clear-cut epistemology, most likely individuals combine a variety of ways of knowing in order to learn about the world around them and most importantly to learn about themselves. This epistemology also allows students the opportunity to discover how they fit into the vast world in which they live.

In the late 1960s Harvard researcher William Perry (1970) studied the intellectual and ethical development of students as they moved through their undergraduate years at Harvard. Perry described a series of stages or positions that he observed in these students as they moved through the education process. He concluded that students go through four stages of epistemological development. These stages, basic dualism, multiplicity, relativism subordinate, and total relativism, seemed to apply to most of the students Perry interviewed. Perry defined *basic dualism* as that point in the learning process when students viewed the world in polarities such as black/white, good/bad, or right/wrong. Here students were passive learners, relying on teachers to provide them with all truths. Eventually students realized that there could be many different opinions and moved to a state of *multiplicity.* At this point students can understand that teachers do not always have all the right answers and that they too can have an opinion. Eventually the teacher challenges the student's personal opinion. The teacher requires evidence and support for that personal opinion and students move to a position of *relativism subordinate.* Here an analytical evaluative approach to knowledge is cultivated particularly in one's academic pursuits. Perry believed that eventually students shifted to full *relativism* where they understand that truth is relative and that knowledge is constructed. At this point students affirm their own personal identity and their own place within the learning process. While this seemed to be the way by which most of the students Perry interviewed came to know things, these results reflected primarily masculine ways of knowing as the majority of the students interviewed were men. Later, Belenky, Clinchy, Goldberger, and Tarule (1986) revised the study to include how women moved through these stages.

In *Women's Ways of Knowing*, Belenky et al. (1986) describes how women come to know all that they know, keeping in mind that the acquisition of knowledge and the ways that women learn to express themselves often come as the result of negative events or experiences throughout their lives. *Women's Ways of Knowing* discusses the ways in which women draw conclusions about truth, knowledge, and authority. Using Perry's epistemological positions, Belenky followed women through the positions of basic dualism, multiplicity, relativism subordinate, and total relativism. Effects from society seemed to slow the rate at which women moved through these same stages.

While it may seem that Belinky's assertions were quite simplistic concerning the intellectual development of women and viewed this development from a very essentialist viewpoint, they may still provide insight into how students both male and female develop ways of knowing as a result of the many events both positive and negative that they experience throughout their lifetimes. Belinky's stages take Perry's work one step further by including the influence of socially constructed femininity on the methods by which women come to know what they know. Belinky described the *silenced women* who have received the message throughout their lives that that they should be seen and not heard. Not only are they not heard but through this silence comes the belief that they in fact do not deserve to be heard. These women begin to take what they are told as gospel and fail to give themselves permission to think for their own person. They accept the stereotyped sex role portraying women as passive and powerless, requiring the presence of a man for survival. The next level of knower described by Belinky is the *received knower.* This is the woman who gains knowledge through listening. Typical of many college women, these women lack the assertiveness to speak what they know. They feel as if this listening is the road to knowledge and rarely doubt what they learn by listening to authorities. Since these women are only listening and not speaking they almost never take advantage of the opportunity to disagree with authority. The assumption is that the information to which they are listening is true. If two authorities disagree, the listener decides on truth based on a variety of things, such as place in society, education, age, etc., which person is the ultimate authority and takes their word as the truth. The messages that have comes across clearly to these women is that they are to be seen but not heard. Unfortunately, the greater society perpetuates itself by keeping the received knower in her place. Additionally, the young women described by Belinky are only exhibiting the educational behaviors taught to them from their earliest educational experiences. In the classroom setting it is often safer for the teacher's comfort level for students to stay in this place, not questioning or challenging the "authority." For women in particular to move out of this place challenges the social structure and male hierarchy in the academic setting.

From very early ages, girls and women are conditioned to think of the "other." Eventually with *subjective thinking*, women begin to find a self and discover their own voice. She is able to listen to this voice in conjunction with outside voices as she makes decisions in her life. As many women move to a position of *procedural knowledge* characterized by reasoned thinking, they are quite ambivalent because while they hope to move beyond their subjectivism they also hope to defend it. It has taken them a long time to discover the voice from within. For many women the move to a more reasoned way of thinking is part of the overall game they must play to get to where they hope to eventually be either personally, academically, or professionally. Women begin to recognize that only relying on their own inner voice can be detrimental to their development.

By thinking more rationally women are able to make more informed decisions. Developing this type of thinking is what Belenky refers to as *procedural knowledge*. Whether through examining impersonal facts and data as does the subjected knower or developing relationships as with the *connected knower*, procedural knowers reason out decisions using given information. Eventually Belenky describes the development of a woman who uses her heart, her head, and her voice to become a connected knower. Her ultimate goal is to become a *constructed knower*. The constructed knower begins to look at things as they really are, she is patient and realizes that everything that goes on around her is part of who and what she is or will become. She moves to a place where she can be more flexible and adapts more easily to change and instead of being threatened by others who disagree with her, she welcomes the difference and the discussion. In the classroom this allows for a dialogue that includes all students and creates a learning environment of equality among students. It creates a setting where women are encouraged not only to begin a discussion but also to follow it through debate and disagreement.

So why is the process of becoming a constructed knower a woman's way of knowing? Why is it that men seem to either step into or quickly move to the epistemology of a constructed knower? Why was there a need for a book to be written about this issue? Is this process of intellectual and personal development truly inherent in the lives of women or are women socially constructed to be as they are in each stage. It appears that in a patriarchal society it is in the best interest of the dominant group for women to remain silenced or at best to remain in the position of a received knower. While it seems that many women move beyond silence in spite of the culture, there appears to be an equal number of women who hear the repeated message to be seen but not heard and never make the steps necessary to move to the next stage of knowing. While Belenky's descriptions of each type of knower do seem to describe many women in some situations, they may also help perpetuate the tight patriarchal box in which many women find themselves. We can only imagine a world in which women, from a very early age, are encouraged and even rewarded for expressing their voice and being heard. In educational psychology it becomes imperative that educators begin early in kindergarten looking at the role gender plays in the learning process and address teaching/learning strategies to move students more quickly to a constructed way of knowing. Maybe it is time to rethink how the lives of women are structured from their earliest intellectual development. Hopefully through increased awareness and education women will not become adults and still be silenced. To do this we must move the awareness into action and create curricula that recognizes and incorporates gender differences in learning. Equally important is the need to include gender-specific teacher training programs that provide teachers with the skills necessary to address and blend gendered styles of learning.

Socially constructed or not, many women develop intellectually through the process. Educators may find the work of Belenky helpful as a tool in the pedagogical processes. If as educators, we develop an understanding of how these women become constructed knowers, we can better tailor our pedagogical methods toward enhancing development of women as well as men to this epistemological stage. At the same time we can encourage women and men to develop a strong sense of self and move through these stages more deliberately at a much earlier age. The goal here is to create students who recognize the contributions of all individuals in the process of intellectual development.

REFRAMING THE GENDER MESSAGE

Margaret Mead defined an ideal culture, as one in which there was a place for every human gift. This ideal culture would allow its members to grow to their fullest potentials, and would allow the culture the maximum use of its members' gifts. Nothing would be wasted. Socially constructed differences between masculinity and femininity exist. Unfortunately, along with recognition of the differences often comes the assignment of social value to those differences. In a pedagogical environment it is important to tailor learning strategies to these differences but it is equally important to use this environment to deconstruct the hierarchal value placed on these gender differences. Amy Guttman speaks of the need for a democratic dialogue in the classroom in order to experience true understanding of these differences. She focuses on dialogue as an avenue to explore cultural, religious, and gender differences. Dialogue also serves as a curricular strategy that demands the rethinking of limitations placed on cognitive capabilities based on gender. Guttman believes that schools have a responsibility to get students ready for citizenship and that public school must be at the center of the debate. Guttman proposes the need to keep the push toward improving self-esteem and mutual respect regardless of gender, in balance. She does not suggest that dialogue will end all of society's problems with gender inequality but it will teach students about their shared citizenship and their shared humanity with all individuals, regardless of citizenship (Guttman, 1996). This conversation gives students the opportunity to have direct experience with who the other is, affording them countless opportunities of the practice of daily democracy.

By encouraging classroom dialogue about difference whether it is race, class, or genders in the school, students are provided with a more solid ground for decision making and value clarification. Students are moved more quickly to the position of a constructed knower regardless of their gender. Individuals must be taught to share mutual respect. This does not mean that all bias will be purged from the educational system nor does it mean that everyone will agree with or accept those differences, but it does mean that there will be an ongoing dialogue that encourages the mutual respect among people. In order for this dialogue to be effective it needs to be framed in such a way as to allow everyone the opportunity to have an equally valued speech, free from the limitations of gender roles. By continuing this dialogue there may eventually be a time when women no longer feel the need to "perform femininity." Once the voices of women in the classroom began to be heard, we begin the reconstruction of access to learning. All students learn how to voice one's opinion free of trivialization or invalidation as a result of one's gender. This in turn leads to varied positions of authority or expertise in the classroom. Students become repositioned as producers and interrogators of knowledge. In the mean time, it is important for educators to recognize how the social construction of gender as well as the performance of that gender contributes to the way students learn, apply, and produce knowledge, and how traditional conceptions of educational psychology has in the past classified gendered ways of knowing that result in counterproductive learning experiences for both female and male students. And of equal importance is the need for educators to recognize their own positionality within this social construction of gender. Failing to do this jeopardizes student learning and perpetuates the positions that educational strategies are meant to overcome. Educators must be aware of the plethora of ways that students learn and specifically include the contributions of gender to the construction of the self, academically, intellectually, emotionally, physically, and socially.

REFERENCES

Belenky, M., Clinchy, B., Goldberger, N., and Tarule, J. (1986). *Women's Ways of Knowing: The Development of Self, Voice and Mind*. New York: Basic Books.

Britzman, D. (1998). Is there a Queer Pedagogy? or Stop Reading Straight. In W. Pinar, *Curriculum Toward New Identities*. New York: Garland Publishing, Inc.

Gilligan, C. (1982). *In a Different Voice: Psychological Theory and Women's Development*. Cambridge, MA: Harvard University Press.

Gutmann, A. (1996). *Challenges of Multiculturalism in Democratic Education*, in Relativism, reason and public Education. Cambridge MA: Harvard University Press.

Orenstein, P. (1994). *School Girls*. New York: Doubleday.

Perry, W. (1970). *Forms of Intellectual and Ethical Development In the College Years*. New York: Holt, Rinehart & Winston.

Walkerdine, V. (1997). *Femininity as Performance*. New York: Routledge.

CHAPTER 81

TEAM: Parent/Student Support at the High School Level

PAM JOYCE

SHOULD PARENTS BE INVOLVED IN SCHOOLS?

Parent connections within schools should be prioritized as a respected and sought after mandatory aspect of all school systems. It should be viewed as a viable and visible force for aiding
student enrichment. TEAM, a parent/student support group at the high school level, addresses
the important aspects of educational psychology in relation to parent involvement and adheres
to the belief that academic ability has multiple dynamics and thus is involved in nurturing the
mind and the intellect. One might query why parents are associated with the topic of educational
psychology but I would counter that inquiry and respond by saying why not? Why not critically
examine parental involvement for the benefit of students? One of the dynamics attributed to
academic ability is parental involvement. The dynamics that are interrelated both with the mind
and with the intellect in the learning process require the support of nurturing and caring parents
along with the help of society to participate in the guidance and knowledge sharing associated
with the education of children.

Education is a complex endeavor involving young impressionable minds and thus should be
approached as a TEAM effort. All parents, regardless of race, class, or gender should be a part of a
team that serves to provide viable resources about their children to the school community. Parents
should be able to use their multidimensional backgrounds as resources for the benefit of the
children and provide ontological as well as psychological insights into the lives of their children.
Parents usually supply the initial foundation of resources to their children because they plant the
seeds of culture, economic status, personal ideologies, and position in a child's web of reality. In
a world defined by multiple "people labels" subjugated knowledges and indigenous ontologies
become lost, devalued, and/or sometimes diminished through physical and mental positioning.
There is an established ideology that accompanies negative labels and categories in reference
to specific parent groups where parent voices are not encouraged in the school community. It
blatantly professes that ostracized parents are not intelligent enough to stand up for their children
and when they attempt to advocate for their children they are ignored. A school stance that ignores
indigenous knowledge espouses arrogance and insensitivity to marginalized groups. TEAM works
to unearth new participation frameworks for parents who do not fit into existing communities of

practice ultimately enabling them to eventually experience portable learning styles, which can be transported into lived world experiences under varied circumstances.

Predispositions, that hinder change, are sometimes contrived concerning specific parents groups. Educators believe that the "hard to reach/low profile" parents due to their lack of participation in school activities are not interested in the well-being of their children. I would argue that when underserved parents and students do not feel they are a part of the dominant community of practice they disengage from the mainstream community. When individuals do not feel as if they are a part of the hegemonic group they are not drawn toward the group and actually shy away. Consequently more than likely they do not have the tools needed to share their voices in unfamiliar and varied contexts. If by chance disengaged parents were able to transport the skills of navigating the system, acquired in TEAM, to new and or existing dominant frameworks, then coparticipate comfortably with TEAM members and also with the mainstream high school parent group, ultimately overall parent involvement would increase. These results of course would be contingent on the level of criticality demonstrated by those involved and the belief in democratic practices.

In order to live critically and pursue democracy for all we must see "what is." Inside and outside the world of academia the placement and assignment of negative categories and labels further serves to alienate parents and this problem can be addressed by pushing beyond the established boundaries or obstacles. Traditionally parents of underachieving and/or underserved students have not been welcomed in the school environment. The situated position of these parents, who are usually minority and lower to lower-middle-income status, has usually been recessed from the forefront and apart from the hegemonic parent group. In this sense race and class aspects of postformalism thinking have surfaced at the school level to be a strategic consideration in comprehending the far-reaching aspects of the lack of parental involvement and also in seeking alternatives to the situation. The critical lenses of postformalist perspectives do not support either isolating parents from school activities nor insulating them from the mainstream parent population. In this sense isolation means being closed out and not being allowed to participate and insulation means being protected from the hegemonic group, basically not being allowed to mingle with them. TEAM reinforces a critical dimension that condones questioning and promotes understanding of the multilogicality of the issues surrounding high school parental involvement. Through this expanded lens parents are exposed to new vistas and comfort zones while the mainstream school population is exposed to the positive aspects of difference both by sharing the lenses of multilogicality. This far reaching intervention serves both populations for the greater good of all with particular focus on the students.

TEAM invests in underserved parents through the power of intervention. Parents are scaffolded into power positions as in Vygotsky's Zone of Proximal Development (VPD) whereby parents and students are guided by interactive, meaningful activities to achieve higher positions within the school community and the ability to self-advocate. In order to achieve a redefined positionality parents reconstruct their reality and mainstream society adjusts their preconceived notions about specific parent groups. A mechanistic psychology assumes parents of underachieving/underserved students are not intellectually savvy enough to orchestrate effective interventions for their children. TEAM presents a more positive scenario of parent/student relationships but hegemonic differences arise with the belief in the existing mindset that underserved parents are unable or less likely to advocate for their children and consequently the children often suffer. Sometimes underserved parents lack the privilege of having a critical ontological vision but if given the opportunity to exercise the right to a broader vision their understandings and insights can support the nature and legacy of their past and the lived world interactions of their present to confidently lead them to productive ends. Acknowledging the ability for transformations due to the fluctuating levels of parental involvement, it is imperative to explore both the historically and socially situated self of the teachers, parents, and students. In order to understand the complexities and interconnectedness of all involved in the school community, simultaneously become aware of the myriad of forces, and strive for the connections that can bring people together, a powerful synergistic relationship must develop. This occurs when TEAM parents form a powerful synergistic relationship with teachers, other parents, students, and community members and eventually construct a power literacy that repositions them and helps them realize their new place within the web of reality. To witness this synergistic relationship is to witness critical democracy at work passionately fighting for the inclusion of parents in schools. It is in essence an honoring of the complete person first within self and secondly outside self, meshing the micro, meso, and macro lived parental worlds.

PARENTAL INVOLVEMENT AT THE HIGH SCHOOL LEVEL

In the twenty-first century starting with Goals 2000 and currently with the No Child Left Behind (NCLB) Act parents have been and continue to be encouraged to get more involved in various aspects of school life. In agreement with Concha Delgado-Gaitan, I also believe school success for many minority children is dependent on the ability of the schools to incorporate the parents and the culture of the home as an integral part of the school curriculum. Presently making a connection between the home and the school is not a usual occurrence and consequently not the norm for underserved parents. As indicated under the NCLB, opportunities are currently available for parents to exert a more visible and viable role in their children's school careers. Due to blatant discrepancies one might ask, is overall parental involvement actually happening? Unfortunately there is a dichotomy between what school legislature purports and what seemingly occurs in reference to parental involvement. In spite of the documented inviting atmosphere of academia toward parents there are still a percentage of parents who choose not to get involved with the school from the K–12 levels for numerous reasons and sadly, historically this lack of parental involvement has been more noticeable at the high school level. The fact that the problem usually heightens at the high school level only tends to exacerbate the need for immediate action. What better time but at the culmination of mandatory formalized schooling, would it be to assist, nurture, and support children if not when they are getting ready to embark into the "real world?"

Noting the culminating aspect of the high school years, I believe adults and/or educators should feel obligated to give high school students tools to help them survive in the real world? It is not only an obligation but also a necessity for society to equip children with what they need in order to be productive citizens. Some educators have accepted the tapering off of parental involvement at the high school level but now more than ever there is a need to unite as a TEAM for the students who have inadvertently been forgotten by the system. We are losing greater numbers of students, therefore, educators need to unite and assist in providing stability for a number of underserved students by helping to increase parental involvement at the high school level.

If a proportionate amount of school attention concerning high school parental involvement can be shifted or redirected from the lower grades to the higher grades and more priority can be placed on student well-being then the focus on the future of young people can be restored and forgotten students can be rediscovered. In the interest of fairness and democratic practice assisting parents to create partnerships with their children, teachers, administrators, and community members is an important and extraordinary combination of human forces, which ultimately enables schools to accomplish more expansive opportunities for underserved students. In this case parents are the missing key component that will enable students to regain perspective but they are not the only missing piece to the puzzle. Further exploration into the causes of reduced high school parental involvement for underserved students needs to be examined.

PARENTAL OBSTACLES

Parental involvement varies across grade levels usually ranging from a higher level in the lower grades to a lower level of involvement in the upper grades. Statistical information over the years documents that parents who fall into the category of "hard to reach" and/or "low profile," in the school system are often from minority groups, such as black, immigrant, non-English speaking, and/or are from the lower socioeconomic strata. In addition the children of these parents are traditionally the underserved population of the school. Therefore, in an effort to understand the underserved parent position it is only fair to take into consideration multiple factors that might cause parental involvement to sink so low. There are personal factors that repeatedly arise that hinder these partnerships from occurring but problematically often at the crux of the problem is the system that continues to underserve the parents of these students and consequently allows them and their children to remain invisible in schools.

Often, parents of students labeled as underachieving and/or underserved feel unwelcome in schools. A variety of factors tend to lead to these feelings subsequently inhibiting parents, preventing them from advocating for their children, and successfully navigating the system to help empower them. Linguistics, economics, logistics, institutional racism, feelings of marginalization, and cultural factors, for example, are a few obstacles that offer a somewhat accurate yet narrow explanation for the lack of parental involvement. Past stigmas, which might be preventing parents from participation in school activities, can be relinquished with rigorous efforts initiated by teachers. Transformative changes can be incorporated in schools in an effort to thwart the unwelcome feelings that labeled parents experience or anticipate when faced with an invitation to participate in various school activities, but barriers inhibiting parental involvement must be addressed.

The information that follows was accessed on the Internet, in a literature review, which guided the development of the South Carolina Parent Survey. It provides information concerning the obstacles affecting parent involvement on three levels, practical, personal, and institutional. Practical, personal, and/or institutional barriers affect parental involvement and contribute to perpetuating low visibility. Underserved parents are faced with practical issues such as lack of time, lack of appropriate childcare, language-communication barriers, juggling of multiple work schedules, and diverse linguistic and cultural practices to name a few. They sometimes experience personal experiences such as reminders of their own past negative school experiences, reawakening of old fears and frustrations, lack of knowledge about how to become involved, and mistrust of the educational system. Institutional barriers also remain a problem for these parents. Many schools fail to examine current school practices that are not effectively promoting parental involvement, which is a number one deterrent for high school "hard to reach/low profile" parents. I would argue that institutional barriers are "hot spots" for educators. These "hot spots" create spaces in school communities that are charged with untapped negative as well as positive energies. I believe educators can tap into the positive energies of "hard to reach/low profile" parents and help to dispel some of the long-standing barriers that have been promoted in the past by developing a counselor's role with parents. In essence, educators in an academic arena have the power to institute transformative change by rectifying the negative results of limited or absent parental involvement. In order to develop TEAM, an understanding of parent background information, with all the obstacles that prevent or limit participation, is needed.

The aforementioned parent obstacles provide the impetus for the interconnected and supportive structure of TEAM. A study of the unique obstacles that confront the parents of specific districts can provide the information needed to bring people together. TEAM opens possibilities needed for parent/school connections. Each TEAM is comprised of at least one parent/guardian, one teacher, one student, and a community member. In essence each student TEAM member is given a personal team to advocate for her and assist her in navigating the system. Students are the most important members of TEAM because they represent the future of our country. Two of the most important goals of the team are one that all students and parents involved eventually learn to navigate the system and two that both students and parents learn to advocate for themselves. Navigating the system and knowing how to self-advocate are basic survival tools which more often than not are missing form the toolkits of the underserved children and parents.

In light of the present day reality of disenfranchised parents and forgotten children, teacher's roles have expanded to that of parent counselor. This role entails building a connection with the "hard to reach/low profile" parents and creating a supportive and nurturing place for them to be seen and heard in the school community. As I discovered it can happen simply by human agency. Teachers can have a strategic impact on building the bridge between home, school, and community. TEAM is an example of an alternative approach for partnering with parents.

SHIFT FOR THE RETURN OF PARENTAL INVOLVEMENT

A reanalysis and reconstruction of the norm must take place in order to discover the remaining missing pieces needed to create a support system for parents that will ultimately benefit under-achieving and underserved students. School communities must be able to admit and see that something is amiss if a percentage of the parent population continues to be invisible. Contradictions abound in education. Teaching involves both intended and unintended lessons, and often the unintended lesson, that parental involvement of the "other" is not welcomed, is the message that is sent by the schools. I argue that the resounding message echoing forth through the walls of academia is that parents who are not involved and subsequently whose voices are not heard are people who are not embraced by the school community. Living in a society that professes democratic beliefs and practices should be an adequate reason to become proactive about this issue. It is morally wrong and undemocratic to allow such an obvious human disconnect to occur when a shift in thinking and the launching of a action plan can make an immediate and significant difference in the level of involvement of high school parents traditionally known as "hard to reach/low profile" parents. A successful shift can make a difference in the lives of many parents and students and have a resounding impact on society. Parents and students can benefit through a renewed faith in the educational system that previously distance them, and then subsequently society can benefit from students emerging into the "real world" with a sense of purpose and direction. TEAM is an example of what a shift in thinking and a commitment to action can produce in answer to the dismal scenario of unwelcome parents and invisible students. Educators can make a difference in high schools with increased parent involvement.

Educators need to shift support for parental involvement at the high school level not only for the sake of the students but also for a productive future society as well. How is it possible to forget underachieving students, become oblivious to their needs, and closed off to all possible means of correcting the situation? Two contrasting ways to address this pressing situation is first: (1) to remain oblivious to the needs of students and ignore the obvious positive contribution that parental involvement can afford to students and schools and (2) to tackle this issue by moving forward with the vision of a critical educator. I decided to move forward with a critical vision and start TEAM, a support group, in an effort to partner with parents for the benefit of the students as well as the society. TEAM stands for Teacher Efforts—Advocating/Motivating. TEAM is a teacher-initiated support group formed for the purpose of giving support to students and parents while advocating on their behalves and motivating them to master navigation of the intricacies and subtleties of the system. The end goal is for the parents as well as the students to be able to have their voices heard and recognized and to encourage self-advocacy for both.

TEAM OVERVIEW

Parent involvement can be referred to in several different terms such as home-school relationships, family-school involvement, home-school collaboration, and home-school partnerships, although these terms encompass a wide range they do not adequately define parent involvement in TEAM. Parent involvement in TEAM has broader implications and relies on graduated life-learning experiences for all members. The broader underlying factor or basis of the group rests in the ability to act individually in some instances and then collectively in others depending on the circumstances in order to accomplish diverse tasks ranging from simple to complex. The individual and collective aspects of TEAM highlight the dual efforts needed to build the connection between the school and the team members. The worth and power of individual and collective endeavors become an opening for personal growth, thus releasing parents and students from invisibility and equally as significant creating space for the exchange of new discourses.

TEAM initially is energized by the individual and collective efforts of teachers nurturing and supporting parents and students and quickly picks up this positive momentum as TEAM membership increases. The goal is for the initial energy of teachers to become infectious and spread to all TEAM members. Consequently, each TEAM member helps to enact difference or change through dedication and participation thereby causing a snowball effect within the communication system of the school arena. The contagious energy level ultimately results in collective and magnified differences in the world and these differences can be instrumental in education if manifested as renewed, revitalized, and/or newly discovered discourses of teacher/parent/student voices. In order to accomplish this endeavor, TEAM focuses on eight essential posits:

- Helping students and parents to navigate the educational system.
- Helping "hard to reach/low profile" parents and students recognize and express their voices.
- Exposing students to options for life after high school.
- Modeling "how to" advocate for self.
- Providing motivating experiences for students and parents to pursue school involvement on multiple levels.
- Encouraging community assistance and participation.
- Enhancing academic achievement.
- Developing leadership skills of students and parents.

Helping students and parents navigate the educational system is essential because this introduces them to power structures and the means to acquire power. TEAM organizes workshops based on parent requests and teacher suggestions. It informs parents how to interact with guidance counselors, teachers, administrators, and other dominant parent groups within the school, while simultaneously advocating for their children. In addition to workshops and informal meetings TEAM teachers volunteer to accompany parents, if necessary, to conferences with school personnel. Parents are aware that they always have the option of requesting teacher assistance in school matters. This type of "in person" hands on parent assistance is necessary at times and involves going the extra mile or going beyond a job description in order to achieve increased parent involvement at the high school level.

Navigating the system requires learning how to schedule courses, interpret report card grades, and knowing what to do when students are not performing well. Navigating the system can be a TEAM meeting topic where guidance counselors can engage with parents in intimate roundtable discussions or in panel format and share pertinent information with parents. Power is key!

The information below is a sample parent information sheet entitled *Navigating the System* that can be revised to suit the needs of any school.

Navigating the System

START UP CHECK SHEET

1. Check the total amount of course credits your child is registered for each year.
2. Check the transcript or report card at the end of the year. Do the credits earned match?
3. Check report cards every cycle.
4. Check report cards for grades of D and F. TEAM Alert!
5. Check for possible tutoring services for student. TEAM can help!
6. Check the mail for warning notices. If parents receive a warning notice schedule a conference.
7. Check the school calendar for parent conferences and Back to School Night (attend).
8. Schedule your own teacher conferences (in person or by phone) to
   - monitor your child's academic progress and/or to,
   - check for unusual lateness or unexcused absences.

Note: request your child's presence at the meetings when appropriate.

9. Schedule a meeting with your child's guidance counselor
   - Know the name and number of your child's guidance counselor.
   - Request the attendance of all teachers.
   - Request summer school information.
   - Request information for summer enrichment programs.
   - Request a four-year layout plan for getting into college, if college is a future consideration.
10. Request your child's transcript at the end of each year. Review the transcript!
    - Less than the required yearly credits accomplished—consult TEAM for guidance.
    - Grades D and F—consult TEAM for guidance.

Helping "hard to reach/low profile" parents and students recognize and express their voices is essential because parents and students need a space in which to be heard. It is imperative that they begin to express their needs and store up enough cumulative energy so that they may become visible and recognized as people who count. In this manner they will not have to assimilate but on the contrary they will create a new and unique place for themselves where the power wielders will take notice and finally they will have a vote that counts and a voice that matters and can be heard. Voice is key!

Exposing students to options for life after high school is essential because it creates the continuity and connectedness that should be associated with high school graduation. It provides avenues and possibilities for continued learning and encourages students to think in that direction. Building connections and modeling the importance of life long learning is one of the strengths of TEAM. Lifelong learning is key!

Modeling "how to" advocate for self is essential because students learn to analyze what they need, speak up for what they want, and then secure what they need all in an effort to establish themselves as productive individuals in the world. Self-advocacy in TEAM requires students to empower reluctant parents or guardians to attend meetings on their behalf and if for some reason parents or guardians cannot attend students are encouraged to go beyond the roadblocks and seek family support from relatives or adult friends approved by the family. As a last resort if these measures are not successful TEAM teachers or community members will support and represent students at a meeting but family representation is the goal. Self-advocacy is key!

Providing motivating experiences for students and parents to pursue school involvement on multiple levels is essential because continuous visibility and physical presence in strategic locations of both parents and students within school walls creates an infectious positive shift in thinking for the dominant members of the school community and thus for the power wielders of education. Involvement is key!

Encouraging community assistance and participation is essential because that level of involvement goes beyond school walls and helps to establish valuable connections for parents and students. For example, if a percentage of the parent population's primary language is not English, they might need legal, medical, and/or translator assistance in order to navigate the system. This is a situation TEAM can address by scheduling meetings with legal and medical representatives and securing the services of appropriate interpreters for the various languages spoken at these meetings. In this case foreign-born parents can be instrumental by creating a multilingual newsletter to assure that parents remain informed on a timely basis about all school events. Community resources are key!

Enhancing academic achievement is essential because through information gathering and sharing students begin to understand the worth of education and how successfully pooling individual and collective efforts can be effective in achieving higher goals. When students attain this enlightened level of academic awareness it is assumed at that point they have developed an understanding that power can be used as a tool to abandon and circumvent all negative labels associated with them thus increasing and opening the likelihood of present and future personal success. Education is key!

Developing the leadership skills of students and parents is essential because it often requires specific "take charge" skills in order to self-advocate and navigate successfully through the system. One goal of TEAM is to have traditionally "hard to reach/low profile" parents expand their school participation to include attendance at parent meetings that involve the larger school parent population and eventually develop enough confidence to assume leadership roles in these arenas. It can be projected that the benefits of these actions will trickle down to the students and spill over into the school community. Leadership is key!

The highlighted eight essential posits of TEAM mentioned above emphasize key underlying components of the group. Its message refutes Piagetian assimilation, whereby deeply embedded parental marginalized perspectives as well as beliefs in the marginalization of specific groups by educators is adhered to. In TEAM we break away from fixed notions about underserved parents and rethink and reconceptualize the framework constituted for these parents. The preconceived notion that nonparticipating parents categorized as "hard to reach/low profile" parents conveniently fit into existing categories which happen to be negative is not acceptable any more. This perspective must be uprooted, extricated, and reconstructed in order to move forward with a new agenda. TEAM is an example of the new agenda because it embraces an alternative mindset one which involves stepping out of the box and moving away from assimilation to accommodation perspectives. In this manner educational psychology expands boundaries from a micro focus to include a meso and macro understanding of underserved high school parents, with all the complexities, in relation to the issue of school involvement.

The focus of the essential posits recognize the changes in cognition needed to honor the new realities of parents and in conjunction it also acknowledges the innovative categories needed to accommodate that information. The educational institution, in an effort to change parent/school relationships, must reevaluate the situation and reconstruct what currently exists. The new realization, which necessitates new dimensions for educational psychology, should include the realities of the twenty-first century, which harbors over stimulation of the senses, high-tech equipment, and prevalent links to hyper-reality. In light of these distractions whether they are deemed positive or negative, it is suggested that educators remember to consider the lived world experiences of parents when reconstructing new partnerships with them. It is inconceivable that schools can continue to think that parents will assimilate to the traditional parental positions constructed which created opposing realities, one of acceptance in print and in contrast one of rejection in practice. There are many dichotomous relationships within the "hard to reach/low profile" parent's web of reality between the parents and the school that continue to manifest.

The dichotomy between the seemingly under-participating parent and the minimally supportive school system with TEAM assistance can lead to a dialectical interaction between the parents and school representatives. The challenge is to maintain the vision and passion of postformalist thinking while attempting to unravel past discrepancies. The problem with the lack of high school parental involvement is not one-dimensional it expands into a complexity of experiences ultimately surfacing through the lived world of each parent. Information obtained about parents changes according to culture, economics, race, gender of the dominant parent and various other factors. In order to process this information it is necessary to think on many levels and to be committed to see the bigger picture and the multilogicality of the context. Joe Kincheloe proposes that with multilogicality every description of the world is an interpretation and there are always new interpretations to encounter. Educators need to be very careful when they hastily interpret the actions of "hard to reach/low profile" parents. Observations have to be made and on one hand we must enter into a multifaceted world similar to the multidimensions of all people and on the other hand acknowledge dissimilar and similar aspects within its unique intricacies. Adhering to Kincheloe's belief that postformalism assumes reciprocity and holism, TEAM makes strides to demonstrate that postformalist viewpoint. In this sense when parents are involved in TEAM they are empowered by position and action. Their contributions to the TEAM help to complete the purpose of the TEAM and the reciprocity or the mutual exchange of ideas among TEAM members reestablishes the importance of the parent as a group member making the idea of TEAM a complete experience.

Joe Kincheloe's postformalism rethinks intelligences, embracing four concepts relevant to TEAM: etymology, pattern, processes, and contextualization. The etymology or personal history of parent TEAM members originates from a common nuclear space. A historical trek back in time exploring the negative and positive aspects of childhood school experiences uncovers the origins of current dispositions. Shrouded in a cloak of misconceptions often parents begin to form life patterns and subsequently transmit these patterns to their children. It is possible that the historical dynamics constructed also helped to create the present situation made apparent by the uninvolved parent or by the compliant educator accepting existing conditions. It eventually becomes necessary, after careful scrutiny, for the interconnecting relationships that shape the similar parent scenarios to be seen in a broader more inclusive and questioning light. Ultimately, the personal histories of parents lead to deep patterns, unique life structures, and in addition expose subjugated knowledges and perspectives typically not found in schools. Sometimes negative labels originate from these circumstances.

In the educational institution the labels of the students become the labels of the parents and vice versa. The ability for parents, students, and school personnel to connect and interact becomes strained under these recurring deficit patterns. TEAM deconstructs these deficit conditions and engages in a process that acknowledges the past and accommodates for new ways of doing and seeing things in the present. TEAM assists parents and students to escape past stigmas and move beyond the devastating and debilitating circumstances of exclusionary practices. The process of deconstruction redefines the information of the existing system and strives to address the needs of parents while recognizing their efforts to affect change in their children. If we dare to challenge the norm we just might be able to alter the negative context and recreate the experience under a new context. With this in mind, TEAM attempts to alter the distorted parent/student context to make it possible for parents of underachieving/underserved students to experience a different reality within the school system. In an expanded context the previously uninvolved parent is no longer labeled or rejected but seen as an asset to the school community. In this context teachers can experience the parents as resources, helpers in exorcizing tacit student potentials, and members in a fluid-learning environment with all members interrelated and learning from each other. TEAM is one way critical educators can incorporate and cultivate postformal thinking in schools.

There are six primary areas that must be addressed in order for TEAM to be successful, which includes setup, pre-event, day of event, post-event, during the year, and projected activities. Highlights concerning the six areas are listed below and section that targets "Underserved Families" provides further information.

The Setup

The setup stage of TEAM requires conscientious planning with sensitivity to the needs, desires, and expectations of parents and students. A primary consideration is to provide varied accommodations for parents to make it possible for them to start to feel welcome in the school community.

TEAM Teacher Recruitment.   It is important to enlist other teachers to join the support team. When teachers initiate additional support systems for parents and students and take an active role in their lives the result is increased parental involvement. In order to recruit the participation of other dedicated teachers,

* send flyers out requesting teachers who are interested in supporting parents;
* create a TEAM responsibility sheet that addresses the areas of expertise of all teacher members (see Figure 81.1)

TEAM Motivational Perks.   Incentives or motivational perks are important and play a strategic role in the continuation of TEAM. Therefore they should be monitored and periodically reevaluated and updated to hold the interest of all TEAM members. For example,

* Parents—babysitting services provided, dinner served for the family, all family members are encouraged to come to the meetings (brothers, sisters, etc.).
* Teachers—professional development hours, free days, stipends, teacher suggestions.
* Students—extra credit for attending meeting with parent, credit for empowering a parent to attend a meeting, credit for completing all assignments connected to the meeting whether on or off site.

Community Involvement in TEAM.   Can come from numerous places depending on what a particular community has to offer. TEAM members should periodically evaluate community assets and establish ways students can give back to the community.

Pre-event Preparation

There are multiple responsibilities before an event takes place and these responsibilities should be dispersed among the Team members.

* Multiple methods of communication should be used to promote the event.
* Introduce the academic aspect of TEAM.
* Choose the event and topics that attract interest—get feedback—have a workshop based on the suggestions
* Students and teachers develop event rules.

Figure 81.1
TEAM Responsibility Sheet

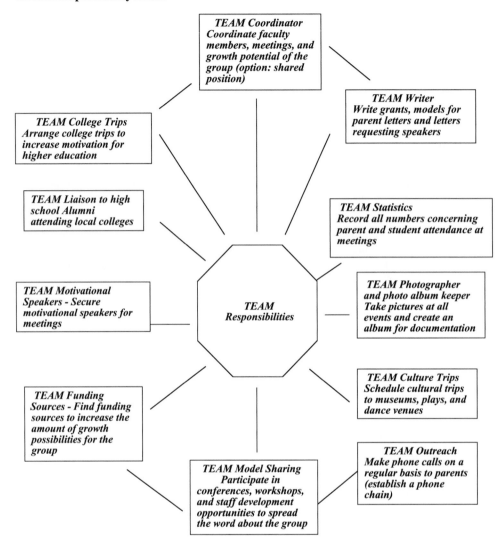

Day of event

On the day of the event responsibilities and trip rules should be dispersed. Transportation, chaperones, teacher/parent/student roles should be reviewed before the event. Sometimes community members accompany TEAM members as guardians to students who cannot find family members to attend meetings with them.

Post-event

Teachers, parents, students, and community members need to know their responsibilities for the event. These responsibilities will vary for each event.

Projected Activities

TEAM Club.   Often underserved students do not join school clubs and this lack of involvement on a social level further alienates them from the mainstream student population. Giving TEAM students the opportunity to join a club where they will not feel intimidated and will be able to have fun and learn how they can give back to society is a nonthreatening way to enhance leadership skills.

Club Ideas:

- Student Newcomer Registry

    1. Photography—photo bulletin board of students
    2. TEAM students become escorts or partners to new students
    3. Write literature about TEAM
    4. Students create profile sheets about themselves
    5. Review new student course schedules
    6. TEAM Students organize community outings for new students
    7. Encourage new students to get involved in the community

- Voicing Room/Ideas

    1. Voicing room can be located in classroom
    2. "Voice Box" will be available for depositing the issues to be discussed
    3. Monthly meetings
    4. Bulletin board for TEAM student club
    5. Encourage TEAM students to Speak Out!

- Community Service Possibilities/Ideas

    1. Students create multicultural materials for TEAM (flyers, etc.)
    2. Students and parents can organize cultural events
    3. TEAM students can read to younger children in different settings/locations

- Election of officers—practice in leadership
- Club advisors—parents and teachers

Projected TEAM Ideas

- Establish a cohort of parents that will encourage consistent attendance and participation in the TEAM program (parent delegates for TEAM).
- Establish a cohort of students that will encourage consistent attendance and participation in the TEAM program (student delegates for TEAM).
- Increase parent and student involvement and ownership in TEAM.
- Disperse teacher responsibilities.
- Gradually increase parent involvement.
- Gradually increase student involvement.

VIP Parents.

- VIP parent letters/correspondence—choose ten to twenty families as the supporting cohort of TEAM (focus on and nurture that cohort)

A sample of a Teacher TEAM responsibility sheet is listed further according to individual areas of expertise.

TEAM Workshop Model.   Building a Support TEAM—Staff Development Workshop—create a personalized TEAM model that will fit your school based on the essential posits. Then share the model with other schools at workshops and conferences.

Time Frame:

Target: underserved families

Objectives:

> - To enhance the leadership skills of our parents and students.
> - To enable the parents and the students to successfully navigate the system.
> - To enhance academic achievement.
> - To act as advocates for students and parents throughout the year.

Questions to think about:

> - Why are a certain percentage of parents absent from school meetings?
> - What can we do to rectify this problem?

TEAM startup worksheet:

1. Build a teacher team (find teachers that share the same students)
   List Partner Possibilities

   _____

2. Identify student population
   List methods of identification

   _____

3. Establish areas of focus to encourage parents to attend meetings
   > - Navigating the school system
   > - Parent/student academic empowerment

4. In class promotion (get students involved—talk about)
   > - Parent/guardian roles with students
   > - Personal ownership of future
   > - Student course credit for participation

5. Plot student geographic locations
   > - Index cards—students write address and location in the town.
   > - Students write their names on the town map indicating where they live.

6. List things that can be determined from the map activity

7. Class Discussion—get an idea of parent availability from students (weekends, evenings, specific days, etc.)
   Meeting location ideas _____
   1st consideration—location should be in close proximity to the majority of parent homes.
   2nd consideration—if special meetings are further away, transportation should be provided.
   List multiple steps for correspondence _____

8. Correspondence #1—send flyers home—give them out in class.

9. Correspondence #2—mail letters with RSVP—get a written response from parents—include self-addressed envelope.

10. Correspondence #3—in addition distribute parent letters to students in class.

11. Correspondence #4—send home student-written post-it notes to put on the refrigerator (reminder) include school telephone number to call.

12. Correspondence #5—make telephone calls—if someone is calling the parents for you make sure to provide a phone conversation script for that person—verbal response from parents

Write telephone script ideas—ask for TEAM volunteers to make calls

---

13. Meeting Accommodations—explore all possibilities
    ➢ Food
    ➢ Babysitting

14. Meeting Agenda—program inclusions
    ➢ Parents—ex-students Parents discuss issues and concerns and share expertise
    ➢ Students—sharing information with parents
    ➢ Teachers/administrators—facilitate / distribute materials/ share expertise
    ➢ Panel discussions
    ➢ Small group discussions—topics can originate from teachers, parents, or students
    ➢ Community representative

Meeting Topics

➢ Immigration
➢ Health care
➢ Transcripts
➢ Guidance counselors as guest speakers
➢ Enhancing the reading experience
➢ After school support programs
➢ Extra curricular activities

Off-site Locations Possibilities

➢ Public Library meeting rooms
➢ Local colleges
➢ Ask parents where they would like the next meeting to be

Note:

➢ Involve parents and students in the planning of the next meeting
➢ Are home visits an option?
➢ What are some options for students without an advocate?

TEAM Trips—College Component. The goal of preparing students for life beyond high school is met when we have succeeded in teaching students and their parents how to pursue avenues of life-long learning. One way to achieve this is to assist in making the college environment comfortable for both parents and students. TEAM arranges visits to a variety of colleges so that a broader view of the range of options that are available can be introduced to TEAM families.

➢ Students participate in classes with their parents,

➢ tour the dormitories on campus,

➢ eat lunch with a special delegation of college students,

➢ are included in the college classes that day,

➢ are expected to participate (professors send work for students prior to the class).

Note:

• Following the classes, the students and their parents meet with university administrators, professors, and college students to discuss EOF, the admissions process, financial aid, college life, and the experiences of the day.

• Seniors are allowed onsite college registration during the visit if the time frame is appropriate with the college admissions office (prearranged by TEAM teachers).

Team pre/during/post college trip activities:

All students develop career planning and workplace skills. At the same time, they use critical thinking, decision making, and problem solving skills. Before participating in a college visit, students are required to do "prework," including self-exploration activities on future goals. They must develop a mock course schedule for college freshman year and support their course choices. Course selections are to be based on where they see themselves in the future and the career path they want to be on in the future. (See basic sample sheet below for during a college visit)

During a College Visit—students receive a worksheet when they arrive at the college with two items on it.

1. Write about something different you experienced in the college class.

2. What was the college lesson about?

TEAM year report

Early documentation is important and yearly reflections are needed in order to upgrade the effectiveness of the program.

Event date	Total student attendance by grade	Total parent attendance by grade	Meeting location	Theme/ agenda	Materials distributed	Colleges acceptances for seniors

Year End Awards Program.   Congratulate and thank parents and students for their various aspect of participation in the program. Both parents and students receive awards. Students can present their parents with the awards as a gesture of thanks for their support.

Team Culture Trips.   Students and parents participate in various cultural activities to enhance aesthetic awareness in dance, music, theater, and visual arts.

Reaching Out to "Underserved" Families TEAM Ideas

Setup/teachers	Setup/parents	Setup/students	Setup/community
– Recruit teachers	– Develop a student/parent master call list	– Help design a TEAM brochure (for credit)	– Teachers find out what community resources are available in the town.
– Build a teacher team			– Students stick pins on a town map indicating locate strategic community sites
– Determine shared "in common" students among TEAM teachers			
– Plot students residencies on a town map (assists with planning meeting locations)			
– Establish teacher/parent/student/ community participation incentives or motivations			
– Develop a student/parent master call list and info sheet			
– Design a brochure			

Pre-event/teachers	Pre-event/parents	Pre-event/students	Pre-event/community
– Discuss upcoming event in class with students	– Receive letters and flyers	– Help plan event	– Teachers check date, time, and room accommodations prior to meeting
– Receive letters and flyers in class	– Parents call teachers about the event	– Help create flyers	– Students research site event on the Internet
– Make-up an agendas Secure a site	– Activate the phone chain the night before the event	– Help package info for distribution	
– Write a letter to parents about the upcoming event	– Have a suggestion box at each event and ask for agenda ideas/meeting topics	– Address envelopes	
– Each TEAM teacher call four or five parents	– Build in a feedback time at meetings for parents	– Complete assignments connected to the event	
– Remind students of all incentives connected to the event		– Discuss upcoming event with students and review strategies on how to empower a parent/caregiver to attend the event	
– Create a flyer about the event for students and parents		– Build in a feedback time at meetings for students	
– Include parent incentives for attending the **event** (ex. Have a raffle) on the flyer		– Collect responses from parents and students	
– Arrange for food, child care, and transportation at the event			
– Xerox information for distribution			

(continued)

Reaching Out to "Underserved" Families TEAM Ideas (*continued*)

Day of event/teachers	Day of event/parents	Day of event/students	Day of event/community
– Give students a written assignment either to complete on event site or off event site (see college example) – Take attendance – Travel with emergency phone list – Teachers must enforce the student dress code – Take pictures at the events (photographer) – Provide transportation	– Adult chaperones required – Parents request transportation in advance – Parents take the place of absent parents – Parent are asked to help enforce the dress code on trips and at events – Parents also should take pictures (photographer)	– Attendance encouraged – Students must empower an adult to attend the event with them (parent, a friend's parent, a relative, or a TEAM teacher) – Students must adhere to a dress code – Students can take pictures (photographer) – Collect assignments	– Locate the key person at the site responsible for the event

Post-event/teachers	Post-event/parents	Post-event/students	Post-event/community
– Write personal thank you notes or call /e-mail parent & presenters thank you notes – Give feedback for TEAM documentation records – Record statistics (see TEAM yearly sheet) – File materials connected to the event	– Give feedback–written or verbal – If verbal record comments	– Write and email thank you notes	– Get feedback and if appropriate discuss dates for next event

During the year/teachers	During the year/parents	During the year/students	During the year/community
– Plan the yearly calendar – Delegate responsibilities (see chart) – Agree on event themes – Confirm event dates – Start a scholarship fund – Establish additional TEAM supports (guidance counselors, administrators, etc.) – Choose a team historian – a person to collect all the data and house it in one location	– Help design a brochure – Parents plan and organize an event – Parents start to attend parent meeting that include the mainstream population – Parents seek membership on school committees	– Students plan and organize an event	– Continue various forms of correspondence with community business owners

Projected activities/teacher	Projected activities/parent	Projected activities/student	Projected activities/community
– Explore funding opportunities – TEAM creates parent officers – Schedule trips out of town(ex. colleges, cultural)	– Parents volunteer for TEAM officer positions	– Students start a TEAM club	– Ask community parents to connect with TEAM parents

CHAPTER 82

Becoming Whole Again through Critical Thought: A Recipe

ROCHELLE BROCK

An often-asked question of teachers concerned with critical thinking is how to "do-it" in their class, in their curriculum, in their pedagogy. I so wish I could provide a fail-safe lesson plan to be used in any and every situation. But of course that's impossible if we understand and except the changing nature and fluidity of critical thought. Instead, I offer an assignment I have given my students, which provides the space to question and reflect on a specific issue utilizing critical thought/critical cognition as the vehicle to understanding.

When working with my students on issues that are difficult to understand I ask them to write a dialogical play, complete with stage directions. The play is written in the questioning Socratic method and the characters (preferably only two) represent the confusion the student feels about the subject matter. Inform your students that the stage directions should convey in a literal and metaphorical visual both the mystification and enlightenment the characters (and by extension the student) experience. The process of conceptualizing and writing the play allows students to question themselves, constantly delving deeper into obscure meanings. As a conclusion for this exercise you can either have certain students perform their play for the entire class or depending on class size and time all the plays can be a performed in a culminating event for the class. Sell tickets, invite the community, open the knowledge to others. After all is not that one of the goals of critical thought in education?

Ingredients to make a Black goddess of Critical Thinking:

* spirit of ancestors
* a healthy dose of angst
* sense of humor
* patience
* theoretical understanding of all and everything
* wholeness of being

Take your ingredients and stir while listening to your favorite jazz tune—preferably Cassandra Wilson. Allow the sounds of a Black woman to seep into your mixture. When everything is smooth (the mixture, not the jazz) get out your old beater and slip a pumpin', bumpin' reggae CD in, turn it up as loud as you can and twirl and dance as you beat the shit out of your mixture—Remember, you are paying homage to those who came before so do it with the rhythm of your past adding your unique flavor to the batter—then beat . . . the faster the better.

And call her Oshun, the African goddess of voluptuous beauty, the goddess of love, the goddess of fertility, the female master of strategy. Oshun is the sweet and sour taste of life. Don't forget to add a little Yemaya for water purifies and is a giver of life . . . new life

A goddess was just what Rochelle needed. Not only a higher power but one from the historical memories of an African past. Created with music and brought to life with rhythm and soul, a goddess with the strength to move the paradigm beyond the margins. She holds a golden chain in her hands, a chain to tie all of her people together.

Together Oshun and Rochelle will write and speak their truth. Oshun brings voice to the silence surrounding Rochelle. Rochelle brings life to the historical memory of Oshun. As one they tell you A Black woman's story . . .

Stage Directions: *Rochelle is sitting at the kitchen table in her apartment, an ashtray, an old battered typewriter and a stack of blank typing paper is on the table in from of her. A lone light hangs over the table forcing the kitchen to be seen only in shadows. There are several candles on the table in varying heights. A bowl of grapes sits in the middle of the table with a coffee pot on one side. One large purple coffee mug is placed in front of Rochelle. Surrounding the table in a semi-circle are four 6-foot bookshelves. Scattered on the floor are books stacked haphazardly and in varying heights. The books represent the knowledge of the leaders in the field of Critical Thinking, Radical Education, and Black Woman's History. Note: The audience should get the feeling of "intellectual chaos" from the books.*

The Players:
Oshun the African Goddess of Critical Thinking
Rochelle the teacher of all students

Rochelle: (*Looking out into the audience.*) Where can I find the power to understand the feelings I have? Who will hold me; help me traverse this hostile world I find myself in? I sit here confused, stuck, barren. (*Extending hands toward the typewriter and then pulling them back, roughly*) I cannot even write a facile sentence in a language not meant for me. It's as if I'm fighting an abstract, stubbornly refusing to engage in these words and thoughts that feel alien. Why?

(*Standing and moving to the front of the table Rochelle begins to pace.*) My head hurts, I cannot fill my lungs with enough air to speak a thought, even one that is silent. I need to turn away, take a mind-rest, at least for a moment, from this malaise. But I can't. It is too important to work my way through, process my alienation from abstract thought, explain and articulate so all can understand. I must write and complete this article on critical thinking as a means to help Black women understand and fight their status in a racist sexist society. But the pieces will not come together in any type of cohesive whole. Instead, I sit, staring at an empty piece of paper, drinking coffee, killing myself with cigarettes, questioning my intelligence, my critical thinking skills. Why? Puffffff.

Oshun: (*As soon as Rochelle utters "Why" Oshun walks out of the shadows onto the stage. Soft jazz and sounds of the ocean can be heard in the background, which should remain for the entire play. Walking to the kitchen table, she reaches one hand out toward Rochelle.*) I hear and feel your pain and I have come to help you process that pain. Go inside of yourself, reach deep, and find the strength to look and think critically about your life. Change your way of thinking of seeing the world. Use those analytical skills of transgressive critical thought to help and guide you. Remember that you are a conscious being and therefore possess the cognitive skills to consciously control the trajectory of your world. Never forget that racism and all its manifestations produce a mind−funk that distorts thought and action. What has enveloped your soul is internalized racism; it's taken away your wholeness. You are defining yourself through it, accepting that because you are Black and a woman your options; your worth is limited. You are forgetting your own power of thought and mind.

Rochelle: (*Still pacing and walking aimlessly while at times talking to the audience and other times talking to self.*) I once read about this thing called mindfunk. Caused by internalized racism, it has encapsulated my thoughts, my entire sense of being until I cannot find the words to articulate the things I know. I have become theoretically challenged, not by outside forces but from the inside. I have allowed the words of others to enter my Being, forgotten that their thoughts do nothing but pull me down. I have been violated. But I must find a way to climb out of and far from this mindfunk. Damn, where is my shelter against the pain? My confusion, anger, and isolation increase as I realize that my critical insight into the constructions of Black womanhood does not insulate me from the daily pain of my otherness. (*Laughing*) But then perhaps if I did not possess a critical understanding, I would be crazy rather than terminally depressed. I don't know.

Oshun: (*slowly and gracefully sits in the chair opposite of Rochelle*) Ahhh yes, you are experiencing racism at its finest my Original World daughter.

Rochelle: (*repeating*) I would be crazy rather than terminally depressed.

Oshun: (*Speaking directly to Rochelle*) You are crying, I am happy. For I want you to never lose your passion. Do not become the rational thinker attempting to scientifically analyze your feelings of incompleteness. Instead, feel deeply and allow those feelings to move you to passionately question your world. Racism works at the decomposition of the cultural integrity of Blackness. Close your eyes, walk with me, and visualize. Decomposition, the breaking into parts, affords a visual, emotive sensation to describe the realities of racism. In order to remain whole, you must keep a constant vigil against internalizing racism. Anything short allows the space to exist where mindfunk can thrive. You must understand that mindfunk is more than a catchy phrase; it is a consuming way of reading the world and reading the self. It fosters the doubt, which stops a person from moving beyond their prescribed boundaries, to break out of Western psychological assessments of who we are as black women. You were not careful enough, not cognizant enough. You let your armor rest a minute too long.

Rochelle: (*Walking over to the bookcase Rochelle speaks while looking at the books. Her back is to the audience.*) Could it be that my soul has been raped? Could it be that my armor has been stolen? Or could it be that I'm tired as hell of constantly having to carry that armor! Whatever the reason it's missing and I have no idea how or where to find it. My position as Black and female hinders the ability I need to think my way out of this oppressive frame of mind I find myself in. I let things inside that I should not have. Western positivistic evaluations of my abilities have found their way into my selfhood. What makes it so difficult is this inner turmoil that is blanketing me is caused by something outside of me. (*Turning toward the audience, but speaking to no one in particular*) I am alienated not only from society but also from myself. And even though I strive for knowledge of my otherness; despite my understanding of subjugated knowledge and objectification; regardless of my awareness and acceptance of critical thinking's transgressive cognition, I still allow myself to be silenced. Does it really matter if that silence is internal or external? I still become too tired to make my voice and thoughts heard. Such an insipid thing, racism can seep into every pore until it feels you with hate, bitterness, and confusion.

Someone please tell me how racism accomplishes the decomposition of the cultural integrity of Blackness? Why am I allowing myself to be silenced and not using the critical thinking skills I have worked so hard to get? How do I find the strength to develop and become a critical agent of change and transformation for all those Black women I come into contact with daily and for myself? How do I re-remember the spiritual strength that aided my ancestors during the years of capture, enslavement, colonization, and exploitation? How do I retrieve my wholeness?

Oshun: (*As angry and confused as Rochelle's words are spoken Oshun speaks in a calming, reflective voice.*) Wholeness is delivered when your spirit is strong. Yes. Re-remembering and reconnecting with that which aided our ancestors is extremely important to your survival and the strength you need. But you ask how do you survive and I answer that you must open your eyes and your heart to all that surrounds you. You must become conscious of the powerful influences, which seek to destroy your understanding of self. You must learn to not only use critical thinking to analyze what is outside of you but more importantly what is inside. (*Reaching for the grapes.*) Dig deep and discover that which gets in your way, hinders you as a Black Woman. (*Rises from her seat and moves to the front of the stage, parallel to Rochelle.*)

Rochelle: (*Moves from the bookcase to center stage and begins to slowly, rhythmically sway. Oshun standing far left moves in unison.*) What is it that keeps getting in my way? Concepts of me as the other. A nonentity. Different, unheard, unwanted, unrespected, unloved, the only, removed, outside of society. My position as a Black woman in America is as *the other*, which is such a strange term to describe a person. What does being the *other* have to do with how I feel about myself? People explain me, they study me, they write about me and if I am not careful I occasionally allow their definitions to seep into my thoughts. Everywhere I look they try to take me out of myself. (*Movement stops.*) There are powerful forces that attempt to construct my identity; place me within an oppressive cage; force me to become the spectacle in their obsession.

Oshun: (*Oshun continues swaying dance.*) The decomposition of the cultural integrity of Blackness is cultivated, in part, through an ideology of the *other*. You are greater than the sum total of your parts. Perhaps it is this knowledge that will allow you to dismiss the attempts at decomposition.

Rochelle: (*Still center stage, perfectly still*) When I disrobe, lay down my shield, rest, I am left with no choice but to use my *otherness* to define the boundaries of my existence. As the *other* I am removed, standing at the perimeters of normalcy helping to clarify a criterion I can never meet. Those who stand at the perimeters of normalcy are constantly demeaned by mainstream education and psychology's regime of truth.

Oshun: (*Walks to center stage several feet from Rochelle, looks at and speaks directly to Rochelle. Rochelle continues looking out into the audience, oblivious of Oshun.*) My child you always have a choice. Yes, you are the other but the other must never define you—resist that regime of truth. A liberated mind is the manifestation of critical thought. Deconstruct the significance of the *other*. The paradox of your life is that as the *other* you are both despised and yet needed. Although your status threatens the moral and social order of society you are also essential to its survival—your position at the margins of society help to clarify those very margins. Black women empower the privileged in dominant culture's norm referenced tests. Without us at the bottom they can't be the superior ones. Know that African American women, by not belonging, emphasize the significance of belonging.

Look for your shield in the knowledge that you are not what they say. Those writings by other people that you speak of do not or should not necessarily mean control. You are giving those who harm you the power to define. Stop! Make clear to yourself the ways in which ideology work.

Rochelle: (*Should be read stilted as if reading from a book in the beginning. As Rochelle reads the words should become more natural, like she is internalizing the knowledge of the many attempts to define and dominate Black women*) I am a political being. My life is politically inscribed. I must make clear to myself the ways in which ideology works. Ideology, socializes us to believe that the taken for granted assumptions are a natural, inevitable function of life. It calls us into being, but a being that is falsely constructed. Historically, Black women have been controlled with an ideology of domination, through legitimization, categorization, reification, mystification, and acquiescence, that ideology has used to subjugate, objectify, and dominate Black women in America since enslavement. Remember that ideology functions in such devious ways. It becomes legitimate when systems of domination are represented as being worthy of support. Likewise, systems of domination are denied or obscured and unequal social relations are hidden–"there's no oppression in psychology's testing industry." In other words, ideological forces ensure that oppressed people are either not aware of their own oppression, or aware but can not necessarily articulate how it operates. Yes, it is becoming clear. Ideology works vis-à-vis fragmentation, which occurs when meaning is fragmented and groups and individuals are placed in opposition to each other and to self. Decomposition. Through reification a transitory state is represented as if it were permanent, natural, or transhistorical. I was becoming that which society said I was. Ideology allows society to believe that the constructed images are valid. And more importantly, it allows the individual/the group to believe that the constructed images are valid. In this ideological configuration IQs are real. I really don't have the ability to make it in the worlds of commerce, academia, knowledge work, technology, helping professions—the hell I don't. (*Read with the pain and joy of giving birth to a new thought*) These forms of ideology are interwoven and occur simultaneously and ultimately work to interfere with my wholeness of being. I can become an intellectually free person.

Oshun: (*Moving closer to where Rochelle stands.*) Once you truly understand and internalize the definitions of ideology you begin to develop the strength and knowledge to fight. Can you now begin to see our recipe for wholeness—connectedness to our ancestors, spiritual strength, power through self-definition, and deconstruction of ideology—that come together when we use critical thinking as a methodology? These are your ingredients but you must still add others, depending on the spiciness you need. Remember the fluidity of critical thought. Move with it. Allow it to take it you where it must. There are times when the moon is right and the ingredients for wholeness are few but at other times the weight of racism will threaten to pull you asunder and you must add the spices of your past. Although difficult to find they will bring about a taste favored by the goddesses.

Rochelle: (*Moving away from center stage and from Oshun, Rochelle resumes her seat in front of the typewriter.*) I will write and think myself away from this. I will prove to me that despite the changing faces of racism spiritual strength and connectedness with the ancestors will and can guide me to wholeness. I will combine all that I know and feel and bring forth my greater truth. I will do it all with the passion that is central to my being. Yes, that is what I will do.

Oshun: (*For the first time Oshun speaks directly to the audience*) The mind-funk, the depression, and confusion which had been smothering Rochelle for weeks began to open, not completely, just enough so that she could see and breath her way into thought.

Rochelle: (*Speaking as she puts a fresh piece of paper into the typewriter. Should be spoken while simultaneously typing*) I can craft words to define thoughts to tell a story that is both personal and political. I can do it all while remaining true to *my* voice. When I stop and breathe and reflect on my life I know the only way to survive is to give birth to my wholeness. I must recreate and redefine me. (*As these final words are spoken Oshun walks to where Rochelle sits, Rochelle rises when Oshun reaches her and for the first time they look directly at each other and become one*) I weave a tapestry for the future with threads of hope and humanity.

FURTHER READINGS

King, J. E. (1994). Being the Soul-Freeing Substance: A Legacy of Hope and Humanity. In M. J. Shujaa (Ed.), *Too Much Schooling Too Little Education: A Paradox of Black Life in White Societies*, pp. 269–294. New Jersey: Africa Free World Press.

Murrell, P. C. (1997). Digging Again the Family Wells: A Freiran Literacy Framework as Emancipatory Pedagogy for African-American Children. In P. Freire, J. W. Fraser, D. Macedo, T. Mckinnon, and

W. T. Stokes (Eds.), *Mentoring the Mentor: A Critical Dialogue with Paulo Freire*, pp. 19–55. New York: Peter Lang.

Yamato, G. (1995). Something About the Subject Makes it Hard to Name. In M. Anderson and P. Hill-Collins (Eds.), *Race, Class, and Gender: An Anthology*, pp. 71–75. New York: Wadsworth Publishing.